PENGUIN BOOKS

MODELS IN POLITICAL EC O

Michael Barratt Brown was Principal of Northern College, Barnsley, from its founding in 1977 to 1984. Before that he was Senior Lecturer in Economics and Industrial Studies at the Extramural Department of Sheffield University. He is now the Chair of Third World Information Network and of Twin Trading Ltd. For a time he worked with the United Nations and in the film industry. He has been a Visiting Professor at the Universities of Aligarh (1972), Hitotsubashi (1976), Papua New Guinea (1979), the University of California in Los Angeles (1987), the University of Alicante (1989), the University of Madrid (1993) and the University of Victoria in Vancouver (1994). He has written regularly for the *New Left Review*, *Tribune*, *Spokesman* and *European Labour Forum*. His books include *After Imperialism* (1963), *What Economics is About* (1970), *From Labourism to Socialism* (1972), *The Economics of Imperialism* (1974) and *Information at Work* (1978), *European Union: Fortress or Democracy?* (1991), *Short Changed: Africa and World Trade* (with Pauline Tiffen, 1992), *Fair Trade: Reform and Realities in the International Trading System* (1993) and *Africa's Choices: After 30 Years of the World Bank* (1995). He is married with four grown-up children, lives in Derbyshire and grows fruit and vegetables as a hobby.

MICHAEL BARRATT BROWN

MODELS IN POLITICAL ECONOMY

A GUIDE TO THE ARGUMENTS

SECOND EDITION, REVISED AND EXPANDED

PENGUIN BOOKS

PENGUIN BOOKS

Published by the Penguin Group
Penguin Books Ltd, 27 Wrights Lane, London w8 5tz, England
Penguin Books USA Inc., 375 Hudson Street, New York, New York 10014, USA
Penguin Books Australia Ltd, Ringwood, Victoria, Australia
Penguin Books Canada Ltd, 10 Alcorn Avenue, Toronto, Ontario, Canada m4v 3b2
Penguin Books (NZ) Ltd, 182–190 Wairau Road, Auckland 10, New Zealand

Penguin Books Ltd, Registered Offices: Harmondsworth, Middlesex, England

First published in Pelican Books 1984
Reprinted in Penguin Books 1990
Second edition 1995
10 9 8 7 6 5 4 3 2 1

Typeset by Datix International Limited, Bungay, Suffolk
Printed in England by Clays Ltd, St Ives plc
Filmset in Monophoto Sabon

Diagrams drawn by Raymond Turvey

CONTENTS

FIGURES AND TABLES

PREFACE

This book is a response to two urgent needs of men and women today who want to understand the causes of mass unemployment, of cuts in living standards and worldwide economic crisis. The first need is to know what all the argument is about between Keynesians and monetarists, those who believe in more state intervention and those who want to let the market do its work. The second need is to discover whether there are alternatives to the capitalist system and whether there is some form of social order that might offer an improvement. For many years socialism has been seen as the alternative, and despite the collapse of the Soviet Union and the counter-revolution in China, socialism is still seen by many as *the* alternative to capitalism. By socialism is meant a society based on social action and social provision with choices determined by popular discussion and decision, in place of the personal choices of the capitalist market, determined as they are by the dictates of capital accumulation for the owners of capital and their associates.

In this book we shall be as much concerned with the ways we produce goods and services – in the home, in mines and factories, schools and offices – and how these are decided, as we are with the way goods and services are distributed between employer and self-employed, wage-earners and housewives, pensioners and workers, employed and unemployed. At the same time, the way these things are studied will not be narrowly economic. Most of the differences between economists and between economic models result from political differences in which fundamental cultural values and philosophical arguments are involved. All models have their own associated ideologies, as these sets of values are termed.

Much of the argument in the media assumes that there is only one alternative to leaving things much as they are in what is called a 'free' society, which relies on the incentives of profits and wages in a free market plus an element of welfare-state spending. This alternative is supposed to be the failed totalitarian state with more and more government intervention, central planning and power in the hands of a few leaders at the top. One response from socialists has been to despair of all central-government and intergovernmental planning and to concentrate their efforts on grass-roots activity in community action, shop stewards' committees, women's groups, black people's groups and local enterprise, or to join the Green movement's total rejection of industrial society. All this is only too understandable, but these groups remain at the mercy of those giant companies and government ministries that have real power in the market and in the state. We need to find another alternative.

In this book, then, we shall look at the different models of capitalist economies, especially the three main ones: the market, Keynesian and Marxist models. But we shall take account of changes in the market model in the present stage of transnational capitalism and of criticisms made by Greens and feminists in presenting their model of the economy. We shall also include some examination of monetarism and of the corporate or fascist model of capitalist economy. After that we shall look at various attempted models of socialist economies, especially the Soviet, Chinese, Yugoslav and African models, comparing them with Marx's original concept of a socialist mode of production. This will I hope enable us in the last part of the book to develop our own models; to see both how far the world capitalist economy can cease to be an arms economy in conflict with socialism, and how far it might be capable of establishing a new and sustainable international economic order. The aim of the book in the end will be to discover a model that links the needs and activities of men and women where they live and work with the big decisions that have to be made about the allocation and distribution of national and international resources.

I do not believe that we have yet worked out such a model, but until we do begin to have a clearer picture in our minds of this model of a decentralized planned economy it will be impossible to move forward towards building a new social order. No one person can draw up this model. What is written in this book has come out of many discussions and much exchanging of ideas, particularly in recent years from the economics seminars in which I have been involved, in the programmes of long and short courses for trade unionists and community activists at the Northern College. Going back much longer, the book takes its place in a continuing dialogue over twenty years which I have had especially with Ken Coates and the late Stephen Bodington but also with other colleagues in the Institute for Workers' Control, Kenneth Alexander, Tony Benn, Mike Cooley, Stuart Holland, Robin Murray, Vella Pillay, Hugo Radice, Regan Scott, Tony Topham, Audrey Wise and Mike Ward. I am especially grateful to Steve Bodington and Hugo Radice for reading through the whole of the book in its original draft and making invaluable criticisms and comments. I must also thank Jean McCrindle for reading the original chapter on the feminist model and Vella Pillay for reading the chapter on the Chinese model, and making most useful criticisms. Without Jean McCrindle there would have been no Chapter 10. If the book encourages the dialogue to continue and draws more people into the debate, it will have done good and we may be that much nearer to finding the model of the future that will really help us to build a new society.

I am indebted for Figure 5 (in Chapter 5) to an article by Professor Arnold Tustin in *New Scientist* (31 October 1957).

The book is for Eleanor Singer, without whose loving but unpaid labour (see Chapter 10), as doctor, nurse, mother, gardener, cook, housekeeper, housemaid – and companion – it could certainly not have been written.

Northern College,
Barnsley, October 1983,
and Derbyshire, May 1994

PREFACE TO THE SECOND EDITION

It is a rare privilege to have the opportunity ten years after its first publication to revise a book on political economy and to be able to rewrite several chapters and add others. It enables one to make corrections for changing events and indeed for the mistakes one has made, but more than this to examine the reasons for incorrectly foreseeing how events would unfold. Political economy is not an exact science. Its models are not those of the physical sciences, and even some of those have been shown to be false. But the study of human behaviour suffers from one very particular difficulty: that human beings are themselves active participants. They can, for example, conceal reality behind a smokescreen of ideology and they can learn lessons from the past so as to falsify prediction made from a correct perception of reality. And yet I have to admit that there are enough errors of foresight in what I wrote ten years ago for some general explanation to be called for.

The first must be a personal confession. To those who would change the world, the Italian socialist philosopher Antonio Gramsci is reported to have recommended optimism of the will and pessimism of the intellect. I recognize that I have always allowed my will to override my intellect. Even to imagine myself taking part in such a great endeavour as 'changing the world' was an act of the will of overweening intellectual arrogance. I feel no regrets; and would do it again. But lying behind the excessive optimism there were certain misjudgements that have to be recognized. They concern my estimates of human capacities and the effect of these on the basically Marxist model of human society with which I was working.

It is clear from anthropological studies that the human race has survived and multiplied through a combination of two conflicting instincts – the one cooperative and the other competitive. I have argued elsewhere that in a hostile environment, such as the

African continent, the cooperative instinct had perforce to be dominant. One may make the same generalization about most of Russia. In more benign environments, the competitive instinct became uppermost. This was especially true in Western Europe and North America. In these regions institutions which encourage competition were developed and then exported to other parts of the world – to a point where the competitiveness generated now threatens the very survival of human and other life on our planet, but it generated enormous productive forces.

I realize now that I underestimated the power of this competitive instinct and the ease with which, in the form of nationalism, it could be regenerated by political leaders like Reagan and Thatcher, or later by a Zhirinovsky or a Milosević. At the same time, I realize that I underestimated the extent to which the cooperative instinct at work in the Soviet Union, in China, in Cuba, in Zimbabwe and in the former Portuguese colonies of Africa could be exploited by individual self-aggrandisement, often influenced and abetted by successful competitive societies elsewhere.

Only One World Model?

When I was writing in 1983, it was appropriate to distinguish three major working models in the world economy: the capitalist model, with more or less state regulation, the Soviet model and the Chinese model. In addition, there were a number of experimental models – in Yugoslavia, in Cuba and southern Africa. My other models remained as critiques of the working models, in people's imaginations only – the Marxist model, the feminist model, the Green model and my transitional and networking models. Today, there is really only one working model – the capitalist model, with variants in the corporate economy, in the arms economy, in Japan and in the developing countries. These are all subject to varying degrees of monetarism, with very much reduced Keynesian regulation in the West and with the hangovers of command structures in the market socialism of the East. Even the imaginary models have lost some of their attractions.

This hegemony of the market model implies a transformation

of major proportions. It is not that the market model is working particularly well. The worldwide recession which began in the 1970s deepened in the 1980s and shows only very slight signs of recovery in the 1990s. I was able to identify it as a low point of the long 'Kondratieff' waves of economic activity which had each lasted for about fifty years in the past, with low points in the 1830s, 1880s, 1930s and 1980s. I had not expected such an extended 'low', given the capacity of governments to take countervailing action. The intermediate 'Kusnets' swing in land speculation and building activity went higher in the 1970s and dropped lower in the 1980s than had been expected, adding amplitude to the regular five- or six-year trade cycle (Tylecote, 1993). Nor had I expected such a massive development of inequality during the 1980s – between developed and developing countries and inside them both. The cumulative pain of impoverishment of whole peoples in entire regions where unemployment and marginalization have taken place, side by side with the enrichment of a few, has created a quite new problem for socialists and a new justification for their concerns.

A new combination of events has taken place which has generated high and continuing unemployment. This is the rise in productivity resulting from the introduction of new technology, but with little or no increase in output. The failure of output to rise more than marginally is only partly accounted for by diminishing resources and by uncertainty about the effects on the environment. There appear to be other reasons internal to the system of capital accumulation in giant companies that we shall have to examine, including the enormous growth of investment in speculation and so-called 'derivatives'. Despite their huge scale of operation and managed markets, the transnational companies still compete with each other. There is no sign of their uniting in what Kautsky foresaw as a stage of 'ultra-imperialism'. United States world hegemony has come under serious challenge.

What Is Left of Socialism?

Because of the evident crisis in capitalism, the collapse of all attempts at socialism in the Soviet Union, China and elsewhere has not altered my personal commitment to a basically Marxist view of history and the need for radical social change to end all forms of human exploitation, nor my faith in collective action and social provision as the only alternative to the anarchy of the system of individual buying and selling in the market. It has, however, to be accepted that the socialist project is in disarray and market solutions are everywhere in the ascendant. To gain credence, any proposal for social control of the economy has to be prefixed or suffixed with reference to the market, as in the weaker 'social market' or the stronger 'market socialism'. It is widely assumed, especially in the former Soviet Union, in Eastern Europe and China, that Marx and socialism went out of the window along with the discredited command economy.

Anyone who foresaw in 1983 the collapse of the Soviet Union, the counter-revolution in China, the disintegration of Yugoslavia, the demoralization of Cuba and the corruption of the leaders of national liberation struggles in southern Africa has a perfect right to pour ridicule on my apparent naivety. But how many people writing in 1983 did in fact foresee these events? I certainly know of none, except those who for sixty years had been predicting disaster for all socialist experiments.

A problem remains because I assumed in the book a clear antithesis between capitalism and socialism, i.e. between private and social ownership of the means of production, and equally I assumed the correctness of Marx's prediction that capitalism was doomed and socialism bound to take its place. Now, even if the failure of the command economies of the Soviet Union and China need not necessarily undermine belief in socialism, the collapse of capitalism is not at all evident. Critics of Marx have proposed that the idea of capital ownership and therefore of exploitation of workers is outmoded. There are now, they say, several 'stakeholders' in companies – their financiers, suppliers, customers, the environment, society as a whole, as well as employees. Obviously, some have larger 'stakes' than others, but all are said to have some property rights. Even the employees have a guaranteed basic income, as well as basic education and health service (Handy, 1994). This is one expression of what is called 'post-modernism' –

like the architecture of that ilk, built up from a mix of different styles. It does nothing to meet the moral case for socialism; in William Morris's words, 'No one is big enough to be another person's master'.

None the less, Marxist writers have followed a similar pluralistic line in reminding us that there was always a problem about the place of a middle class and an under class (Marx's *lumpenproletariat*) in any two-class analysis of society. It is better, they believe, to think of different 'economic locations', which carry rights to a share in the surplus realized in the production of goods and services above the cost of the production of labour. This surplus can derive from special skills and abilities as well as from the ownership of capital (Wright *et al.*, 1992). Surpluses can be capitalized, so that we see all the time new entrants to the capitalist class. For this reason, Roemer has suggested that both inherited wealth and surplus from the exercise of skills should be separated by law as 'stock money' to be distinguished from commodity money, if a halfway house between capitalism and socialism, some sort of market socialism, were to be established (Roemer, 1994).

Corrections of Judgement

In the revised edition of this book I describe the failed forms of social organization in the Soviet Union and in China as 'attempted socialism'. I refer to fundamental social change as implying the end of human exploitation. The social change in the Soviet Union and China was not complete because, while resources were owned socially and not privately, control remained in the hands of a few who benefited from the exploitation of the many. It was therefore confusing and incorrect to speak of Soviet, Chinese or Yugoslav models of 'socialism'.

In this respect, there are a number of correct judgements which I can claim to have made in the earlier book. I recognized the certain disaster for the USSR of engagement in a galloping arms race with all its costs and terrors, the danger to China of the failing food supply under collective agriculture, combined with a democratic deficit, the threat to Yugoslavia of the debt burden and increasing economic inequalities, the rising corruption of one-party rule in Africa and Cuba. At the same time, I also identified positive trends which were to establish themselves in the growth of the women's movement, in the Green campaigns, in the first signs of a revival of Keynes's thought after the failures of monetarism were becoming clear and in the wide spread of networking as an alternative to either market relations or authoritarian commands. None of these models has been set to work on a large scale in the last decade, but they have greatly influenced popular thought and even found some response here and there in government policy-making.

There is, however, a deeper failure of judgement to which I plead guilty. This went beyond an excess of will over intellect. It lay in my too-ready acceptance of the progressive character of Marx's evolutionary model of the succession of social formations. I am not questioning the evolutionary model. Far from serving as a refutation of Marx's thought, the collapse of the Soviet Union only reinforces Marx's argument. He never expected that a socialist society would emerge from the least developed of capitalist societies, and in his letters to the Russian revolutionary, Vera Zasulich, specifically ruled out the possibility of a direct leap from the Russian commune to communism (Shanin, 1983). But Marx did expect the breakdown of developed capitalism to create the conditions for a new social order. He did not say when, but he clearly believed that it would not be so long delayed.

In the book, I did not accept the likelihood of an early emergence of a socialist society out of the contradictions of capitalism, and certainly not that Soviet society was any form of socialism, except in the narrowest sense of planned allocation of resources. I was careful to reject the very nineteenth-century belief shared by both Marx and Engels in the infinite powers of human reason and the unlimited extent of nature's resources. Yet there was an assumption running through the book that social progress was inevitable once some major, even revolutionary, corrections had been made in economic and political structures.

I do not for a moment renounce my belief in the power of the human instinct for cooperation, however much it has, in places, been overlaid by competitiveness. What I had clearly failed to come to terms with, however, was the profound implications of acts of human violence, not only of masters towards servants, of employers towards 'their' employees, but of men towards women, of whites towards blacks, of competitors in every field. The gulag and the holocaust and Pol Pot had taught us all how frightful these could be. I had explanations for these horrors in terms of economic failures. The revival of fascism in the late 1980s as a worldwide phenomenon can again be related, as in the 1930s, to unemployment and economic collapse. But the spread of violence to games, the viciousness of football fans, the internecine murders in Yugoslavia, the excesses of terrorism – could all these be accounted for wholly by the contradictions of capitalism and similar contradictions in other economic systems?

The Causes of Rising Violence

However vehemently conservative governments may deny it, the connection of unemployment and poverty with crime and violence is now well established. But the extent of the violence, the massacre of whole populations in civil wars between peoples who had lived together for hundreds of years in relative peace, seems to require further explanation. The holocaust and the gulag were too easily explained by economic collapse plus the paranoia of tyrants and the addiction of psychotics who became their accomplices. It had to be accepted that there were dark places in the human make-up that political economy had to allow for, even while maintaining that it was economic collapse which had revealed them.

The turning-point in my thinking about this came from the war in Yugoslavia. It so happened that I spent the last months of the Second World War and the first years of the peace after 1945 in Bosnia. I had no difficulty in 1990 in understanding the causes of the disintegration of the Yugoslav federation in terms of the total collapse of the Yugoslav economy and the natural instinct of the much richer member republics to abandon a sinking ship. What was hard for me to explain was the murder and rape and arson which exploded among peoples who, despite religious differences, had managed to live together relatively peacefully in the same towns and villages over several centuries. Nothing that the German and Italian occupation had done between 1941 and 1945, in encouraging Croats to turn upon Serbs and both on Moslems, could account for the bloodbath that followed the recognition of Croatia first by Germany and then by the European Community in 1990 and the military response of the Serbs.

When I entered Bosnian territory as the Germans withdrew, I saw the results of the German scorched earth policy, but most of the Orthodox and Catholic churches and the mosques in each town and larger village were still standing. They are not today. I saw enough to know that what was happening between 1941 and 1945 was a war of national liberation, in which all the separate nations and religions had united under Tito's leadership to defeat the occupation forces of Germany and Italy and their allies. After the war ended, the new Yugoslav federal constitution enabled all the Yugoslav peoples to work together in rebuilding their war-torn country. The Moslems of Bosnia, Macedonia and Serbia sought recognition as a nationality and the Albanians of Kosovo sought greater independence within the federation, alongside their Serbian, Croatian and Slovene brothers and sisters. By and large they got it. (Barratt Brown, 1994.)

How was it, then, that when the Yugoslav economy collapsed in the late 1980s, such terrible hatreds were let loose? It seems that jungle instincts take over once the gap between rich and poor widens beyond a certain point, as it did in ex-Yugoslavia, in the old Soviet Union, in parts of Latin America. One can ask a similar question about central Asia, about northern India, about Somalia and Rwanda, Peru and southern Mexico, and – nearer home – about Algeria and Northern Ireland, where civil wars prevail.

Unemployment and economic disadvantage and discrimination must be part of the answer. But the framework that is needed to hold human beings together in a cooperative mode is evidently more than just an economic structure. The development of political forms, the whole structure of social, legal and political relations which Marx called the 'superstructure' has clearly to enter Marx's model at a more fundamental level than he allowed for. What, then, is left of the model which identifies the contradictions between developing productive forces and existing relations of production as the dynamic of social change?

Politics or Economics at the Base?

It can still be plausibly argued that contradictions between new technology and old economic structures, often taking the form of class conflicts, prove to be the chief reason why men and women build alternative economic structures, which require new social, political and legal superstructures to contain them. But the necessity for a revolutionary restructuring of the economy *prior* to changes in the superstructure seems unproven, and the possibility of adaptation within old economic structures, as lessons are learned from previous contradictions, much more likely than Marx envisaged.

In other words, social change comes more directly than Marx believed from the consciousness of the need for change that men and women gain from experiencing these contradictions. Marx proposed an almost automatic sequence of contradiction and economic change when he insisted in the Preface to the *Contribution to the Critique of Political Economy* that the 'transformation of the economic conditions of production can be determined with the precision of natural science', and when he relegated to 'ideology', 'the forms in which men become conscious of this conflict and fight it out' (Marx, 1904).

It seems to be much more likely that changing the superstructure and changing the economic structure have to go together. The experience of public enterprise and of social provision is an essential part of the learning process which can lead on to fundamental social change, to end human exploitation. Establishing space in our societies for such cooperative activity must be the first task of socialists. This is not at all the same thing as the social democratic view, well represented in a collection of *Political Quarterly* essays (Crouch and Marquand, 1993), that changing the superstructure comes first and economic restructuring can follow.

This is the obverse of Marx's view. Nor should one underestimate the power of false consciousness, perceptions based on ideology, which Marx saw as concealing reality in the struggles that human beings engage in. But a growing consciousness is developing today of the absurd, even obscene, contradictions of capitalism: that it is possible, for example, to land a man on the moon while we are unable to provide enough food for a quarter of the world's population; that in the richest countries in the world one-fifth of the people are in absolute poverty.

The implications of such growing consciousness appear not only in people's minds, but in their forms of organization. There was always something of this idea present in Marx's thinking of starting to create nuclei of future superstructures through trade-union and cooperative organization. When, for example, he addressed the First International in 1864, he welcomed the Eight Hour Act and the birth of a cooperative movement in Britain as victories of the political economy of labour over the political economy of property. This recognition of workers' power distinguished his later writing from that of the *Communist Manifesto*, when he and Engels stated their belief that, unlike previous classes which have challenged an existing ruling class, the working class had 'nothing of their own to secure and fortify'. It has become evident in recent years that organizations of working people are essential for their collective well-being, indeed for their personal self-advancement also; and the destruction or reduction of such organizations has been for them a terrible loss.

What Is New in This Edition

After issuing these cautionary words, I have left the introductory chapter, 'On Models in General', almost intact, as an acceptable statement of a certain largely Marxist position on models in political economy. In the chapters on the Marxist model and on Marx's model of socialism, I develop a rather sharper critique than before of Marx's method, and this more critical stance pervades the subsequent chapters on the Soviet, Chinese, Yugoslav and African models in Part Two, which I have now called 'Models of Attempted Socialist Economies'. I have left the order in which models are studied very much as before, but I have added a Japanese model and I have moved the Arms Economy model back into the models of capitalism. Its place in transitional models was always a tenuous one, depending upon a particular view of the East–West struggle. It can have no place today in any kind of transition, except to perdition. The chapters on the Soviet Union, China, Yugoslavia and Africa have been considerably expanded to take in recent events.

In Part Three, 'What Models Do We Need Now?', in the place that was occupied by the Arms Economy model I have extended the chapter on 'Models for Understanding Transnational Capitalism', adding a new first part on the breakdown of the nation state; this is followed by a revision of what I had written before, leading up to some new suggestions for the basis of a new international order. Even more than ten years ago, the nation state is now under attack. It has begun to succumb to attacks both from above, as in the advancing powers of the European Union and global economic integration, and from below, as in the disintegration of the Soviet Union, Yugoslavia and Nigeria. At the same time, the activities of big transnational companies are more and more concentrated within the already industrialized countries. Yet it must be noted that these companies have had to face challenges, both from newcomers in East Asia and from smaller companies everywhere with greater innovatory capacity. The decline of IBM must be a warning to all the other giants.

With the disappearance of the Soviet bloc and the marginalization of Africa, spheres of influence are being strengthened around the three main industrialized centres: North America, Europe and Japan; and only China shows the dynamism needed to demand a restructuring of the world order. The last chapter but one, called 'Models in the Transition to Socialism' as it was written in the early 1980s, reads ten years later like a description of the flowers of yesteryear. Despite the many warnings given about the shallowness of their roots, a great number of plants have unexpectedly died. Undoubtedly, something remains in the ground to send up new shoots, but distinguishing the quick and the dead requires more ruthless pruning than was attempted before. The framework for encouraging new growth, for a new social order, has certainly to be different from preceding models; and the revision of this chapter is an attempt to discover alternative views on what should be different. The emphasis in the arguments that are being advanced remains on local initiative, but the existence of a wider framework of regulation has been shown to be more than ever necessary if increasing inequalities and ecological damage are to be avoided.

The last chapter, then, is more modest than the one ten years earlier on the prospects for democracy and socialism: first, because the human situation greatly worsened during the 1980s for the overall majority of men and women under capitalist regimes in developed and developing societies; secondly, because the actual outcome of socialist attempts during these years to create a new social order was a great worsening in the lot of the poor and disadvantaged. Attempts that were made to build socialist alternatives in industrialized countries like Britain on the basis of trade-union initiatives and Labour-led local government collapsed almost completely under the hammer blows of Mrs Thatcher's monetary counter-revolution. Marx's 'reserve army of the unemployed' became separated from the working class in a way that Marx never envisaged and was not true of the nineteenth-century periods of recession. Marx had often said that there was 'only one thing worse than being exploited; and that was not being exploited' – referring to the unemployed. But he did not imagine a whole part of the population in industrialized countries and in the world as a whole being thus marginalized and permanently excluded from active social life.

At the same time, despite growing unemployment, something must be said on the positive side. Developments in alternative trading and consumer consciousness combined with the democratizing capacities of the new information technology have begun to open up fresh opportunities for democratic management and social provision. The opportunities have still to be realized in much of industry and commerce, where technology has been exploited to introduce new managerial techniques of controlling labour time and labour processes, especially through supplanting trade-union shop steward controls by 'team leadership' and a structure of mutual pressurizing of worker by worker. What has to be recorded is that the techniques have not been entirely successful. There are stories from Japanese plants, as we shall see later, of workers' resistance in the UK, and in the USA and Canada as well as in Japan itself. Capital is not obviously succeeding in developing a profitable labour force along with the new technology (Garrahan and Stuart, 1992).

At the same time, there is something in the nature of a consumers' revolt. The demand for organic and 'green' products and for fair trade has come from the shoppers; it was not created by the suppliers. Public spending for social provision is still popular. A sequence of opinion polls in Britain in the early 1990s showed that, despite politicians' fears of raising taxes, a growing proportion of the population (65 per cent in 1994 compared with 32 per cent in 1987) would be prepared to pay more taxes to obtain more benefits in public provision. The electorate is not so keen on privatizing everything. Even in the pages of academic journals the 1960s and 1970s are looked back on as the Age of Equality (Robinson, 1991). Old Marxist ideas about 'socially necessary labour time' have been revived as a measure of fairness in wage determination, to counter the uneven development of market economies. Still older Athenian ideas of choosing rulers by lot have been resuscitated in an effort to counter rising discontent with the performance of parliamentary democracy (Held, 1987; Cockshott and Cottrell, 1993). The conclusion for socialists is to make it small, to act democratic and not to despair because progress is slow.

FURTHER READING

BARRATT BROWN, MICHAEL, 'The Question of a Third Balkan War', *End Papers*, Spokesman, 1994

COCKSHOTT, PAUL, and COTTRELL, ALLIN, *Towards a New Socialism*, Spokesman, 1993, pp. 177ff.

CROUCH, COLIN, and MARQUAND, DAVID (eds.), *Ethics and Markets: Cooperation and Competition within Capitalist Economies*, Blackwell, 1993

GARRAHAN, P., and STUART, P., *The Nissan Enigma: Flexibility at Work in a Local Economy*, Mansell, 1992

HANDY, CHARLES, *The Empty Raincoat*, Hutchinson, 1994

HELD, DAVID, *Models of Democracy*, Stanford University, 1987

MARX, KARL, *Contribution to the Critique of Political Economy* (Preface), Kerr, 1904

MARX, KARL, and ENGELS, FRIEDRICH, *The Communist Manifesto*, Lawrence & Wishart, 1948

ROBINSON, SIR AUSTIN, 'The Economics of the Next Century', *Economic Journal*, Vol. 101, No. 404, January 1991, p. 96

ROEMER, JOHN, *A Future for Socialism*, 1994

SHANIN, TEODOR, *The Late Marx and the Russian Road*, Routledge, 1983

TYLECOTE, ANDREW, *Riding the Long Wave*, Employment Policy Institute, 1993

WOLLEN, PETER, 'Our Post-Communism: The Legacy of Karl Kautsky', *New Left Review*, November–December 1993

WRIGHT, ERIK OLIN, *et al.*, *Reconstructing Marxism*, Verso, 1992

1 INTRODUCTION: ON MODELS IN GENERAL

It has become fashionable to speak about models where once we might have spoken of systems, theories, abstractions, hypotheses, paradigms or conceptual frameworks. The word 'model' is rich in meaning. As a verb it means to fashion or shape and, because this implies a new shape or fashion, we have 'this year's model' and the idea of a model as a standard; and by transference those who show off this year's shapes become 'models'. In scientific usage – both in the natural and social sciences – model has now taken on the further meaning which concerns us here. It describes in a simple way how some complex organism or organization works. Children can build scale models of cars that reproduce on a small scale many of the working parts of a real car; best of all if they reproduce the essential working parts, for example of a steam engine in which water is actually heated in a tiny boiler to produce steam which drives a piston and turns wheels. In this way the model shows in a simplified manner the essential relationship of the various parts in a complex structure. The pieces are not thrown together in a random way like a pile of spillikins, each of which can be extracted by careful manipulation without disturbing the others. The pieces are parts of a whole which has been designed with a purpose and, as we would say of a child's model, it actually works.

Models to Represent Moving Parts

Applying the word 'model' to an economy, we are suggesting, then, that we can abstract the essential relationships between the parts that make it work. We are implying that there may be different kinds of economy that work in different ways, though some may look at first sight rather the same – just as the essential parts of a steam engine, an internal-combustion engine and an electric engine will work in very different ways, although each could be used to power a very similar-looking car. In each engine we have some form of energy – coal, petrol or an electric current – which can be turned into power by heating water, by internal combustion with an electric spark or by magnetic attraction and some connection of pistons, cranks and gears that will turn wheels round to make the car move. So in an economy there has to be some motive force which generates the production and distribution of goods and services.

Except in a few places where it is possible for people, like the lotus-eaters of the old myths, to lie under palm-trees and pick up the falling coconuts and bananas for food and drink and idly weave the leaves for clothes and shelter, human energy has to be expended to get a living; and not only by individuals but in groups. This requires some organizational structure even at the simplest level of collecting roots and nuts, chasing animals and spearing fishes, cooking them and making simple clothes and shelters. It also requires some cultural bonding to reinforce the structure. As agriculture and animal husbandry, stonemasonry and metalworking were developed, much more complex structures were needed. Today, with the huge range of goods and services that we regard as essential for a decent living, the structure has become immensely and bewilderingly complex, and we tend to think of cultural bonds as something separate. Nevertheless, it should still be possible for us to sort out the several parts of the structure and to reveal their essential relationships in a model of how the economy works, and to integrate the political, cultural and economic aspects of the whole social formation.

Let us stay for a moment with our mechanical comparison. Human energy has to be harnessed so that it works. The very word 'harnessed' suggests to us one way in which this was done – literally by yoking men and women together to pull ploughs or haul stones. Historians have distinguished different social formations and economic systems according to the tools that men and women used and the power that they had at their disposal. In this way we can distinguish different economic models.

Models of Economies in History

The peasant household which produces its own food and clothing and shelter is based on a division of labour between members of an extended family of several generations. They may join together with other families in a primitive commune for certain larger tasks of forest clearance, flood prevention or irrigation on the basis of age sets, each age group having a task allotted by custom. It is then the sense of community, reinforced by verbal tradition in songs and dances and religious practices, that harnesses the human energy, directs it into set tasks and distributes the products of labour among the people in ways that are accepted as fair. When that sense is lost, with the coming of individual literacy and buying and selling in the market, 'things fall apart', as we may read in Chinua Achebe's book about Nigeria with that title or in George Thomson's story of the desertion of the Blasket Islands off the west coast of Ireland.

Slavery gives us another model of an economy based on human labour. To produce a surplus for building cities and temples, great houses and great monuments to the dead, as well as for flood control and irrigation works and metal crafts, slaves are harnessed together under the lash of the whip or the spell of superstition. In that wonderful allegory of the founding of capitalism on the basis of the slave trade, Daniel Defoe describes how Robinson Crusoe bound Man Friday and his fellow islanders to him by the combined power of the gun and of God, to produce sugar for export from his plantations.

We need different models to understand economies which have developed on the basis of successively more advanced forms of energy brought under human control: water and wind, steam, internal combustion, electricity, nuclear power, wave and solar energy. 'With the windmill we have the feudal lord and with the steam engine we have the industrial capitalist,' said Marx; and Lenin added that 'Planning plus Electrification equals Socialism.' Of course, neither of them meant that the social systems and the model of their economic workings followed exactly or depended totally on the new sources of energy. Unfortunately, these state-

3

ments have been taken by some socialists in a dogmatic manner to provide a sort of final proof of the inevitability of the coming of socialism. This kind of deterministic abstract model-making has been criticized, especially as it was developed by the French Marxist philosopher, Althusser. But to criticize all economic models in historical analysis is to throw the baby out with the bath water. For the late E. P. Thompson, for example, in *The Poverty of Theory*, to make the criticism by reference to drawings of mechanical 'orreries'* of the eighteenth century, which showed the movements of the planets round the sun, is to substitute ridicule for reasoned argument.

What Marx really meant in analysing the social formations of different epochs was that we need different models to understand the different economic structures that human beings have built in developing and using new technologies; but he also meant that old structures could hold back this development and would have to be overthrown if development was to continue to fulfil the aspirations of humanity. Capitalist profit from labour and the incentive to accumulate capital had made possible the progress of the first industrial revolution, which feudal landownership and serfdom had held back. In its turn capitalist ownership in our day acts as a fetter on the fulfilment of the second industrial revolution. Social ownership alone, Marx believed, would release the new powers that human beings had developed – for their enrichment, not their impoverishment. It is this method of Marx's, not the predetermined conclusion, that has informed the writing of this book.

Marx summarized his model of the distinctive social formations of different epochs of human history in his Preface to *A Contribution to the Critique of Political Economy*, published in 1859. At the base he placed the struggle of human beings with nature and their discovery of progressively more advanced forces of production. But these could only be developed within an appropriate economic structure of production relations of ownership and control that would correspond to the level of technology. Produc-

*The name is owed to an Irish peer, the Earl of Cork and Orrery, who invented one.

4

tive forces and relations of production thus formed what Marx called the mode of production: Asiatic, ancient (slave), feudal, capitalist. Each mode, however, required a corresponding superstructure for its fulfilment, i.e. of social, legal and political institutions. This combined with the mode of production made up a total social formation – what we might now call a social order (see Figure 1).

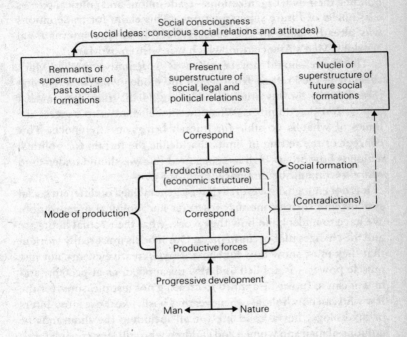

Figure 1. Marx's model of social structure and development (from Lange, 1963, p.33, after Marx, 1859)

Our ideas, our social consciousness, said Marx, do not create this social order, as the German idealist philosopher Hegel had proposed. Marx turned Hegel on his head. It is how we get our living, Marx said, our social existence, that determines our ideas, not the other way round. Our ideas emerge, however, not only from the present social formation but also from the remnants of the superstructure of past social formations and from nuclei of superstructures of future social formations. This is where we find the dialectic in Marx's materialism, i.e. the possibility of change. For these nuclei arise from the contradictions and conflicts which developing technology raises for people's consciousness of their place in the relations of production. Class struggles lead to workers under capitalism building their own organizations – trade unions and political parties – as nuclei of future superstructures. (This claim for trade unions was already made in the 1866 Resolution of the International Working Men's Association, which was written by Marx.)

The figure should not be taken as a definitive model. Marx called it in the Preface, from which the model is taken, a 'guiding thread' only for his studies; and Lange's diagram may indeed appear too deterministic. What the model does is to suggest the limits of what is possible for human beings in any epoch. This concept of the setting of limits that define the terrain for political action is how Stuart Hall has suggested that we should understand Marx's economic determinacy (Hall, 1983).

It is not enough, however, to have a general idea of different social systems and their economic structures and political organization. We have to understand how they work, what their actual limits are and the changes that occur in them. Our models must really work in that they must show how human energy – creative energy not just muscle power – is applied and also misapplied, as at present; and how it can in future be applied to creating not just pleasures for the few who can now holiday whenever they wish, like those lotus-eaters of mythology, but a good life for all including the thousands of millions of men and women and children who still lack enough food, pure water, good health, clothing and shelter to give even a modicum of comfort and dignity and who only survive by back-breaking toil and constant anxious care for every grain and fruit they produce.

Models of Political Economy and Econometric Models

Marx's view of social formations is of course only one of many views that we shall meet in this book. It happens to be the view that this author has found most helpful in guiding him through the problems of political economy. Other views have in common the rejection of the central importance that Marx gave to labour, to the way we get our living, the techniques we use and the relations between human beings at work, in determining both the institutions within which we work and the ideas that we have about the world. Some, by contrast, will emphasize the importance of the institutions that human beings have created over long periods of time – the family, the market, forms of government, monarchy and Parliament, the churches, courts of justice and so on. These are seen as continuing and abiding despite apparently revolutionary changes, and their importance will be supported by all that is conservative in our make-up. Others will emphasize with Hegel the paramountcy of ideas and of the individual creative human spirit, forever experimenting, inventing, discovering, changing as well as conserving. This spirit is seen to transcend institutions, to know no bounds of place and time, so that the words of writers and thinkers who have been dead for two thousand years and more can reach out to us afresh to inspire us today. All that is liberal, in the sense of freedom-seeking and generous in our make-up, responds to this view of the world. (The reader is referred to Raymond Williams's *Key Words* for more insights into the origins of words like liberal and conservative.)

Ideas, however, can imprison and constrict as well as liberate and inspire. It is part of Marx's revolutionary vision that our present ideas, our consciousness of our own times, are not a good indication of reality. These ideas are made up from many hang-overs of the past as well as from Utopian visions of the future. 'Men make their own history,' says Marx and he means not only great men but thousands and thousands of ordinary men and women, 'but not just as they intended it.' For history is made by many men and women with separate wills and interests. There is 'not as yet', says Engels (in a famous letter to H. Starkenburg in 1894), a 'collective will' or 'collective plan' involved even in any one given society. Reality is concealed from us by a veil of false consciousness which reflects the surface phenomena, giving us only a partially true picture. It is such 'necessarily false consciousness' that Marx calls ideology. It was, Marx believed, his task to reveal the workings of a model of capitalist economy that lay behind the everyday appearances of capital, land and labour and their 'rewards' in profit, rent and wages in the market.

Marx's emphasis on the importance of the economic element in all the complexity of interacting wills and events is always set within a total view of any social formation. It is already obvious that our models will have to be political as well as purely economic. Marxists do not make the distinction, but speak, as the early classical economists did, of political economy. In other words, what Marx called the superstructure, the political framework of the state, of Parliament and local government, of the laws of the land, and of international institutions, will have to be seen not only as setting constraints on the economic model, influencing and sometimes even controlling the way it works, but as an integral part of it.

This means that we shall have to distinguish the models we are examining from those econometric models that governments of market as well as planned economies use as the framework for computer calculations. From these they seek to predict the results of their interventions in the national economy, since such computerized models are made up of equations and correlations representing quantities of money flowing through different sectors of the economy. They allow statisticians on the basis of past experience to measure what the effects will be, say, on employment or prices of increasing or decreasing government taxes and expenditure or of raising or lowering the interest rate or exchange rate. The predictions are not expected to be very accurate and certainly not for more than about six months or at most a year ahead. To look further there are too many variables that are not allowed for in the model.

Now there is no doubt that as these models are refined they become more and more useful to government planners. But they do not really help us very much, for two reasons. First, such models do not tell us how we may change the correlations, for example how output per person working with similar machinery may be increased by better organization, different ways of working, incentives, etc. It is noteworthy that, in the measurements that statisticians make of differences in rates of economic growth between countries, by far the largest element is always the residual factor, that is, the unknown element after inputs of capital and of labour, the scale of production and the mix of industries and agriculture and so on have all been accounted for. Secondly, such models do not tell us what the results might be of major changes that could arise in economic expectations and so in economic activity as a result of government planning. To take two examples: What might the effect be on trade-union wage demands and on price inflation if the government greatly increased the social wage and transferred more control over its spending to local authorities, including community groups? And what might be the effect on the level of world trade exchanges if national governments agreed to introduce an element of long-term planning to expand international trade, instead of each country holding back the growth of its imports so that they are balanced by its exports?

These are among the many questions to which we shall hope to find models of political economy to answer for us at the end of this book. To sum up, then, our models can help us to describe reality as in the natural sciences; but they do more than this in the social sciences. They help to organize social relations, to define social duties and justify the social structure. Even if our models do not give us precisely measurable data, they may give us the courage to start making the changes in political and economic structures necessary to improve the conditions of life and work of the poor and hungry the world over. For we are part of the model with all our personal and cultural strengths and weaknesses, class, gender and national differences.

It is the strength of the Marxist tradition that it not only provides a theory of historical evolution but an analysis of social relations *and* a message for the future. Eric Olin Wright has described these three nodes of Marxist theory as a 'historical trajectory', a 'class analysis' and a 'normative view' of emancipation from class rule (Wright *et al.*, 1992). It was the way in which each reinforced the other, he insists, that gave Marxism its strength. We shall need to raise questions about each one of the

9

nodes in Marx's thinking, but the attempt to combine historical evolution with social analysis will inform all our efforts to understand the possibilities of a fundamental social change which would end human oppression.

There are some who will challenge the very idea that oppression is an economic problem rather than a political one, i.e. depending on economic relations in production rather than on forms of government. Exploitation of human labour in different ways has been central to all economic and social systems. Labour is exploitable because unlike any other of the factors of production which can be exploited – land, energy, materials – it is not a technical coefficient that determines the relationship between the ratio of the value of the factor consumed to the value of the factor produced: for example, how much oil or coal is required to produce a given quantity of oil or coal. What a human being consumes in producing value is socially determined, but there is no given technical coefficient which determines how much value he or she can produce at work. This will depend partly on the tools and machines in use, but largely on the effort and skill applied, and the reward for this will depend on the relative bargaining strength of the owner of capital and the owner of labour power. But this is a matter which will engage us again and again in our studies of models in political economy.

FURTHER READING

BODINGTON, STEPHEN, *Computers and Socialism*, Spokesman, 1973

COHEN, G. A., *Karl Marx's Theory of History: A Defence*, Oxford University Press, 1979

ENGELS, FRIEDRICH, *The Origin of the Family, Private Property and the State*, 1884 (first published in English 1940); Lawrence & Wishart, 1972

HALL, S., 'The Problems of Ideology', in Betty Matthews (ed.), *Marx: A Hundred Years On*, Lawrence & Wishart, 1983

LANGE, O., *Political Economy*, Pergamon, 1963

MARX, KARL, Preface to *A Contribution to the Critique of Political Economy*, 1859; Lawrence & Wishart, 1971

MATTHEWS, BETTY (ed.), *Marx: A Hundred Years On*, Lawrence & Wishart, 1983

SHANIN, T. (ed.), *The Rules of the Game*, Tavistock, 1972

TEAL, F., and OSBORN, D. R., 'An Assessment and Comparison of Two Econometric Model Forecasts', *National Institute Economic Review*, No. 88, May 1979, pp. 50–62

THOMPSON, E. P., *The Poverty of Theory*, Merlin Press, 1978

WILLIAMS, RAYMOND, *Key Words*, Fontana, 1976

WILLIAMS, RAYMOND, 'Base and Superstructure in Marxist Theory', in *Problems in Materialism and Culture*, Verso, 1980

WRIGHT, ERIC OLIN, LEVINE, ANDREW, and SOBER, ELLIOTT, *Reconstructing Marxism*, Verso, 1992

1 MODELS OF CAPITALIST ECONOMIES

THE MARKET MODEL:
A. WITH COMPETITION ON A
NATIONAL SCALE

A market, as everyone knows, is a place where goods are brought to be bought and sold. But in a capitalist economy the market has a much bigger role than that of a shopping centre. One of the earliest victories of capitalists (of the townsmen or bourgeoisie) over feudal landowners was to end the payment of dues and tolls to them and to free the movement of produce from the countryside into the market towns and from town to town. An even more important capitalist victory came when labour was freed to enter the market and land could freely be bought and sold. For it is not only goods for consumption that have markets. There are the relics of wool markets and cloth markets, a cattle market and a corn exchange in most old towns. In London and other very big cities there are commodity markets of many sorts where food and minerals and raw materials from overseas can be bought and sold: rubber and tin and copper, furs and wool and cotton, sugar, cocoa, coffee, tea and spices. These are called commodities because they are produced for sale in the market. They are cash crops and not for the growers' own consumption. Often these commodities are not even imported into London; they are held in warehouses for re-export and only samples are tested.

Far beyond these in importance, however, for a capitalist economy are the markets in the factors of production themselves: markets for labour in what used to be called the Labour Exchange; markets for land and property in auction rooms and sales rooms or simply in the back room of the local public house; markets for capital in a Stock Exchange and money markets everywhere so that bankers can phone each other to find the going rate of borrowing and lending. In this great system of markets we can discover the economic model of a market economy. It is the model that is introduced at the beginning of every economics textbook and has been canonized with the authority of Adam Smith, the founder two hundred years ago of British political economy.

The market model is based on very simple assumptions. There are millions of producers and millions of consumers all in competition with each other. All go to their various markets to sell or to buy. The buyers can pick and choose from many sellers of roughly similar goods or services. In the process of bargaining, prices are set for the day. Some goods and services will have sold better than others as buyers balanced price and quality. Some sellers will have covered their costs, others may have had to sell at a loss. We have to notice at once that buyers and sellers are being thought of as separate individuals each making his or her own choice. There is no collusion among sellers or common decision-making among buyers. This is quite unrealistic today in relation to the sellers, but it is increasingly true of the buyers of final goods in the shops, since so many common services are being replaced by private goods. While there are fewer and fewer sellers, operating often in collusion, nearly all buyers in shops and other markets will be acting on behalf of an individual household. Facilities for sheltering, bathing, laundering, gardening, exercising and entertainment, as well as for feeding, are all purchased and used in the home. Yet almost nothing is now made in the home, not food or drink or clothes; all is bought in.

The result of this individuation in the market is that, while personal choice is greatly extended, there are increased dangers of two well-known drawbacks occurring. The first is the so-called 'tragedy of the commons'; the second is comparable to the 'prisoners' dilemma'. In the tragedy of the commons, individual villagers decided to introduce more and more cattle and sheep to the common grazing, until all users of the common land found that their animals were suffering. On a world scale, we can see the results of individual overdevelopment in global warming and in the destruction of the rain forests.

In variants of the prisoners' dilemma in a zero sum game, there might be, for example, only one full-time job or two part-time jobs available for two candidates for employment. If each goes for a full-time job, one is going to remain unemployed. They do not know each other and have no chance of making contact. If they both go for a part-time job, both will benefit, although not as much as the winner of the full-time job. Since there is no mechanism for discussion between them, they will compete for the one full-time job and are unlikely to choose the job share. Such encouragement of competition leads inevitably to increasing inequalities (see Figure 2).

		Second applicant	
		Full-time job	Part-time job
First applicant	Full-time job	+2 −2	−1 +1
	Part-time job	−2 +2	+1 +1

Figure 2. The prisoner's dilemma in choosing a job (adapted from Meek, 1971, p.152)

Nevertheless, so long as there is competition, the market performs three essential resource functions: it fixes a price which clears the market, whether for potatoes, land, labour or capital; it encourages producers to reduce their costs; and it allocates resources to those who could make best use of them and for lines that have proved most popular at the price. The profit-makers will produce more of the same; the loss-makers will switch lines, reduce their costs or go out of business. Land, labour and capital go where the profit indicators in the market are signalling. This is what the market enthusiasts claim, and although the signals are now prearranged it is still argued that they reflect people's needs. The profit motive and the search for a good bargain are still supposed to ensure that what is produced is what is wanted.

'It is not', said Adam Smith, 'from the benevolence of the butcher, the brewer, or the baker, that we expect our dinner, but from their regard to their own interest.' All are obliged to bring the results of their efforts 'into a common stock, where every man may purchase whatever part of the produce of other men's talents he has occasion for'. (Adam Smith, *Wealth of Nations*, Bk I, Chap. 2.) The market does the job of distributing the common stock. And Smith goes on,

> Every man, as long as he does not violate the laws of justice, is left perfectly free to pursue his own interests in his own way, and to bring both his industry and capital into competition with those of any other man, or order of men. The Sovereign* is completely discharged from a duty, in the attempting to perform which he must always be exposed to innumerable delusions, and for the proper performance of which no human wisdom or knowledge could ever be sufficient; the duty of superintending the industry of private people, and of directing it towards the employments most suitable to the interests of the Society. (ibid., Bk IV, Chap. 9.)

All these duties can only be performed in the market, where every individual 'intends only his own gain and is in this as in many other cases led by an invisible hand to promote an end which was no part of his intention' (ibid., Chap. 2). To think otherwise is to be deluded, says Smith.

At the same time, Adam Smith's 'invisible hand' is not, as many people suppose, some sort of magic wand guiding the workings of the market. Stuart Holland has made this point abundantly clear in his *The Market Economy: From Micro to Mesoeconomics* (Holland, 1987). Smith had developed his concept of an 'invisible hand' in his first book, *The Theory of Moral Sentiments*, some years before he published his more famous *Inquiry into the Nature and Causes of the Wealth of Nations*. He understood only too well that 'people of the same trade seldom meet together even for merriment and diversion, but the conversation ends in a conspiracy against the public or in some contrivance to raise prices'. Only the force of 'sympathy' (we might say solidarity) provided a framework within which competition was restrained. Smith, writing for the aristocratic society of the eighteenth century, saw such moral sentiments as stemming from 'the sympathetic feelings of the impartial and well-informed spectator'. In a democratic age, they have to come from popular control and regulation

---

*i.e. the government – M.B.B.

of the market. All the recent moves towards deregulation made in Britain by Conservative governments, for which Mrs Thatcher claimed the authority of Adam Smith, have been in the very opposite direction from that in which Smith was pointing. The market was seen as international by Adam Smith and as such even more in need of solidarity. By contrast, in our day deregulation on an international scale through the latest agreements in the Uruguay round of GATT is likely to have the most adverse effects on the balance of nature and the equality of human beings.

Smith was above all anxious to remove royal monopolies that restricted free trade between nations. None the less, he still saw the home trade as more important and argued for agricultural self-sufficiency. He started from the basis of the nation state; his book is concerned with the wealth of nations. He believed in a strong navy to protect national interest. But within these limits it was free competition that he looked to as the guarantee of welfare. The model of the market was an organizing model of great historic power, which many people saw as liberating them from the social and economic bonds of feudal and autocratic societies. Free competition came to be seen as the foundation of democracy.

Historically, Adam Smith's model was undoubtedly of enormous importance in liberating human enterprise from the dead hand of royal monopolies and feudal restraints on trade. Inventions that had lain dormant in the minds of gifted craftsmen could be taken up and applied to production as capital was freed from the hands of the merchants and labour from the lands of the lords. A new group of 'outsiders' had already broken into the merchant monopolies in seventeenth-century England and begun to build an empire based on trade rather than on pillage. Tenant (capitalist) farmers were enclosing land throughout the eighteenth century to carry through an agricultural revolution as precursor to industrial revolution. But it needed the ideological power of Adam Smith's model of free competition in the market to release all the forces that were to create the first capitalist economy in Britain. To remember the misery of those who were driven from their cottages into the slums of the new towns should not lead us to forget the transformation of human productive power that capitalism effected.

Marx and Engels, writing their *Communist Manifesto* in 1848, paid tribute to the effects of the opening up of a world market to capitalist enterprise:

> The bourgeoisie, during its rule of scarce one hundred years, has created more massive and more colossal productive forces than have all preceding generations together. Subjection of nature's forces to man: machinery, application of chemistry to industry and agriculture, steam navigation, railways, electric telegraphs, clearing of whole continents for cultivation, canalization of rivers, whole populations conjured out of the ground – what earlier century had even a presentiment that such productive forces slumbered in the lap of social labour?

The whole passage should be read as a remarkable vision of what was to come in the next century. Stephen Hymer (1975) has suggested that it is only necessary to substitute 'multinational corporation' for 'bourgeoisie', in the passages preceding the one quoted, to bring the story up to date.

Even before it ceased to be true that there were large numbers of competing suppliers in most markets – and we shall look at monopolies in the next chapter – there were already some major difficulties in accepting Adam Smith's model as a fully adequate analysis of the real world. First, there are limitations on what is available in any market. As communications improved, this was not a serious problem since most goods became widely distributed. Some goods, however, cannot be bought in the market but require public provision. Town planning and public parks are examples. What is more serious, some 'bads' are not avoided by the market. Pollution of the environment is the obvious example. The market does not provide for public welfare.

Secondly, there is the fact of inequality. In the market model it is assumed that producers are rewarded for their efficiency and their contribution to consumers' satisfaction; but this leaves out differences in endowment. Adam Smith himself was quite hardheaded about inequality of inheritance. The owner of capital provided the dynamic for industrial development which neither landowners nor royal monopolies could assure. Later apologists for capitalism explained capital ownership as the reward for saving through abstinence. What is true is that Smith's model required that capital should be in a limited number of hands so that it could be laid out on employing men and women in large-scale mining and manufacturing enterprises, which were at the centre of the process of industrialization. It should be noted here, however, for our future consideration that the division of labour which Adam Smith extolled in the pin factory, where every worker was reduced from having general skills to performing one small detail of the job of pin-making, was not the only possible way of applying machine power to manufacture. It was indeed the best way to divide the work-force and maintain the capitalists' centralization of control over the work-force, but no more.

It is sometimes suggested in economic textbooks that distribution of wealth, income and power are moral questions, of human values, and should be distinguished from economic questions. Economics is said to be a positive (what is) science and not normative (what ought to be), in the sense that it accepts that ends are a matter for the politicians and economics is thus concerned only with means. We have made it clear that for our part we are looking at political economy, in which we cannot expect to separate ends and means. We can see this in two particular respects. First, it is worth saying here in advance of later chapters (in Parts Two and Three) that differences in income, wealth and power have crucially important effects on workers' motivations in such matters as discipline, absenteeism and productivity. The second point gives us our third major critique of Adam Smith's model. Unequal distribution of incomes results in market behaviour quite different from what we should find if the incomes of all who came into the market were the same. Not only is there a range of different qualities of goods, with luxuries for a few and necessities for the many, but there is a distortion in the pull on the market. The pull is of money and not of people.

We can see the results of unequal distribution of income in the impact of different shoppers in the market. A family coming to market with £100 has the same pull as ten families each with £10. For the first, the cost of necessities is a small part of their total expenditure and if the price of potatoes rises this will not stop

21

them buying. For the ten poor families such a price rise may well reduce their purchases, though not completely, because potatoes may still be the cheapest basic food. The distortion in the market is that prices of necessities tend not to be reduced as much as prices of luxuries, if there are enough families prepared to go on buying necessities whatever the price (what the economists call demand that is 'price-inelastic'). At the same time every effort will be made by producers to bring the price of luxuries down so as to expand their sales (the economists' 'price-elastic' demand). Capital will tend to be attracted into supplying rich consumers who have discretionary income to spend, thus further reinforcing inequalities.

The fourth major critique of Adam Smith's economic model is that it assumes that the only relations between one national economy and another are through trade in goods and services and that labour and capital do not cross national boundaries. He was particularly anxious to encourage investment in industry in Britain rather than in overseas adventures. The advantage of trade exchanges was that each country concentrated on producing what it was best at. Adam Smith's great successor, David Ricardo, developed this idea into a law – that of 'comparative advantage' – which said that each country should concentrate on producing the goods in which its comparative advantage was greatest. Then total output would be higher as the result of reallocating resources through foreign trade. This may well be true, but it does not say that the benefits of the extra output will be equally shared between the two or more parties to the exchange. That will depend on the relative bargaining strengths of the two. Colonies which have concentrated on producing their one best crop will find themselves at a disadvantage in relation to an industrial country with a wide range of goods to sell; particularly if there are other colonies producing the same crop and it is perishable and its production not easily mechanized. The GATT Uruguay round again provides a good example: the World Bank estimated that 67 per cent of the benefits would be enjoyed by the industrialized countries, with 15 per cent of the world's population; 85 per cent of the people would thus get 33 per cent of the benefits.

There is still one more major critique of Adam Smith's model to consider. This was one that Ricardo spotted, and his insight has led to a whole school of neo-Ricardians growing up in Cambridge in the 1970s. The flaw in the model appears where Adam Smith assumes that producers who find their goods failing to sell can switch their capital into new lines of production. The problem is that the original capital was sunk in plant and machinery and cannot, without considerable losses, just be switched. The result is that there may be delays in recovery and stunted growth, particularly where many producers overestimate demand in the market at one and the same time. A further result is very tiresome for the apologists of capitalism – it appears that profit cannot be regarded as a return to a certain value of capital. On the contrary, capital only has value according to whatever profit it makes.

These major criticisms of the working of Adam Smith's model do not suggest that it is useless, at least for explaining the establishment of British capitalist industrialization. It is also worth remembering that the free-market mechanisms avoid the nonsense of fixed prices and high output levels in planned markets like the Common Market for agricultural products in Europe, within which prices are kept high in order to support the farming community. Since these prices are well above what people can afford to pay, mountains of butter, beef and sugar, and lakes of wine, are thus created and the products of cheaper producers outside the Common Market neglected.

Our criticisms do, none the less, suggest that we need to look more closely into the economic engine, the productive process itself, where profit is made and bargains are struck between workers and employers, between food producers in the colonies and manufacturers at home, and where income distribution is determined, which evidently has such a big effect on the allocation of resources. It was Marx, building on the work of Smith and Ricardo, who first saw that we had to turn our attention from the market to the work-place to discover a true working model of capitalist economy. Before, however, we turn to Marx we need to look at the modifications in the market model which have had to be made to bring it more into line with the real political economy of capitalism as it has spread from Britain and Europe across the whole world and become concentrated in a few giant transnational industrial companies and their financial associates.

It will be one of the main themes throughout this book that alternatives to the market as a system of allocating resources are not easy to discover and may well be not only less efficient but less just in operation, given that resources are scarce (whether we are thinking of food or housing or parking space as examples): the market provides a system of rationing – by the length of the purse. It has the huge advantage which lies at the heart of capitalism: it motivates those who are able to make money to take to the market. By the same token the rich tend to become richer and the poor poorer. But alternatives have other drawbacks. Rationing by coupon, especially of basic necessities, may appear to be more just, but there are always extra coupons for special categories, followed by queues and a grey market, and then a black market. Goods become available under the counter and special shops may be opened for special customers. Those with connections and protection do well; those without will be down to queuing for the basic ration. It is not for nothing that critics of economies that replace the market by planning have described this as the 'road to serfdom'.

This was the title of a famous book by the Austrian economist, Frederick von Hayek, whose criticism of Soviet planning in the 1930s became the bible of East European reformers after 1990. The assumption was that the capitalist market was a necessary condition for political freedom. The well-known United States economist, John Kenneth Galbraith, was provoked to comment that the 'economics of Professor Friedrich Hayek . . . was not a design which in its rejection of regulatory, welfare and other ameliorating action by the state, we in the United States or elsewhere in the nonsocialist world would find tolerable' (Galbraith, 1991).

The Market and the Nation State

Historically, markets began as local fairs, expanding to serve regions, then nations and finally the whole world. In the process peoples came together to form nations marked off by natural frontiers of seas or mountains. But the main promoter, guarantor and extender of the market throughout history has been the state. Nations are the result of the fusion of peoples – as with the Picts, Friesians, Angles, Saxons, Danes and Normans who made up the English nation. By contrast, states are the creation of ruling groups in one nation which sought to bring their own nationals into one market and to bring other nations also under their control. It is the state which has destroyed all internal barriers to trade, established common currencies and weights and measures, built roads, defended frontiers and sea lanes, promoted national products and protected its citizens in the pursuit of their business at home or overseas. (See Murray, 1975.)

Absorption of other nations into one market was supposed in classical economic theory to lead to the elimination of national differences and sectional inequalities. It is a matter for question, however, whether the Celtic peoples have ever been absorbed into a British nation despite the Acts of Union with Wales in 1536, Scotland in 1707 and Ireland from 1801 to 1921. Certainly the hundreds of nations that were brought under the British state as colonies of the empire were not thus absorbed. And, if we may not be entirely surprised that cultural differences survived, there must be a question why economic inequalities should have been perpetuated.

A central element in the neoclassical market model that needs to be critically scrutinized is the assumption that economic development is universally diffused through the workings of the market. (This has been criticized at length in Barratt Brown, 1974, Chap. 2.) Since it is an obvious fact that economic development is at very unequal levels in different parts of the world, and even in different regions inside nation states, some other explanation of this untoward fact must be sought. The explanations offered range from sheer geographical distance between the periphery and central markets, through a variety of cultural factors which might obstruct adequate responses in face of market forces, to the deliberate resistance of some peoples to the operation of market penetration. Examples can be drawn from apologetic writings on

India or on Ireland with their typical references to irrational customs and taboos and inflexible social caste structures. The fatalism and other-worldly values of the religions of these peoples are contrasted with the English Protestant work ethic. Without necessarily accepting that only material explanations have validity, the question has to be asked how such values arose in the first place and why they persisted among some peoples and not among others.

When we come to study the world economy in the last part of this book we shall note the fact that, far from the market automatically diffusing economic and political change everywhere, all countries that have successfully achieved economic development have had to cut themselves off (at least temporarily) from the world market to do so. Differences in levels of economic development have otherwise persisted just as much inside nation states as between them. There is much evidence that the core of English economic and political development around London and the Home Counties has never been fully diffused to the regions, except in a dependent mode. Wales, Scotland and Ireland have remained at lower levels of economic development and as a result of quite specifically discriminatory political and economic measures of the government and financial authorities in London. Examples are the penal laws in Wales and Ireland, and in Scotland to a lesser extent, prior to unification of the kingdom; the Test and Corporation Acts which excluded Roman Catholics from all offices of state; and the restriction on Irish trade in the crucial decades prior to 1800. England had her internal colonies in the Celtic fringe before she embarked on world conquest and retains them after the imperial era has ended. In reply to neoclassical assumptions it has indeed been argued with a wealth of supporting evidence that Celtic sectionalism is more the result than the cause of unequal development. (See Hechter, 1978.) Nationalist parties re-emerge in Britain as elsewhere as soon as general economic difficulties re-emphasize regional inequalities.

Models in political economy can never then be pure economic models of the neoclassical market. Alongside and above the market there is the state and the power of those ruling groups which control the state. The aim of these groups must always be to strengthen their own position against other classes but also to extend the natural frontiers, to subordinate other national groups either by incorporating their leaders or by making them dependent, always to assert their economic, cultural and political hegemony. While they will by their very nature as a dominant group be in antagonistic relation both to the cultural or ethnic groups and to the individual classes which they subordinate to their interests, they may have the choice of incorporating rather than repressing.

Historical evidence suggests that opposing class interests are more easily incorporated within the process of economic development by industrialization than are opposing ethnic interests within national expansion by colonization. Ethnic differences are especially resistant to assimilation where these have a regional base and are reinforced by exclusion from the centres of economic development. The example of the war in Yugoslavia is only too horribly apt. The increasingly uneven development between the northern and southern republics, with the north having the major industrial growth and access to foreign currency while the local currency was steadily devalued by inflation, opened up ethnic and national divisions that had lain dormant for many years.

The southern republics of Yugoslavia also illustrate an important fact about unequal development. Agricultural and other primary producers have everywhere fallen behind the living standards of those peoples which were able to industrialize. This is particularly true of colonies which were deliberately exploited as raw-material producers for Western European and North American industry. An artificial division of the world into core and peripheral regions resulted. A colonial sub-model of the capitalist market emerged and will need to be distinguished in the last part of this book. What has to be noted at this point is the effect of the working of the market on status and class differentiation in the core and periphery.

A crude model of differentiation by status (ethnic/cultural) and by class (economic/industrial) in relation to an industrialized core and an underdeveloped periphery can be indicated diagrammatically (see Figure 3). The model can be used to explain where the interests of different groups and classes may be expected to lie. The interests of the industrial working class are assumed to coincide with those of the ruling group so long as this class also benefits from industrialization. The model is complicated by the diagonal axis of periphery and core. Some parts of the industrial working class will be found in the periphery and will share working-class interests at the core if the benefits place them above the agricultural producers. Where these benefits fail, the interests of agricultural and industrial workers in the periphery will coincide – a most dangerous situation for the ruling group. Similarly, some of the agents of the ruling group will be near to the ruling group, some further away. The interests of the latter will normally coincide with those of the ruling group, but if the benefits in the periphery fail they too may ally with the colonial producers against their rulers. From such alliances have grown all the varied national liberation movements. Behind every appeal for cultural independence and national sovereignty will lie the claim to a fairer share in the benefits of economic development.

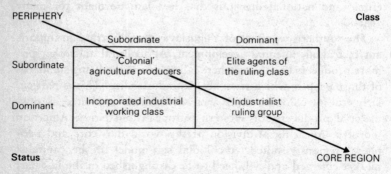

Figure 3. A model of (ethnic) status and (industrial) class differentiation in relation to economic development in a core region

FURTHER READING

BARRATT BROWN, MICHAEL, *The Economics of Imperialism*, Penguin Books, 1974 (see Chap. 2).

GALBRAITH, JOHN KENNETH, 'Economics in the Century Ahead', *Economic Journal*, January 1991, p. 45.

GORZ, ANDRÉ, *The Division of Labour: The Labour Process and Class Struggle in Modern Capitalism*, Harvester, 1978

HAYEK, F. A. VON, *The Road to Serfdom*, Penguin Books, 1976

HECHTER, MICHAEL, *International Colonialism: The Celtic Fringe in British National Development*, Routledge, 1978

HICKS, JOHN, *A Theory of Economic History*, Oxford University Press, 1969

HOLLAND, STUART, *The Market Economy: From Micro to Meso-economics*, Weidenfeld, 1987

HUNT, E. K., and SHARMAN, H. J., *Economics – An Introduction to Traditional and Radical Views*, Harper & Row, 1981

HYMER, S., 'The Multinational Corporation', in H. Radice (ed.), *International Firms and Modern Imperialism*, Penguin Books, 1975

MEEK, RONALD L., *Figuring Out Society*, Fontana, 1971

MURRAY, ROBIN, *Multinational Companies and the Nation State*, Spokesman, 1975

ROBINSON, JOAN, *Economic Philosophy*, Penguin Books, 1962

WINCH, DONALD, *Adam Smith's Politics*, Cambridge, 1978

3 THE MARKET MODEL:
B. WITH MONOPOLIES ON AN
INTERNATIONAL SCALE

In Adam Smith's day the major condition of market competition was met. No single seller or buyer was big enough to affect the price by entering or not entering the market. Even though capital was limited in its distribution to a relatively small number of owners, these could be counted in their tens of thousands, each combining the roles of owner, manager, inventor and of financier too. There is no doubt that the drive behind Britain's industrial revolution at the end of the eighteenth century came from these men like Arkwright and Hargreaves, Watt and Stephenson, Boulton and Paul, Darby and Huntsman. But as the first generation passed, companies took the place of individual entrepreneurs and the roles of owner, inventor, manager and financier divided out. With increasing size of plants, to expand sales and reduce costs, the amount of capital required by an industrial company steadily grew. In the 1860s companies were given by law the special privilege of corporate personality and of limited liability. In this way the savings of the rich could be gathered together as shares in the process of capital accumulation, without the danger of such shareholders being liable for a failing company's debts beyond their own shareholding. We saw in the 1970s how Sir Freddy Laker and his associates could survive even when Laker Air Lines incurred huge debts which it could not pay; for, it was the company that went bust, and not Sir Freddy.

By the last decades of the nineteenth century a new model of market capitalism was emerging. This was based on the accumulation of capital by financial groups, including banks, with interests in many companies and often with state backing. This was especially true of the newly established capitalist states of Germany and central Europe and also of the USA, but a similar process was developing in Britain too. In this model, goods and services were still bought and sold through the market, and so were the factors of production. But the state was intervening more and more. Labour Exchanges in Britain were first established after 1906 and the Stock Exchanges in London, New York, Paris and Berlin became increasingly important especially for the borrowing of governments not only in Europe and North America but in the colonies and new nation states overseas.

Capitalism as a World System

Capitalism had become a world system. No corner of the globe could escape the penetration of money values, the manufactures of the industrial countries replacing local artisan products, the pull of the market everywhere exercising its force on local communities. Capital became international, often entering by force lands like China and Japan that attempted to resist its spread. Great migrations of labour took place, often of communities uprooted under pressure on the land or driven by taxes to earn money in mines and plantations. The driving force in this new international market model was still seen by 'market economists' as a bargain in the market, based on profit from the production and sale of goods, but on an ever-expanding scale, with costs reduced by the application of ever more advanced technology.

The reality was nearer Marx's picture of continuous accumulation of capital in larger and larger monopolistic units. Far from competition establishing an equilibrium in the market, it is a cause of violent disequilibria. As Marx described it, 150 years ago, in *The Poverty of Philosophy*, 'Monopoly produces competition, competition produces monopoly ... monopoly can only maintain itself by continually entering into the struggle of competition' (Marx, 1900). The same point was made by a Keynesian writer much later. Gunnar Myrdal, a Swedish economist and first secretary-general of the UN Economic Commission for Europe, criticized all self-equilibrating models of capitalist economy and described its essential working as 'a system of cumulative causation' (Myrdal, 1954).

For over the last hundred years we have seen the concentration

31

of production in larger and larger plants and the centralization of capital in larger and larger companies. Although this has taken place in jerks – with spates of mergers and take-overs at the end of the great booms of the 1870s, the 1920s and 1970s – the process has continued. Today there are only a few hundred companies that dominate the world's markets – like the oil companies, producing and refining the raw materials, shipping them, manufacturing products from them, distributing them, with their operations spread over every part of the world. We call them monopolies, although they are not strictly the only sellers in the market. There are at least seven great oil companies and several smaller ones. What is left then of Adam Smith's model of competing producers in the market? Not that much, you may say; but the market economists would reply that 'that much' is crucial and should be preserved from further erosion and especially from state-owned oil companies, in the interests of freedom.

What kind of competition is it then that remains between these giant companies? It is evident that they do not always compete in price. Changes in petrol prices generally move in line. Although the major oil companies no longer fix the price, there are only fifteen of them in the market. In some markets there are but three or four. The oil-producing countries – OPEC – decide together now on their price for crude oil, and the oil companies' price for petrol follows, with a small margin for retailers to play with at the pump. Yet, if the oil companies continue to spend huge sums of money on advertising the tigers they can put in your tank or the extra miles you can get to their gallon, there must be *some* competition. There is: they *do* want to expand their sales, if necessary at the expense of the others, but not by price-cutting, which is a dangerous game; nor by expanding everywhere at once, which might leave them all with unused capacity.

Such companies may then form a cartel and meet regularly to divide up the world's markets between them. If one company can show that it has increased its share of oil sales, say in Britain, it can claim that it should build the next new oil refinery in Britain. They won't all want to build new refineries in Britain or they will certainly have excess capacity. Another may have increased its shares of the market, say, in North America, and will claim a new pipeline development there. Between them they will agree on a worldwide package acceptable to all. But it is an uneasy truce in a continuing war. They will be back again with new sales figures next year to bargain with. Of course, when facing the oil-producing countries or their workers, they will try to maintain a common front through joint ventures between them and by long-term contracts with the suppliers (Jenkins, 1987), but in competition for your custom no holds are barred except for price-cutting.

It would be a mistake to suppose that the model of the open cartel is universally typical of the operations of giant transnational companies. It applies well enough to the steel, mining, oil and chemical companies, which have been in the business a long time and have reached ways of living together and managing competition over many years. At the growing points of technological advance things are very different. Here the competitive struggle is still vicious, and is fundamentally a price-cutting war. Between 1950 and 1980 the price of the new information technology – computers of many sorts – calculated in instructions per second, fell at 25 per cent a year from $100 to $0.01. So long as markets expanded, the growing number of firms could be accommodated as they entered each of the sectors of the market: chip manufacture, systems assembly, program writing, storage-unit manufacture and all the computer services and consultancies. But in 1980 growth stopped.

What had happened? The price of components had been cut to the bone by increasing the number of circuits etched on each chip and by employing cheaper labour in the Far East or from minority groups for longer hours, in loading the chips on to carrier assemblies. Profits in 1981 dropped dramatically. Manufacturing companies turned to governments for protection. The Japanese government had always protected its computer industry: the United States government defence agencies were now persuaded to operate blocking mechanisms on the import of the most advanced memory chips from Japan. The European Community had always operated a 17 per cent tariff on imported chips, but within the EEC no one government can protect its own industries.

Though the French generally do use protective devices, the British government has usually stuck to the rules. In 1981, however, even the Thatcher government felt obliged to rescue the British computer firm ICL by underwriting City credits to the tune of £200 million – a minute sum compared with the giant United States IBM's gross investment of $11,000 million. (See Duncan, 1982). Yet IBM was to fall, and not to a bigger company, but to a smaller, more innovative one that made what IBM did obsolete. A Harvard Professor of Business Administration has argued that the 'scale paradigm has passed'. 'The company that wins today is the company that moves fastest at improving its processes, its quality, its services, its features and its technologies throughout the business' (Porter, 1993). It must be added that, while this may be true of manufacturing, in finance, trading and retailing the scale of operations remains large and a few companies dominate each field of activity.

Cartels and Nation States

Now it is evident from this that, if we do not necessarily get the cheapest petrol, it may be claimed that we do get dynamic and enterprising companies pioneering technological advances in deep-sea drilling, pumping and piping from the frozen north, in new chemical products, in microchips, etc. Of course, if they all agree to put lead in the petrol for higher performance or all develop toxic weed-killers, we suffer. What is rather more damaging for the case of the market economists is that there is little or no evidence that any giant company was ever responsible for any important new technological invention. The evidence shows that the giant companies have always taken over and developed the research work of small companies and educational institutions. For such development work they have, of course, the necessary resources. Nor does it seem that the cartel system actually succeeds in avoiding the duplication of capacity that must inevitably result from the free working of a market system. The dozen or so giant motor-car companies in the world were known for decades to have a capacity to produce something like twice the number of cars that they were selling. If the market model were working, they should cut their prices and the firms that survived would be the ones with lowest costs and highest competitive efficiency. Why don't they do it?

To understand this we have to explore a little more deeply into the working of the market model in the economy as it is today, with monopoly on an international scale. There have been two main periods in the development of the process of concentration and centralization of capital over the last century. The first took place very much in the protective arms of the nation state; in the second, the giant companies have spread their wings and are quite opportunistic in their relations with the states in which they may once have grown up. When Lenin described 'imperialism' as the 'highest stage of capitalism', he was writing in 1916 about the first period, which lasted from the 1870s into the 1930s. Lenin saw it as being marked by the development of a monopoly stage of capitalism, by the growing export of capital rather than of goods from the advanced industrial countries, by the merger of finance and industrial capital, by the division of the world market among giant capitalist combines and by the partition of the world into colonies of the industrial powers. The links between finance and industrial capital and the nation state were regarded as crucial.

The model fitted German and French and US development better than it fitted the British case. The British empire had been originally incorporated earlier and by British capitalist enterprise which, because it was first in the field, did not need state protection. Although the British navy was an essential support for opening up the world's markets and defending the colonies, British manufacturers could rely on free trade because their goods were the cheapest. Those who followed after needed to break into the market with state aid and protection against British exports. If they could not do that, they remained underdeveloped and economically if not politically dependent. When German and US industry established a lead over Britain, the British themselves in 1931 withdrew behind a system of imperial protection which Joseph Chamberlain had tried and failed to create thirty years earlier. That Chamberlain had failed was due largely then to the continuing strength of British capital, based on the City of London, in financing the trade and development not just of the British empire but of the whole world capitalist system.

In the 1940s this system entered a new phase. On the one hand, the USA emerged during the Second World War as overwhelmingly the dominant capitalist economy. On the other hand, under the umbrella of US power and fed by a steady excess of US spending the world over, paid for by dollars backed with gold, not only did US companies thrive and grow ever larger but so did those based originally in other lands: Japan, Germany, France, Italy, even Britain. The annual net income of some of these companies began to equal and even to surpass the annual product of any but the largest nation states. The sovereignty of all but the super-states – the USA and the Soviet Union, which had also emerged as a great power after 1945 – came under threat. The European nations were driven to form a Community which looked to the establishment of a United States of Europe; and even Britain was forced to join it. Outside these three only Japan and possibly China had the economic strength and resources to plan on a national basis. At the same time the appeal of nationalism ('Buy British' and support 'our' companies) began to lose its meaning as it became increasingly hard to know where the goods came from.

The market model can, admittedly, help to explain the growth in the size of companies, their competitive buying and selling throughout the world, and by extension the competition of nation-state centres of capital accumulation, with their own banks and financial markets; and even to explain the international connections of trade and services between nation states balanced and adjusted by exchange-rate changes and movements of gold. But what we have now to explain is something quite different: a world of giant companies not simply trading across the world but producing as well as selling in many countries, moving their capital to develop raw materials in one place, employ cheap labour in another, take advantage of special skills in a third and everywhere standardizing production and consumption to their patterns. The concepts of the national market model – of the terms of trade, of exports and imports, of the balance of national payments, of unequal exchange between raw-material producers and manufacturers – make little or no sense in a world in which the movements of goods and services now take place largely inside the giant transnational companies themselves; and in which these companies take a quite opportunistic view about the governments they associate with. When a handful of companies decide what we eat and drink and wear and sing and use for heat or transport or entertainment and how we develop our economies, not only in the capitalist world but in the Soviet Union and Eastern Europe and even in China and Cuba, then we need a new model to explain the new ways of working of such gigantic forces.

Critique of the National Market Model

We shall look for such a model in Part Three, but we need here to summarize how the national market model is supposed to work and how it works in reality. In theory the market ensures that what is produced is what we want. We can take the argument through its various stages and add our own critique at each stage (see Figure 4).

The transnational companies operate, in a world market, as if they were still the butcher and baker of the market town. The market model remains the dominant model of the capitalist system. Indeed, the system of production for profit in the market is still what organizes production. But the hand is no longer invisible, decisions are no longer unplanned. It is increasingly obvious that the hand is the hand of the managers of a few giant companies playing the market and planning the use of the world's resources to make money rather than to meet wants. More and more people can see that this is so, and have felt the very tangible boot of unemployment, as Ken Coates has described it, even if they cannot see the 'invisible hand' that dismisses them.

The result, we now know, can only be described as a ghastly failure: failure to use resources fully, failure to employ all who wish to work, failure to grow crops which all can enjoy, failure to operate the machines to full capacity, failure to meet our needs

Stage One We have wants, which are God-given.

But, of course, these are now created for us by advertising and not only do we not know what we might have and are not offered, but the market cannot supply us with clean air, clean parks and unpolluted streams (unless we can afford to buy Chatsworth Park), and we are discouraged from public spending by the nature of the tax system. [We do not really need to proceed through all the stages of our critique now, because at the start we have discovered that what is produced determines what we want, not the other way round. But let us continue nevertheless.]

Stage Two Wants plus money make demand effective.

But income is unequally distributed and not at all according to our contribution to meeting people's needs. Rather the reverse; many who are the most idle have most, and those who do the most useful jobs have least. Moreover, unequal incomes make for price distortions, with prices of luxuries more likely to be cut than prices of necessities.

Stage Three Demand meets supply in a competitive market and, as a result of the costs of the various suppliers and the bargaining of the buyers, prices are set.

But, in fact, monopolies today fix prices and, although there is some competition about brand quality between them, the price does not reflect this.

Stage Four Where prices are high in relation to costs, profits are made, and where they are low, losses are incurred, so that the market signals what lines should be produced and what firms have the necessary efficiency.

But profits depend mainly on monopoly positions which may not reflect efficiency or inventiveness but only size and power over capital and markets.

Stage Five Profits attract capital and losses repel, so that capital moves to meet what the market has signalled is most profitable and therefore most needed and most efficiently produced.

But capital is concentrated in the hands of a few giant companies and their associates and they will invest where monopoly positions exist, not where people's needs have been shown to exist.

Stage Six Labour follows capital into the most profitable activities.

But labour is very immobile when capital may be moving all over the world and when new technology may be labour-saving.

Stage Seven Goods are produced which people want because that is where the profits are made and the capital and labour have moved to meet them.

But, for all the reasons shown above, the goods are produced which giant companies believe can be most profitably sold by advertising from monopoly positions, and no account has been taken of whether at the end of all this people have enough money to buy the goods produced, nor whether all available resources of labour and machinery have been fully used (and without creating 'bads' as well as 'goods' in the process).

Stage Eight What is possible on a national scale is extended, as the market grows, to encompass the whole world, bringing together the myriad points of production to meet the wants of hundreds of millions of consumers.

But what happens in the world market only exaggerates local inequalities. Wealth attracts new investment and poverty repels, in a cumulative process of polarization. Rich areas grow richer and the poor grow poorer.

Figure 4. Critique of the national competitive market model

without destroying the environment, failure to create goods for people's livelihood without appalling waste and the diversion of vast resources to stockpiling weapons of destruction that can end all life on earth. It is a terrible condemnation of the market and not less because no one wills that it should work like that. We evidently need other models to find answers to some of the criticisms made above. We shall turn to these in the next chapters.

None the less, one more attempt was made in the 1960s and 1970s, even before the rise of monetarism, to rescue the market model in the face of such realities. This was the construction of a sub-model for what were euphemistically called 'developing countries'. When colonial rule was ended and great numbers of newly liberated people emerged with post-colonial governments committed to raising their economic position, it was natural for them to seek new models for their economic development. They were told by leading economists in the imperial countries that they needed only to follow the market model in their masters' footsteps as junior members of the capitalist club. Any ideas they might have of following something like the Soviet model, outside the capitalist system, were denounced as folly and treachery. W. W. Rostow, who wrote the much publicized book *The Stages of Economic Growth* in the late 1950s, specifically subtitled it 'a Non-communist Manifesto'.

A British Communist writer, Bill Warren, accepted much of the argument and proposed a model of 'imperialism as the pioneer of capitalism', spreading systems of capital accumulation throughout the world. He pointed to the NICs (newly industrializing countries) in Latin America and East Asia, all making headway with capitalist development (Warren, 1980). Peter L. Berger, an American sociologist, sought to retrieve the celebration of capitalism's successes for the anti-Communists in a euphoric claim for the 'capitalist revolution' that it had brought 'prosperity, equality, and liberty' wherever it had been established (Berger, 1987). What was quite clear to the ex-colonial peoples, however, was that, while most of them might not wish to accept the forms of communist economic growth, only a few could hope to follow slavishly the capitalist growth path of their one-time masters.

Some East Asian countries succeeded after Japan in establishing their own self-generating capital accumulation, as we shall see notably in South Korea and Taiwan. But colonial rule in its political and economic forms had left most with economies distorted and confined to meeting the continuing interest of the imperial powers in supplying food and raw materials. Industrial development from this basis was not going to be easy for them in a world where the industrial products of the imperial powers were already well established. One socialist economist, Geoff Kay, had much earlier responded for the Marxists that it was because most colonial countries had been *insufficiently* exploited that they were backward (Kay, 1975).

The development model which emerged from this debate and was soon widely accepted in the ex-colonial countries, with the support of most of the new profession of development economists, contained the following features: (a) it was agreed that strong government involvement would be needed in fostering economic growth; (b) but this should not be allowed to obstruct the opening-up of all economies to the world market; (c) major emphasis was to be placed on industrialization, including a base of heavy industry in the larger countries like Brazil and India; (d) encouragement was to be given to ensuring a high rate of domestic saving both by government and individuals; and (e) what was not allowed was that governments should place any limit on the role of foreign capital in the economy or the share of foreign imports in the market.

One result of the working of this model is that the giant transnational companies have benefited most from government activity in developing the economies of ex-colonial and other underdeveloped countries – by employing the savings of these countries and by selling manufactured goods to them in exchange for their raw materials. For a time in the 1960s and early 1970s some economic growth was realized with this model of development, but this came to an end in the collapse of raw material prices in the late 1970s and 1980s. Since then, large parts of the developing world, and especially Africa, have become marginalized and capital investment has increasingly taken place *within* the already industrialized countries. Worldwide flows of capital grew faster than movements of goods in the 1980s, but both goods and capital were increasingly concentrated in exchanges inside the Triad, as the economies of the USA, the European Union and Japan are described by the United Nations Center on Transnational Corporations. Thus by the end of the 1980s intra-Triad trade and investment came to account for over 70 per cent of world exchanges (even, that is, excluding flows inside the European Union). This is a change of historic proportions, which will engage our attention in the third part of this book.

At the same time, we shall have to note the increasing volume of speculation in world markets. There may be a few principal buyers and sellers, but there are thousands of speculators, some big, some small. Tim Green, the leading authority on the gold market, gives three key figures as an example in the gold market: annual newly-mined gold worth $30 billion; *daily* turnover in currency markets of $1,130 billion; futures options, swaps and other 'derivatives' (the new name for speculation) in New York markets, $10,000 billion. Speculators are interested in volatility, not stability. If the price of any commodity settles down, the speculators look elsewhere. Managers of futures funds have some $20 billion at their disposal. According to Green, they think nothing of 'zipping in and out of the market' for 100,000 ounces of gold (at $400 an ounce) or even more at one clip. I have described in detail elsewhere the workings of the commodity markets (Barratt Brown, 1993) and had cause to recall Keynes's warning that 'when the capital development of a country becomes a by-product of the activities of a casino, the job is likely to be ill done'.

FURTHER READING

BARRATT BROWN, MICHAEL, *The Economics of Imperialism*, Penguin Books, 1974

BARRATT BROWN, MICHAEL, *Fair Trade: Reform and Realities in the International Trading System*, Zed Books, 1993

BERGER, PETER L., *The Capitalist Revolution*, Wildwood House, 1987

BEST, MIKE, *The New Competition*, Polity Press, 1990

CAVANAGH, JOHN, and CLAIRMONTE, FREDERICK, *Merchants of Drink: Transnational Control of World Beverages*, Third World Network, 1988

DUNCAN, MIKE, 'The Information Technology Industry in 1981', *Capital and Class*, No. 17, Summer 1982

GAMBLE, ANDREW, *Britain in Decline*, Macmillan, 1981

JENKINS, RHYS, *Transnational Corporations and Uneven Development*, Methuen, 1987

KAY, GEOFFREY, *Development and Underdevelopment: A Marxist Analysis*, Macmillan, 1975

MARX, KARL, *The Poverty of Philosophy*, Twentieth Century Press, 1900

MURRAY, ROBIN, *Multinational Companies and the Nation State*, Spokesman, 1975

MYRDAL, GUNNAR, *Economic Theory and Underdeveloped Regions*, Duckworth, 1954

PORTER, MICHAEL, 'The Wealth of Regions', *World Link*, 1993

RADICE, HUGO (ed.), *International Firms and Modern Imperialism*, Penguin Books, 1975

SAMPSON, ANTHONY, *The Seven Sisters*, Hodder & Stoughton, 1975

UNITED NATIONS CENTER ON TRANSNATIONAL CORPORATIONS, *The Triad in Foreign Direct Investment*, New York, 1991

WARREN, BILL, *Imperialism, Pioneer of Capitalism*, Verso, 1980

4 THE CORPORATE MODEL: COMMAND OR DEMOCRATIC ECONOMY?

National capitalist groups have always been perfectly willing to abandon the market model in times of national emergency – during a war or in face of revolution – as well as in carrying through the first stages of industrialization. We have already noted how in Germany and Japan capitalist groups drew upon state aid and state protection to establish their own centres of capital accumulation independent of Britain or the USA. When the job was done, all the state enterprises, except for posts and railways, were handed back to private owners; but the links between the state, including government and civil service, and industry and finance, remained extremely close. Of course, in Britain too there has always been an 'old-boy network' of ministers, top civil servants, industrialists and bankers meeting in London clubs and on Scottish grouse moors. How close this might be was revealed some years ago by a tribunal inquiring into a leak of information concerning a Bank of England decision to cut the bank rate. The story was written up in an issue of the *Manchester School* (1959).

Merchant bankers in Britain, who are private bankers managing large sums of trust funds including unit trusts, have always had the role of coordinating the investment policies of giant British companies with each other and with government policy. Conservative ministers and top civil servants often retire to sit on the boards of merchant banks. Merchant bankers are frequently found to be chairmen of the clearing banks and of big insurance companies as well as of large industrial and overseas companies.

The Linking of Government, Industry and Finance

Several studies have revealed groupings of British banks, insurance companies and industrial companies. A detailed study for the

1960s by this author was published in Coates (1968) and was brought up to the 1980s in a Northern College Research Unit Occasional Paper. It still appeared that about four hundred top directors straddled the boards of nearly all the large banking, insurance, industrial and overseas companies based in Britain, sharing between them over two thousand major directorships – and this despite the declining loyalty we noted in the last chapter of the giant companies for the country of their origin. There is evidence of a new generation of self-made business leaders who emerged from the Thatcher years in Britain, but no evidence of any change in the preponderance of men (hardly any women) educated at private schools and Oxbridge in leading positions in the City of London, in Conservative cabinets and in the higher ranks of the civil service.

These links in Britain between government, banking and industry are an important aspect of the British capitalist state. They fall far short of the tight bonds that hold together the top echelons of Japanese government, banking and industry or of similar links in Germany, Italy or France. Stuart Holland has for long insisted on the importance of the close interconnections of the graduates of France's *hautes écoles* in sustaining what he defined as the 'meso-economy' between macro- and micro-economic activity (Holland, 1978). It is one of the myths of British Tory spokesmen that economic success outside Britain is attributable to the greater freedom there from government interference.

Japanese success, as we shall see, has always depended greatly upon the close ties of government with a few giant banking and industrial combines. It is said that in the Parliament building in Tokyo the president of Mitsubishi – Japan's largest banking and industrial corporation – has an office next door to that of the Prime Minister. It is inconceivable that any important investment decision by any large company in Japan would be made without the closest consultation with MITI (the Ministry of International Trade and Industry). The failure, for example, of the motor-cycle industry in Britain would have resulted not in Mr Benn's meagre £3 million in aid in 1978 to rescue Triumph-Meriden, but in massive subventions from banking and the mobilization by the government of widespread resources of research and development in universities and government institutions. Mr Benn was nevertheless accused by the British civil service of 'Bennery', that is, excessive interference by government in industry, in the very meso-economy where the Japanese and the French were being so successful.

Wartime Controls and Controllers

In wartime even British governments are prepared to act in this way. It surprised many people that in the assembling of a task force to save the Falkland Islanders from Argentine rule it was possible within a few days for the government to requisition luxury liners, container ships and cross-Channel ferries, cancel the sale of an aircraft carrier, reopen dockyards that had been closed and call back workers declared redundant only the week before. There are, of course, emergency laws to cover such actions, but the main point is that in a war situation it is assumed that there is an overwhelming national consensus in favour of the government's actions, which cannot be assumed in any other circumstance. It is not that governments cannot act to rescue the motor-car industry, as they rescued the Falkland Islanders, but they do not wish to risk the criticism of their opponents if their efforts are unsuccessful or disturb vested interests.

In a prolonged war such as the Second World War direct action by government in the economy went much further. Men and women were called up to the forces and directed to essential work. Factories and offices were requisitioned and government orders given priority. A whole network of state-owned enterprises grew up, including even 'British Restaurants'. Rationing was introduced and government ministries established direct control over all foreign trade, and imposed price controls with quality standards. The departure from the market model of an economy could hardly have been more complete. We have called this wartime model the corporate model, not only because the whole of the nation's economic activity was incorporated within state controls, but also because the state incorporated the main contending classes of employers and workers within its institutions.

We can best understand the working of this model if we note the way in which industry moved into government in Britain during the Second World War. Under a Tory Prime Minister (Winston Churchill) and Labour Deputy (Clement Attlee), with a Tory (Anthony Eden) as Foreign Secretary and a Liberal Home Secretary, key ministries were held as follows: Chairman of the Home Affairs Committee of the Cabinet: Sir John Anderson (previously chairman of Vickers steel and shipbuilding combine). Minister of Supply: Sir Andrew Duncan (previously director-general of the British Iron and Steel Federation). Minister of Production: Sir Oliver Lyttelton (previously chairman of British Aluminium). Minister of Transport: Lord Leathers (previously chairman of William Cory Lines). Minister of Aircraft Production: Lord Beaverbrook (owner of the *Express* newspapers). Minister of Information: Brendan Bracken (owner of the *Financial Times*). Minister of Food: Lord Woolton (previously chairman of Lewis's stores). And – not to be omitted – Minister of Labour: Ernest Bevin (previously general secretary of the Transport and General Workers' Union).

At the same time, department managers of large companies moved into the government ministries – from Unilever into the Food Ministry, from ICI and Courtauld's into the Department of Trade, from the iron and steel trades into Supply, from British Aluminium into Production and so on. These were the experts; they were needed to supplement and complement the regular civil service. But, in exchange, they controlled the rationing of scarce resources and particularly of the very limited imports of food and raw materials. These were rationed on the basis of previous consumption, which meant, of course, that existing companies and particularly large companies were protected, and new enterprises had to enter under the protection of the well established. What came to be called a 'new feudalism' grew up. It is well described in a book by Peter Shore and A. A. Rogow entitled *The Labour Government and British Industry*.

Those who criticize left-wing Labour Party policies for planning and other controls by government over prices and foreign trade often refer to these policies as the 'Siege Economy' and ask if people want to return to wartime rationing. It is generally assumed that we don't. We should in any case not need to, as imports would not have to be cut but only prevented from growing, to ensure the viability of planned economic growth. The fact is, though, that the average consumption of meat per head under rationing in wartime was larger than it is today. The alternative to rationing by coupon is rationing by the purse. This conforms to the market model but does not allow for inequalities in the length of purses. This is not to say that the corporate model is one that those who believe in freedom and equality should necessarily adopt. On the contrary, the power of the state in this model is undoubtedly excessive and such state power is rightly feared by most people in Britain.

The Fascist States

The dangers of the corporate model are only too clearly seen by looking at it in its totalitarian forms, under the fascist regimes of Germany, Italy and Japan before the Second World War. There have been many descriptions of the way in which the *zaibatsu* – the top industrial and financial groups in Japan – established the military government of the 1930s and of how the leaders of German heavy industry put Hitler into power and how the *padroni* financed Mussolini. What is less well known is the nature of these fascist economies. As in wartime Britain, the major industrialists moved into the seats of government under the political leadership they had established. Even more than was the case in Britain, the great departments of state became in effect arms of the largest companies – particularly in Germany the steel, coal and chemical combines. It was these companies themselves which were given the concentration camps to run and draw their labour from, until the order came for the final holocaust.

The incorporation of labour was, of course, far more complete than in Britain. The trade unions were destroyed and their leaders gaoled. New organizations were formed, under state control, that every worker had to join. Every citizen was organized into some part of the state–party structure – the children's Pioneers, the

Hitler Youth, workers' Strength Through Joy, women's circles, pensioners' clubs. The armed services were reinforced by armed guards and storm-troopers and special police. The unity of one people, one party, one state incorporated all. And the role of the market was steadily reduced even before Goering pronounced that the nation had chosen guns in place of butter. Production was almost wholly to government order, and distribution was increasingly made through the party and state organizations – as rewards for loyal behaviour, in producing children, increasing output, saving materials, spying on neighbours. Finance was supplied through the two or three major banks, the Jewish banks having been expropriated. Foreign trade was frequently reduced to barter, as Hitler's financial wizard, Hjalmar Schacht, discovered that Eastern and Southern European governments were happy to exchange their grain for arms and military advisers. Once the war began the barter was replaced by loot and plunder. Foreign companies and whole industries were incorporated into the German economy under the direction of German bankers. A German soldier's ditty ran thus: 'Who marches behind the last German tank? Why, it's Dr Deutz of the Dresdner Bank!'

A similar description could be given of the working of the Japanese and Italian fascist economies before and during the Second World War. Total mobilization involved total central control, reaching down through descending ranks of authority to the least and poorest of the people. None could escape the eye of the police and its auxiliaries. All were incorporated in the national effort and great numbers believed in it. The weaknesses lay in the smothering of independent initiative, the destruction of some of the most talented citizens, the all-pervading fear of stepping out of line. German scientists fled the country, and Germany, the very home of atomic physics, failed to develop an atomic bomb. Those who compare favourably the free working of the market with the totalitarian authority of the corporate economy are thus far justified in their judgement.

Even short of fascism and war we have to conclude that there are inherent tendencies to corporatism in capitalist economies. These emerge most strongly in times of crisis. In Britain we can instance the class collaboration that was called 'Mondism' in the 1930s and the tripartite system of the 'Neddies' of the 1970s. *Mitbestimmung* in West Germany was another example of the attempt to incorporate Labour into the inner workings of capitalism. Sir Alfred Mond (later Lord Melchett) was the founder of ICI and made the first moves towards industrial collaboration after the 1926 General Strike by engaging in talks with Ben Turner and Ernest Bevin of the TUC General Council. These led to the setting up of a joint committee of employers and the TUC for improving the efficiency of British industry.

More recently the National Economic Development Office (NEDO) was set up on the lines of other quangos (quasi-autonomous non-governmental organizations) as a tripartite body of government, employers and unions. NEDO was in fact created in 1963 by Harold Macmillan, Conservative Prime Minister and a Tory collectivist from the 1930s. It soon sprouted little Neddies with ministers in the chair and civil servants, employers and trade-union leaders for each section of industry to recommend ways of improving British competitiveness. These Neddies were revived by Edward Heath in 1972 as an instrument of national consensus, but they tended to be ignored under the more partisan Wilson and Thatcher governments. They sought other models to guide their policy-making, of a respectively Keynesian and monetarist orientation.

Nationalized Industry and Social Planning

There is some element of command economy in all capitalist states today, namely the public sector, represented not only by the social services but also by the railways, post office and telephone services, electricity supply (including atomic power), airlines, coal and steel production, armaments production and key services of other manufacturing industry. These industries and commercial services were generally 'nationalized', as it was called, in the 1950s. This resulted partly from pressure by workers against ruthless and greedy employers, partly from the need to ensure basic supplies to the rest of industry in sectors where the scale of investment or the time-scale of return to capital were beyond the scope of any individual capitalist. Once they are profitable, bits of such utilities can be sold off to private capital. Inevitably, the nationalized industries are regarded as prototypes of social owner- ship and a socialist society. This view is mistaken. They are state- owned and subject to government command but do not operate within a framework of social planning with social aims and social criteria, let alone a democratic structure. They have in effect a market structure and market aims and operate by market criteria; they lack only the discipline of market profit. The result is an unfortunate hybrid prone to inefficiency, corruption and waste, which became the justification for their privatization in the 1980s.

The armed services form by far the largest element of the command economy in capitalist states. They are sometimes re- garded as admirable examples of efficiency and self-discipline. This view is wholly mistaken: waste of resources and overmanning are typical, as anyone who has served in the forces will know. Success is achieved in peacetime as in war only because of the sheer scale of resources available and the overriding priority given to military requirements. When we look at the command economy in the Soviet Union we shall see that the military complex which launched the Sputniks, flew the MiGs and designed the SS20s can reckon these as its shining example – and for the same reasons, its albatross.

The public social services, including the health service and education, may equally form part of the corporate model. They are often regarded by socialist critics as quintessentially used to incorporate working-class aspirations within capitalist state con- trol. To the extent, however, that these services have social aims, social criteria and a somewhat democratic structure the so-called 'welfare state' must be seen as a forum for struggle between socialist and capitalist forces. It is neither an arm of the capitalist state like the police force nor yet a bastion of socialism. The cuts made by the Thatcher government showed to many just how important it was to defend what had been won by working people in this field in achieving a universal service based on need rather than on the pull of income in the market.

At the same time, the economic collapse of the Soviet Union and Eastern Europe revealed societies where the health of men and women and the conservation of the environment had been neglected and there was no protection for the unemployed. Socialism is not about equality by regimentation, but about democratic choice through social planning. It is not enough that the command economy is directed by representatives of a revolutionary class. We shall have to recognize here that, whatever we think of the deformations of central planning in the former Soviet Union and Eastern Europe, some central framework of planning will be needed in a society within which men and women seek to open up and protect the potentialities of grass-roots initiatives for building socialism.

The attack on state planning by Mrs Thatcher and her friends, along with the rhetoric of the enterprise of the 'small man' and of 'buy British' in the new *Great* Britain, has served only to conceal the reality of planning by the giant transnational companies which the Thatcher policies legitimated. Before the monetarists took over, governments had done much to correct the failure of the market in order not only to rescue capitalism but also to ensure that resources were fully used and that people's wants were met. In so doing they had shown that public enterprise and social provision were of the essence of that endeavour and despite structural weaknesses could be brought under democratic control. The QUANGOs manned (*sic*) by the Tory faithful, with which the Thatcher and Major governments replaced locally elected authorities, reveal the corporate state at its most blatant. But democracy would not be better served if the seats were occupied by Labour supporters with no change in the structure of accountability.

The German Model

Germany, the Federal German Republic as it has developed since the Second World War, is generally regarded as a model of democratic corporatism. The journalist John Palmer has likened the whole system to the Mercedes car – large, powerful, luxurious and dependable, but expensive and in need of a change (Palmer,

1994). The corporate elements are obvious enough even to the casual visitor: shops close at 6.30 on weekdays by law, legal regulations cover all aspects of life as well as business, all those that British governments have been busy deregulating. Employers belong to industry associations which regulate their members' competition and workers belong to industry unions which run closed shops defending skills and quality standards. The two negotiate centrally on wages and hours. Consensus and not confrontation is the watchword. The democratic element is less obvious; it is nonetheless there, not only in elections for the federal Parliament, but in the extent of decentralization to the regional state governments and to local authorities, all guaranteed by the constitution and not at the will of the leader of a party with a majority in Parliament and the support of 40 per cent of the voting population, as in Britain.

Even the much-feared independent board of the German Central Bank turns out to be made up of a representative from each of the Länder and to have a constitutional requirement to maintain economic growth as well as to curb inflation. The emphasis of all German institutions of political economy is on *Ordnungspolitik*, a 'framework of rules and machinery of impartial supervision which a competitive system needs as much as any game or match if it is not to degenerate into a vulgar brawl' (Ropke quoted in Palmer, 1994). This is precisely what Adam Smith had in mind in proposing the regulatory effect of the 'invisible hand' of moral sentiment in the market.

There is a strong democratic element also in the corporatist arrangements for managing industry through *Mitbestimmung* ('deciding together') between management and workers on the supervisory boards of companies. These boards make major policy decisions, while an executive board carries out day-to-day management. The worker representatives are not trade-union delegates, but rely on union power for the strength of their voice. John Palmer calls it a 'cosy corporatism' and questions whether it gives enough flexibility to stand up to sharper competition in a recession and particularly in relation to low-wage competition from East Germany. It could hardly present a greater contrast to the deregulatory policies of British Conservative governments. David Goodhart of the (British) Institute for Public Policy Research describes Germany's 'social market' institutions as constituting 'a far more radical affront to the common sense of the Anglo-American market model than is often realized ... German labour markets are chock-a-block with rigidities, the freedom of capital is severely curtailed, company ownership is often lost in a blur of cross-holdings, taxes are high and unions are strong' (Goodhart, 1993).

A critical review in 1993 of British government measures of deregulation demonstrated that, by following deregulatory and anti-trade-union policies over a fourteen-year period, British economic performance had been reduced to the bottom of the league table in growth, competitiveness and employment. Those countries, including Germany, having higher taxes, more public spending and denser trade-union membership had all done better than the average (Coates, 1994). That was the record in the past (see Table 1, Chap. 6). Today, however, there is no doubt that new competition from the East as well as the threat of social dumping by the UK, exploiting its opt-out of the social clauses of the Maastricht Treaty, is causing Germany's leaders to rethink their commitment to market regulation. In a major report for the forthcoming German and French presidencies of the European Union, in mid-1994 the two governments called for the linking of pay to productivity, adopting more flexible (i.e. longer) working hours and lowering barriers to cheap imports. Could this really, as the report claimed, reduce chronic unemployment? Keynes would have said 'No!'; he would have agreed with those who supported Jacques Delors's programme for public spending on Europe's decaying infrastructure to stimulate economic recovery.

FURTHER READING

BARRATT BROWN, MICHAEL, *From Labourism to Socialism*, Spokesman, 1972 (see Chap. 3)

BRADY, ROBERT A., *The Spirit and Structure of German Fascism*, Gollancz, 1937

COATES, KEN (ed.), *Can the Workers Run Industry?*, Sphere, 1968

COATES, KEN (ed.), *Deregulation: The Dismal Truth*, European Labour Forum, Spokesman, 1994

GOODHART, DAVID, *The Reshaping of the German Social Market*, Institute for Policy Research, 1993

HANNAH, L., 'The Rise of the Corporate Economy', *Manchester School*, Vol. 26, No. 1, January 1959

HOLLAND, STUART (ed.), *Beyond Capitalist Planning*, Blackwell, 1978, pp. 150ff.

MARTIN, J. S., *All Honourable Men*, Little, Brown, 1950

NORTHERN COLLEGE, *Sheffield Industry and Capital Ownership*, 1981 (Occasional Paper No. 3)

PALMER, JOHN, 'Model Vision: A Survey of Germany', *The Economist*, 21 May 1994

ROGOW, A. A., and SHORE, PETER, *The Labour Government and British Industry*, Blackwell, 1956

ROPKE, WILHELM, 'Germany in Transition', *Daedalus*, American Academy of Sciences, Winter 1994

SOHN-RETHEL, ALFRED, *Economy and Class Structure of German Fascism*, Conference of Socialist Economists, 1980

5 THE KEYNESIAN MODEL

John Maynard Keynes began and ended his working life in the employment of the British Treasury. In between times he had a distinguished career as a fellow of King's College, Cambridge, and, simultaneously with a Polish economist called Michał Kalecki, developed the model of a capitalist economy that takes his name. During Keynes's first spell at the Treasury he was concerned with the negotiation of reparations that were to be paid by Germany to the victorious Allies at the end of the First World War. It became clear to Keynes that such reparations would only do harm to the Allies. Germany would use up so much of the earnings from her exports in making the payments that she would be unable to purchase imports from the Allies, and their industries would suffer. Thus was laid the seed of the idea, which Keynes was to develop, that the capitalist market model suffered from an in-built tendency for effective demand for goods to be inadequate to make use of the available capacity to produce them, and thus for investment opportunities to dry up at the very centre of the system of capital accumulation.

It was not surprising that Keynes should have continued to work away at this idea during the 1930s when the whole capitalist world was in the depths of the most severe slump since the late 1870s. Not only had banks and stock markets collapsed through lack of confidence, but wheat was in fact being burnt and coffee and sugar crops destroyed for lack of a market, while millions were unemployed and starving. The conventional wisdom was that each country should reduce its spending and cut back its imports, but these were of course some other country's exports. Such beggar-my-neighbour policies led to a vicious downward spiral of trade contraction, until by 1933 the level of world trade had fallen to less than a half of what it had been in 1929. The market model, said Keynes, might always lead to a balance of sales and purchases, but it could not guarantee at what level that balance might be achieved – and the chances of it being at the full-employment level were evidently not very good. Moreover, once the downward spiral had begun, people out of work were unable to buy as much as when they were in work; and this had a multiplier effect putting even more people out of work. Far from the market providing an equilibrium effect, there was a multiplier effect that continued until prices were reduced to rock-bottom levels. By this time many millions were unemployed in the industrial countries and still more millions in the colonies and other primary-commodity-producing countries, which were receiving prices for their crops that hardly left them enough to live on. Keynes's aim was frankly to rescue the capitalist system; but socialists were no less anxious to find ways of averting fascist solutions to these problems.

Keynesian Demand Management

Keynes proposed to turn the conventional wisdom upside-down. Governments instead of cutting their expenditure in a crisis should increase it, to spend their way out of the threat of slump. The first country to adopt such a policy was Sweden. My first economics lesson as a small boy was learnt when my family was being driven along a beautiful new road in Sweden which suddenly terminated in a rough track. 'Why doesn't it go on?' I asked and was told that work would be restarted when the government needed once more to find jobs for unemployed workers. The US President, Franklin D. Roosevelt, was influenced by Keynes's ideas in introducing the so-called New Deal, to turn back the rising tide of unemployment in North America. This was designed to put federal government money into large-scale road and river development and land-reclamation projects, of which the Tennessee Valley Authority became the most famous. Neither Conservative, Labour nor National governments in Britain took any notice.

Keynes thought that it was especially important to put government money into investment in such things as roads and power projects and schools and hospitals. This was partly because these did not compete with manufacturers' goods in the market, partly because he had noted that in booms and slumps the rise and fall of employment in the capital-goods industries (making plant and machinery, etc.) was much greater than in others. He distinguished a consumption sequence and an investment sequence in the market economy and compared purchasing power with consumption in the one and savings with investment in the other. In a boom he noted that the proportion of income going to savings rose, so that there were more funds available for investment – by which he meant actual purchases of capital goods. For a time capital investment rose, but if consumption did not rise in line with this new capacity to produce goods, a crisis arose. Capital investment was suddenly stopped as stocks of unbought goods built up.

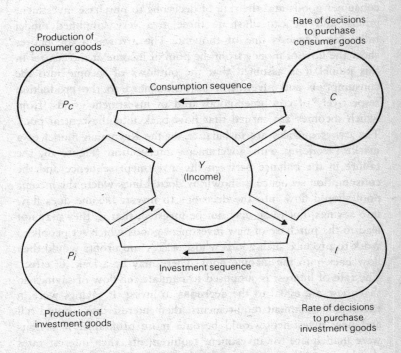

Figure 5. Simplified Keynesian economic model (after Tustin, 1957)

There was nothing in the market model to ensure that the balance between savings and consumption was equal to the balance between investment in capital goods and the production of consumption goods.

In discussing this Keynesian critique of the market model some years ago I adapted a model prepared by an engineer to illustrate Keynes's concept of the interconnection of the flows of consumption and investment sequences in a capitalist economy. I have reproduced the model here (see Figure 5), together with my own interpretation of the way governments use Keynesian demand management to maintain the balance between saving and investment at the highest possible level (Figure 6).

When we speak of consumption and investment in the economy we are really talking about the rate of decisions to purchase consumer goods and the rate of decisions to purchase investment goods, and we can illustrate these in a very simplified model following Keynes's line of thought. The arrows in the figures show the flow of money from the pool of income at the centre. In this model it is assumed that the outflows of income into the consumption and investment sequences lead to the production respectively of consumer goods and of investment goods, from which incomes are earned that flow back into the central pool. The two sequences are in balance. In the Keynesian model of a market economy with government intervention (Figure 6), the failure in the balance between the investment sequence and the consumption sequence is shown by dotted lines where the income pool should flow into the decisions to invest. Income does flow into savings, but these may not be invested; that is, they may not lead to the purchase of new investment goods which set people to work to produce such goods whose wages and profits would then flow back into the income pool. There may be a leak, in effect. The rate of interest is supposed to regulate the flow of savings so that these are equal to the decisions to invest. If savings were in excess of investment requirements, then interest rates should fall and new investment would become more profitable. If savings were inadequate for investment requirements, then interest rates should rise and so attract new savers.

Figure 6. Keynesian model of a market economy with government intervention

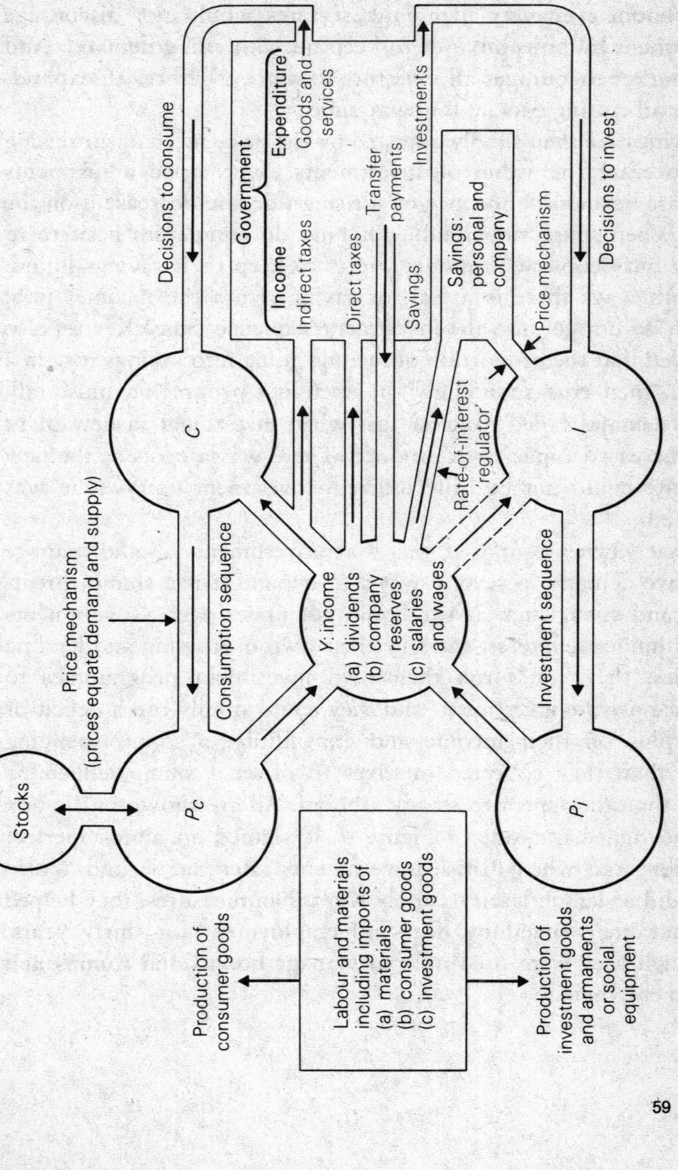

Unfortunately, the interest-rate regulator is sticky. If in a slump there was much excess capacity, no reductions in interest rates would be enough to encourage investment in new plant. Similarly, in a boom even very high interest rates would not discourage investment by firms anxious to keep up with rising demand. And the market encourages all investors to move together, all expanding or all cutting back at the same time.

Savings are then simply adjusted by the price mechanism raising or lowering the value of investments. Such price adjustments increase business confidence on a rising tide and decrease it on the ebb. When share values fall, not only do companies hesitate to invest but people with money prefer to keep their savings liquid. In both ways there is a leak of savings from the incomes pool which do not get into the investment sequence. Since Keynes also believed that the proportion of income going into savings rose in a boom, then correspondingly the spending proportion must fall. Thus demand failed to grow just when investment in new plant had increased capacity to produce. There was a crisis as the new capacity could not be fully utilized. Investment everywhere was checked.

What Keynes proposed was that governments should manage effective demand in several ways: to expand it if a slump threatened and cut it back as the boom got under way. Governments could influence interest rates by their own borrowing and lending policies; they could run their own investment programmes to balance private investment; and they could simply run a deficit or a surplus on their income and expenditure account, spending more than they collected in taxes to offset a slump, collecting more than they spent to steady a boom. All are shown in the box on the right-hand side of Figure 6. It seemed an almost perfect solution; and when British governments after the Second World War did at length learn to apply Keynesian measures, they helped to guarantee something near full employment for thirty years, although they were used only to manage booms and slumps and not to end them.

Keynes and the International Economy

Keynes's last years were spent negotiating on behalf of the British government with the USA in order to try to establish an international framework for the Keynesian demand management he proposed for use inside individual national economies. It was clear to him from the experience of the 1930s that, if each national government tried in a period of economic difficulty to reduce its imports and expand its exports, either by cutting the value of its currency or by cutting purchasing power at home, then the whole world economy spiralled downwards. It was also clear to him that it was necessary to have a world money for clearing accounts between nations, and that this could not be the currency of one particular country, whether or not it was convertible into gold.

For hundreds of years gold had been the world's money and an increase in gold supplies had encouraged every expansion of international trade. But Keynes saw that mining more gold was not an adequate means of financing increased trade. At one time the pound sterling and later the US dollar had indeed become a world money, which could be expanded in supply beyond the gold holdings of each country. These currencies could be tied to gold at a certain rate and converted into gold if necessary, but there had to be no danger that all holders of pounds or dollars might want to change them into gold at the same time.

Keynes's idea was that to avoid this danger all countries should join an International Monetary Fund and set up a World Bank. The Bank would issue its own money – called Bancor. Member nations would be able to draw automatically on Bancor from the fund, up to certain agreed limits, whenever they found themselves in deficit on their balance of payments with other countries. In this way, they could avoid the beggar-my-neighbour cutting back of imports of the past. National currency rates of exchange would be fixed in relation to Bancor and only changed by general agreement so that there could be no beggar-my-neighbour rate-cutting either.

Countries that were less developed and suffered from long-term deficits on their payments could apply for aid from the Fund or long-term investments at the going interest rate from the World Bank. These financial arrangements would be combined with an International Trade Organization designed to expand world trade exchanges. This would be linked to the policies of the United Nations Food and Agriculture Organization for storing food surpluses and managing commodity stocks and prices. The whole scheme would be run by an international civil service under the general umbrella of the United Nations. The USA, having most of the world's gold in its coffers and the largest proportion of the world's income, absolutely and per head of population, would be expected to finance the larger part of the scheme's operations.

It was hardly likely that the United States, having supplanted Britain as the dominant capitalist power and having in fact become as a result of the Second World War overwhelmingly the most powerful nation on earth, would now hand over the management of the world economy to a group of international civil servants; and as for giving its dollars away automatically to any country that failed to run its economy properly, that was just absurd. What emerged in 1944 from the agreements reached at Bretton Woods in the USA among the Allied governments was a compromise. There was to be an International Monetary Fund and a World Bank, but there was to be no Bancor. The US dollar, convertible into gold at $35 per ounce, would be the world's currency. National exchange rates would be tied to the dollar and only changed by general agreement. Much later, Special Drawing Rights (SDRs) on the Fund were established as a sort of very limited world money and all currencies were related to the value of SDRs, but that was after the dollar had ceased to be convertible in 1971 and exchange rates had ceased to be fixed.

Member nations, it was agreed in 1944, would be able to draw upon the International Monetary Fund for dollars, or other foreign currencies, if they needed them, according to the sums of their own currency which they had deposited with the Fund; but these drawings would be subject to supervision by the Fund's officials. The World Bank would provide loans for countries with long-term balance-of-payment problems; but, as with the Fund, the sums were to be much smaller than Keynes had wished and the overwhelming voting power of the USA among the Bank's governors, with a direct line to the US Congress, would ensure the domination of US government policies. The International Trade Organization was reduced to a General Agreement on Tariffs and Trade (GATT), which was designed to ensure only that in future tariffs and other obstacles to free trade were reduced, or at least not raised. This was an obvious benefit to the industrial countries with the lowest costs of production, but positively disadvantageous to developing countries which needed protection for their infant industries – a 'one-way street', as an Indian delegate at a GATT meeting once put it.

What Maintained the Post-War Boom and What Ended It

So the market model was reintroduced into the world capitalist economy at the end of the Second World War. Goods moved to where the richest markets were; capital and labour followed them. Development took place in the already developed economies and in the most developed parts of them. The gap between them and the underdeveloped widened. Gunnar Myrdal, Swedish economist and director-general of the United Nations Economic Commission for Europe, described it as the law of cumulative causation: 'Wealth attracts and poverty repels'; 'Unto him that hath shall be given and from him that hath not shall be taken away even that which he hath.' Economic growth, especially in underdeveloped economies, but also in economies like Britain's with a high dependence on international trade, was held back by constant anxiety about the foreign trade balance. Japan with a surplus (initially from US purchases and no defence budget) could expand indefinitely. Britain with a recurring deficit grew slowly and haltingly. Inside each country favoured areas boomed and others declined. The south-east of England and north-west of Europe attracted migrant capital and labour. The north of England and Scotland, Wales and Ireland, southern Italy and Brittany declined; and not even unemployed skills and low wage rates could overcome the attraction of the rich markets of the lower Rhine.

How then was it that for nearly thirty years after the Second

World War with modest ups and downs the capitalist world as a whole enjoyed almost continuous boom conditions? There are many answers: the reconstruction of industrial plant destroyed in the war, the extension of mass production and consumption from the USA to Europe and Japan, the defeat of labour movements in Germany and Japan which permitted high profits to be earned, the opportunities for investment in the new industrial revolution of automated production. One answer is a very Keynesian one, though it is not quite the answer Keynes had sought. For nearly all of these years the United States did in fact spend more than it earned abroad and paid in gold. Year after year US government aid and military purchases expanded the level of world demand – very unequally, concentrated most unfairly in the more rather than in the less developed countries, favouring regimes that would protect US capital rather than the more progressive. Although the remittances of income from US capital invested abroad generally exceeded US investment, the difference was more than made up for by US government aid in grants and loans. But this could not go on for ever.

On 15 August 1971 the US Senate declared that enough was enough. The stock of gold in Fort Knox had dwindled to an irreducible minimum. The dollar would no longer be convertible into gold, even for foreign governments, at the fixed rate of $35 per ounce. The gold window was closed. For some time no one worried. The USA continued to spend more than it earned, even greatly so during the Vietnam war. Dollar balances were built up outside the USA; and, even if these could not be converted into gold, was not the USA the greatest power on earth and its economy the strongest? Moreover, these dollar balances could be used for trade outside the USA and a market in these Eurodollars, as they were called, was opened, with rates of interest according to the length of the loan and the currency of deposit. Soon finance in Eurodollars supported much of the whole world's trade, and giant companies moved their earnings into and out of accounts with a dollar sign at the top according to their needs and their expectation of the future value of other currencies.

Uncertainty, however, had now re-entered the world market.

The dollar was not convertible and there were huge quantities of these Eurodollars, in effect no more than IOUs, sloshing around. For, added to the balances of the giant companies had now come the new earnings of the oil states from the rise in oil prices that had been imposed through OPEC, the oil producers' cartel established after the Yom Kippur War in 1973. These were held in dollars too. What was worse, the US economy began to look vulnerable. The USA is the largest importer of oil in the world; and, far from US exports expanding to pay for this, German machinery and Japanese cars were penetrating the US market itself as well as capturing US markets elsewhere. As a result the dollar was actually devalued in 1974 in relation to other currencies and the era of fixed exchange rates came to an end. The world was back to beggar-my-neighbour policies as each nation state sought to expand its exports and reduce its imports either by cutting the value of its currency or by curtailing its citizens' purchasing power by deflation.

In this atmosphere of uncertainty the giant companies and the big oil producers moved their funds into whichever currency seemed strongest, unless they could be tempted by high rates of interest to balance an increased return against reduced security. So there began a period of high interest rates *and* price inflation, of balance-of-payments deficits *and* recession. The economics textbooks always said that you could not have in one country both inflation and recession, both a balance-of-payments deficit and high interest rates. Each would balance the other. Recession or slump would mean lower prices as demand was reduced. A foreign-payments deficit would mean reduced demand for home-produced goods and therefore presumably less borrowing for home investment. The only exceptions in the textbooks were underdeveloped and dependent economies from which capital was being drained; and it appeared that more and more countries were entering that category – not only the Argentine, Poland and Mexico, but Britain too.

Governments in both capitalist and socialist countries increasingly had to borrow to maintain oil imports, to balance their foreign payments and to sustain their economic development. As the international sources of finance – the IMF and World Bank – failed them, they turned to the commercial banks and, behind them, to the giant companies. But the bankers' price was high. The effect of governments' importunity and the opportunism of the transnational companies is that the companies move their funds around seeking the highest rates of interest, especially to compensate for the risk and uncertainty of failing economies or where future expectations of growth are lowest. High rates of interest, however, raise costs and prices and make exports less competitive. 'Stagflation', as it is called, becomes the typical condition – stagnation *and* inflation. For a government to lower interest rates in order to encourage recovery only leads to an outflow of capital, seeking better terms elsewhere.

Keynes, Inflation and Full Employment

Keynes is generally criticized because he is said to have had no real answer to the problem of inflation. The fact is that he regarded it as a political rather than an economic problem:

> I do not doubt that a serious problem will arise as to how wages are to be restrained when we have a combination of collective bargaining and full employment. But I am not sure how much light the kind of analytical method you apply can throw on this essentially political problem. (Keynes, 1936)

Governments have attempted to solve the problem by the introduction of incomes policies. These have been relatively successful in economies where productivity was rising in line with the rise elsewhere and there was a national consensus about how the extra income should be distributed between wages and profits, as in Scandinavia and the Netherlands. They failed in the UK, partly because productivity here was lagging behind rises elsewhere and partly because there was no curb on profits and, with one exception, increases in incomes were proposed as a percentage on existing levels, and this was seen as being unfair to the lower-paid. It was a Conservative Keynesian minister, Sir Ian Gilmour, who commented: 'Certainly, in this country incomes policies have not always worked well. But then not having an incomes policy has not worked well either' (Gilmour, 1983). And that, of course, is also an incomes policy, one that leaves income distribution to power in the market.

Keynes's prescriptions for full employment had come up against further limitations: first, the sheer scale of government spending – over 50 per cent of the national product compared with 30 per cent in the 1930s; second, the increasingly high proportion of output coming from high-productivity industries whose demand for labour is shrinking; third, the absence of an international framework of growth within which national measures can operate. Governments were expected by Keynes to transfer wealth, obtained by taxation, borrowing or through owned resources, from the productive, mainly private industrial sector into non-productive public services. So long as the size of the national cake grew, rich employers and the richer workers would be prepared to exchange their larger shares of a smaller cake for a smaller share of a larger cake. The model in Figure 7 shows how governments have to transfer wealth from the private to the public sector.

If the public sector, however, has to be continually extended to maintain full employment, as increases in productivity reduce the number of productive workers, then to employ them on non-productive services governments will need to increase taxes, raise more funds by borrowing or increase their owned resources. So long as the cake grows increased taxation may be acceptable provided the share of income taken by taxes is unchanged, but if the cake fails to grow, then taxes will cut into the shares of profit and wages. Companies will take their capital abroad and better-off workers will complain of reduced take-home pay. For a time governments can borrow, but if their owned resources are limited they will soon be in trouble, spending more than they receive, with inflationary results. So the monetarists said that Keynes had failed, and that the crisis was due to excessive government spending and borrowing. Full employment is impossible, they say, except at savagely reduced wage rates. But if all governments cut their spending then economic activity must decline worldwide, as it has done. This is why Keynes argued for international action to support full-employment policies. The absence of such policies gave some credence to the monetarists' critique, but the Keynesian model was looked at again when monetarism failed.

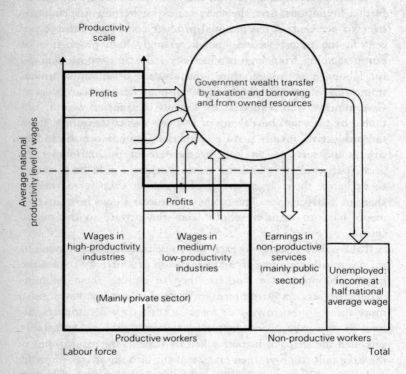

Figure 7. A model of wealth transfer in a market economy having high-productivity industries, with productive activity mainly in the private sector and non-productive in the public sector (from Barratt Brown in Coates, 1979, p.71)

1994 marks the fiftieth anniversary of Bretton Woods. The revival of support for Keynes's ideas means that his memory will certainly be honoured. It seems to be less likely that his original prescriptions for concerted international measures to ensure full employment will be applied, although the world economy is once again in deep recession. But circumstances are more propitious for joint action than they were in 1944, when United States world hegemony was overwhelming. Today the United States is no longer the world's banker and the dollar the single secure currency. The US foreign balance of payments is in deep deficit, US industry under severe challenge from Japan and from Germany. The balance of power is more even, as it was when Keynes first thought about an international economic order. The situation in 1994 cries out for joint government action by the leading industrial countries, the so-called Group of Seven (G7). They meet annually and so do their finance ministers, but to what avail?

The response of these leaders at their summit meetings has been wholly in the monetarist mode – to call for balanced budgets to reduce interest rates to curb inflation. In addition, Japan was asked in 1993 to cut back her foreign trade surplus by increasing demand at home. Japan had in fact in that year launched a $100 billion recovery programme, equivalent to between 2 per cent and 3 per cent of national product. Although the actual implementation of this programme was slow, it caused worldwide interest rates to rise. The European Union had agreed in December 1992 on a $15 billion investment fund, a third of the Union's total budget, but the budget itself was then less than 1 per cent of the combined national products of the member countries. Again, for fear of raising interest rates action was hesitant in implementing expenditure, let alone doubling the budget to strengthen recovery, as proposed by European Commission president, Jacques Delors.

There was no concerted G7 action to stimulate recovery during all the years of recession. Despite levels of unemployment in the seven countries equivalent to 8 per cent of the labour force (over 10 per cent in the European Union), there was in effect no concerted action of any sort, apart from agreement to supply some measure of aid to Russia. Curbing inflation by lowering interest rates was thought to be all that monetarist policy required, together with the opening up of all markets to free trade. What was agreed in the international forum, therefore, was more free trade and the conversion of GATT into a World Trade Organization (WTO). This came at the end of the long-drawn-out Uruguay round of GATT negotiations to include agriculture and services within GATT's purview. But WTO in no way corresponded to the International Trade Organization (ITO) which Keynes had envisaged fifty years earlier. Far from having as its main concern cooperation to ensure worldwide full employment through support for economic development, as the ITO had, the WTO is a monitoring organization to ensure that trade agreements are complied with. And its establishment came at the end of a round of negotiations on the freeing of trade in goods and services, which gave most of the benefit to the already industrialized quarter of the world's population.

To many Keynesians and others, it appeared that action was needed for development on a world scale, not least because ecological limits are appearing to put in question the continued growth of consumption in the industrialized countries. There were brave efforts in the European Parliament to revive the spirit of Keynes during the celebration of the fifty years of Bretton Woods, but no sign of the new and more equitable international economic order, which had been under discussion for a decade or more. Too many of the world's leaders were still in thrall to the arguments of the monetarists. What, then, was their fatal attraction?

FURTHER READING

BARRATT BROWN, MICHAEL, *The Economics of Imperialism*, Penguin Books, 1974

BARRATT BROWN, MICHAEL, 'Money, Debt and Slump', in Ken Coates and Michael Barratt Brown (eds.), *A European Recovery Programme*, Spokesman, 1993

BEVERIDGE, W. H. *Full Employment in a Free Society*, Allen & Unwin, 1944

COATES, KEN (ed.), *What Went Wrong?*, Spokesman, 1979

DONALDSON, PETER, *Economics of the Real World*, Penguin Books, 1973

GALBRAITH, J. K., *The Affluent Society*, 2nd edn, Penguin Books, 1970

GILMOUR, SIR IAN, *Britain Can Work*, Martin Robertson, 1983, pp. 178–9

HOLLAND, STUART, *Towards a New Bretton Woods: Alternatives for the Global Economy*, Spokesman, 1994

KEYNES, JOHN MAYNARD, *General Theory of Employment, Interest and Money*, Macmillan, 1936, p. 271

MYRDAL, GUNNAR, *Economic Theory and Underdeveloped Regions*, Duckworth, 1954

POLLARD, SIDNEY, *The Wasting of the British Economy*, Croom Helm, 1982

ROBINSON, JOAN, and EATWELL, JOHN, *Introduction to Modern Economics*, rev. edn, McGraw-Hill, 1973

TUSTIN, A., 'The Mechanisms of Economic Instability', *New Scientist*, 31 October 1957

6 THE MONETARIST MODEL

The monetarist model of the economy was fundamentally a revival of the old market model, with a new twist to turn the tables against what were said to be failed Keynesian policies. Inflation had become the enemy No. 1 and not unemployment. There is no evidence, of course, that an economy suffers worse from inflation than from unemployment. Rather the contrary. A steady rate of inflation of between 3 per cent and 4 per cent a year accompanied the boom years of the 1950s and 1960s, when the rate of unemployment never rose in Britain above 4 per cent and averaged around $2\frac{1}{2}$ per cent. Annual price increases of 10 per cent a year in Britain in the early 1970s, however, accelerated to peaks of 15 per cent in 1974 and 25 per cent in 1975 and to over 20 per cent again in 1980. These rates were above those in most other capitalist countries. Unemployment in Britain rose at the same time to over 5 per cent in 1976, to over 10 per cent by 1981, and 15 per cent by 1982. The Keynesians were said to be in disarray in the early 1970s. Increased government expenditure, especially by the Labour government in 1974–5, was not increasing employment; and prices continued to rise. Mr Healey, Labour's Chancellor of the Exchequer, accepted the logic of the monetarists and cut public spending, mainly in the government's capital programmes.

What then was the monetarists' model that the British Treasury accepted in 1975 and Mrs Thatcher made her very own after 1979? Inflation is said to be caused by an excessive increase in the supply of money. If it was required to reduce the inflation rate to a level similar to that of Britain's competitors so as not to be undercut, then it was necessary to reduce the money supply. This is the quantity theory of money, which is expressed in the equation $MV = PT$. The supply of money (M) multiplied by the annual turnover or velocity of circulation (V) equals the price (P) of transactions (T), i.e. of all goods and services in any year. If money supply increases, prices go up, unless the velocity of circulation falls as the money supply rises, as it may very well do. Unemployment can only be checked from rising, according to the monetarists, when the price of British goods is once again competitive at home and in foreign markets.

At the centre of the model is the money supply. This is made up of notes and coins in circulation plus private short-term deposits of sterling in banks (i.e. current accounts) and a certain proportion (assumed to be 60 per cent) of items in transit between accounts. This is called M1. A more widely used definition of the money stock is called M3. This includes, together with the M1 items, also longer-term private deposits of sterling in banks (deposit accounts) *and* all public-sector deposits. A minor variant (M4) includes UK residents' deposits in banks which are in non-sterling currencies. Notes and coins in circulation (Mo.) were distinguished as an object for control by government when it proved hard to control any of the other monetary measures. The monetarists' model works on the assumption that the velocity of circulation of money is unchanging, so that an increase in supply with the same goods and services to be bought pulls up prices and needs to be controlled. It is the old explanation of inflation – 'too much money chasing too few goods'.

Money supply is supposed to increase in advance of money incomes and expenditure, and it is the extra money that pulls up prices. But the Keynesian reply is that there is no evidence that the increase in money supply *causes* the increase in money incomes. It is in every way more likely to be the other way round, i.e. that changes in economic activity *result* in changes in the money supply. Professor Milton Friedman's revival of this quantity theory of money overlooks both the possibility that there may be unused productive capacity to draw on as incomes rise and that money may circulate with different velocities at different times and in different countries. Professor Nicholas Kaldor showed conclusively in his lectures on *The Scourge of Monetarism* (1982) that this is just what does happen. Controlling the growth of the money supply, as Professor Kaldor insisted, is only a fig-leaf to cover a policy of general deflation of the economy, so far as (a) to reduce the demand for imports and (b) to attack the bargaining power of labour.

The result in the UK has been to ruin more and more of the country's industry. For the central fact of government intervention in the capitalist economies since the Second World War is that government spending – on capital works, housing, roads, etc., on transfer payments, pensions, etc., on public employment, of teachers, health workers, etc. – is what has sustained the Keynesian mixed economy against the collapse of investment. Take these away and you take away half the national income. Since the greater part of this is spent on purchases from private business, the result must be disaster. And so it turned out as the 1980s unrolled: lower growth, worse export competitiveness *and* higher inflation than in other industrial countries. (See Table 1, p. 87.)

What is true is that governments have tended to increase their spending sharply in periods leading up to elections. This has raised expectations about increased real incomes. Wage bargains and other earnings have then moved up well ahead of increases in output per person (what is called productivity). Prices have been pushed up by rising costs with wages chasing after them. The incoming government has tried to check the process by incomes policies, which have been seen as an unfair assault on the bargaining power of labour and have been challenged. For many years it seemed that there was a trade-off between unemployment and inflation – what was called after an economist at the London School of Economics a 'Phillips curve', which showed the inflation rate rising as the unemployment rate fell. Governments could reduce inflation by allowing unemployment to rise – but by how much? Keynesians had said that inflation could be controlled by investment to increase productivity in the long run and by incomes policies in the short run. The monetarists said that what was needed was that the money supply be reduced by cuts in government spending.

The Monetarist Strategy – Cutting Public Expenditure

To reduce the quantity of money, the monetarists argue, first, that interest rates must be raised (they can be brought down only as the policy succeeds) – at higher rates of interest private persons and firms will borrow less and make less use of credit; and second, that government spending must be cut, since much government spending – and, as we have seen, increasingly more and more government spending – is financed by borrowing. In her more excitable moments Mrs Thatcher promised that she would never print money as the Labour government did. All governments of course print money, but what she meant is that she would not spend more than she collected in taxes, rely on borrowing, and thus increase what is called the Public Sector Borrowing Requirement (PSBR). Again, all governments borrow, just as any business does to meet its capital expenditure. Keynes's recommendation to governments to budget for a deficit did not mean that he recommended borrowing to meet current spending, and indeed only in one year (1978) did the Labour government run a deficit on current account. Keynes's advice to governments was to expand capital spending by borrowing in face of a recession. This, unfortunately, the Labour government on Treasury advice did not do in 1977, as we have seen, but instead cut the government capital-investment programme by 10 per cent in order to halve the PSBR.

The next step in the monetarists' strategy follows the argument that, with less money and credit available, firms, and public authorities also, will have to resist the wage demands of trade unions or face bankruptcy. It is part of the monetarists' model that wage rises are the main element in the money increases that cause inflation. The resistance of employers can be strengthened by government legislation designed to reduce the power of the unions. But there is a third step in the strategy – this is that the cuts should deliberately create unemployment whenever firms or workers 'price themselves out of jobs', as it is called. Wage pressures will be further reduced and inflation will, in the Thatcher speech-writers' terminology, be literally 'squeezed out' of the economy. As the inflation rate declines, within two to three years (it was originally hoped to be within six to eighteen months) interest rates will fall and 'healthy' growth can begin. In the event base rates of interest rarely fell below 10 per cent throughout the 1980s, with a range between 8 per cent and 17 per cent, although the official inflation rate after 1982 was held below 5 per cent for most of the rest of the decade. Such high *real* interest rates, which we shall look at further, had to be a disincentive to recovery from recession.

The final stage of the strategy is growth which, when it does recover, will be in the demand for goods and services of the private sector. 'Slimmed-down' firms will be in a position to compete successfully with their foreign rivals in home and export markets. The profitable parts of the nationalized industries will have been sold off and the 'wasteful and inefficient' public services forced to improve their performance. The objective was nothing less than a massive reversal of thirty years' growth of social provision – back to the market model of individual producers and consumers. At first, public expenditure actually rose as increased payments of benefit and social security were required to provide for the much increased numbers of unemployed. Only later did a reduction in individual payments, especially to pensioners, to-gether with the rate capping of local authorities, actually bring public spending down so that taxes could be cut. And it must be said that the redistribution of income from the poor to the rich under Conservative governments has gone further than the Labour government's promised 'irreversible shift in power and wealth from the rich to the poor' ever did. For this we have to understand that there are good reasons in the culture of the British people and in their traditional institutions. We said at the start that we had always to include in our models of the political economy the reinforcing elements of culture and ideology.

The Appeal of Thatcherism

What then was the appeal in Thatcherism (or for that matter in Reaganism) of the monetarist model? Negatively, there is little doubt that it was a protest against the power of the state, of the proliferation of government officials, of the horrors of town planning, of the apparent inefficiency of nationalized industries. This was combined with a strong resistance to the increasing share of income going in taxes. When British government expenditure amounted to between 40 and 50 per cent of the national income, as in the 1950s and 1960s, that was one thing, but when it rose to over 55 per cent in 1975 this was too much. It was especially unsupportable because higher government spending was increasingly being taken out of the same overall income. Workers discovered that their wage increases were being eroded not only by higher prices but also by higher tax rates and the inclusion of ever lower incomes in the tax net. (See Beddoe, 1981, and Townsend, 1994, for detailed figures.) Labour's attempt to publicize the advantages of the social wage carried little weight against the massive appeal throughout the media for more money to spend on all those private goods so attractively displayed in the glossy magazines and on television.

Negatively, it has also to be recognized that the image of trade-union power has steadily deteriorated for large numbers of people, including even trade-union members. From being one of the leading defenders of the disadvantaged and a main exponent of democratic solidarity, the image of the unions became one of resistance to change combined with sectional infighting. Much of this lay in the way the media coded the message, but there was enough truth in the picture to make it stick. Still worse was the failure of the Labour Party, especially on the left, to present a coherent alternative economic strategy. What was said about the Alternative Economic Strategy sounded either like much of the same as the mess that ended with the 'winter of discontent' in 1978–9, plus import controls, or else like wartime controls and rationing and more power for state officials. It cannot be denied that even before the Falklands adventure the positive appeal of Thatcherism to very large numbers of British working people had been to the values of individualism – individual initiative in business, in finding a job and keeping it, in self-improvement, in making your own choices about how you spend your money, in standing up to officialdom. For those who were securely in work in Britain – and this was still the majority – things went well. Real wages rose steadily year by year; but, while the numbers of unemployed were for a time reduced, the total numbers employed did not recover during the decade to the figure recorded in 1979.

There came to be a deep divide in the British nation between those who had the security of regular employment and those who had not. Not only was an average 10 per cent of the workforce (2.8 million) unemployed on the government's official figures and another 4 per cent on the earlier basis of calculation (another 1.2 million), but one and a half million new jobs, a million of them for women, were part-time, replacing three million lost full-time jobs for men. Each job, whether full-time or part-time, counts as one in the statistics, but in terms of hours and pay the part-time job amounts to no more than half of the full-time. Thus the apparent re-establishment by 1990 of workers in employment to 23 million, the 1979 figure, should really be reduced by 750,000, since each part-time worker is equivalent to almost exactly half a full-time worker (Hughes, 1994). Such part-time jobs in the UK carry no insurance and pension rights and no security of employment. There was, moreover, during the decade a huge increase in the numbers of self-employed in Britain – from two million to three and a half million. Few of these have any job security or pension rights.

The actuarial implications of this loss of contributions must place the whole contributory basis of the national insurance scheme in jeopardy. The number of non-contributors, four million unemployed – two and a half million of these for over a year – plus six million half-time workers and three and a half million self-employed, amounts to nearly half the total labour force. Moving towards such an abandonment of the basis of Britain's post-war welfare state, laid down in the much-vaunted Beveridge Report on Social Insurance of 1943, evidently implies more than just short-term political thinking. The stated aim of Conservative government in the 1990s was to encourage privatization – not only of nationalized industries, but of health, education and social security, including old age pensions. It is a radical agenda – nothing less than dismantling the whole of the welfare state – for which monetarism was but a means to an end, and an agenda which has won the support of a large enough proportion of the population to win elections, given the divided state of the opposition. But can it work – in purely economic terms – to achieve sustainable growth by eradicating inflation?

Myth and Reality in Monetarism

In the first edition of this book, it was suggested that by 1983 the Conservative government's monetarist experiment in Britain was already failing. Ten years later, it has lasted for long enough – some fifteen years – for it to be possible to judge certainly of its success or failure. The experiment has to be judged on two grounds: first, whether it worked in the way it was supposed to and, secondly, whether it worked at all, except in fulfilling the hidden agenda. The aim was to eradicate inflation once and for all, so as to ensure stability at home and competitiveness abroad.

The means used were to be a sharp reduction in government spending and borrowing, if necessary creating unemployment – 'a worthwhile sacrifice', as one Chancellor of the Exchequer put it before he himself lost his job. Businessmen were then expected to respond to incentives from the supply side, i.e. from reduced taxes on profits and salaries, an end to the 'crowding out' of private by public investment, reduction of state debts and deregulation of state controls. Keynes, by contrast, although he placed great faith in the regulation of interest rates, had always believed in working on the demand side, to encourage businessmen to invest as a result of the prospect of increased purchasing power in the market, especially to recover from conditions of slump.

There were three stages in the British monetarist experiment. The first was the Medium Term Financial Strategy (MTFS) launched in the 1980 budget. This did not follow the advice of the more extreme monetarists like F.A. von Hayek, who recommended a sharp shock to the whole system by slashing state spending and taxes and weakening trade-union power through the repeal of the 1906 Trade Disputes Act, so as to break at one stroke, as he believed, the whole inflationary psychology. Such shock tactics had been proposed by Milton Friedman and other monetarist economists of the Chicago School in the USA for General Pinochet to adopt in Chile after the fall of the socialist government of Dr Allende. It was perhaps because of what followed in Chile – the massive increase in the rate of inflation, from 20 per cent to 400 per cent, as plants were operated down to half their capacity and interest rates were jacked up; the phenomenal rise in unemployment, from 3 per cent to 25 per cent, even though a million workers fled the country; the reduction of minimum wages by 8 per cent a year in real terms; the doubling of the public debt; and exports overtaken by imports despite food being exported from a starving population – that made the British government proceed more cautiously.

The aim of the Medium Term Financial Strategy was to reduce monetary growth through cuts in the public sector borrowing requirement (PSBR) in the medium term. In the event, for four whole years the money supply maximum target range was exceeded by a margin of 10 per cent. Even though the government borrowed less, the private sector increased its borrowing, in order to maintain purchases or to fend off bankruptcy. To discourage borrowers, interest rates were raised to an unprecedented base rate of 17 per cent in 1980, 16 per cent in 1981. Industrial output then fell by nearly 20 per cent. The rate of inflation, fuelled by an increase in VAT, and falling use of industrial capacity on top of the rise in interest rates, exceeded 21 per cent in mid-1980, but fell back again thereafter to leave *real* interest rates at high levels throughout the 1980s. Unemployment in the UK rose sharply – from 5 per cent in 1979 to 12 per cent in 1982.

The shock had been delivered. The stage was set for the second phase of the monetarist experiment. Massive unemployment – up to three million, over 10 per cent of the workforce, for the first time since the 1930s – was doing its work. Union membership, and with it union power, was falling. Old plant was being destroyed, but even first-class innovating firms were being driven to the wall by lack of markets. Appeals to the small man provided rhetorical cover for the highest rate of company liquidations ever known in Britain. Failing private companies were bought up for a song by British and foreign-based transnational corporations, the only ones to benefit from the destruction of much of British industry. What was left, however, began to look slimmer and fitter. Productivity rose. The more profitable parts of the nationalized industries could be privatized. And at length in 1983 the rate of inflation came down to below 5 per cent – and stayed there, apart from a blip in 1985, for almost the rest of the decade.

So the experiment was a success? In fact, inflation rose again in 1990 and only came down to historically low rates – below 2 per cent – in 1993, when a new recession had brought unemployment once more back up to almost 3 million (over 4 million on the old basis). By then it was a success – at least on the objective set of reducing inflation – although nobody expected early in 1994 that such a low rate of inflation could continue as the economy recovered. But what had been the effect on the competitive strength of the British economy? After the first two phases of shock and slimming down, the third phase was supposed to be recovery and expansion. Mr Major was expected to build on the inheritance Mrs Thatcher had left him – the lucky boy! Or was he?

The inheritance included a manufacturing industry which had not achieved its 1979 output again until 1988, and which in 1989 went into a further recession from which it had barely recovered to 1988 levels by the end of 1993. There had been no increase in manufacturing output in fifteen years. But productivity had been increased, two million workers having been shed from manufacturing employment. So British manufacturing was once more competitive? – apparently not so! Britain's relative export performance, that is the volume of British exports of goods relative to world trade, declined between 1979 and 1992 in comparison with Britain's main competitors. The rest of British industry, apart from oil and gas, fared no better.

According to Mrs Thatcher the British economy was now a service economy. So exports of services had done better? Unfortunately, again not so! In 1986, for the first time since the 1930s, except during the war years, the so-called 'invisibles', income from abroad from services and investment, failed to cover the non-government 'visible' deficit on imports and exports of goods. Thanks to North Sea oil and gas, Britain's foreign payments account had been in balance in the early 1980s. But by 1989 the deficit was £22.5 billion, over 4 per cent of GDP. It was reduced steadily thereafter, but was still over £10 billion in 1993. Exports of goods were still having to meet three-quarters of the import bill. The contribution of income from services actually fell.

In no industrialized country have living standards been raised without a base of competitive industry. This is true even of Switzerland, which enjoys a large service and investment income. The devastation of the British manufacturing base can best be seen by examining the investment in manufacturing industry over the years 1979 to 1991. In real terms at 1985 prices, this was just over £10 billion at the beginning and also at the end of the period. Between 1980 and 1984 it was on average somewhat less, only £8 billion a year, and between 1988 and 1990 somewhat more, just under £12 billion. Investment in all plant and machinery throughout the British economy was raised from just over £19 billion a year between 1979 and 1983 to just over £31 billion between 1988 and 1991 (Barratt Brown, 1994). The increase was in retailing and distribution, not in manufacturing.

During the same period, while on average some £35 billion was being invested in British companies at home, direct investment by British companies overseas was running at £10 billion a year with another £10 billion going into overseas portfolio investment. It amounted to a fairly massive export of capital, although there was at the same time an inflow of foreign capital of £6 billion a year in direct investment and about the same in portfolios. This pattern of cross-investment between the advanced industrial economies is typical of our era; but Britain was maintaining a net outflow of long-term investment mainly into the USA and Europe, and to do this even with North Sea oil earnings, it was necessary to borrow short-term money from abroad to cover the deficit.

What Makes for a Competitive Economy

This was the Achilles heel of the monetarists. Borrowing from abroad meant offering attractive interest rates to foreign lenders. A regime of high interest rates, however, is not conducive to low rates of inflation after the initial shock to employment is over. Interest rates are a cost to industry, and Japanese industry, enjoying rates of 5 per cent to 7 per cent, was likely to be more competitive on that account alone than British industry, borrowing at 11 per cent to 12 per cent. This is where we have to take note of the many other causes of inflation besides the one simple explanation of the monetarists, excess money supply. Several may be distinguished – import prices, tax rates, under-capacity working, as well as the interest rate regime.

In regard to import prices, the Labour governments of the 1970s had faced a trebling of oil prices before North Sea oil came on stream and a doubling of the prices of other imported raw materials. Conservative governments after 1979 not only had the bonanza of North Sea oil and gas, but the benefit also of declining raw material prices worldwide, which continued throughout the 1980s apart from a couple of blips in 1987–8. The rates of indirect taxes were sharply increased by Conservative governments after 1979, partly to make up for the cut in direct taxes and partly in order to reduce purchasing power. The immediate effect was to raise the rate of inflation to an unheard of 21 per cent in 1980, even though it was thereafter brought down. The most serious impact of monetarist policies on prices, however, was caused by the reduced level of capacity working in industry. General deflation of demand means reduced sales, but until capital equipment is written off and less efficient firms are bankrupted, costs of production must rise. Overheads have to be paid from reduced earnings of production and one of the chief overhead costs is the payment of interest.

This is the explanation for the apparently paradoxical fact that since the Second World War prices in Britain have always risen fastest in periods of deflation and slump. Prices have risen more slowly in each of the boom periods, when rising money demand might have been expected to pull them up. In fact whenever governments have deflated the economy because of balance of payments difficulties they have used tax increases and higher interest rates to do the job; together with the rising unit costs of operating industry below capacity, these very deflationary measures were the cause of prices rising.

The main source of funds in the modern world are the giant transnational companies and their financial associates. They have the power not only to fix prices but to set interest rates in any country by their movement of funds into and out of different currencies. For these companies are the price-makers, the rest of us the price-takers. If interest rates rise big companies benefit, and they cannot lose from rising prices for their products. The true beneficiaries of monetarism were thus the giant companies. Under Labour governments in the mid-1970s real interest rates – that is, interest rates discounted for the rate of inflation – were actually negative, with base rates of interest at 11 per cent and annual inflation in the UK at 16 per cent. They were briefly negative again in 1980, but under the Conservatives the real interest rate rose steadily from nil to 6 per cent in 1983 and continued at over 5 per cent right through to 1993. There was one unfortunate twist to interest rates and inflation in the late 1980s. Because of the government cutback in house-building, house prices rose almost as fast as the rate of interest, so that for a time the real cost of borrowing to buy houses was nil and the property market boomed to unsustainable heights.

The Thatcherite model of monetarism required that interest rates be lowered in any one country by the government reducing its own borrowing and its citizens' private borrowing. But while governments are national, the market is global. Interest rates are set internationally. To bring rates down, all governments would have to reduce their borrowing. The G7 have generally agreed at their meetings to do so. In the event, each government hoped to be the one to make the big cut, only to find that the big companies then withdrew their funds. An uncompetitive economy like Britain's stood to fare worst and to have to maintain comparatively the highest rates in the hope of attracting the companies' funds.

It was a vicious circle: higher rates, less competitiveness; less competitiveness, higher rates. The only way out for a government was to devalue the currency, so that the country's exports became once more competitive. There is always a balance to be struck here. A devalued currency means more competitive exports but it also means more expensive imports, which if they go on being bought push up prices. British governments have tended to try to maintain a high international value for the pound sterling. It is often said that this is because the City of London can then deploy sterling as a strong currency worldwide. Today, it is more likely that the big transnational companies based in Britain want to be able to buy plants and companies overseas with their earnings of sterling.

It is certainly an advantage for large British-based companies to have a strong pound and no disadvantage for them if this means a regime of high rates of interest, since they have the funds to lend. It is not so good for medium-sized and small companies, who must rely on borrowed money and cannot compete abroad if their goods are valued too high in pounds sterling. In the early 1980s the value of the pound was sustained by sales of North Sea oil and gas, but then declined from a level of two dollars to the pound until by 1985 it reached almost one dollar to the pound. A regime of high interest rates brought it back to $1.80 in 1988 and enabled the pound to enter the European Exchange Rate Mechanism in 1990 at the very high level of £1 to 2.95 DM (Deutschmarks). That level proved unsustainable, but instead of requesting a general realignment of European currencies – several others were in trouble in relation to the Deutschmark – the British government attempted to hold it with interest rates at around 14 per cent. When rising unemployment required interest rates to be lowered, the pressure on the pound became too great and the pound was toppled by the speculators on 'black Wednesday', 20 September 1992.

Deregulation

The moral would seem to be that monetarism cannot, any more than Keynesianism or socialism, be pursued in one country. But the British monetarists were not discouraged. Their conclusion was, first, to press on to win still further freedom from state regulation for the British market; and, second, to convince their fellow Europeans to follow suit, and not only in Western Europe, but in the recently 'liberated' East also. There was still much to be done to fulfil the original intentions of the monetarist campaign.

Twenty monetary economists, most of whom had shown rather

right-wing reactions over long periods in the past, explained their views in *The Times* of 9 January 1980, in answer to a manifesto from 356 anti-monetarist economists. The gist of their argument, using mainly their own phrases, was that there are three obstructions to monetary policy. The most ubiquitous is the monopoly power of trade unions in the market for labour. The second is monopoly in the market for the products of industry, which so long as protection against foreign imports is resisted 'cannot be too serious'. The third and by far the most entrenched obstruction is the monopoly in nationalized industry, which only the removal of 'legal barriers against new competition in postal services, road transport and even in electricity generating and coal (opencast) mining' can offset. Finally, 'the most pervasive obstacle is the government itself as a monopoly employer in a vast range of national and local services'. 'Restoring "public revenue" to private pockets whence it came and putting personal services supplied by government into the market is . . . essential', i.e. by raising charges 'for personal private family services which we estimate to account for over half of total government spending'.

Most of this programme had been completed by the Thatcher and Major governments between 1979 and 1994. The outcome of this British monetarist experiment is of some importance because it was being offered by the British government in 1993 to Britain's partners in the European Union as a model for them to copy. In a Green Paper entitled *Growth, Productivity and Employment in the European Community*, the British government recommended almost total deregulation of the labour market, as a cure for unemployment and for greater competitiveness in world markets. The argument in the Green Paper can be summarized as follows:

The upward trend in EU unemployment cycle by cycle since the late 1960s, and an increasing proportion of long-term unemployed, are evidence of inflexibility in, and over-regulation of, labour markets. All regulations impose a cost on business. Social spending implies a burden of tax and public borrowing on public finances and employers' costs. The costs of public social protection – social assistance and health care – are already very high in the

Table 1. Comparisons of economic performance, 1979–1992 (countries in reverse order of growth performance)

Country	GDP growth (1979 = 100) 1992/1979	Consumer prices (1979 = 100) 1992/1979	Export performance (1980 = 100) 1979	1992	Unemployment rates % 1979	1992	Taxes and social security contributions as % of GNP 1981	1991
UK	122	244	100	91	5·0	9·9	39	37
USA	130	187	91	99	5·8	7·3	30	30
France	131	219	97	95	5·9	10·2	42	44
Italy	132	341	109	95	7·6	9·8	32	39
Germany	133	147	100	96	3·2	4·8	41	41
Canada	134	210	98	114	7·4	11·2	34	39
Japan	165	139	65	98	2·1	2·1	28	32

NOTE: Export performance = export volume relative to world trade
Unemployment rates standardized
Sources: National Institute, *Economic Review*, 3/93, Tables 14, 15 and 17; *Economic Trends*, February 1994, Chart 1, p. 92, for taxes, etc.

EU compared with those of Britain's main competitors and have been rising faster than the capacity of our economies to sustain them. Temporary and part-time jobs can be a route back into work, enabling people to move into more traditional full-time jobs later if they wish. There was no case for any further increase in European Union research and development spending. An EU Directive on working time will reduce employers' flexibility. A European Works Council Directive would delay vital business decisions.

Trade Unions are not even mentioned in the Green Paper; nor is there any reference to the demand side. Presumably the unions are not thought to have any role in a strategy for growth, competitiveness and employment. If British experience in the previous fifteen years had been brilliantly successful, the advice proffered would have to be taken seriously. The reality was that British economic performance had been the worst of all in the G7 in respect of economic growth, export performance and increasing unemployment, and second to worst in the crucial matter of inflation. At the same time, three of the states which had done markedly better than the UK – France, Germany and Italy – had higher levels of those 'burdensome' taxes and social security provisions. These facts are of such importance that they are reproduced here in the form of a statistical table (Table 1).

If the experience of other industrialized states were included in the table, this would show a similar correlation of trade-union density and high state spending with high economic growth and low unemployment – the very opposite of what the monetarists would have expected.

The same experiment has been applied by the Chicago economists of the IMF and the World Bank not only in Chile but in most of the indebted countries of the Third World. The result has been almost universally disastrous, especially in the poorest countries of Africa, for which the monetarist treatment has been almost terminal. The one part of the world where growth was continuous throughout the 1980s, and unemployment minimal, was East Asia, where Japan and the four 'little dragons' – Hong Kong, South Korea, Singapore and Taiwan – have been breaking every monetarist rule and World Bank prescription in the book. How could this be?

FURTHER READING

BARRATT BROWN, MICHAEL, 'By Their Deeds Ye Shall Know Them', in Ken Coates (ed.), *Deregulation: The Dismal Truth*, Spokesman, 1994

BEDDOE, ROBIN, 'The Budget: from Bad to Worse', *Workers' Control Bulletin*, No. 3, 1981

COATES, KEN (ed.), *What Went Wrong?*, Spokesman, 1979

FRANK, ANDRÉ GUNDER, *Economic Genocide in Chile: Monetarist Theory versus Humanity*, Spokesman, 1979

FRIEDMAN, MILTON, *Free to Choose*, Penguin Books, 1980

HUGHES, JOHN, 'How Deregulation Kills Jobs', in Ken Coates (ed.), *Deregulation: The Dismal Truth*, Spokesman, 1994

JOSEPH, SIR KEITH, *Monetarism is Not Enough*, Centre for Policy Studies, 1976

KALDOR, NICHOLAS, *The Scourge of Monetarism*, Oxford University Press, 1982

PANIC, M., 'Monetarism in an Open Economy', *Lloyds Bank Review*, January 1982, pp. 36–51

TOWNSEND, PETER, 'Think Globally: Act Locally', *European Labour Forum*, No. 13, Spring 1994

WALTERS, A. A., *et al.*, *Dear Prime Minister*, Institute of Economic Affairs, 1974

7 THE JAPANESE MODEL

Everyone now recognizes the 'East Asian miracle', although its causes are not generally supposed to be supernatural. By 1993 it achieved the accolade of a 400-page World Bank report under that title, with the significant sub-title of 'Economic Growth and Public Policy'. During the 1970s and 1980s the economic growth of Japan and the four 'Little Dragons' or 'Little Tigers' (Hong Kong, South Korea, Singapore and Taiwan), and of Indonesia, Malaysia and Thailand, surpassed that of corresponding countries with similar levels of development. Japan continued to move ahead of North America and Europe, and the 'Little Dragons' doubled the rate of developing Asia; Indonesia, Malaysia and Thailand were also well ahead, while Africa and Latin America actually declined in *per capita* income in the 1980s. The differences were sufficiently startling and sufficiently unexpected by the doctors of monetarism to have elicited some soul-searching.

At the same time, it has to be said that there was no chapter on the Japanese model in the first edition of this book. It seems impossible ten years later that it was not widely foreseen that Japan's worldwide trade balance in 1980 of $US 2 billion, with a negative overall balance on trade and services, should have become a surplus of over $80 billion every year between 1986 and 1988, only declining thereafter to half that level and recovering once more in 1991 to $80 billion. Perhaps more understandable is the failure to foresee the massive rise in exports – five- to tenfold – from the 'Little Dragons' and from Malaysia and Indonesia during the 1980s.

It is necessary to confess that the meteoric rise of the Japanese yen in the 1960s was regarded by many, including myself, as no more than recovery from wartime devastation and the continuing Japanese export successes in the 1970s as but one among many examples of unequal development in capitalism, in Japan's case supported by a powerful state bureaucracy and United States military spending. The 'Little Dragons' were written off, quite incorrectly except perhaps in the case of Singapore, as enclaves of United States and other transnational companies' investment in free-trade enterprise zones drawing on cheap local labour. In explaining the general experience of East Asia, nothing could have been further from the truth.

Economic Growth and Public Policy

It has taken the world, at least the world of the economists, a long time to recognize what was actually happening in East Asia. The President of the World Bank, introducing the report *The East Asian Miracle* in 1993, writes:

> The report breaks new ground. It concludes that in some economies, mainly those in North-East Asia [i.e. Japan, South Korea, Taiwan – MBB], some selective interventions contributed to growth . . . within the context of good, fundamental policies [i.e. monetarist policies – MBB]. (World Bank, 1993, p. vi)

The authors of the report go much further, recognizing that

> In most of these economies, in one form or another, the government intervened to foster development and in some cases the development of specific industries . . . targeting and subsidizing credit . . . keeping deposit rates low . . . protecting domestic import substitutes, subsidizing declining industries . . . making public investments in applied research . . . developing export marketing institutions . . . (World Bank, 1993, p. 5)

About ten years earlier, two World Bank Staff Working Papers, *The Japanese and Korean Experiences in Managing Development* (1983) and *Capital Accumulation and Economic Growth: the Korean Paradigm* (1985), had said all this; but the message had not been accepted in the official World Bank Development Reports or in the World Bank's prescriptions for developing countries. The result of this failure was quite devastating for the countries the Bank was advising. Yet the message from the Staff Working Papers could not have been spelt out more clearly. In these papers, the successive economic plans of Japanese governments from 1955 to 1979 were detailed and the key role of the Ministry of International Trade and Industry (MITI), especially in the 1950s and 1960s, was emphasized. By the mid-1950s MITI had been given powers over foreign exchange, foreign capital flows, imports, technology and licences, access to domestic credit and selective taxation and authorization to form cartels.

> In particular [MITI] encouraged mergers; and it coordinated investment behaviour and specialization through formal (legislative) and informal (administrative) measures. MITI's industrial policy thus ran counter to the orthodox Western approach to development, which favoured a free market and competition. (World Bank, 1985/574, p. 20)

Ten years later, the authors of the 1993 report recognized the Japanese emphasis on cooperation among private firms; but they insisted that this did not rule out competition, and claimed that government activism was concerned with the 'fundamentals' of low inflation and fiscal discipline where it was both 'effective and carefully limited'. They quoted from the Bank's *World Development Report* of 1991:

> In the 'market friendly' strategy it articulates, the appropriate role of government is to ensure adequate investments in people, provide a competitive climate for private enterprise, keep the economy open to international trade and maintain a stable macro-economy. (World Bank, 1993, p. 10)

So be it, but this is all a long way from the monetarist requirement of reducing government intervention to the minimum, to let money work in the market, and even then it much understates the role of government in both Japanese and East Asian economic development.

The Japanese Role in East Asian Development

The World Bank Staff Working Paper of 1985 on Korea is quite specific in its abandonment of neoclassical development theory to explain Korea's capital accumulation and expanding exports:

Planning *à la* East European economies or even China was never attempted by the Korean government. But planners utilized the entire register of policy instruments that economists of a *dirigiste* persuasion had laboured to compile and there was no reluctance at all to intervene in pursuit of industrial, export and growth objectives. In many respects, Korea is a paradigmatic case of a managed economy in the non-socialist sense of the term. (World Bank, 1985/712, p. 9)

The experience of both South Korea and Taiwan in advancing over a period of thirty years from undeveloped colony to an economy generating its own capital accumulation is of special importance for developing countries elsewhere, for it totally contradicts all the advice given to them by the World Bank and the market economists. It was the several stages of extended state intervention that took the economic development of South Korea and Taiwan from land reform and massive investment in education *via* selective controls on manufactured imports to the subsidizing of exports, finance for research and development and provision of low-interest loans from the state for introducing new technology.

Even more important were the stages of industrialization and export concentration through which South Korea and Taiwan developed – from resource-intensive mineral products *via* labour-intensive products like textiles and footwear to capital-intensive heavy industry of steel and engineering, and finally to technology-intensive production of motorcars and electronics. Without the transfer of technology from Japan and Japanese transfer of markets to South Korean and Taiwanese companies as Japan's own industries moved upmarket along this route, such development would have been impossible. These transfers did not necessarily take place through Japanese subsidiary companies but through licensing and Original Equipment Manufacturing (OEM) arrangements. What Japan had done for Korea and Taiwan, these two did for Malaysia and Indonesia. The result was a booming co-prosperity area in East Asia, in marked contrast to the declining economies of Africa and Latin America where export-led industrialization had come up against barriers to reciprocal trade with North America and Europe.

Market and Plan

A major explanation for the failure of Western economists to understand what was happening in Japan and East Asia lay in the total antithesis they assumed between market and plan, private and public enterprise, competition and cooperation. Khrushchev's attempts to introduce market mechanisms into Soviet planning in the early 1960s, and the more radical ideas of planned markets developed by Professor Ota Sik, the Czechoslovak Minister of Economic Planning in the 1968 'Prague spring', had explored the marriage of plan and market. The exposition of such ideas in the first edition of this book and in an earlier book of mine, *What Economics Is About*, had been widely dismissed as a bizarre fantasy. And yet, all the time, this was what the Japanese were doing.

The institutional invention which the Japanese had come upon was a combination of cartels or 'control associations' for each industry and 'deliberation councils' for each sector, composed of private and public officials meeting on a permanent basis under MITI's auspices. Cooperation not only between government and industry but between major companies in drawing up economic plans was combined with inter-company competition in executing those plans. Contests between companies were encouraged by MITI for finance, for import licences and for export permits, once a common strategy had been agreed. It is these contests that the World Bank report seized upon, but in doing so underestimated the strength of the cooperative framework within which they take place.

This all sounds very like the British Labour Party's National Plan in the 1960s and Planning Agreements in the 1970s, the early German 'Social Market Economy', the Italian 'Programme Contracts' and the French *Contrats du Plan* of the early 1980s, which were abandoned in face of the cold blasts of monetarism. What was different in Japan? The first difference was the dominant position for many years of MITI, which possessed controls over credit and foreign exchange which were the preserve elsewhere of the Ministry of Finance. The British Treasury had only reluctantly agreed to the establishment of a Ministry of Economic Affairs, made sure that it had no real powers and saw it off as soon as it decently could. This in itself reflected the much greater power of active intervention granted to civil servants by Japanese governments. Behind this lay the whole ethos of Japanese society, from which the concept of an overriding national industrial policy of economic recovery and capital accumulation derived.

Keynes's ideas were overwhelmed in Europe and North America during the 1980s by the monetarist onslaught, but it was not simply Keynesian intervention that Japanese economists held on to. They had learnt not only from Keynes but also from Joseph Schumpeter, and what they had learnt concerned the revolutionary nature of capitalism in constantly altering the processes and organization of production. Abandoning text-book theory of tendencies towards equilibrium in marginal demand and supply of resources and in marginal costs of the factors of production, Schumpeter in his great work on *Capitalism, Socialism and Democracy* described a real world of 'Creative Destruction: a process of industrial mutation . . . that incessantly revolutionizes the economic structure *from within*, incessantly destroying the old one, incessantly creating a new one'. Price competition in itself and resulting profitability cannot create the innovation in new products, new processes and new forms of organization that make for survival in the capitalist system. Schumpeter believed in the role of the individual entrepreneur in the system's success. His Japanese disciples extended this to collectivities of entrepreneurial activity.

The Entrepreneurial Firm in Japan

Renunciation of Keynesian thought in both the East and the West led to concern for the supply side of the economy, but while in the West it was deemed by the monetarists to be enough to free private enterprise from the clutches of the state, in the East this concern was seen more positively. The state could not of itself be entrepreneur – the Soviet Union showed that – but it could harness the entrepreneurs from both private and public sectors and drive them forward. It is an interesting commentary on Western economic thought that there is only one small section in the whole of the World Bank Report, *The East Asian Miracle*, which is concerned with technical processes and procedures. In it the authors recognize the importance of 'export-push policies' in 'tapping world technology' so as to increase total factor productivity (TFP), and go on to make the following observation: 'It stretches credibility to suggest that the large cumulative effects of TFP growth in Japan, Korea, and Taiwan could have been achieved by the plant floor innovations proposed as important sources of productivity growth at lower TFP rates' (and they quote the authors of a background paper prepared for the Report as the proposers of this suggestion) (World Bank, 1993, p. 317). Yet it is not only credible but a fact that what are described here as 'plant floor innovations' have gone far beyond a mere tapping into world technology, and have given the Japanese, South Koreans and Taiwanese the means to conquer the world.

There is an irony in the reference to 'world technology'. The Japanese attribute the rebirth of Japanese industry to a certain W. Edwards Deming who had worked during the Second World War in the US War Department on statistical quality control (SQC) and seen it abandoned by American industry at the war's end in favour of a return to 'Taylorism'. Frederick W. Taylor was the engineer at the Bethlehem Steel Corporation in the 1890s who fathered what was called 'scientific management'. This meant carrying Adam Smith's faith in the division of labour as the source of wealth to its logical conclusion. Tasks in the process of production were subdivided and subjected to precise measurement and control by 'time and motion study', with the twofold aim of speeding up the throughput of products and ending the control that the skilled craftsmen had over the process. At the same time, the mental work of planning and organizing production was taken 'upstairs', leaving manual work on the shop floor. Information from studying best working practice was used to standardize procedures, reduce costs and control the labour force.

American industrial success was built upon 'Taylorism' and 'Fordism', the latter adding to the detailed division of tasks, the flow of the assembly line and the achievement of mass production.

The be-all-and-end-all of American big business became the reduction of costs through the sheer scale of production. Quality was secondary to quantity. Such technological imperatives had implications not only for industrial organization but for economic and political structures, as we should expect from our introductory study of models. Michael Rustin in a study of 'Fordist' and 'Post-Fordist' modes of production has spelt them out for us (Rustin, 1989). Under 'Fordism', large scale meant long runs on fixed product lines, a low level of innovation and mass marketing ('any colour you like as long as it's black', as Henry Ford said of the 'tin Lizzie'). It also meant a hierarchical structure in the company, with central planning, vertical lines of command and bureaucratic rules. In response, workers organized in mass unions, engaged in centralized wage bargaining and saw themselves as a unified class. Rustin goes further and suggests that this implied national political parties based on class, universal forms of welfare, prescribed courses in education and standardized assessment.

The ideas of W. Edwards Deming, which Japanese industry made its own in the 1950s and 1960s, challenged every part of this – from the technology upwards. Michael H. Best of the University of Massachusetts, who has charted this challenge, summarizes the differing uses of the information that Taylor collected and Deming required, as

> representing two contradictory approaches to work organization. The purpose of Taylorist information is to minimize direct labour costs in the production of a standardized product. It is the heart of the mass production paradigm. The purpose of Deming's information is to provide a basis for continuous upgrading of production methods and product quality. Deming's message was that quality and productivity are positively related, contrary to the trade-off presumed by orthodox economic theory and adherents to the mass production paradigm. (Best, 1990)

Most of the new technology has become well known and widely practised: the incorporation of quality control into every stage of production, involving teamwork in place of individual detailed tasks; the pull from below rather than push from above, both by the final consumer and by the workers on the floor; the delivery of products and of parts 'just in time' instead of 'just in case'. Much of this was made possible because the Japanese had designed computer controlled machine stations which could be re-jigged without any 'down-time' to meet several different shapes, sizes and colours of the product. Defective products were almost eliminated, time wasted in transferring parts between work-places

Table 2. Production of vehicles and number of employees, Toyota, 1955–1988

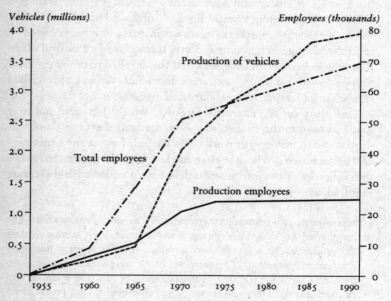

Number of workers required to make a small car, 1988

		Toyota	Europe (*av.*)	Europe (*best*)
Number of workers per shift –	*direct*	350	1024	643
	indirect	60	1012	355
	Total	410	2036	998
Numbers of workers per car		1.1	5.4	3.2

Source: J. Womack, D. Jones and D. Roos, *Report on the World Auto Industry*, MIT, 1992.

greatly reduced, stockholding cut back to the absolute minimum. Meanwhile Deming's belief was realized for the worker, that 'his right to do good work and to be proud of himself may be the single most important contribution of management to poor quality and loss of market' (quoted in Best, 1990, p. 160).

The result in increased productivity was shattering for the competing firms in the United States and Europe. By 1988 each Japanese auto worker was producing five times as many cars as the European average and three times as many as those in the most advanced plants in the USA and Europe, with only two to three times as much capital equipment per worker. Three years later, it was estimated that 'European producers need to "take out" 150,000 jobs (from a total workforce in the auto industry of about two million) in order to become competitive with Japanese producers.' (Holland, 1993). The rise of the Japanese motorcar industry can be illustrated in the figures of Toyota's production, reproduced in Table 2.

The 'Post-Fordist' Mode of Production

Just as the technology of 'Taylorism' and 'Fordism' needed corresponding economic and political structures for it to develop, so it is with the new technology. Michael Rustin has again outlined for us how these might be characterized – under 'Post-Fordism'.

Flexible automation creates the possibility for accelerated innovation, shorter runs, product variety and diversification of markets. In the work-place, hierarchies are flattened, autonomous profit centres are established to encourage entrepreneurial activity, with internal markets within the company and networking to outside suppliers. Markets can be deepened rather than widened – two- and three-car families instead of more families having a car. The workforce is divided, wage bargaining is local and often individual, with major differences between core and periphery. Poorer consumers, indeed poorer countries, can be marginalized and abandoned except as a reserve army of labour. Class formations break up into ethnic and regional groupings or into multi-party systems of fragmented political clients. Consumer choice is introduced into welfare, health and education, with different levels and standards of provision.

The fact that in all these ways economic and political structures are adapted to the new technology, as they very evidently are in Japan and in South Korea, does not mean that all contradictions and conflicts disappear. Far from it; the very differentiation between core workers with lifetime guarantees of employment at the work-place and the peripheral workers, on first, second, third or fourth level sub-contracts, with widely varying standards in consumption and welfare provision, makes for inequality and instability. The absence of democratic and egalitarian traditions in Japan, and equally in South Korea and Taiwan, has made the Japanese model much more acceptable there than in Europe. But even lifetime employment in the big Japanese companies has come to cover an ever shortening span, as the age of 'retirement' is brought down. Then there is nothing for the retired but early unemployment, unless they enter the sweat-shops on the periphery.

Enthusiasm for team work, which sets worker against worker, is, however, weakening. Reports from Japanese motorcar plants, not only in the UK, the USA and Canada, but in Japan itself, have begun to tell of resistance to the pressure of the new techniques of management. Strikes in the Mazda plant in Detroit, in the Suzuki-GM joint venture in Ontario, and rising union militancy in the Toyota-GM plants in the USA and the Nissan plant in the UK in the early 1990s began to reveal growing worker dissatisfaction. In Japan itself, the Japanese car workers' union federation recorded in 1991 that only 4 per cent of workers at Nissan would recommend their children to get a job in the industry and 67 per cent were not satisfied with their working environment (Kilminster, 1994).

Even more serious for confidence in the system than the rise of union militancy in the car industry is the fact that from 1991, for the first time in thirty years, the output of Japanese industry ceased to grow, and actually showed a fall of 20 per cent over the next two years. One explanation for this check to growth is a very Keynesian one: the failure of demand. High rates of saving among the core workers and low incomes of the subcontracting family workers on the periphery have meant that home demand has failed to keep up with rising productivity. Up till 1991 exports filled the gap, but net exports had been declining as a percentage of Japan's gross national product for some years before 1992, when their volume actually fell. Because the yen was revalued, export earnings still grew and Japan's foreign payments surplus with it. But while this expanded still further the massive Japanese stock of overseas investment, and increased investment incomes in Japan, this benefited the big companies and the rich, and that does not necessarily increase demand for the products of Japanese industry. The rich choose foreign travel, not more goods.

Even the booming East Asian market could no longer absorb the results of higher productivity brought about by the new technology. In 1993 the government of Japan was forced to undertake a major programme of Keynesian measures of investment in public works and housing loans, but stopped short of cutting taxes. When an economy as large and as healthy as the Japanese is caught in a trap between the increasing capacity to produce and failing capacity to buy back the extra production, it must be clear that the economic and political structure is still failing to correspond to the new technology. This is a very Marxist type of explanation and one with worldwide implications. Since the United States economy had become heavily dependent upon Japanese capital, retention of this at home left less for the USA and pushed up US interest rates, which in turned raised interest rates in Europe, so that economic recovery there was held back.

We have to add one further explanation, proposed by Richard Koo, for rising interest rates in Japan checking economic growth and for the delay in implementing the Japanese 1993 economic recovery plan (Koo, 1993). This is that the construction industry in Japan has always served as the conduit for government counter-recessionary spending. This industry was closely linked to government through the big integrated finance and industrial companies and the Liberal Democratic Party (LDP), which had been the ruling party continuously since the war, using 'big business' money to bribe electors for votes. In exchange, government contracts were handed out in a manner that could only be described as scandalously corrupt. Revelation of these scandals finally brought down the LDP, but also ended the principal means of stimulating the economy. The problem was aggravated by the legally required assets-to-loan ratio for Japanese banks, which encouraged them continuously to increase their holdings of property. Rising land prices combined with extra borrowing for its recovery programme forced the government to concede higher interest rates. This, as we have seen, was immediately translated into higher interest rates worldwide, since Japan has for long been the major source of capital for the United States and US interest rates determine rates in Europe and elsewhere. Capitalism is a global system of accumulation and the contradictions in that system which make for instability and uneven development between nations and regions are at the very heart of the Marxist model of political economy.

FURTHER READING

BEST, MICHAEL H., *The New Competition*, Polity Press, 1990, pp. 158 and 160

GEORGE, MIKE, and LEVIE, HUGO, *Japanese Competition and the British Workplace*, CAITS, Polytechnic of North London, 1984

HOLLAND, STUART, *The European Imperative*, Spokesman, 1993, p. 64

KILMINSTER, ANDY, 'New Management Techniques: The British Experience', *International Marxist Review*, no. 15, Spring 1994

KOO, RICHARD C., 'Why Monetary Policy Has Lost Its Punch', *Economic Eye*, Keizai Koho Centre, Tokyo, Autumn 1993

NIESR, *National Institute Economic Review*, NIESR, April 1993

OECD, *Economic Integration*, OECD, Paris, 1993

RUSTIN, MICHAEL, 'The Politics of Post-Fordism', *New Left Review*, No. 175, 1989

SCHUMPETER, JOSEPH, *Capitalism, Socialism and Democracy*, London, 1943

UN CENTRE FOR TRANSNATIONAL CORPORATIONS, *The Triad in Foreign Direct Investment*, New York, 1991

WORLD BANK, *The Japanese and Korean Experiences in Managing Development*, Staff Working Paper No. 574, Washington, 1985, p. 9

WORLD BANK, *Capital Accumulation and Economic Growth: the Korean Paradigm*, Staff Working Paper No. 712, Washington, 1985

WORLD BANK, *The East Asian Miracle: Economic Growth and Public Policy*, Oxford, 1993, pp. vi, 5

8 THE MARXIST MODEL

Marx's model of capitalist economy has had a much greater influence on economic thought than is generally acknowledged. There is a vast literature of Marxist writing on political economy, which Ernest Mandel summarized in his contribution to *Marx: The First 100 Years* (McLellan, 1983). Several non-Marxist economists have acknowledged the influence of Marx on their thinking. The Austrian Joseph Schumpeter is the most famous, but John Kenneth Galbraith in the USA, Gunnar Myrdal in Sweden and Joan Robinson in the UK provide other examples. At the same time, many writers on economics have felt the need to introduce their books as a critical response to Marx. W.W. Rostow's *Stages of Economic Growth* is subtitled *A Non-Communist Manifesto* (Rostow, 1960). Peter L. Berger in his *Capitalist Revolution* devotes the whole of the Introduction to refuting Marx's model (Berger, 1987). Galbraith in his *History of Economics* writes: 'Telling of how Marx was wrong . . . has become a small industry in the service of those for whom Marx continues to be a glowering threat' (Galbraith, 1987).

Marx himself has to be seen as a member, albeit a dissident member, of the school of classical political economists along with Adam Smith, David Ricardo, John Stuart Mill. They came to be criticized in the latter half of the nineteenth century by Alfred Marshall and others for failing to distinguish economics, which should be regarded as value-free, dealing only with means in a scientific manner, from politics, which was about values. These critics called themselves the 'neoclassical school'.

Today, it is customary for writers on economic issues – in World Bank publications, for example – to distinguish 'neoclassical' economic analysis from what is termed 'revisionism'. Maynard Keynes and Milton Friedman, who were politically active while being poles apart on much of their economic analysis and therefore on the economic policies to be followed by governments, nevertheless saw themselves as part of the neoclassical tradition. The revisionists have made their revisions following Joseph Schumpeter and Gunnar Myrdal, who questioned the whole concept of an equilibrium in economic affairs, and it was they, as we saw, who greatly influenced Japanese economic policy.

Marxists are regarded as quite another species and one that is altogether outmoded today. Yet many revisionists have come under the influence of Marx, whose works are widely and seriously studied in Japanese universities. Schumpeter has been called a 'bourgeois Marxist' (Catephores, 1994). He certainly differed from Marx in seeing technical innovation rather than the exploitation of labour as the central dynamic of capitalism. The models which we have been examining so far fall short of providing adequate explanations for the phenomena which we have observed. They fail, in particular, to reveal economic and political structures which would enable the new technology to develop fully and universally. Of course, it betrays a very Marxist way of thinking to speak of economic and political structures 'corresponding' to the progressive development of technology. But we adopted this way of thinking in our Introduction, 'On Models in General', and, unfashionable as it now is to say so, it remains my view that the Marxist model of capitalism works better in explaining what is happening in the national and world economy than any of the others we have looked at.

In the Marxist model we look behind the market and the sphere of circulation, as Marx called it, to study the sphere of production itself, now increasingly contained within the giant transnational companies. It is here that the profits are made and the capital accumulation takes place, which all governments are desirous of getting their hands on through taxation or borrowing. The Japanese model also starts from the point of production, where the new technology is being applied, and it reveals the relationship between government and industry, but it fails to explain the inner dynamics of the capital accumulation of the transnational companies. We had to look for other explanations for the check to Japanese growth in the 1990s.

Marx begins his analysis of the capitalist mode of production with the commodity, because the commodity, something produced for sale – land, labour, materials, goods, tools and machinery, money – holds within itself the essence of the market economy: first of all, a value derived from its use and from the 'congealed labour time' contained in it; secondly, a value derived from exchange. The value of a commodity relative to that of other commodities depends on the labour time needed to produce it at current levels of productivity. Whereas all other commodities also have a value in use, money, however, has only exchange value (that is money as money; gold or silver have also a use for other purposes, in industry). Most of us use the one commodity we have, our labour power, to sell in the market for money with which to buy commodities to live on. Those (capitalists) who have money to start with, however, will buy commodities – land, labour, materials, buildings, plants, machinery – in order to make more money. They may hoard their money or use it as a merchant does to buy and sell with, but it is the essence of industrial capitalism that money should be used productively – to produce goods and services – in order to make more money.

Money to Make Money

The capitalist, then, sets his capital to work, buying land, labour, machines, materials, to produce goods for sale. But where does the extra money come from? Not, says Marx, like the merchant's profit from haggling in the market or from establishing a monopoly position, because nearly all capitalists, and not just monopolists, appear to make money. It is in the process of production that the capitalist's money is made. Here is where Marx's understanding of the congealed labour time in a commodity becomes important. Workers are paid not for their labour but for their labour *power*. This means that they are paid, like everything else in the market, for what it costs in labour time to produce them, in this case, as labour power – food, clothing, shelter, maintaining a family (so that the labour force is reproduced) and anything else that is needed to make workers work well. But the value of what the worker actually produces with his or her labour may well be more than the value of their labour power. The surplus accrues as profit to the capitalist. Of course, the goods have to be sold; but the profit is produced in the process of production itself. It is concealed, however, behind the 'veil of money'. The worker receives money for selling his or her labour power (to spend on buying the necessities of life) without ever knowing the actual value that he or she has added by labour in the productive process.

Each capitalist is driven on to make more money in production by the competition of other capitalists, not necessarily even in the same line of business, but in the use of money as capital. Marx speaks of the 'law of value' which equalizes the profit from capital everywhere by driving out those who fail to keep up with the going rate of profit, evening out differences in labour time used in production and attracting new capital into fields where the return is above the going rate. This does not mean that at any time there will not be wide divergences in profit rates between and within different sectors. The driving force of the system is capital accumulation. 'Accumulate, accumulate! That is Moses and the Prophets,' wrote Marx. This is generally quoted as if Marx was talking about personal motivation. But Marx is clear that 'we shall see first how the capitalist, by means of capital, exercises his governing power over labour; then, however, we shall see the governing power of capital over the capitalist himself'. This comes from Marx's earliest work on economics, *The Economic and Philosophical Manuscripts* of 1844. Writing later in the first volume of his great work, *Capital*, Marx emphasizes that competition for the capitalist 'compels him to keep constantly extending his capital, in order to preserve it, but extend it he cannot, except by means of progressive accumulation' (*Capital*, Vol. I, Chap. 24, Sect. 3).

There are many ways in which capitalists can increase their profit. Marx distinguishes between 'absolute' and 'relative' surplus value. The first arises from stepping up the intensity of work, so that with the same labour power and machinery more goods are produced. There is much talk today of increasing productivity in this way in British industry. As a result of the slap-down on trade unions and the threat of redundancy we have a British Leyland employee at Longbridge car-assembly plant talking like this (Glyn, 1982):

> In the past management couldn't shift you without the agreement of the union; now it's done without consultation . . . In the old days the target was set by timing the operator, now the target is based on the 'gross potential' of the machine, that means they set the machine as fast as possible, the only limit being quality, and you have to keep up with it. They give you targets you can't reach. The gaffer comes to check your counter every hour; blokes have been suspended for failing to have an adequate explanation of why they haven't reached their target.

Despite the new methods of flexible automation and 'lean production' introduced from Japan in the 1980s, the intensive use of labour through 'speed-up' being reported from British Leyland in 1982 was apparently still continuing a decade later. Hours of work in Japanese plants are higher than elsewhere and often include 'voluntary' overtime. Some of the car's components like seats and cushions and some of the first stages of metal work are still subcontracted to sweat-shops. A 1992 report from the Massachusetts Institute of Technology on the world auto industry came in for strong academic criticism for understating the 'classic exploitation of labour' (quoted in Holland, 1993, pp. 168–9). It remains the case that the new technology has at least halved the overall labour time, including that of component suppliers, in the comparison of a typical Japanese plant with a typical European one. This is the result of each worker having on average twice the European equipment to work with, but it will be much more than twice in the main assembly plant.

One might have been forgiven for supposing that the introduction of labour-saving machinery on a large scale would have made possible a great reduction in hours of work in manufacturing and commerce. In fact the very opposite appears to have been occurring, not only in Japan but also in the UK. Hours of work of full-time employees in the motorcar industry, in mining and generally across all UK industries rose steadily during the 1980s. The drop in 1991 and 1992 may reflect the general decline in economic activity in those years. At the same time, there was a great increase in part-time employment for both men and women. The increase in the application of machinery led to unemployment, not to shorter hours for the employed. Nor did it lead to any increase in output. With little change in output over the 1980s, there was a reduction in the UK of three million full-time male employees, mainly in manufacturing. This was offset by an increase of one million female and half a million male part-time workers, mainly in service industries. The UK is to some extent exceptional among industrialized countries in its long hours of work and a low rate of economic growth. But the lesson we learnt in the chapter on the monetarist model was that deregulation of the labour market in the UK did nothing to advance output or export competitiveness.

This failure of British capitalism to provide full employment in the 1980s is not only a tragedy for British workers, it means that British capital has faced a real problem of creating a profitable labour force. Investment in manufacturing industry in the UK was steadily falling below levels in Japan and also those in the USA and Germany. In 1976 it would have required an investment of £100 billion to catch up with Japan, but the annual rate of investment in UK manufacturing industry was at that time running at only £10 billion. It was actually cut back in the first years of the 1980s and averaged about £10 billion a year thereafter. By that time, Japan had moved far ahead, with an investment level in relation to national income about twice that in the UK. But it should not be supposed that all was well in Japan and the United States or in the rest of Europe. In the last chapter we saw how workers in Japanese plants in the UK, the USA and in Japan itself were demonstrating widespread resistance to new techniques of management which involved increasing labour intensity. Schumpeter's faith in technological innovation had come up against limits to the exploitation of labour which Marx insisted was the foundation of the capitalist system.

Those who would argue that capital exploits many factors of

production (the land, energy resources, raw materials, as well as labour), and by technological advance can increase the margin in each case between the factor consumed in production and the final output, have to face the fact that the owners and managers of capital themselves know that it is with labour alone that they can increase the rate of exploitation. Marx believed that labour values – that is, socially necessary labour time – determine the prices of commodities. Many of his followers have shown how this can be demonstrated with computer analysis of national accounts (see Cockshott and Cottrell, 1994). What matters is that the profit for capital must come from the difference between the value which the worker produces and the bundle of consumption goods and services that the worker needs to produce and reproduce. That is a social and not a technical question. Workers have somehow to be prevented by the owners and controllers of capital from rendering themselves unexploitable.

It can easily be seen from the UK figures how competition drives competing capitalists to reduce costs in every possible way – not only by increasing investment in machinery, but by reducing the costs of machinery and of raw materials used in production. In the end it is labour time that must be saved so that only that which is 'socially necessary', as Marx called it, is used up at any time. The microchip has not only greatly extended the processes a machine can perform without human supervision, and so can keep machines running more continuously, it has greatly reduced the cost of each machine, as anyone buying a micro-computer today knows very well. This is not to say that the great manufacturing companies do not make use of cheap labour in Hong Kong and Singapore and elsewhere for the actual assembly of the microchips. They look to reduce costs in every way they can. We can now see how inevitable it was that competition should itself lead to plants that were more and more capital-intensive and to giant companies accumulating the capital necessary to finance them and their interrelation, although it was a powerful test of his model that Marx could predict this in the 1860s.

The Economics of Imperialism

Capitalists, in Marx's model, have both to produce surplus value from exploitation in the process of production and realize it by selling their products at a profit in the market. This leads to a contradiction between keeping workers' wages down and at the same time expecting them to be able to afford to buy their own increased production. The problem is only solved so long as purchasing power, including credit, just rises to match increased productivity. But there is a further and more serious contradiction in the capitalist system, according to Marx. As more and more capital is introduced with each unit of labour, changing what Marx called the organic composition of capital, it will be more and more difficult to maintain the rate of surplus per worker and so profit rates will tend to fall.

Marx saw that this tendency could be counteracted by cheapening the cost of capital equipment or of workers' wages. New machinery and equipment were not necessarily more costly per unit of output. Raw materials could be bought cheaper from overseas and workers' wages could be reduced by obtaining cheap imported food. Both the last two movements involved increased foreign trade and most advantageously trade with colonies where markets could be captured from local producers and cheaper labour could be exploited.

We saw in Chapter 3 how the growth of giant companies and their integration with the banks and the state apparatus itself had been seen by Lenin as the cause of the imperialist expansion of Europe and North America at the end of the nineteenth century. What we can now see is the source of that pressure outwards. Lenin emphasized that the pressure came from the necessity to export capital for investment in colonies overseas when opportunities for profitable investment at home were declining. In fact, as I have argued in The Economics of Imperialism, the figures do not really show that. The investment overseas consisted always of reinvestment of profits already made overseas: most of British capital investment overseas was in the USA, Canada, Australia, South Africa, Argentina and other independent states; and the

111

levels of home and overseas investment tended to rise and fall together rather than alternately.

The advantage to the individual investing overseas was not necessarily a higher rate of return, but a government guarantee of the return. What overseas investment did undoubtedly provide for British capital in general was a cheapening of the inputs into the productive process: cheaper food for the workers, cheaper raw materials for industry. In both cases, the USA, the dominions and other independent states were the main sources of supply opened up, but many of the smaller colonies were developed for their single crop or mineral supplies and India became an important market for exports of railway equipment and port installations, as well as a source of tea, cotton and mercenary armies.

Today, most of the European colonies have gained political independence, but, like the Spanish colonies in South America before them, they remain largely dependent economically on US, European and Japanese capital accumulation. The great strength of the Marxist model is that by concentrating our attention on the process of production it helps us to explain the strength of the North American, European and Japanese industrially developed nations and the weakness of the rest of the world. This is not simply or mainly the result of bargaining strengths between industrial and agricultural producers, of unequal exchange in the terms of trade or even of guns. It is the result of the fact that the profits are made and the actual accumulation of capital takes place *inside* the American, European and Japanese companies. Where this capital should be invested is decided in New York or London or Tokyo or Berne and not in Delhi, Buenos Aires, Ibadan or Singapore, and not in government offices either, but in the head offices of the giant companies.

Marx foresaw the increasing concentration of capital into fewer and fewer hands:

> The battle of competition is fought by the cheapening of commodities ... Commensurately with the development of capitalist production and accumulation there also takes place a development of the two most powerful levers of centralization – competition and credit. At the same time, the progress of accumulation increases the material amen-

able to centralization, i.e. the individual capitals, while the expansion of capitalist production creates on the one hand, the social need, and on the other hand, the technical means, for those immense industrial undertakings which require a previous centralization for their accomplishment ... In any given branch of industry centralization would reach its extreme limit if all the individual capitals invested there were fused into a single capital ... either in the hands of a single capitalist or a single capitalist company (Marx, *Capital*, Vol. I, Chap. 25, Sect. 2).

This has not happened yet, but the corollary which Marx assumed is already clear, that 'the additional capital formed in the course of further accumulation attracts fewer and fewer workers in proportion to its magnitude'. Not only are whole working populations inside the industrialized countries being excluded from employment but whole countries are becoming marginalized. A single Triad of just three economic entities – the USA, the European Union and Japan – is now responsible for 80 per cent of the flows of world investment and 65 per cent of that takes place between themselves. They are also responsible for about two-thirds of the world's trade (in trade in manufactures it is three-quarters), even though they comprise only 15 per cent of the world's population. In the years 1983 to 1989, moreover, while world output and exports both rose at an average annual rate of 8 per cent to 9 per cent, world foreign direct investment rose at no less than 30 per cent a year (UNCTC, 1991).

The Marxist model also helps us to understand the uneven development of capitalism, growing first in Britain, then in the United States, Germany, France and Italy, later still in Japan, South Korea and Taiwan – not because of the political power of the governments of those countries or even because of the size of their markets, though both were important supportive factors, but because of the economic strength of their industrial concerns. The very independence of the giant companies today and their increasingly opportunistic attitude to the nation states of their birth, which we have already noted, is the final proof. And while it may appear that the great banks and financial institutions have power independent of the producing companies, we need to note that, although the City of London could for a time protect British transnational companies, the British economy steadily declined once the productive base of British industry had been undermined. Indeed, it is the view of several Marxist economists that it was the very strength of British financial institutions, investing funds in ventures all over the world, that led to neglect of the necessary investment in British industry first in the 1920s and again in the 1970s.

So much was clear when this book was first written and two Sheffield economic historians, Andrew Gamble and Sidney Pollard, could be quoted as having already convincingly argued the case against the City of London (Gamble, 1981; Pollard, 1982). But what they then described was nothing to what was to follow. Employment in manufacturing industry in the UK had fallen by a million in the 1970s; it fell by over two million in the 1980s to a total of less than five million. The Thatcher government believed that the UK could become a service economy. Academics were found to argue a new set of theses against the Marxist interpretation of history which had put production at the centre of society: that the industrial revolution was much exaggerated and Britain's role as the world's workshop was very short-lived; at least since the 1870s the British economy had always been a service economy and the British Empire had been built on the provision of financial services.

All the facts go against this new interpretation of history and support the Marxist view of the industrial base of British capitalism's imperial expansion. Throughout the nineteenth century and for the next forty years the share of industry in the national product was generally nearly twice the share of commercial activity (including trade and transport but not the income from foreign investment). The value of exports of goods was always five times the value of exports of services; re-exports and shipping earnings were roughly equal to those of the services. The Empire provided the main markets for exports and source of materials, for the mining and transport of which most of the investment was directed. This is not a picture of a service empire. The current account of foreign payments was generally in balance, so that income from past investments could be partly repatriated and partly re-invested (Barratt Brown, 1994).

All this ended with the Second World War. Much of the investment had to be sold to pay for arms from the USA before Lend-Lease arrangements were introduced. British capitalists have tried ever since to restore that overseas nest egg, but the result has been to destroy the goose at home that laid the golden eggs. The consequent reduction of investment in British industry has led inevitably to the decline of the British economy. Even Switzerland, which is often quoted as the supreme example of a successful service economy, depending on tourism and banking, has in fact always maintained a highly competitive export business in precision instruments and machine tools. While there was a great increase in world trade in services in the 1980s, it no more than kept up with world trade in goods. For the UK Professor Rowthorn has shown that in the 1980s income from exports of services only amounted to one tenth of exported goods, and the share had been falling. There was, he believed, no future in a purely service economy (Rowthorn, 1994).

The Causes of Booms and Slumps

The accumulation of capital not only takes place unevenly between nations and companies; it takes place unevenly over time. A cycle of booms and slumps can be traced back to the early years of Britain's industrial revolution. It appears that throughout the nineteenth century they had an amplitude of eight to ten years. They have continued throughout the twentieth century but with rather shorter periods between the tops of one boom and of the next. The whole capitalist world is caught up in their rhythm. At one time they were associated with the ten-year cycle of sunspots which influence the earth's weather and therefore our crops; but the timing was found to be out! William Beveridge at the end of the nineteenth century proved that the cycles were a phenomenon of industry and due, he thought, to the failure of labour to move to new industries after technological change had caused unemployment. He therefore proposed the establishment of Labour

Exchanges and the payment of dole during unemployment, so that mobility was improved and in the meantime effective demand was not so severely reduced in periods of recession.

Unfortunately, slumps grew deeper despite the introduction of Labour Exchanges and the payment of dole to the unemployed. The slump of the 1930s was the worst ever. We saw in Chapter 5 how Keynes proposed to increase government investment in a recession. This was because he believed that the cause of the crisis was the rise in the proportion of income put into savings during a boom, so that as a result there was inadequate demand for the products of the boom-time investments. The facts, however, showed that this was not always true. People often saved more at the beginning of a recession, presumably out of caution as an insurance against the future. What was true was that during a boom profits rose more than wages. Marx had said this all along.

Marx's understanding of the boom was that new plant and machinery was installed by capitalists all acting at the same time to keep up with each other as if there were no limit to the size of the market. Profits rose from the reduced costs of the new production processes, and what followed was over-production. The boom was often fuelled by speculation and rising prices; but a crisis was inevitable if too much money was going into building new machines and too little into the wages of the workers who were expected to buy the products of the new machines. The crisis led to a slump as workers were laid off, and to bankruptcies of companies and the writing-off of old plant and machinery. After that prices fell again through cut-throat competition for the limited market and through the elimination of the companies and plants that produced at higher cost. With lower prices, purchasing power picked up and a new boom was on its way with a further advance in cost-saving technology.

By noting that the time that capitalists allowed on average for depreciation of their buildings, plant, machinery and tools was about twelve to fifteen years, Marx was able to explain the periodicity of the cycles. An eight-to-ten-year cycle would roughly allow for twelve to fifteen years from the time when new plant was introduced in the middle of one boom to the time when it was written off in the slump that followed the next boom. We can add that the shorter cycle today corresponds with shorter depreciation periods during years of more rapid technological change.

Later Marxist economists, especially a Russian economist called Kondratieff, detected a much longer cycle of fifty years, with periods when the booms were bigger and the slumps shallower, in the 1760s, 1820s and 1860s, followed by periods when slumps were deeper and booms smaller. Schumpeter, and then Ernest Mandel, showed that the cycles continued with long booms in the 1920s and 1960s, followed by long declines. In the early 1990s it is not clear when and how recovery will be established after the slump of the 1980s. The booms related to the introduction of new technology: successively, textile manufacture, railway building, electricity and shipbuilding, the motor car and aeroplane, the computer and automation. Ten years ago, it seemed that nuclear power could give capitalism its next upswing, or end in human disaster. Today, nuclear power is discredited, but the possibilities of flexible automation and the potentially revolutionary development of information technology open up new vistas of technological advance.

Recovery from the slumps, however, requires that old plant shall be written off. In the past it has taken a major war to do that, and such an eventuality cannot any longer be contemplated with impunity by the human race. This may mean, at the very best, some delay in worldwide economic recovery, even if other problems were overcome. The profits for those who were in first with the new technology carry the boom onwards; but, as more and more producers come into the business, competition brings profits down. There is obviously much evidence for Kondratieff's long waves, but the cycle is nothing like as precisely fixed at forty to fifty years as Kondratieff suggested. Nor is it certain that the cycle will keep repeating itself. The causes of the cyclical movements have always been conjunctural – wars of destruction and redistribution, voyages of discovery, the introduction of new minerals, a stream of inventions and innovations. It is far from certain that such cycles should recur with the reliability of the seasons and the movements of the planets around the sun.

This leaves us with an important point to make about the

Marxist model of the economy. Marx was greatly influenced by Isaac Newton as well as by Charles Darwin. He sought to discover 'laws of motion' of the capitalist economy similar to those which Newton discovered within the solar system. He saw in the commodity certain properties corresponding to mass and velocity in the heavenly bodies. 'As the heavenly bodies, once thrown into a certain definite motion, always repeat this, so it is with social production,' he writes in Chapter 25, Section 23, of the first volume of *Capital*, and earlier in Chapter 2 he says, 'In the form of society now under consideration, the behaviour of men in the social process of production is purely atomic,' and in Volume 3, Chapter 51, 'The law of value is called a "blind law". Only as an internal law, and from the point of view of the individual agents as blind law, does the law of value exert its influence here and maintain the social equilibrium of production in the turmoil of its accidental fluctuations.' Sometimes in his more prophetic moments Marx allowed these comparisons to suggest the inevitability of capitalist development – towards deeper and deeper crises, the reserve army of labour rising with every new slump until the 'centralization of the means of production and socialization of labour at last reach a point where they become incompatible with their capitalist integument. The integument is burst asunder. The knell of capitalist private property sounds. The expropriators are expropriated' (*Capital*, Vol. I, Chap. 32).

Trotsky took up some of this dramatically fatalistic manner of writing and even of thinking. Others have done so since. In the Introduction we noted E. P. Thompson's attack on Althusserian models and his ridicule of Newtonian 'orreries'. But Marx was always cautious enough to indicate counteracting tendencies. For he was well aware that *we* are inside the models of political economy. Our increasing consciousness of the conflicts between what could be and what is, between technological advance and the economic structure, leads to change and not only to revolutionary change, but to all sorts of adjustments and accommodations.

We have looked at such adjustments in the measures proposed by Keynesians and by the Post-Fordists. Some are not at all what Marx might have expected. The crisis of 1929 and the slump of the 1930s did not sound the death knell of capitalism. It almost looked as if they might, but a fascist distortion of capitalism was the main result of 1930s unemployment. The 1980s witnessed a further worldwide recession of 1930s proportions which has continued into the 1990s. Fascism has again emerged as a widespread response. Capitalism has certainly not collapsed, but recovery is slow and, given the nature of modern armaments, humanity can no longer afford the 'creative destruction' of a world war.

What we may learn from Marx is that small-scale adjustments are not enough to adapt to a major technological revolution. A revolutionary change is needed in the whole social formation, although this does not need to be accompanied by violence. Most revolutionary social changes have involved very litle violence. It is the social breakdown that follows a failure to change that engenders violence. But for the whole social formation to change, a new model of the political economy is needed which is clearly understood and grasped by men and women as an inspiration for making the change. None of the existing socialist models has appeared to fulfil Marx's expectations, but this may be because we have been looking in the wrong direction for an alternative to the capitalist market.

Marx assumed that there would have to be a revolutionary change in ownership of the means of production to end the economic exploitation of wage slaves. The failures of attempted socialism in the Soviet Union and China combined with the survival of capitalism elsewhere have led both Marxist and non-Marxist writers to reconsider Marx's concept of polarization of capital and labour and their antagonistic relationship (Handley, 1994; Olin Wright, 1994). It is argued that labour has won property rights – in a guaranteed basic income, basic health, basic education – and many workers have shares in private companies either as direct shareholders or through pension funds and unit trusts. The middle class has grown in size throughout the industrialized world. While Marx saw the self-employed peasantry and small business class declining, a new self-employed class has arisen in the household economy that has followed from male unemployment. It is not only that there are many more jobs for the wives and that membership of the professions has boomed, professional husband and wife teams can be found exploiting their skills and knowledge to win a surplus well beyond the costs of production and reproduction, which they can capitalize and thus join the capitalist class.

A far more subtle change has taken place in many working-class households where the man has become unemployed and the wife has kept her job or taken on outside employment for the first time. Studies in the North of England where male unemployment is very high have shown not only that men are doing more of the housework, but that households have engaged in small business activities, which though not necessarily more rewarding financially than life on the dole are infinitely more acceptable for the family's dignity and sense of purpose (Wheelock, 1994). Some, including car boot sales, come close to a black market.

At the same time there has been created not only a vast impoverished peasantry and exploited proletariat in the Third World, but in the industrialized countries an even larger excluded class (Marx's *lumpenproletariat*) than in Marx's day. This amounts in many countries to a fifth of the whole population – immigrants, lone families, unemployed youths and older workers, as well as those disabled and on pensions – who have become marginalized and excluded from the solidarity of class consciousness. Marx's prophetic picture of the future seen from the 1880s, of a failing, broken capitalism and a rising self-conscious proletariat, bears little resemblance to the actualities of the 1990s. On the other hand, the continuing failure of capitalism to meet the needs for a decent life for the overwhelming majority of the human population, or to provide the conditions for sustainable life on earth in the future, must leave Marx's insistence on the need for social change unchallenged.

Within Marx's general view of the historic evolution of classes and social formations, one must ask whether there is some alternative to the social change he expected. Before we look at alternatives, there is a major argument to be considered between Marxists about the way in which capitalism might be expected to give way to socialism through the permanent arms economy, and there are two important critiques of Marx also to be considered, from the feminists and from the Greens.

FURTHER READING

BARRATT BROWN, MICHAEL, 'Marx's Economics as a Newtonian Model', in T. Shanin (ed.), *The Rules of the Game*, Tavistock, 1972, pp. 122–45

BARRATT BROWN, MICHAEL, *The Economics of Imperialism*, Penguin Books, 1974 (see Chap. 3)

BARRATT BROWN, MICHAEL, review of *British Imperialism* by Cain and Hopkins, *Spokesman*, 1994

BERGER, PETER L., *The Capitalist Revolution*, Wildwood House, 1987

CATEPHORES, GEORGE, 'Schumpeter: A Bourgeois Marxist', *New Left Review*, No. 205, 1994

COCKSHOTT, P., and COTTRELL, A., 'Empirical Test of Labour Theory of Value', *Socialism and Beyond*, Conference of Socialist Economists, 1994

FREEDMAN, ROBERT (ed.), *Marx on Economics*, Penguin Books, 1962

GALBRAITH, J. K., *A History of Economics*, Penguin, 1987, p. 139

GAMBLE, ANDREW, *Britain in Decline*, Macmillan, 1981

GLYN, ANDREW, in: The Committee on Joint Studies in Public Policy, *Slow Growth in the Western World*, Heinemann, 1982 (quotation from *Militant*, 23 April 1982, repeated in the *Economic Review* (National Institute), August 1982)

HANDLEY, CHARLES, *The Empty Raincoat*, Hutchinson, 1994

HODGSON, GEOFF, *Trotsky and Fatalistic Marxism*, Spokesman, 1978

HOLLAND, STUART, *The European Imperative*, Spokesman, 1993

MANDEL, ERNEST, *Late Capitalism*, Verso, 1978

MARX, KARL, *Capital*, Volumes 1–3 (ed. Ernest Mandel), Penguin Books, 1976, 1978, 1981

MCLELLAN, DAVID, *Marx: The First 100 Years*, Fontana, 1983

POLLARD, SIDNEY, *The Wasting of the British Economy*, Croom Helm, 1982

ROSTOW, W. W., *Stages of Economic Growth*, Cambridge, 1960

ROWTHORN, BOB, 'Brave New World of Services', *Guardian*, 23 May 1994

SCHUMPETER, J. A., *Business Cycles*, McGraw-Hill, 1939

SCHUMPETER, J. A., *Capitalism, Socialism and Democracy*, Cambridge, 1943

UN CENTER FOR TRANSNATIONAL CORPORATIONS, *The Triad in Foreign Direct Investment*, New York, 1991

WHEELOCK, JANE, 'The Economic Character of Households at the Margins of Employment', Conference of Socialist Economists, 1994

WRIGHT, ERIC OLIN, 'Class Analysis, History and Emancipation', *New Left Review*, No. 205, 1994

9 THE PERMANENT ARMS ECONOMY MODEL

All Marxists would agree that competitive private accumulation of capital in the developed countries, even on a transnational scale, would inevitably involve uneven development, economic and political rivalry, bitter class struggle, colonial resistance and global crisis. Marxists are, however, divided on the nature of the crisis. It is possible to distinguish three main schools of thought, although there will be some among them who would wish to combine elements of the models of two or more of these schools. The first we shall call 'overproductionists'. They regard the crisis as the bottom of a Kondratieff cycle in which increasing competition between giant companies with state support has driven down the rate of profit and forced the accumulators of capital to compete for more intensive exploitation, for rationalization of plants and a restructuring of capital that will re-establish acceptable rates of profit. Such competition breaks out from time to time in minor wars, results in huge so-called 'defence' budgets and threatens an internecine Third World War among the capitalist powers.

A second school we shall call 'underconsumptionists'. They emphasize not so much the failure to generate an adequate surplus but rather the failure to find ways of absorbing the huge surpluses generated. On this view, expenditure on arms – the permanent war economy – has been the saving of the capitalist system. We looked in an earlier chapter at the wartime capitalist command-economy model as a structural model of economic organization. We now have to consider whether the gigantic element of military expenditure in the budgets of all states since the Second World War has not in fact provided a command economy within a wider market economy.

The third school of thought we shall call 'Third Worldists'. They also start from the high levels of arms spending but see this in terms not of the competition of rival capitals but of a global struggle between the declining power of capitalism and the rising strength of socialists the world over. They did not ever believe that this lay so much in the Soviet Union and Eastern Europe as in China and the Third World, where they expected to see successful revolutionary struggles.

It seemed best to test these three different schools by their respective power to explain the desperate condition that humanity had arrived at, in which the superpowers, and some other states also, had arsenals of bombs which could in a few minutes destroy all that human beings have constructed on the earth's surface in five thousand years and wipe out most of the human race. All our studies so far have suggested that we shall need to look behind the popular explanations that a few wicked men, whether in the Kremlin or in the Pentagon, are responsible, or alternatively that it is the foolishness and ambition of their advisers that must be blamed. Behind Hitler stood the barons of German heavy industry and their links with the Reich. Behind Reagan stood the giant transnational companies and their links with the United States government. Behind a Brezhnev or Andropov stood an economic structure linked to the Soviet state.

Internecine Struggle of Rival Capitalist Powers

The division of the world between the capitalist powers was at the centre of Lenin's model of imperialism; and there is no doubt that the challenge of German industry to France and Britain and to the USA for markets and spheres of influence led to the First World War. The challenge once again of the 'have nots' to the 'haves' in the 1930s led to the Axis powers' attack on the capitalist allies in 1939 and 1940. But the Second World War became something more than a war between rival centres of capitalism, both because of Hitler's invasion of the Soviet Union and because of the revolutionary nature of the national liberation struggles in Europe and in Asia which the war generated. Some young historians (like Anthony Barnett in his book *Iron Britannia*) have characterized the very wide national support for the war effort in Britain as 'Churchillism' – a bargaining of some social reforms for the preservation of British capitalism. In doing so they omit the implications of an anti-fascist struggle in which British soldiers fought side by side with the French and Dutch resistance and with Yugoslav and Italian partisans, whose aims were openly revolutionary. (Basil Davidson's *Special Operations Europe* provides the necessary corrective.)

From this anti-fascist element in the Second World War there emerged the liberation of China and of Yugoslavia and the dismantling of the British and French empires, as well as a Labour Britain, none of which Churchill welcomed. It has to be added that the revolutionary social change that many hoped for elsewhere in Europe, or in Asia and Africa, was not realized.

We have to note Stalin's decision in 1943 to terminate the Comintern and to negotiate for spheres of influence with Churchill and Roosevelt. Eastern Europe went into the Soviet bloc, Germany was divided; but social revolution elsewhere was left for the Allies to abort as best they could. Western Europe was united under the shield of Nato. Neo-colonial regimes replaced colonial rule. Frontiers in Asia were less clearly established. Taiwan was separated from China; Korea and Indo-China were both divided into North and South after wars involving the superpowers; and in the end, after the most vicious of all colonial wars, the whole of Vietnam and Cambodia was liberated from the capitalist sphere of influence.

Despite these major wars and the threat of major war, for example, over Cuba, Syria, Egypt, Iran, Iraq or Afghanistan, it can still be argued that the main source of conflict in the world today comes from the unequal competitive development of the capitalist states themselves. This is the 'overproductionist' case. For many years (until the USA sought superiority) *détente* held, if only just, between the superpowers, while their dominant position was being steadily challenged – the Soviet Union's by China, that of the USA by Japan and Germany. Even if other nation states are dwarfed by the giant transnational companies, these five stand out above them in economic and political power. Though much of Germany's power comes from its leadership of the European Economic Community, it is German industry just like Japanese industry that has been challenging the US hegemony.

The first two world wars followed within two years of German exports surpassing those of the United Kingdom. German exports did so again in 1958, and in 1962 they surpassed even those of the USA. Twenty years later Japan's exports of manufactures also surpassed those of the United States. The Japanese threat to United States industry has been well understood, but it is complicated by three new features of inter-capitalist rivalry: the threat comes mainly from Japanese plants inside the USA; the United States trade deficit with Japan arises mainly from imports of automobile parts; and the deficit is mainly covered by Japanese investment in the US economy. The giant transnational companies have become increasingly opportunistic in their attitude to nation-state governments. In times of crisis they look to the superpowers for protection and this now means, among the capitalist states, to the USA, Japan and the European Union.

Since the possibility was first broached by Ernest Mandel in 1968 in his book *Europe versus America*, there is no doubt that the hegemony of the USA has been challenged by Germany and Japan. The dollar ceased to be convertible in 1971 and was devalued in 1974. It has tended to fall in relation to other currencies (though with ups and downs) ever since. Of the three outcomes envisaged over twenty years ago (by Bob Rowthorn for example – see Rowthorn, 1971), which were, respectively, continued US domination, an imperialist coalition of relatively autonomous capitalist states and the intensification of imperialist rivalry, the last seems nearest to what has happened. The obvious global crisis of recession and unemployment from 1979 onwards has led to successive meetings of the heads of the capitalist states, with absolutely no results in action. That was written in 1983 and remained true in 1993.

A suggestion that I made in 1974 (in the last chapter of *The Economics of Imperialism*) that, if the nation states could not agree, perhaps the giant companies might, has been realized at least in one respect. The bankers who manage the funds of the giant companies have so far succeeded, by joint action, in preventing an international banking crisis of the kind that triggered the crash of 1929. (The bankers themselves are writing the best books on the international economy today. Nobody who wants to under-stand international finance can afford to miss reading Paul Erdmann's books, *The Billion Dollar Killing* and *The Crash of '79* – which so nearly came true – but they need also to read his more recent book, *The Last Days of America*, to reach their own conclusion about the German threat to US hegemony.)

Many people would regard the possibility of war between Europe and the USA or between Japan and either as unthinkable. Most wars since 1945 have been either wars within the Third World (Iran and Iraq, the Biafran war, the Israel–Arab wars, the Bosnian war), or wars between the capitalist powers and Third World countries (the Korean War, the Vietnam War, the war in the Falklands, the Gulf War), or between the communist powers and Third World countries (the Soviet Union's Afghan war, the Chinese Vietnam war). Direct confrontation between capitalist and communist powers has been avoided since the Korean war and the Cuban crisis in 1960, but an element of communist–capitalist rivalry has been involved. This is the foundation of the argument of the Third Worldists. But inter-capitalist rivalry has been even more evident, short of open war.

As the minerals in the earth's crust, metals as well as oil and gas, are rapidly exhausted the competition to control them could be expected to become ever sharper. 'Beggar-my-neighbour' actions reminiscent of the 1930s have come to typify relations between the major powers, and smaller countries have been caught up in the antagonisms. The argument between the USA and the European Union which for many years held up completion of the Uruguay round of negotiations under GATT is but one example. There has been much talk of a New World Order fifty years after Bretton Woods, but no action has been proposed to revise the Bretton Woods institutions, from which GATT derives its powers. Most serious for the survival of the planet itself is the lack of any common commitment to fulfil even the quite modest requirements of the Treaty of Rio for global ecological protection. The recent failure of the great powers to sign a Law of the Seas, which would put under international control the mining of the ocean beds, and the renewed interest of the individual states, including Britain, in the future of Antarctica, the last unexploited continent, do not bode well for those who believe in peaceful capitalist development.

The Permanent War Economy

If doubts remain about the inevitability of war between the capitalist powers, perhaps we should remember that Orwell's *1984* began with a sudden switch, which none of those in power had explained to the public, from 'Oceania's' alliance with 'Eurasia' to alliance with 'Eastasia'. There is certainly no doubt of the continuing pressure to increase military spending in the USA, in Britain, France and Japan, and throughout the capitalist world generally – and the Marxists we called 'underconsumptionists' offer a straight economic explanation for this. The rationale of Soviet military spending will be looked at in the next section of this chapter. The explanation of these Marxists is that far from the capitalist states competing for a declining surplus, the problem remains that of disposing of an excess surplus – which only a permanently expanding arms economy can absorb.

It could be that the two models are not so completely contradictory. On the one hand, the surplus is mainly in the hands of a few giant companies, while the rest are suffering from severe competitive pressure on profits. On the other hand, the giant companies compete quite ruthlessly for armaments orders not only in their countries of origin but throughout the world. On either view, the assumption of a dangerous threat, first assumed to be from the Soviet Union and then more obviously from fascism and terrorism, everywhere has to be sustained in order to keep up the commitment to continued military spending.

It is argued that military equipment has immense advantages as a capitalist product in that it (a) becomes obsolete almost as soon as it is produced (if it hasn't done so already); (b) does not compete with other goods in the market; and (c) can be presented to the taxpayers as a life-and-death requirement for national defence, not to mention the defence of such ideological concepts as 'the free world'. This was the view of Rosa Luxemburg, revived by Michael Kidron in his book *Western Capitalism since the War*, published in 1968. Thereafter, for many years, so-called defence expenditure has been estimated to take up every year something like 8 per cent of world output (USA 7.5 per cent, UK 6 per cent and Soviet Union 15 per cent – much higher in some Third World countries). It accounts in many countries for a third of all government spending; and half of all expenditure on research and development goes into military budgets in the USA and UK. It is a strangely untoward result that Japan and West Germany, with the lowest military spending, have far outstripped the USA and UK in industrial competition, leaving them, in Britain's case at least, without the advanced industrial base to defend even their native capitalists. The greatest irony of all is that the USA has been rearming Japan, its major competitor, to sustain the only thriving industry – the arms industry.

The model of excess capitalist surplus absorbed by armaments, however, leaves other important questions to be answered. First, it has been argued by Professor Seymour Melman, Professor of Industrial Engineering at New York's Columbia University (Melman, 1974), that while the arms industry may absorb surpluses, it does so at the expense of investment in new capital equipment. As a result, countries like the USA and Britain, in which arms spending is the equivalent of one-third of industrial capital investment, fall behind in competitive productivity, while Germany, in which arms spending is the equivalent of only one-fifth, and Japan, in which it is no more than 4 per cent of capital investment, forge ahead. President Reagan's military plans for the USA raised the figure to 87 per cent in 1988, above even the 60 per cent in the USSR, which has been so disastrous for Soviet economic advance.

Melman argues that it is not only that arms spending pre-empts scarce skills and resources, but that the cost-plus basis of military contracts in the USA provides one of the main built-in causes of inflation, since this spills over into the non-arms economy also. While costs in civilian industry have been held down by increased productivity, costs have risen in the arms industry, measured for example in cost per lb of aircraft. Melman concludes: 'Since the elemental task of an economy, any economy, is to organize people to work, it is evident that the military economy of the United States is an anti-economy. Independently of intention, the military economy of the US disables the competences ordinarily required for the conduct of economic life.'

Melman's view of the over-powerful state as the source of the arms economy differs from the Marxist view of an 'underconsumptionist' cause. The debilitating effect of an arms economy does not disprove the 'underconsumptionist' argument. On empirical grounds, the more serious problems for this view lie in the absence of any clear correlation between unemployment and arms expenditure and of any apparent deliberate intention of governments to increase military spending to absorb unused industrial capacity. Since the ending of the Cold War, spending on so-called defence has been reduced in nearly all industrialized countries, in spite of a worldwide economic recession. With the 'Soviet threat' removed, it did not prove to be true, as was claimed in the first edition of this book, that 'defence is the one form of government spending that appears to have overwhelming popular support and has had strong trade-union support to date'.

Reduction in expenditure on armaments has not, however, led to expansion in welfare expenditure. The resources involved in the production and sale of arms still far exceed those devoted to the relief of poverty at home or abroad. It was calculated in the 1980s that the military expenditure of the eighteen richest countries in the capitalist world, with 16 per cent of the total world population, was equal to the total income of the poorest thirty-six countries, with 50 per cent of the population (Sutcliffe, 1983). That means that if all the arms had been converted into ploughshares, the income of these last countries would have been doubled. The end of the Cold War could have realized a great peace dividend. But in the event the huge stores of arms and the capacity to produce arms led to a massive expansion of the arms trade with the Third World. The World Bank has published lists showing that over half of all developing countries were spending more on arms than on health and education together in the late 1980s.

The Gulf War revealed that it did not need any Soviet threat for the launching of great armies and support forces to secure the oil supplies of the West. And the ending of that war revived demand for military supplies in the Middle East to the extent of an estimated $30 billion. Nevertheless, spending on arms has been cut back even in a recession. There has been some political and trade-union resistance to cuts in military establishments, especially where these were concentrated in a limited area as in Scotland, south-west England and certain regions of France and Germany. The fact is, however, that in most capitalist countries there is no such thing as an arms industry. Military production is a part of the aerospace, shipbuilding, motorcar and engineering industries. The only difference is that the orders for arms come from governments.

Representatives of workers attending international trade-union conferences on arms conversion in the 1980s wanted to know what form of government spending was going to keep them in jobs. It has been the misfortune of such workers that armament orders have fallen off in a period of general recession in the industries involved, when governments have been applying monetarist policies of retrenchment rather than Keynesian policies of expansion. The distinguished British economist Frank Blackaby has argued that arms conversion has to be tackled by specific measures of government spending, not because the arms industry is different, but because, just like any other major industrial change, it cannot be left with impunity for market forces to adjust (Blackaby, 1989).

Apart from the empirical evidence to support the concept of the permanent arms economy, or otherwise, there is a theoretical question mark over the Luxemburg underconsumptionist thesis concerning the cause of economic crisis. The famous quotation from Marx does leave some room for doubt. 'The last cause of all real crises always remains the poverty and restricted consumption of the masses as compared to the tendency of capitalist production to develop the productive forces in such a way that only the absolute power of consumption of the entire society would be their limit' (*Capital*, Vol. III, Chap. 30). I have discussed the view Marx took of overproduction and underconsumption at some length in *The Economics of Imperialism* (in Chapter 3). If the 'underconsumptionists' imply that workers' wages (and peasants' prices) are set too low for them to buy back the products of their own industry, then Keynesian methods of demand management designed to correct any underconsumption on a national and international scale ought to be in the interests of both capitalists and workers.

Those who believe that overproduction is the essence of the Marxist view of capitalist crisis are drawing attention to the competition between each of the centres of capital accumulation – the trusts and giant companies. This competition leads them all, especially in boom times, to invest in new productive capacity, much of which cannot then be operated profitably. When they all discover this they all act together to cut back, lay off workers, write off old plant and a slump ensues, as we saw in Chapter 5. If governments then turn to war it is to divert their people, not to absorb unused capacity; but preparation for war is also the inevitable logic of the competitive ethos of capitalism. This may be the explanation for the somewhat disturbing fact that Japan has been increasing its military spending, albeit from an exceptionally low level, and for the rearmament drive throughout the Far East and Asia. According to one British arms exporter, arms spending in the Pacific Asia region will outstrip that of Western Europe by the year 2010 and equal two-thirds of that in North America, which in 1992 accounted for almost half of world arms demand.

A Historical Epoch of Social Revolution

Some Marxist writers, like the editors of the American journal *Monthly Review* – Harry Magdoff and Paul Sweezey – combine an underconsumptionist model of capitalist crisis with the view that the fundamental conflict lies between the developed and the underdeveloped countries. 'Since the Second [World] War', Sweezey wrote in the *Monthly Review* of June 1971, 'it has become increasingly clear that the principal contradiction in the system, at least in the present historical period, is not *within* the developed part but between the developed and underdeveloped parts.' This is the 'Third Worldist' view. In this article, while Sweezey allowed for some challenge from German and Japanese firms to the dominance of US capital, he was ruling out the significance of class struggles within the developed capitalist countries 'in the present historical period'. Looking out at the world from the quiescent state of the American labour movement this might seem to be a realistic judgement, but it overlooked the level of class struggle in Europe. The apparent overwhelming strength of United States capitalism (at least prior to the 1970s) and the deep divisions in American labour – ethnic, religious, cultural and geographical – have tended to lead American Marxists to see the contradictions of capitalism as occurring outside the USA.

This view of the centrality of the conflicts between US imperialism and the Third World is part of a world view of the present historical epoch as being marked by the struggle between the two camps of socialism and capitalism. Most people would acknowledge the USA as the last bastion of capitalist power. Some, equally on the Right and on the Left, saw the Soviet Union as the first bastion of socialist power. This view collapsed with the disintegration of the Soviet Union, but some Marxists, who regarded the Soviet Union as less than socialist, none the less always saw it as a counterforce to the United States' capitalist hegemony. This even included some who regarded the Soviet military industrial complex as equally responsible with the United States military and industrial leaders for the 'exterminism', as the late E. P. Thompson called it, of the nuclear arms race (Thompson, 1982).

It hardly seemed to be a very Marxist type of explanation that would have such a similar military industrial complex emerging from such different social formations. Mike Davis, a Marxist historian from the United States, in debating with E. P. Thompson, rejected the shared origin of 'exterminism' but insisted strongly (despite the mixed metaphors) on the thesis of the 'two camps'. 'The Soviet Union's role in world politics as the material and military cornerstone of further subtractions from the Empire of capital has been largely involuntary.' So Davis wrote, but he went on to argue that 'the Cold War in its wider sense is not an arbitrary or anachronistic feud staged essentially in Europe, but a rationally explicable and deeply rooted conflict of opposing social formations and political forces, whose principal centre of gravity has been for some thirty years now the Third World'.

Most of what were called wars of 'national liberation' had a Marxist inspiration without necessarily having overt socialist aims, let alone Soviet prompting. There can be no doubting the succession of revolts against colonial or neo-colonial rule from 1945 onwards. Even if we exclude the countries whose decolonization was relatively peaceful, this starts with Yugoslavia and is followed by China, Vietnam, Algeria, Kenya, Egypt, Cuba, Iran, the Portuguese colonies, Zimbabwe, Nicaragua. Mike Davis contrasts the success of these revolts with the socialist failures of the inter-war years and adds: 'Since 1945 there has been, as the American far-right never ceases to point out, a socialist revolution on the average every four years.' This is to assume that every national liberation struggle against colonial rule has been a socialist revolution, and our studies in Part Two of this book lead us to doubt this. The world military economy cannot then be so easily characterized as a model of struggle between developed capitalism and developing socialism. How then should we explain it?

It would be possible to construct a model which combined the competitive rivalry of giant transnational companies for armaments orders with their worldwide search for the necessary raw materials and cheap labour in the Third World as well as for markets the world over. This would be very much in line with Marx's own view of counteracting tendencies brought into play against the tendency to falling rates of profit, particularly if we allow for the ideological cover which Marx would have expected to be employed to conceal such barefaced exploitation. The ideology in this case was the picture of the Soviet Union as the source of all revolutionary actions, even of all protests against the deployment of nuclear missiles whether inside or outside the territory of the USA.

This model of capitalist imperialism is not adequate on its own, therefore, without some model of the Soviet response. This response consisted of a concentration of resources on defence which took a far larger proportion of the Soviet national product than arms spending in the USA. Combined with the command economy, which was necessary to carry through a forced process of industrialization in backward Russia after the devastation of two major invasions, this created a highly centralized and authoritarian political and economic system. E. P. Thompson quotes the Polish economist Oscar Lange's phrase that 'the Soviet has always been a war economy' (Thompson, 1982). Defence, as we have seen, provides a simple priority in a command economy. This might be a wholly rational response with which one could treat, and not the exterminism which Thompson conjures up from the postures of both the superpowers. The Medvedev brothers have argued forcibly that the Soviet arms drive was a rational response to superior US nuclear technology.

This is to insist that there was no symmetry, such as Thompson proposes, in the equal and opposite drives of the military complexes in the USA and USSR. Such a proposal hardly allowed for the collapse of Soviet power within the decade. But already in the 1980s it was obvious that there was no clear two-camps division between the USA and the capitalist states on the one hand and the USSR and the Third World on the other, such as both Soviet and US propaganda suggested. To start with there was China, which was a member of neither camp and claimed that it and not the USSR led the Third World. Apart from the Chinese quarrel with the USSR it was evident that there was a whole range of conflicts that could not be reduced, as President Reagan liked to insist, to a basic US–Soviet clash of interest. China fought Vietnam, which had Soviet support against the USA. Iraq fought Iran. Iraq was said to be armed by the USSR but also by France and the UK; Iran since the fall of the Shah was no friend of the USA. Syria was fighting Israel and Syria was said to be armed by the USSR and Israel by the USA. But there is still a question about US support for Iraq, until US interests in Saudi Arabian oil exploded in the Gulf War. Even then they did not involve Soviet support for Iraq.

Looking nearer home, what connection has either the USA or the USSR with the civil war in Northern Ireland? In the Yugoslav war, the US appeared to be supporting the Bosnian Moslems and the Russians the Serbs, but nobody supposed that the war had anything to do with some lingering remnants of a two-camps division between the USA and Russia. Support by Russia for the Serbs may involve some consideration of the balance of power in the Balkans as well as of Slavic brotherhood. It was clear even before the break-up of the USSR and of Yugoslavia that wars arise as much from frustration and misery as from the pursuit of conquest. But the major powers – the USA, Russia, China and Germany – do not consent readily to the loss of influence in spheres that they regard as their own, whether on economic or political or strategic grounds. Thus local wars can soon blow up into global conflict where accepted spheres of influence are disturbed, whether it is in South-East Asia, the Middle East or the Caribbean. The danger lies in the enormity of the instruments of mass destruction in the hands of the several nuclear powers.

The Two Camps as Ideology

Rational behaviour within the social structure as it is – competitive profit-making on the one hand, defence of spheres of influence on the other – is certainly on all sides covered up by ideology, as Thompson suggests. Soviet ideology, as Royden Harrison (1981) has proposed, consisted of a false consciousness spread among the Russian people that the Soviet Union was in fact a socialist society already and the vanguard of socialist advance the world over. Although we have seen every reason to doubt both these propositions, their widespread belief served only to reinforce capitalist ideology that the Soviet system was what you could expect from socialism and that the Soviets were indeed behind every revolutionary action and every anti-capitalist struggle everywhere. This was simply untrue, but there is a more important point. Over many years, we can conclude, as in the earlier edition, that it is not at all the case that all the major world conflicts have been *au fond* between the USA and the USSR, nor was their main arena the Third World. What the disintegration of the Soviet Union demonstrated was not so much that one side in the arms race lost and the other won, but that neither was able to solve the world's economic problems. Both were more involved with struggles inside their own so-called 'camp' than with divisions between the two of them.

If the arms economy is a central element in both market and command economies, it is not because it is a necessary component of both systems or because of ideological differences; it is because there was a quite capitalist type of competition between them for markets and spheres of influence. This conflict is between the capitalist powers themselves – Japan's and Europe's challenge to the USA not only in exports of goods, but increasingly in exports of capital – and was between the Communist powers themselves – between the Soviet Union and China. It was a cynical but perceptive comment of Henry Kissinger to say that the Soviet Union was the only country to be surrounded by hostile Communist states.

It would still be wrong to ignore the reality of peoples' struggles in almost every part of the world for a new and better life and for a safer world. But these are struggles of peoples against their governments, much more than between states of whatever political colour, and this can prove far more potent than any inter-state rivalries. Even in the early 1980s, before Gorbachev pulled out of the arms race, there was something unreal about the concept of the 'two camps'. In Africa, where it was particularly the case that the United States and the Soviet Union each had their client states, there had been no detectable differences between them in social structure. Defence of these alliances was half-hearted except in southern Africa, where the special interests of the apartheid regime in the Republic led to continuous cross-border military intervention. Africa after the Cold War ended became increasingly marginalized from world trade and investment, abandoned to the World Bank to collect the outstanding debts. Where the United States found revolution on its doorstep in Nicaragua, El Salvador or poor little Grenada there was a sharp response, but revolutions further away, in Eritrea or in Sri Lanka or in East Timor, were of less concern – and no one really supposed that they were fomented by the Soviet Union.

The reality was made clear in the Gulf War. Whether the

danger came from rising local discontent with the Saudi rulers or from Saddam Hussein going just too far in Kuwait, the threat to United States control over Middle East oil supplies brought an overwhelming military response, in which America's allies joined in. The message from the developed to the developing countries was clear: You can have what government you like, and we certainly don't want to be responsible for colonies, but we will always preserve our access to strategic industrial supplies – if necessary, in the jargon of the day, by 'taking them out'. There is, of course, behind the surface battles a real division between the concept of a socialist commonwealth, which is beginning to seize the hearts and minds of tens of millions of people, and the actuality of capitalist exploitation of human beings and of natural resources. This is not a division, however, that can be subsumed under the concept of the two camps.

FURTHER READING

BARRATT BROWN, MICHAEL, *The Economics of Imperialism*, Penguin Books, 1974

BARRATT BROWN, MICHAEL, *Fair Trade: Reform and Realities in the International Trading System*, Zed Books, 1993

BARRATT BROWN, MICHAEL, 'The Question of a Third Balkan War', *European Labour Forum*, Spring 1994

BLACKABY, FRANK, 'Conversion and Industrial Change', in M. Barratt Brown (ed.), *Conversion: Can We Really Disarm?*, Spokesman, 1989

ERDMANN, PAUL, *The Billion Dollar Killing*, Arrow Books, 1974

ERDMANN, PAUL, *Crash of '79*, Sphere, 1979

ERDMANN, PAUL, *The Last Days of America*, Sphere, 1982

HARRISON, ROYDEN, 'Marxism as Nineteenth-century Critique and Twentieth-century Ideology', *History*, Vol. 66, June 1981, pp. 208–20

KIDRON, MICHAEL, *Western Capitalism since the War*, Penguin Books, 1968

LOVERING, JOHN, 'A Post-Military Economy', in Ken Coates (ed.), *Drawing the Peace Divided*, Spokesman, 1993

MAGDOFF, HARRY, *The Age of Imperialism*, Monthly Review Press, 1969

MAGDOFF, HARRY, and SWEEZEY, PAUL, 'The Multinational Corporation', *Monthly Review*, October–November 1969, June 1971

MANDEL, ERNEST, *Europe versus America: Contradictions of Imperialism*, New Left Books, 1970

MANDEL, ERNEST, *Late Capitalism*, Verso, 1978

MANDEL, ERNEST, *The Second Slump*, New Left Books, 1978; Verso, 1980

MELMAN, SEYMOUR, *The Permanent War Economy*, Simon & Schuster, 1974

ROWTHORN, BOB, 'Imperialism in the Seventies – Unity or Rivalry', *New Left Review*, No. 69, 1971, pp. 31–54

ROWTHORN, BOB, 'Mandel's "Late Capitalism"', *New Left Review*, No. 98, July–August 1976, pp. 59–84

SUTCLIFFE, BOB, *Hard Times: the World Economy in Turmoil*, Pluto Press, 1983, p. 13

THOMPSON, E. P., *et al.*, *Exterminism and Cold War*, Verso, 1982

10 THE FEMINIST MODEL

Ten years ago, it seemed necessary to explain why there should be a chapter with this title in a book on models of political economy. For some it may still seem strange, but there is now a large and ever growing literature on feminist economics and the political economy of women's subordination. The chapter was placed near the end of the first part of the book, which is concerned with models of capitalist economy, for two reasons: first, because it provides an important corrective to all models of capitalist economy and, secondly, because it offers the most profound critique of the Marxist model. It is not simply, however, itself a model of capitalist economy but an intersection of the whole question of women's subordination into models of pre-capitalist, capitalist and post-capitalist societies. The feminist writers have reminded us that Engels in *The Origin of the Family* predicted, first, the decline of the family, as more and more women were drawn into social production under capitalism, and then the liberation of women in common with men in the socialist society to come. While the first has been realized to an extent unanticipated ten years ago, the second has not. Feminist writers, even though Marxist in their method and socialist in their aims, have looked behind economic forms at more continuing sources of patriarchy. We place discussion of the feminist model here but we shall come back to it again in looking at socialist models and in the last part of the book when we look into the future.

The women's liberation movement has drawn our attention to three aspects of women's subordination under capitalism which are of particular importance in political economy. The first is the inequality of payment for the same job; the second is the inequality of employment opportunities for women – the crowding into particular occupations which then become low-paid and the absence of women in the higher-paid and more influential jobs; the third is the undervaluing, indeed the non-valuation, of women's work in the home. The first two aspects of subordination women share with oppressed people everywhere – in poor countries and among minority groups in rich countries also. The third is the main claim that feminists are making for a revaluation of the place of women in the political economy. For the assumption that women can do two jobs, one outside and one inside the home, with child care falling almost wholly on the women, seems to them to be the most important issue to be examined.

In Britain as in most rich countries in the capitalist world, and in societies claiming to be building socialism also, some advances have been made towards recognizing the disadvantaged position of women under the first two aspects of subordination. Campaigns in Britain supported by legislation for equal pay, followed by an Equal Opportunities Commission backed again by legislation, have at least recognized the problem. More effective results have been achieved by positive programmes in companies and government departments to establish equal opportunity, including flexible working hours, as is more common in the USA. Some progress has also been recorded in establishing equality before the law in relation to children, state benefits and taxation, the ownership of property and so on. Most informed persons would say that there is a long way to go in Britain. Recognition of the third aspect of woman's subordination – the place of housework in the political economy – has barely begun. Dad's contributions in washing up, mowing the lawn and doing odd jobs around the house and on the car, pay lip-service. These are not to be taken as any equivalent, averaging as they do no more than ten hours a week in relation to the forty-to-fifty-hour week that most women put into housework and child care even on top of a part-time and sometimes of a full-time job.

Housework in Political Economy and the Family Wage

I have twenty or more textbooks on economics on my shelves and an equal number of basic works on political economy. Almost without exception up to the last decade, I find that reference to the chapter headings and to the indexes of these books reveals no mention of housework and only references to homework and domestic economy as precursors of manufacturing industry. John Ruskin's essays on political economy (*Unto This Last: Four Essays on the First Principles of Political Economy*, 1862) are the most dismissive in this respect. The essays open with the following sentence: 'As domestic economy regulates the acts and habits of a household, political economy regulates those of a society or state, with reference to its means of maintenance' – and that is the end of that. The exception is, of course, in a book by a woman – not I regret to say by H. M. Scott (although she does mention on the first page of her *Approach to Economics* that the work of women in their own homes is economically important, only to omit it from the rest of the book), or by Vera Anstey or by Joan Robinson, who are more recent writers, but by one who wrote on economic questions over a hundred years ago.

Charlotte Perkins Gilman was an early American feminist and in 1889 published *Women and Economics: A Study of the Economic Relation between Men and Women as a Factor in Social Evolution*. The book is evidently directed at men as well as women in its plea for women's liberation. In the 'Proem' that opens the book the author cries, 'Loose her now, and trust her! She will love thee yet!' It is a passionate plea for freedom from dependence on men and it faces the reader frankly with the facts of women's hours and conditions of work in the home, which are no better than those of slaves, however 'well kept'.

Charlotte Perkins Gilman was perhaps the first to make the point that a man could buy each of the services his wife supplies but it would be exceedingly costly – and none of the servants, she adds, except perhaps the mistress, could hope for a very high standard of life. Gilman also thinks of course that this would be degrading. The only other reference to housework I could find in all my texts is a jocular reference by Sir John Hicks in *The Social Framework* (4th edn) to the reduction in the national income that would be caused if a man were to marry his housekeeper. But here is the essence of the matter. The work that a woman does in bearing and bringing up children, in the whole range of household duties, is literally not valued in our economic calculations.

After I had written that, I found the whole subject developed at great length by Marilyn Waring in a 1989 publication, *If Women Counted: A New Feminist Economics*. Marilyn Waring had chaired the Public Expenditure Committee of the New Zealand Parliament and had discovered that there was something called the United Nations System of National Accounts (UNSNA), which was used as a measure of national economies. She learned, she says, that the things she 'valued about life in [her] country – its pollution-free environment . . . national parks, walkways, beaches, lakes . . . absence of nuclear power . . . all counted for nothing . . .' and 'Hand in hand with the dismissal of the environment, came evidence of the severe invisibility of women and women's work'. UNSNA, which is adopted by all governments and international institutions, draws what is called in the accompanying *Studies and Methods*, Series F, No. 2, a 'production boundary'. This, she found, excluded almost all women's work in the household, even in peasant subsistence farming households.

The production boundary is of great importance in economic measurement, especially of agricultural economies. The relevant paragraph of *Studies and Methods* makes it clear that the goods produced by 'primary producers, that is those engaged in agriculture, forestry, fishing, mining and quarrying, whether exchanged or not . . . are included in the total of production'. 'Home ownership is regarded as a trade' and is included. But the paragraph continues: 'In practice, no other imputations of this kind are made since primary production and the consumption of their own produce by *non-primary producers is of little or no importance*' [emphasis added].

'In other words,' Marilyn Waring draws the conclusion, 'women's work is of no importance.' It might appear that she is jumping to conclusions, but she is able to quote a Working Party of African statisticians who made recommendations in 1960 about non-monetary activities, which were incorporated into the revised UNSNA in 1968. These included work that is generally men's work in peasant households – house-building, landworks, and the transportation, processing and manufacture of non-food household products. The only women's work in the household that was thus included was the carrying of water. All the other women's household tasks were excluded – household management, catering, cleaning, child care, vegetable-plot sowing and weeding, cooking and food processing, including the fetching and carrying of firewood, storage and carrying and distribution of food in the compound and outside in the subsistence economy.

According to UNSNA definitions, the household is not a family-operated enterprise, because it does not produce income. Yet the great majority of households and enterprises in the Third World were, and are still, family-operated enterprises. In many Third World countries, the woman is the head of the household and the farm manager, because the man is away in the cities or in the mines or on the plantations. Moreover, in the towns the so-called informal economy or black economy is where many women work, and this by definition does not appear in any statistics. There is one peculiar twist to the national account statistics which Waring noted. If women live longer now, as they do especially in the Third World, and their contribution to the economy is not counted, then the national income per head may fall, although from a welfare point of view longevity might be regarded as a bonus.

It is not only in the Third World that women's work is excluded from the calculations of national income. Households are similarly excluded from the scope of production in the 'material product' accounts which were employed for national income calculation in the Soviet Union and Eastern Europe. Women's work in the home is equally excluded in capitalist economies. If prepared food is bought or baby milk powder is used, for example, that indeed is accounted for, but women's work in food preparation or in breastfeeding is not. And why does reproduction not come within the production boundary? If a woman can employ a nanny or pay to put her child in a day nursery, those payments enter the national accounts, but there is no entry for women who stay at home and perform these services.

More is involved in all this than national accounting. Housework is devalued. Women at home are classified as 'unoccupied' or 'inactive'. It is enough to make you laugh, but it is not so funny when it comes to estimating compensation for desertion or the sharing of property rights in the event of divorce. In pre-capitalist societies a peasant household would have a structure of authority which might still leave the women subordinate to the men, though not always so. But the women's work would tend to be equally skilled and to be valued equally with the men's in the division of labour and in the distribution of the household products. Once the man goes out to work for a wage everything changes. Unlike all the animals 'The female of *genus homo*', as Gilman has it, 'is economically dependent on the male. He is her food supply.'

It is possible to calculate how much it would cost a man at current rates to employ servants to do all the work that his wife now does. This was variously estimated in the 1980s at between £300 and £500 per week, or about twice the average weekly wage of manual and non-manual workers respectively. Even if the wife went out to work and contributed to the cost there are few families who could afford such a sum; and the few who could do so probably have servants already anyway. It may be that, if men henceforth refused to maintain their wives, the number of women coming into the market would, as the economists argue, bring the price of household services down. The fact remains that we now set a value on the cooking, cleaning, baby care, housekeeping, companionship, etc. provided by women in the home which is very much greater than the wage a man hands over to·his wife for the household, even if it is the whole wage. To demand an increase in the man's wage would do nothing to remedy the subordination of women.

This problem has been compounded by an unprecedented increase in the employment of women during the 1980s, while the unemployment of men has been rising. This is partly but not entirely associated with an increase in service industry employment as employment in manufacturing and mining has declined. In the UK 2 million more women went out to work in 1992 compared with 1979, while 1 million fewer men found work. Almost as many women were employed or self-employed as men in 1992 – 11.4 million women compared with 14 million men. But nearly half the women were working part-time, four-fifths of them married women, and only 7 per cent of the men were working part-time. The same trend has been apparent throughout the industrialized world. In the European Union nearly 70 per cent of women between the ages of twenty-five and forty-nine went out to work in 1991 compared with 55 per cent in 1983. In France and the UK the figure was 75 per cent, while in Denmark it was nearly 90 per cent.

This trend in women's employment might have been expected to increase the contribution of men to household work, but the evidence in the UK is that this only happens when the woman works full-time, and even then the proportion of men taking a less traditional attitude to household work as being women's work is quite small. On the other hand, we noted in an earlier chapter that in some parts of northern England where male unemployment has continued at a high level for many years, a new economy of the household has been developing, built around the part-time work of the wife or around a small family business involving all members of the family, as has been typical of family shops in France, Spain or Italy for many years. The conclusion from the English study was that financially such families were no better off than they would have been on receipt of state payments, but their morale was infinitely higher. It still remains the view of most feminists that the search by women for employment which permits them to continue to manage their household work combined with the low wage and low regard associated with part-time service employment ensures women's continued subordination.

It is independence that women are seeking; but they are also protesting at the use of an economic model which excludes household services that are valued in the market at something well in excess of (probably not less than double) the value of men's wages and salaries. There is a vicious circle here: women's work is low-paid work and low-paid work is women's work.

There are three responses. The first is to call for adequate wages for housework as socially productive work. But this leaves most women and a very few men, as things are now arranged, in a ghetto of housework with other work opportunities still further removed. The second is to accept the principle of the family wage and to call for increases. The third is to separate out the legal aggregation of man and wife for taxation and grants and property calculation so that each party to a marriage is equally independent.

To reply that the cost of the woman's services is already allowed for in the wages of the man since this payment must cover both his maintenance and reproduction is not to meet the criticism. In the first place, women, including married women, have always been part of the labour force, albeit often part-time and generally underpaid. Secondly, men receive the same wages whether they are married and have children or whether they are bachelors – and no more than a third of the male labour force, in Britain at least, appears to have wives and dependent children. Thirdly, there is much evidence that it has never been possible for the majority of working-class families to manage on one income.

There is a strong feminist argument against the principle of the family wage, which trade unionists have historically fought for, although there are problems in finding an alternative. Articles by feminists have caused outrage in trade-union circles by dismissing trade unions as not only male-dominated and male-chauvinistic, but as actively damaging to the advancement of women. This is a harsh judgement which runs counter to recent growth in UK white-collar unions and much valuable experience of men and women in common struggles of the trade-union movement over the years and in the working-class pride they have developed together. There is an obvious danger of a gap opening up if the trade-union argument for a family wage were abandoned before the establishment of an alternative independent source of income from the state for women. In a capitalist market economy everything is valued in the market. Providing for use values outside the market requires the social action of government.

It is evidently necessary to consider what alternatives to the family wage might be obtained through such social provision within capitalism. There are differences of view about this. One line of advance would be through a great increase in the family allowance payable to women (or to men who choose to stay at home while the woman works outside). Another might be through the introduction of negative income tax for women both with and without children, when their income from employment is below a certain level. The strength of the feminist argument is that these are unlikely to be won without major changes of attitude to men's and women's work. Unless trade unions change their attitude to the primacy of the family wage and fight for direct benefits equally with their wages and also for women's job opportunities and flexibility equally with men's, this could hardly succeed. What would be an adequate allowance not only during periods when maternity benefit might be applicable, but during child-rearing and even prior to maternity, is a further question which would need to be examined in relation to all the current arguments about social security and low pay. Again, it is argued by many feminists that equity is likely to result more from the struggle to overcome men's traditional patriarchy than from legislation about allowances or minimum levels of payment. But it also implies unity with men in the same struggle against polarizing tendencies of the capitalist market.

If the market gives us no satisfactory valuation of housework, then maybe a Marxist analysis will help. Socialists have always assumed, with supporting quotations from Engels's *Origins of the Family* as we noted earlier, that with the replacement of capitalist society by socialist society the subordination of women would be ended. Feminists find little either in Marxist theory or in the experience of countries which claimed to be building socialism to support this assumption. State provision – whether capitalist or socialist – has not guaranteed equal opportunities despite crèches, maternity leave and family planning. It has often only incorporated women, depriving them of the will to struggle for real equality. The fundamental questions of the persistent sex-typing of men's and women's labour in political economy and of the continuing non-socialization of housework remain to be answered.

It is particularly unfortunate for the progress of women's emancipation that a division has arisen in the women's movement between those who wish to raise the status and emphasize the special qualities of women's work, including housework, and those who want to compete on an equal footing with men in all occupations and all fields of activity. It is, of course, only right that women should claim equal pay for work of equal value. It is also true that women are debarred from many occupations, the construction and engineering industries for example, for which many women are as well suited as men. This is not the same thing as saying that any woman can do all the jobs that men normally do, any more than that any man can do all the jobs that women normally do. Some can; some can't – in both cases. The danger of arguing that men and women should be equal is that it can come to mean that they are the same rather than that they should be treated as of equal value. Emphasizing sameness conceals the possibility of gaining from the rich differences between the qualities of men and women. The problem for most women in establishing respect for their special qualities remains the stereotyping of women's work and its fatal association with the unpaid status of housework (see Mitter and Rowbotham, 1993).

Marxist Value Theory and Women's Work

The Marxist model should be the most helpful in understanding the place of housework in the economy, always assumed to be done by women, because it is based on the labour time socially necessary to produce use values. Given any mechanical aids now available like washing-machines, which were unknown in Marx's day, the labour time expended by women in feeding, housing and in other ways caring for workers and in reproducing them should measure the value of women's work as a cost of production of labour power, and should then enter the equations in the law of value. One might almost suppose that none might be more important. Yet women's work appears neither as productive labour nor as non-productive labour in the writing of Marx, nor in the other works of classical political economy of Smith, Ricardo or Mill. It is simply ignored. Productive labour is that which creates wealth, i.e. for Marx the surplus which can be accumulated as capital.

Unproductive labour produces no commodities but only consumes them.

The nearest perhaps that Marx came to recognizing the existence of women's work is that he distinguishes the labour of a cook when it is bought by a capitalist hotel proprietor to make him a profit – and is therefore productive (of profit); and when it is bought by Marx to cook meat for his enjoyment as a use value only and not as 'a value-creating element' – and is therefore non-productive (of profit). (See Marx's *Theories of Surplus Value*, Chap. IV.) But what element, you might ask, could be more 'value-creating' than a woman who cooks and cares for the worker and produces and reproduces the very labour which can then be bought as a productive commodity?

Profit, we saw in Marx's analysis, arises from the use values *produced* by labour power that exceed the use values *consumed* by labour power. These last of course include the work of women at home. Marx sees only that 'man's' labour power has been exploited at work by the capitalist. Women should, then, presumably join with men in winning back that part of the man's work which is unpaid. 'But', say the feminists, 'if we analyse things differently, and say that the mysterious "use value of labour power" (that "unique quality" of labour power as a commodity in Marx, that enables it to produce more than its "costs of reproduction") is quite simply and unmysteriously the appropriation of unpaid female labour by the male worker, then the idea of women supporting them in their trade-union and labour struggles seems, quite simply, perverse, "false consciousness" of a kind which is itself anti-woman, and repressive of female work.' (Quoted from Bradby, 1982.)

It is this assumption of unpaid women's labour by the male worker that is at the heart of the feminist critique of the models of political economy, together with the ideology that surrounds it. It can hardly be denied at the same time that women produce a surplus of value over what they consume in the same way that men do in working for an employer and that this too enters into the capitalists' profits. This has become more important than ever now that such a high proportion of women are entering the labour market, even part-time, and are being paid at rates well below those of men.

The mystification that money wages make of the actual process of exploitation depends, we saw earlier, on workers' ignorance of the actual value which they add to the product by their work. This ignorance is deepened and strengthened by the ideology of the free worker and the free bargain with the employer. What the feminists are saying is that it is even further reinforced by the ideology of the male breadwinner and the family wage, upon which women are dependent.

The relegation of women to work at home cannot simply be explained by demonstrating the advantages for capital of having an unpaid labour force in the home nor yet of having a reserve army of part-time married women workers to call upon. These were, and are, certainly valuable assets for individual capitalists. History, however, including recent history, is not made by individual capitalists but emerges from the struggle between capitalists and workers (competition among capitalists and among workers also), with the capitalist state and its ideology reinforcing the power of capital. The feminists have worked their way through to a crucial correction of the Marxist model that explains the failure of Engels's prediction.

The work of women and children in factories and mills in the early nineteenth century exemplified Marx's concept of the extraction of *absolute* surplus. Such work foundered on the declining physical condition of the working class. The Mines and Factory Acts of the 1840s were designed to restore the workers' reproductive capacity, although it did not happen just the way the capitalists wanted. The miners' wives were tucked away at home and kept there for more than a century; but the men used the reduced labour force to organize unions to protect themselves against the owners. In the rest of industry capitalists introduced more machinery to replace labour and to increase the extraction of *relative* surplus; but not without the resistance first of Luddites and then of the skilled workers in their trade unions protecting their skills against the employers' continuous drive to de-skill labour. Inevitably this protection was turned also against the so-called unskilled labour of women; and in fact women continued to provide cheap labour, not least in domestic service and in those industries which became ghettos of women's work.

The most interesting contribution of the feminists to the rewriting of nineteenth-century labour history is their emphasis on this defence by men of their skills (against the degradation of labour by capital), as the chief source, however ironical it may seem, of the degradation of women. An article by Michèle Barrett and Mary McIntosh convincingly argues this case and shows how the classification of jobs as men's and women's jobs seriously undervalues the skills of women and almost always relates them to the tasks of the home: child care, nursing, cooking, cleaning, laundering, valeting, sewing, mending, packing. This is where the ideology reinforces the division of labour, not from any conspiracy of capitalists, but because, as we saw earlier, the social framework moves towards correspondence with the mode of production. But women thereby suffered a double degradation. Confined to their homes, dependent on the male breadwinner, they were only to find that the skills of the home were taken from them too. The clothes they made, the bread they baked, the beer they brewed, the simple medicines they concocted were transferred to factory production. Professional doctors, nurses, teachers and social workers took over their tasks of child care and training. Women were reduced to parasitism, as sex objects and child-bearers.

This was the awful conclusion of Olive Schreiner writing on *Women and Labour* at the end of the nineteenth century. How much more is it so today with every kind of convenience food and household gadget? These have certainly reduced some of the drudgery of housework, and released women for work outside the home; but, apart from the act of childbirth and child care, what is left inside and outside the home is mainly the unskilled dusting, tidying and cleaning. What should have been liberating turned out to be confining in both the work at home and the jobs that women could enter outside, at best in the social services, at worst – and for most married women – to do more cleaning and tidying in some other house or office. The skills of the home are devalued, first, because they are over-represented in the market, which reduces their exchange value as well as their use value. But, secondly, it is the ideology of the market, even more than its economic valuation, that has held women at home in the role of unpaid servants of their men and devalued the work of nurses and teachers outside the home. And ideology in Marx's sense is chiefly *false* consciousness.

Clearing the false consciousness from our eyes is one thing, and this chapter is designed to help do just that; finding another way of incorporating women's (or men's) housework and care of the family and of meeting Olive Schreiner's claim for women that 'all labour is our province' in a model of a socialist economy is something else. But we must come back to that problem in the last chapter. We shall look to see what help we can find in the next part of the book when we look at existing models of the socialist project. The feminists believe that the facts revealed little real advance in women's position in the societies claiming to be building socialism.

On the one hand, the constitutions of these countries granted all the essential provisions to ensure equality before the law for men and women, equal pay and equality of educational and employment opportunities (with some restrictions on heavy manual work) and socialization of a part at least of domestic labour, the care of young children. On the other hand, the family was still regarded as the 'basic cell of society', and in most families the result of greater employment opportunities for women was that women simply worked a double shift: one in the factory or office and one at home. The sexual division of labour in employment persisted and though there were soon more women doctors and teachers, their pay was relatively lower than in capitalist countries.

The image of women on the posters might be that of the Cuban women's emblem of a woman with a gun in one hand and a baby in the other, like the statue of Anita Garibaldi in Rome. The reality was different, in part because, as the feminists pointed out, there was no corresponding image of a man with a gun in one hand and a baby in the other. Men continued to hold all the top positions. Women's representation in the USSR at Politburo,

Central Committee or ministerial level amounted to barely one in twenty, in the Party itself to one in four. Maxine Molyneux, writing on women in socialist societies, revealed the basic weakness of women's position. They were not encouraged to develop their own grass-roots organization. The Party organization excluded all others and was a wholly top-downwards affair (Molyneux, 1981). Even in Yugoslavia, where there was freedom of speech and publication, there was no pluralism of civic society. In this case the result led to disaster, and Yugoslav women have insisted that this was chiefly because there was no forum for discussing the problems of ethnic and national differences (Korać, 1993).

The experience of women in societies where the attempt was made to build socialism serves to reinforce the argument that gender issues cannot be subsumed under a simplistic class analysis. It also reveals that outside of China no attempt was made at the sharing of life and income in common, and the attempt failed in China. It seems to be a historic fact that all attempts at communal living and income-sharing have failed except among celibate religious communities. In view of the very considerable reduction in the costs, at least in labour time, of housing and house maintenance, child care and care of the aged, cooking, cleaning, and laundering, let alone of the sharing of swimming pools and other leisure facilities, which can be obtained as a result of the potential economies of scale, this failure is surprising. The cost savings are not, of course, as great as they would be if labour time was fully costed, because of the non-payment in family households for domestic services, which are mainly provided by women. Even then, there is an opportunity cost of wages forgone by not going out to work full-time, or at all.

Why then do communes fail? The assumption that most people prefer living in nuclear families is breaking down in face of the growing number of single-parent households. In the UK by 1990 one-fifth of all families with dependent children were headed by a lone parent. One explanation provided in a robust argument of the case for communes comes in a book by Paul Cockshott and Allin Cottrell, *Towards a New Socialism* (1993). This is that insufficient attention has been given in the past to determining a fair 'exchange rate' between the labour time of commune members expended inside the commune and that 'exported' into the national economy. A fair rate would involve calculations of Marx's concept of 'socially necessary labour time' for which so many work units would be allocated. The Chinese communes applied such a system and we shall have to see what happened to them. That is not to dismiss the matter out of hand. A society capable of building a new socialism would have room for new types of living, where women and men were truly equals.

FURTHER READING

AMSDEN, ALICE H. (ed.), *The Economics of Women and Work*, Penguin Books, 1980

BARRETT, MICHÈLE, and MCINTOSH, MARY, 'The Family Wage', *Capital and Class*, No. 11, Summer 1980, pp. 51–72

BEECHEY, VERONICA, 'Some Notes on Female Labour in Capitalist Production', *Capital and Class*, No. 3, Autumn 1977, pp. 45–66

BRADBY, BARBARA, 'The Remystification of Value', *Capital and Class*, No. 17, Summer 1982, pp. 114–45

COCKSHOTT, PAUL, and COTTRELL, ALLIN, *Towards a New Socialism*, Spokesman, 1993, pp. 165ff.

ENGELS, FRIEDRICH, *The Origin of the Family, Private Property and the State*, 1884 (first published in English 1940); Lawrence & Wishart, 1972

FEMINIST REVIEW (ed.), *Waged Work: A Reader*, Virago, 1986

GILMAN, CHARLOTTE PERKINS, *Women and Economics: A Study of the Economic Relation between Men and Women as a Factor in Social Evolution*, 1889; Harper & Row, 1966

KORAĆ, MAYA, 'Women in the Balkan Wars', in K. Coates (ed.), *Drawing the Peace Dividend*, Spokesman, 1993

MARX, KARL, *Theories of Surplus Value*, Lawrence & Wishart, 1951 (originally published as *Theorien über den Mehrwert*, Dietz, 1905–10)

MITTER, SWASTI, and ROWBOTHAM, SHEILA, *Dignity and Daily Bread: New Forms of Organising among Women in the Third and First Worlds*, Routledge, 1993

MOLYNEUX, MAXINE, 'Women in Socialist Societies', in Kate Young *et al.* (eds.), *Of Marriage and the Market: Women's Subordination in Historical Perspective*, Conference of Socialist Economists, 1981, pp. 167–202

MORRIS, LYDIA, 'Domestic Labour and Employment Status among Married Women', *Capital and Class*, No. 49, Spring 1993

PHILLIPS, ANNE, and TAYLOR, BARBARA, 'Sex and Skill: Notes towards a Feminist Economics', *Feminist Review*, 1980, pp. 79–88

ROWBOTHAM, SHEILA, *Homeworkers Worldwide*, Merlin Press, 1993

SCHREINER, OLIVE, *Women and Labour*, 1911; Virago, 1978

SECCOMBE, WALLY, 'The Housewife and her Labour under Capitalism', *New Left Review*, No. 83, 1974, pp. 3–24

TRADE UNION RESEARCH UNIT, RUSKIN COLLEGE, *In Defence of the Family Wage*, 1982 (Occasional Paper No. 72)

TROTSKY, LEON, *Women and the Family*, Pathfinder, 1970

WARING, MARILYN, *If Women Counted: A New Feminist Economics*, Macmillan, 1989

11 THE GREEN MODEL

In the early 1980s it was not yet regarded as necessary for economists to take into account the criticism of their theories by ecologists, any more than of those made by feminists. Ten years later all references to economic growth had to be prefixed by the qualifying adjective 'sustainable'. Definitions of what is sustainable and how the concept could be incorporated into their calculations had become a central issue of the economists' analysis. Protecting the stock of natural resources for future generations had to be taken into account. The bounties of nature were not inexhaustible. Neither the market of the neoclassical economists nor the planning of the Marxists had allowed for giving a value to nature.

Neoclassical economics should have recognized the omission since its central interest, according to one of its leading exponents, Lionel Robbins, had always been in the 'relationship between human ends and scarce means which have alternative uses'. One of the main founders of neoclassical economics had been Stanley Jevons, and his concern with scarcity had arisen from recognition of the possible early exhaustion of Britain's coal reserves. Thomas Malthus had warned much earlier of the possibility of population growth outrunning the food supply. But these warnings had been forgotten in the optimism of economic development. The potential exhaustibility of nature was concealed in the economists' construction of a system of elastic substituting of factors of production at the margin. Rising prices would warn of increasing scarcities, and cheaper substitutes would be found by new investment.

Marx had dismissed Malthus as isolating only one cause of rising population. The observed effect that rising food consumption in the richer countries actually reduced the rate of growth of population seemed to be reassuring. 'Malthusiasm', as it came to be called, reappeared in the 1950s when it was revealed that populations in the poorer countries were rising ahead of the food supply as consumption increased. This discovery by a Brazilian economist, Josué de Castro, led him to emphasize in his book the *Geography of Hunger* the need for relating economic growth to nature. It was taken up by American writers William Vogt and Fairfield Osborne, who were mainly concerned at the erosion of the land as a result of irrational agricultural practice. These fears led to a whole series of studies of the effects of such practices on the land and rivers, outstandingly Rachel Carson's *Silent Spring*. The emphasis was not only on malpractice but on the resource limits to economic growth. This was most famously expounded in the Meadowes' *Limits to Growth*, published in 1972 by the Club of Rome.

All these warnings were treated as pessimistic jeremiads by Marxist writers, who extolled the Soviet Union's giant irrigation and afforestation schemes and set these and Russia's fraternal association with its one-time colonies in contrast against the imperialist exploitation of resources in the Third World by the capitalist powers. The German Green movement was the first to draw attention to the failure of communism to protect the environment any better than capitalism. They called themselves 'Green' because their aim was to keep the earth green with plants and trees as an abiding habitat for the interdependent survival of human and other living things. They attacked industrialization wherever it was found – in capitalist or communist countries alike.

Their belief was put in its bleakest form by Rudolf Bahro (1982), the East German communist dissident who became a West German Green Party leader:

> If the industrialization of the world were to be completed, life on earth would be destroyed. This might take a hundred years more or less. The main problem is not resources, which may not run out soon enough, but rather what is called the environment. This is really the biosphere which we are killing off.

This biosphere is the totality of life-support systems on earth upon which human life depends and from which it has evolved. The ecology movement is above all else concerned to protect the balance of nature in our habitat, which industrialization is destroying. It is not only, as Bahro says, that we are using up the non-renewable mineral resources – coal and oil and metals and rocks – in the earth's crust. Worse than that, we are destroying the basis even of the renewable resources – in the forests, fields, lakes and rivers and even oceans – from which we draw our food. The worst example Bahro gives is the deforestation – to graze cattle for beef production – of the Amazon basin at a rate that destroys an area of forest equal to the size of Germany every two and a half years. This is forest that we are told provides the reserve of climatic moisture for most of Europe's rainfall.

The Failure of the Industrial System

The Green movement argued that there was only one industrial system – the capitalist industrial system – in the East as well as in the West. 'The system', said Bahro, 'is inherently deadly.' The Green model follows Marx in identifying capital accumulation as the dynamic, driving force of the system. Accumulation of capital means also accumulation of capital equipment: more and more, bigger and bigger plant and machinery to make more and more, bigger and bigger cars, lorries, ships, aeroplanes, blocks of flats and offices, cities, power stations, guns, rockets – and bombs. This is the heart of the Green critique of industrialism – capitalist and so-called socialist alike. The 'Greens' see industrial society as a dead end – like the giant dinosaurs in evolution – and so reject it totally. Capital accumulation means reducing costs by exploiting labour, exploiting all natural resources, exploiting the biosphere, and in the end *without* the result that Marx hoped for – the revolution that would establish a socialist commonwealth.

The Green model excludes this optimistic outcome for three reasons. First, as we have already noted, the whole environment is expected to be destroyed in the process of industrialization. This is because accumulation of capital, accumulation of capital equipment, accumulation of the material things that this equipment produces, far from meeting human needs, increasingly obstruct and frustrate the ways in which most people's needs could be met. Obvious examples were individualized transport, prescribed medicine, drugs and pills instead of natural foods, mechanical reproduction of music displacing traditional singsongs and local music-making, tower blocks dwarfing our houses, power stations and refineries polluting the air, giant machines dehumanizing human skills. Secondly, the very essence of industrialization was to be seen in the desperately dangerous production and proliferation of nuclear weapons, weapons that could easily bring destruction even before the biosphere is made uninhabitable in other ways. Thirdly, the industrial workers, far from becoming – as Marx supposed – the grave-diggers of the capitalist system, had become its chief support. We will consider this third point in a moment. The other two need first to be considered.

The evidence that industrialization must destroy the environment is in fact conflicting. Many would agree that capitalist development destroys social provision but would not therefore agree that industrialization *must* follow this line of development. Zero growth seems to them too negative an objective, if growth embraces well-being and not just money incomes in national accounts (see Bodington, 1976). Some growth is essential if population expansion is to be allowed for, and, moreover, if *per capita* growth is proposed to be nil, this simply cannot be applied to the developing countries with low standards of living.

The point is well made by the Greens that measurements of GNP, as we saw in looking at the feminists' critique of national accounts, are extremely unhelpful in measuring welfare. Christovam Buarque, a leading Brazilian economist, in his stimulating critique *The End of Economics* contrasts the positive value in GNP per head ascribed to the pregnancy of a cow and the negative value ascribed to a woman's pregnancy; and goes on to challenge the association of production with well-being. Civilization is more than the quantity of available goods, even if account is taken of the corresponding availability of 'bads'. Above all, a civilized life implies a balanced relationship with nature as part of the heritage and the environment of human livelihood.

The optimists still have a case to make. The Meadowes' second Club of Rome report, *Beyond the Limits*, demonstrates that the predictions made twenty years earlier had been fulfilled. If present trends continue we face the certain prospect of global collapse, with decline in food production, industrial capacity, employment opportunity and life expectancy. But the report shows at the same time that sustainable growth is still technically and economically feasible, *if* the growth path is changed and growth in material consumption and population is reduced and the efficiency in the use of materials and of energy is greatly increased.

Those, moreover, who argued that the earth's mineral and energy resources would run out have had to revise their views. It appears that the sea-bed and the Antarctic continent contain huge untapped resources which modern technology can now exploit. It appears that energy from the sun and from the waves and the winds could be harnessed to replace the carbon deposits of coal and gas and oil in the earth's crust. The ecologists will remind us that these are not in fact the new sources of energy that industrial capitalism is devoting huge resources to developing. The chosen new source of energy was nuclear power. For this has the great advantage for capital that like oil it can be monopolized. Its mining, refining, transport and utilization all require vast capital resources that only the giant accumulators of capital possess. Here there are major implications for the biosphere.

A massive global increase in steam-power generation such as the industrialization of the world would entail could be expected to have a major effect on the atmosphere. Expert opinion has concluded that the gradual warming of the seas from the 1960s onwards is man-made. There is clear evidence that the polar ice-caps are retreating and there is a real danger of flooding for all the major coastal towns and cities. It is supposed that barrages can be constructed for their defence in the industrialized lands, but such defences at the mouths of the great rivers in Egypt, Bangladesh, Thailand, Burma and China present a huge engineering challenge and massive potential financial burden. The increase in the number and severity of hurricanes appears to have the same origin and has an incidence largely confined to the tropical lands of the Third World. The dangers to human beings from the sun's radioactivity as a result of the destruction of the ozone layer by the release of aerosols is now well understood; and belated efforts are being made to stem the release and to adopt protective measures. Capitalism can certainly survive without aerosols, as it has learned to survive without DDT.

The destruction of the tropical forests is still believed to have serious implications, however, not only for the human and other forest-dwellers, but for the whole planetary ecosystem. In bewailing the failure to check this damage, Manfred Maxneef, the Chilean economist, has described man as the only 'stupid animal', which cannot reproduce itself without destroying itself. But he would not wish to blame the Chilean or Brazilian people or other tropical peoples for the sale of timber to pay international debts or for burning forests to clear land for food-growing. The blame must lie with the banks and governments of the industrialized countries who are demanding their pound of flesh, and with the logging and ranching companies who are exploiting the tragedy so as to make money (Maxneef, 1982, 1992).

More serious even than the threat to the tropical forests is the danger that competition for dwindling resources prior to the discovery of alternatives will engender increasing international tension and that this could set off a nuclear disaster. P. Peeters (1979) spelled this out in his book *Can We Avoid a Third World War around 2010?*. Such a disaster could not be called a war but rather a holocaust. Nobody doubts that the explosion of even a minute proportion of the nations' current stockpiles of nuclear bombs would render a very large proportion of the earth's surface uninhabitable, destroy most of what human beings have constructed on the earth over five thousand years and incinerate perhaps as much as half the population, leaving millions of others to die more slowly from famine, disease and radiation. If such an eventuality is intimately linked with the process of industrialization, as the Green model suggests, the prospect is awful.

Exterminism, as E. P. Thompson called this prospect and its roots in the military industrial complexes of the superpowers, was the subject of an earlier chapter (Chapter 9) when we looked at the arms-economy model. The Green movement sees the danger rather in the spread of industry to the Third World and the nuclear challenge of a Third World nationalism to the 'have' nations of the North – both East and West. What can be said here is that even the Green movement appears to see more hope in the avoidance of a nuclear holocaust, at least in Europe, than in the avoidance of environmental destruction by industrialization. 'Nuclear weapons', says Bahro, 'have given us advance warning of the exterminist character of the entire productive system.' The reason for their hope lies in the Green model view of the motivation of men and women in seeking to make a fundamental change in the system to meet this danger.

The Collapse of the Workers' Movement

It was Marx's view that the capitalist system would be ended by the struggle of workers in protest at their exploitation at the hands of a small and dominant employing class. As more and more men and women lost their independent livelihood off the land and were absorbed into the process of exploitation, crowded together in great factories and offices, alienated from the results of their own work, thrown on to the streets when they were not wanted, capitalism created its own gravediggers. The Green movement replies quite simply, as the feminists do, that the workers' movement has failed. There has been no breakthrough either when the workers were fully employed in boom times or when relegated to the reserve army of labour in the slump. There was no historical necessity, they say, for the workers to build socialism.

The reason, says Bahro, for the failure is that the premise, namely 'that workers would become politically active via the process of abstract reasoning that Marx had pioneered', was false. They were expected to look, according to this process that is, beyond 'the outward appearances – what directly affects people – down to the point where the exploitation can be proven'. Bahro argues, against this, that 'what really motivates people is indeed all these phenomena at the surface of the economic process'. Marx's prediction failed, he says, because it needed theorists to explain to workers by theoretical argument how it was that they were exploited. Some workers in any case always enjoyed comparatively good living conditions even while most others were suffering increasingly adverse conditions, especially in the colonial Third World.

By contrast with the failing consciousness of capitalist exploitation, the Green movement points to the growing obviousness of ecological disaster, which needs no abstract analysis to understand and which affects all alike.

> The system already fails to deliver the standard of living it defines as normal [says Bahro]; economic growth no longer brings any real gain, and most products are not just relatively superfluous but actually harmful. It is precisely the key products of this technology that are completely deadly. Nuclear weapons, reinforced concrete, many products of the chemical industry, which no one can pretend any longer to control in advance; so that more and more people come to realize, even without a deep abstract analysis, that the whole system is no longer viable.

As examples of useless and dangerous employment, Bahro cites the products of his own city of Bremen: ships to carry cars into Bremen from Japan and out to the USA, ships and aircraft, half for military, destructive purposes, the car industry itself – 'Germany's economic miracle' that creates jobs but 'does not in any way serve human needs'.

This is the point at which one begins to ask how obvious in fact all this is to workers who can't understand exploitation without professional analysis. Bahro admits that half the Green Party puts the maintenance of jobs first and only one wing of the party says that 'it's necessary to dismantle this industrial capacity altogether'. This division among the Greens between the fundamentalists like Bahro and the moderates has been the cause of the failure of Green parties after their initial electoral successes to maintain the momentum of their political advance. On the one hand, all parties now claim to be 'green'. On the other, the true Greens failed to present a coherent policy on all issues, which would rally a jaded electorate. The assumptions that were made about a potential green consciousness have proved to be true of the middle classes, who look for green labels in the supermarkets.

There would seem to be far more evidence that exploitation –

job speed-up, health hazards, low wages, the threat of the sack –
is better understood by workers than the exhaustion of finite
mineral resources or the effect on the atmosphere of aerosols or
deforestation or even the threat of nuclear disaster. One response
of the Greens to such comments is that all peoples equally are
threatened by ecological and nuclear disaster – North and South,
East and West, workers in jobs and the unemployed. It would be
a strong argument if everyone realized what was in store for
them. The fact is that the Amazon forest, the ozone layer, the
polar ice-cap and even the nuclear bomb seem totally remote or,
like death, simply unthinkable to most people. The fact also is
that exploited workers have not developed the political will to
change the system.

A major criticism of workers' movements made by the Green
movement is that they have always been nationalistic. 'The mass
of the population have never in history', says Bahro, 'acted
altruistically towards faraway people they have never seen.' Workers' organizations and especially trade unions have defended their
own jobs and happily supported colonialism and 'their' capitalists
against foreign varieties. Trade unions have indeed, only a little
less than the capitalists, supported the industrial system and its
imperialist extension, being in fact interested in even more capital
accumulation than the capitalists are, since there are more of
them and their need for jobs is the greater. By contrast, so the
Greens go on, the whole world population can unite against the
assault on the ecosystem that threatens to destroy their very
existence.

Creating such a measure of unity between the North and the
South is a strong point in the Greens' programme. 'What is at
stake is the existence of the very next generation. Or if perchance
the bombs from the South don't come,' says Bahro, 'then the
existence of the generation after.' This reflects the Greens' preoccu-
pation with the rising competition of an industrialized 'South'
complete with nuclear weapons to break free from the shackles of
the North. For the Green movement sees the main line of 'class'
division running between North and South. It is a difficult analysis
to deal with, as we shall see in Part Three of this book. For

Bahro, like others in the United States peace movement as well as in West Germany, uses the categories of nation states and even of hemispheres as if they were economic classes engaged in class struggle – Underdeveloped against the Developed, South versus North, West and East. In each case these categories contain such wide mixtures of working classes and many other groups that the analysis is hard to follow. No working model emerges except a stereotype of hemispheric boxes – North, South, East, West; Blue, Red, Green – which are presented as shown in Figure 8 (taken from Galtung, 1980).

This was a model prepared by Galtung in a crude form for blackboard exposition, based on a United Nations University article. It showed no agency apart from the Green movement, and failed to notice not only the workers' movements as agents of labour but even the giant transnational companies as agents of capital accumulation. It grossly exaggerated, moreover, the shift of the centre of industry to the South-East from the North-West. Although this tendency did become more marked in the late 1980s and early 1990s, the share of manufactured goods exports from developing Asia had not quite reached a fifth of the world total in 1994 and Japan's share was somewhat less.

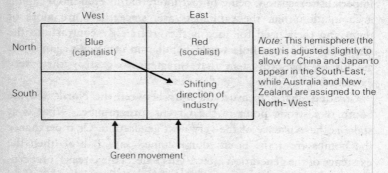

Figure 8. Green model of global political economy (by hemispheres)

Destroying the Industrial System for What?

The aim of the fundamentalists in the Green movement is quite explicitly to destroy in the long run the whole industrial system – red as well as blue: 'First to block, hinder and delay the expansion of the industrial system, i.e. further investments, wherever this is possible, without sorting out in advance which are good technologies and which are bad ones.' The Green Party in Germany, says Bahro, has stopped the expansion of the nuclear-power industry, delayed capital investment at home, stopped the export of capital to the Third World. This sounds rather a negative success, but the second aim is positive – 'We need', says Bahro, 'social and political space for the development of the alternative movement.' They could use the subsidies, he says, which are now given to industry,

> to give to every unemployed person, and every working person too, the practical opportunity to completely drop out of the industrial system that produces for the world market and construct an alternative way of life in the direction of a self-reliant society. This is an opportunity for those people from the working class who are mentally ready for the change.

For the rest 'there is a tremendously important process of social learning'.

The whole of this model of political economy sounds idealist in Marx's and Engels's original sense, unless somewhere someone is producing the tools and machines that we have come to rely on to ease the back-breaking toil – of baking bricks and cutting timber to build houses, of mining coal to heat these homes, of growing cotton and picking it, of minding sheep and shearing them, and weaving the yarns to clothe our bodies, of laundering and ironing, above all of growing food, preserving it, preparing it and cooking it to keep ourselves alive. And even if we forswear the private car, are there to be no public transport, no tractors and trailers, no sea and air travel to visit distant lands and people? Have the men of the Green movement consulted their wives about the abandonment of washing-machines, refrigerators, vacuum cleaners and other household aids? Are we to abandon the vast potential of information technology and return to the use of the abacus with masses of people adding up figures and copying texts to make a living?

We may think that we could be happier with fewer possessions, with more social provision and less private purchases, with greater sharing of work and wealth and less competitive scrambling. But to throw it all away, the baby with the bathwater? The medical advances with the quackery, the labour-saving aids with the gadgetry? The potential of safe nuclear power one day (perhaps) with the bombs and plutonium? Why should we in effect *not* be allowed to choose between good and bad technologies? Why *not* use automated devices for some of the boring routine jobs? Why *not* expand our energy resources using wind and tides and the sun's rays in large- as well as small-scale plants? Why *not* turn the information system contained in the computer and satellite signals to the service of extended human communication? Why *not* explore the universe and feed the people with all the skills that we can deploy? Why must we choose, moreover, between the workers' movement and the Green movement?

Luddism is a natural protest against the destruction of old certainties and against new competition. It cannot be sustained as a positive policy for future fulfilment of human creativity. It is a bewitching myth that there was once a 'Merrie England' of peasants in clean white linen shirts and dresses dancing round Maypoles and calling in the cattle and geese from the common, while their children learnt the ABC from the squire's daughter, and in the towns Guilds regulated the market on principles of fairness and justice for all. The reality was very different. For many it was the life of a serf, if not of a slave. 'The serf serves; he is terrified with threats, wearied by forced services, afflicted with blows, despoiled of his possessions' – so wrote Pope Innocent III in the reign of the English King John. And if one of the king's subjects was a tenant, his lot was little better, 'charged with a crew of children and a landlord's rent', as William Langland's picture of Piers Plowman described it. And most of the hardest work of hoeing, fetching water and gathering firewood fell on the poor man's wife who had the crew of children to care for and had to give personal services to the landlord to meet the rent. In the towns 'Johnnie could earn but a penny a day', sewage ran down the streets, cholera was endemic and goods were mainly carried on human backs. This is how things are still for many of the people in the Third World, and it is a monstrous arrogance to propose denying them the mechanical aids that we have at our disposal.

The Critique of Development

From the assault upon industrialization the fundamentalist Greens moved on to arraign all 'development' as minor variants in imitation of the capitalist model of industrialization. Starting from a critique of Rostow's *Stages of Economic Growth*, they argued that all such growth was fatally flawed. We have already condemned the Rostow model for its neglect of the rich variety of existing social formations, which he dubbed 'traditional' societies and from which a universally similar 'take-off' was to occur, and for its failure to recognize the distortion of economic development which colonial rule had left behind. But while these considerations would certainly lead one to expect that a different model of development would be appropriate in ex-colonial countries, the fundamentalist Greens rule out all forms of development towards industrialization (Sachs, 1990).

The European model of development is not necessarily suited for others to copy; it is probably very unsuited. But it is for the people of the ex-colonial countries to decide the direction in which they wish to develop, and it certainly is unfortunate that so many such countries are ruled by élites which are tied into the capitalist model, albeit as dependent suppliers of raw materials for the industrialized lands. However, it is really not for those who prepare their learned papers on word processors and jet round the world delivering them to international conferences to tell people who do not have these benefits that they are ephemeral and should not be sought.

It is unfortunate that the voices of the fundamentalists are so strident and their arguments so extreme, because they have a point to make of great importance. Development must start from the actual conditions and social practices of each people. This is not either to exalt them or to suggest that they are better left unchanged. It is just to recognize that all peoples have a rich experience of living and surviving in the particular natural environment into which they are born. Practices in the South in agricultural production, in household organization and in social activity including local marketing should not be lightly overthrown in favour of some practice that has proved beneficial in the very different conditions of Europe and North America. Great mistakes have been made in development programmes by assuming that the North knows best.

This is not, however, to conclude that the whole of northern technology and what is called 'Western' science, mainly in fact drawn from the East, should be rejected. There is a particularly ignorant campaign being waged in some Green and feminist circles against Francis Bacon, the father of Western science. By selective quotation he is supposed to have begun a tradition of imposing man's (and not woman's) will upon nature. A more careful examination of what he wrote would show that his whole philosophical criticism of Aristotle was based upon the need to start from experience and to work with the grain of nature. 'We cannot command nature except by obeying her' was his motto. Less well known is the fact he had to go to the Arabs to learn his mathematics and taught himself and his sons their language in order to do so. There is a case which the Greens are right to insist upon for questioning the mechanical laws of Newtonian physics, which only really apply to the solar system, but Western science has always had its critics of mechanical systems from G. W. Leibniz to Joseph Needham.

The Greens' Critique of Economics

The more moderate Greens have a far more devastating critique of economics, both neoclassical and Marxist, than the root-and-branch rejection by the fundamentalists. This consists in their questioning of the importance attached in both models to increases in labour productivity. Economic growth is for the neoclassicists an increase in output per person, and for the Marxists labour is the sole source of value. What the Greens have shown us is that in almost all cases the source of increased output is the application of non-human energy, derived mainly from fossil fuels. This is as true of the tractors, machinery and artificial fertilizers used in agriculture as in the successive use of steam-coal power, petroleum, gas and the electric power derived from them in industrial production and transportation. The Greens are able to explain the conundrum of industrial countries subsidizing their shrinking agricultural population because agriculture has largely been converted into agribusinesses, which are major users of fossil fuels and a source of the oil companies' profits.

What the Greens' analysis of economic growth has demonstrated is that our economy is basically a fossil-fuel economy, and as such is not sustainable, because resources are being used up and not replaced. Nuclear power they reject as inevitably harmful. Short of massive investment in wind, wave and solar power, shrinking fossil resources will bring the epoch of economic growth to an end. They are able to show, moreover, that in agriculture more and more fertilizer has to be applied each year to maintain the same yields, let alone increase them. The structure and life of the soil is being destroyed by the application of chemicals, and the run-off into our rivers and lakes is killing the fish and other living things. At the same time the fossil fuels provide the essential base of the modern artificial fibre industries – all the nylon, plastics, fibreglass and other materials in our clothing and bedding and buildings.

An Energy Theory of Value

If the using-up of scarce reserves of energy finds no place in the calculations of the market or in the labour theory of value, then it is argued by some Greens – notably Robin Jenkins – that we need an alternative, an energy theory of value. Jenkins argues that it is not man who creates use values, not even woman, but nature. The sun is our only source of energy, until we can safely control nuclear fission and fusion. The sun's energy is converted into energy that human beings can use chiefly by the photosynthesis of plants, including all that energy laid down in the coal and oil and gas deposits that we are now squandering. If we use up the plants' storage of energy faster than they can be rebuilt, then we are setting a finite limit to our economies, whether they be capitalist or socialist in orientation. Jenkins goes further and argues that labour is an 'optimizing agent' rather than the 'active principle' in production (Jenkins, 1984).

This goes back to an old argument among the early writers on political economy. The first true model-maker in economics was the eighteenth-century French physician at the court of Louis XIV,

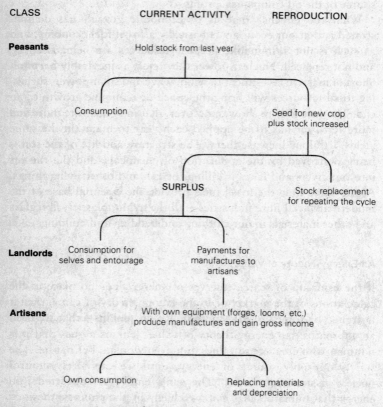

Figure 9. Quesnay's Tableau Économique

François Quesnay, who prepared a *Tableau Économique* to demonstrate the primacy of the land in wealth creation. From this model the French school of physiocrats drew its inspiration and one can say that the riches of the land in France have always led the French to give supremacy in economic policy to agriculture. The argument in the *Tableau* is that the peasants each year use their harvest partly for their own consumption and partly for seed corn for the next year, but this leaves a surplus, which is paid to the landlords. Part of this surplus is consumed directly by the landlords and their entourages, part they use to buy the products of the artisans who own their own equipment – forges, looms, etc. The artisans produce the manufactured goods, again using the grain they receive partly to feed themselves and partly to replace the materials and equipment they use as it depreciates. Thus, the only source of surplus is the land; and the essential distribution of the surplus is carried out by the landlords. So the land must be protected, the peasant should not be taxed and the landlord should be encouraged to improve the land and the techniques of production. More generally, the system of feudal land ownership is justified.

Ricardo had argued against this model by insisting that labour was the sole source of wealth. Writing as a protagonist of the new capitalist class, he wished to challenge the rents and the powers of the landlords, who, he believed, were creaming off the manufacturers' surplus through their power over the peasantry. Without labour the land yields nothing and remains undrained, unirrigated and unproductive. Moreover, the landlord gets a rent even from unimproved land. Marx followed Ricardo and quoted an earlier English writer from the seventeenth century, Sir William Petty, who called labour 'the active principle', 'the father of material wealth and the earth its mother'. As we have seen, later writers were to insist that capitalists were the true wealth-creators. Marx made jokes about the products of the tricks that Mister Capital and Mistress Land got up to.

It must seem almost a semantic question whether labour is described as the 'optimizing agent' or the 'active principle', but the question is whether labour time or energy consumption should be the measure of value in economic calculations. Capitalism chooses to exploit labour, as we saw earlier, because the rate of exploitation is not a technical coefficient but the result of relations of power. In a society without exploitation, it would be necessary to have a measure of socially necessary labour time to establish fair rewards to producers within the technically most energy- and resource-conserving processes of production.

Such a measure will be seen to be essential to Marx's model of socialism when we come to study it. The planned economies in the Soviet Union and China were not in fact based on calculations of labour values, but on an artificial construction of wages and prices set by the state and designed simply to balance supply and demand over fixed periods of time. The planners did not even have a rate of interest to assist them in calculating rates of discount over time and the opportunity cost of capital employed in using up more or less resources per unit of output. Although attempts were made, as we shall see, in Yugoslavia and Czechoslovakia in 1968-9 to introduce a value for stored-up labour into their shadow prices, it did not prove possible to relate wages to the value added by current labour. But there should have been no difficulties, except those resulting from the theory and practice of a command economy, in imposing a tax on energy consumption as well as incentives to reduce resource use.

Pricing Nature in the Market

In a market economy, the introduction of an energy tax and other taxes on the use of depleting resources should present no conceptual problems. Economists like something to measure, and there is no problem in measuring the amounts of energy or other scarce resources used up in production. The rate of tax could be determined by current interest rates, as with other cases of discounting the future, or a more positive rate could be chosen. This rate could be set against the value of output, enterprise by enterprise, industry by industry and sector by sector, so that increased output could be discounted for increased energy used. A new set of national accounts would become available. This would do something to offset the result of current taxation policies in most industrialized countries where more than half the tax-take comes from charges on labour. Economic growth could be calculated not only in terms of output per unit of labour input but in terms of output per unit of energy input.

David Pearce, Edward Barbier and Anil Markandya have gone further and argued in their *Blueprint for a Green Economy* (1989) in favour of using the market to value and to price the use of all environmental capital. Not only would energy use and the depletion of other non-renewable resources be priced, but so would the saturation of the soil, seas, rivers and air with waste products, and the irreversible destruction or degradation of the environment in global warming, ozone-layer destruction, and reduction of biodiversity in plants and seed types. In this new economics, money values can be placed on the loss of production, on the cost of correction of damage to human health and to the land, seas and rivers, and also on property prices and costs of travel to work when these are affected by environmental nuisance like road traffic and airport noise. These costings could be supplemented by surveys of what a sample population would pay for environmental improvements. Instead of governments relying on commands and controls and prohibitions, they would require that polluters pay compensation to society and that prices for goods and services include the costs of 'bads' and disservices now and in the future.

An innovative proposal made by Pearce and his colleagues was that governments should issue quotas for pollution, for example from carbon emissions, which clean and efficient firms within the quota could sell to the 'bad boys'. It would be important for property rights in the land to be granted to local people, so that they could defend themselves against exploitation. It would not be possible for any single nation to tax itself in this way, or its costs would be raised in competition in the world market; and this is why none of these proposals shows any sign of being adopted. But international agreements could be reached on such measures; and by introducing national accounts *net* of environmental depletion and damage, allowing for discounted natural capital, the 'clean' growers could claim to top the league tables instead of the fast growers (Pearce *et al.*, 1990).

It seems highly commendable to devise a green market akin to the social market, the possibilities of which socialists have been exploring. But it inevitably reminds one of Ptolemy adding ever more epicycles to his model of an earth-centred system to account for the movements of the sun, the moon and the planets in relation to the earth when all the time the earth and the other planets were revolving round the sun. Neoclassical economics places the individual at the centre of the market, the consumer with his or her needs which producers seek to satisfy with ever more new technology. What we call 'consumerism' is the end result of this orientation. All the taxes, quotas, compensatory payments and price adjustments being proposed by the moderate Greens are designed to alter individual behaviour, when it is our social behaviour that should be at the centre of the model. The planned economies of the Communist countries placed social needs at the centre, but an authoritarian élite determined what these should be – often just what suited their own interests.

Models which place society and not the individual at the centre of the economy are the subject of the next part of this book. But we have learnt from this chapter that it is not necessary to abandon all modern technology and look back to some golden age which never was but in our dreams. We have somehow to find a way to make technology the servant and not the master, to take the long view, to put social survival before individual greed and find growth paths for all to follow that are sustainable, using our immense accumulation of knowledge to relieve the poverty and misery, the fears and cares that afflict the great majority of the world's people. There will be no simple solutions and much will have to be learned from those who have tried and failed to find an alternative to the unequal societies which surround us.

FURTHER READING

BAHRO, RUDOLF, *The Alternative in Eastern Europe*, New Left Books, 1979

BAHRO, RUDOLF, *Socialism and Survival*, Heretic Books, 1982. Summarized in: 'Capitalism's Global Crisis', *New Statesman*, 17/24 December 1982, pp. 26–9; and 'A New Approach to the Peace

Movement in Germany', in E. P. Thompson *et al.*, *Exterminism and Cold War*, Verso, 1982

BARRATT BROWN, MICHAEL (ed.), *Resources and the Environment*, Spokesman, 1976

BODINGTON, STEPHEN, *What is Economic Growth?*, Spokesman, 1976 (pamphlet No. 32)

BRUNDTLAND, GRO HARLEM, World Commission on Environment and Development, *Our Common Future*, Oxford, 1987

BUARQUE, CHRISTOVAM, *The End of Economics? Ethics and the Disorder of Progress*, trans. from the Portuguese by Mark Ridd, Zed Books, 1993

EKINS, PAUL (ed.), *The Living Economy*, New Economics Foundation and Routledge, 1986

GALTUNG, JOHAN, *Basic Needs and the Green Movement*, United Nations University, 1980

GALTUNG, JOHAN, 'World Conflict Formation Processes in the 1980s', in *Project on Goals, Processes and Indicators of Development*, United Nations University, 1981

JENKINS, ROBIN, *The Road to Alto*, Pluto Press, 1979

JENKINS, ROBIN, *The Production of Value in Agriculture*, mimeo, 1984

MAXNEEF, MANFRED, *From the Outside Looking In*, Uppsala, 1982, and Zed Books, 1992

MEADOWES, DONELLA H., and DENNIS L., *The Limits to Growth*, Club of Rome, 1972

MEADOWES, DONELLA H., and DENNIS L., *Beyond the Limits*, Earthscan, 1992

PEARCE, DAVID, BARBIER, EDWARD, and MARKANDYA, ANIL, *Blueprint for a Green Economy*, Earthscan, 1989

PEARCE, DAVID, BARBIER, EDWARD, and MARKANDYA, ANIL, *Sustainable Development*, Earthscan, 1990

PEETERS, P., *Can We Avoid a Third World War around 2010?*, Macmillan, 1979

SACHS, WOLFGANG (ed.), *The Development Dictionary*, Zed Books, 1990

URBACH, PETER, *Francis Bacon's Philosophy of Science*, Open Court, 1987

2 MODELS OF ATTEMPTED SOCIALIST ECONOMIES

12 MARX'S MODEL OF SOCIALISM

It is often insisted, and rightly so, that Marx did not lay down a blueprint for the building of socialism. Human beings would have to find their way forward in quite specific conditions depending on where they were when they began to make a radical break with the old social order of capitalism. But Marx suggested some important signposts. First, there are the *Communist Manifesto*'s references to the socialization of labour under capitalism, as a condition of building socialism, since 'the various interests and conditions of life within the ranks of the proletariat are more and more equalized' – references that were repeated in *Capital*. Secondly, we have Marx's *Critique of the Gotha Programme* of the German Social Democratic Party in 1875 and Engels's chapters on 'Socialism – Utopian and Scientific' in his *Anti-Dühring*. But there is a particularly important reference to socialism in Marx's *Capital* (Vol. I, Chap. 2). Marx speaks there of

> a community of free individuals carrying on their work with the means of production in common, in which the labour power of all the different individuals is consciously applied as the combined labour power of the community . . . Labour time would in that case play a double part. Its apportionment in accordance with a definite social plan maintains the proper proportion between the different kinds of work to be done and the various wants of the community. On the other hand, it also serves as a measure of the portion of the common labour borne by each individual and of his [*sic*] share in the part of the total product destined for individual consumption. The social relations of the individual producers, with regard to both their labour and to its products, are in this case perfectly simple and intelligible and that with regard not only to production but also to distribution.

No veil of money conceals the value of what is added by each worker's work. The labour time required is known and different levels of technology can be measured and compared, so that all is open and intelligible. But that happy state implies certain prior conditions.

The Necessary Conditions for Social Accumulation

The main assumption of Marx and Engels was that socialism would be built on a basis of well-developed productive powers in industry and agriculture. They expected such powers to have reached a point where capitalist structures had become a fetter on their further development, and where accumulation by consent would have to replace accumulation by exploitation. They might have been surprised that a capitalist economy could one day land a man upon the moon: but they would not have been in the least surprised to be told that at the same time a third of the people on the earth were starving, or on the verge of starvation, wanting the bare necessities of life; and that some of these lived in the very economy from which a spacecraft could take off for the moon. Their assumption was clear. The expansion of human productive powers created both the possibility and the necessity for revolutionary change in social formations. Without such resources, any attempt at building a socialist commonwealth was a Utopian dream. With such resources it could become a scientific reality. So Engels writes in *Socialism: Utopian and Scientific*: 'The division into classes has a certain historical justification . . . It was based on the insufficiency of production; it will be swept away by the full development of the modern productive forces.'

Accumulation of resources for technological advance in the past has always meant exploitation – either by the open extraction of surplus from slaves or serfs or by its extraction through wage labour concealed behind the veil of money. Accumulation by consent would require that men and women had enough to live on to make a voluntary decision to set aside some of today's bread for jam tomorrow. 'So long', wrote Engels, 'as the sum of social labour yielded a product which only slightly exceeded what was necessary for the bare existence of all – so long was society necessarily divided into classes.' Engels was writing more than a hundred years ago but he felt able to go on to say that the possibility of securing for every member of society through social production, an existence which is not only fully sufficient from a material standpoint, and becoming richer from day to day, but also guarantees to them the completely unrestricted development and exercise of their physical and mental faculties – this possibility now exists for the first time, but it does exist.

That we are so far from this situation more than a century later might lead us to doubt whether even now the possibility exists. But then we have to recall that at least one-tenth of the national incomes of all countries – rich and poor, capitalist and socialist alike – is devoted to the production and exercise of instruments of mass destruction and that at least another tenth is squandered on uses of energy and materials which are not only wasteful, as in the waste of heat from power stations or in superfluous packaging or in private motor transport, but are immensely costly in their effects on the environment and in the reclamation activities they necessitate. We could add no less than a further tenth to our incomes by using the unused resources we already have: the unemployed workers and under-utilized productive capacity. It is a great mistake, which nineteenth-century economists led us into, for us to imagine that the normal economic condition of human societies is scarcity. It is not; it is surpluses.

If all the resources at our disposal were actually set to work to fulfil the basic needs of decent human existence, then few would doubt that Engels's possibility exists. But we have seen that the supporters of the Green movement doubt precisely this, and they have a point in reminding us that consumption of private goods on the scale attained in rich capitalist societies could not be universalized. Most people would not want so much private consumption if public services were adequate. Marx and Engels were not so greatly concerned with the concept of abundance as with the development of productive capacity to ensure that basic needs were met. This enables them to escape some of the criticism directed at them by writers like Alec Nove (1983) that they were not in fact scientific socialists but Utopian dreamers.

Given the development of the productive forces, the first

necessary condition for building socialism was seen by Marx and Engels to be the transfer of the means of production into social ownership. This may seem obvious enough to anyone who has thought about the meaning of the word socialism and its implication of social production and social provision. But we are so well aware of the awkward fact that nationalization of industries in a capitalist economy has failed to bring the expected benefits to workers or consumers that we have become doubtful. Our doubts have been reinforced by the evident rejection by both workers and consumers of the conditions and products of state-owned industries in countries that attempted to build socialism. It was an untoward development, not anticipated by Marx and Engels, that social ownership should be established and the building of a socialist order begun in countries whose economies were very far from having developed productive forces and which had little experience even of capitalist development. Their problems will be looked at in the following chapters.

What we need to say now is that Marx and Engels would not have expected such countries to become socialist without more-developed productive forces. Unfortunately, as we shall see, in developing these productive forces from a very low base they, like all other countries, had to accumulate resources through exploitation. There was no alternative. Although the direct use of slave labour in labour camps might have been avoided, the concealed exploitation of wage labour and collective labour behind the veil of money in commodity production almost certainly could not.

The Alternative to Commodity Production

It was just in the ending of commodity production that Marx and Engels envisaged the drawing aside of that veil of money that conceals the exploitation of the workers' labour power. The source of profit and the accumulation process can no longer then be concealed.

'The seizure of the means of production by society', Engels writes immediately after the last passage we quoted, puts an end to commodity production, and therewith to the domination of the product over the producer. Anarchy in social production is replaced by conscious organization on a planned basis. The struggle for individual existence comes to an end ... The objective external forces which have hitherto dominated history will pass under the control of men [sic] themselves ... It is humanity's leap from the realm of necessity to the realm of freedom.

Unfortunately, there is little or no evidence in those countries where the means of production were seized by the state that commodity production was ended. The extension of social provision beyond the range of social services, where it is already established in capitalist states, was minimal. Free supply had not even begun to replace the market. The veil of money continued to conceal the exploitation of workers and peasants, who remained ignorant of the value they added by their labour; and society's control over the state in which men and women can fully exercise their faculties was little developed. We shall see this in detail in the next chapters. We need only repeat here that Marx and Engels would not have expected it at the low levels of productive power in these countries.

But is there not planning in these economies, it will be said, in place of the rule of market forces? Engels specifically contrasts the anarchy of the market and the conscious organization of social production on a planned basis. Did not the five-year plans of the Soviet Union and the short-term and longer-term plans of the other countries, where the means of production were seized from the capitalists, reveal the very essence of the difference between capitalism and socialism? The answer must be that planning by itself does not build socialism. We have seen how the giant corporations now plan their strategies and how in wartime Britain planning replaced the market in allocating resources, how in the corporate economies of Hitler's Germany, fascist Italy and Japan there was total planning of the economy. Marx and Engels make it clear enough themselves that when they talk about conscious organization of social production on a planned basis under the control of men (sic) themselves they do not mean under the control of one man (sic) or of a few all-powerful men (sic). It is all humanity that was to make the leap from necessity to freedom, not a new elite replacing an older one.

This is made abundantly clear in one of Marx's early works, *The Poverty of Philosophy*, when he says 'the working class in the course of its development will substitute for the old order of civil society an association which will exclude classes and their antagonism, and there will no longer be political power, properly speaking, since political power is simply the official form of the antagonism in civil society'. But this still leaves important decisions to be made about the use of the cooperative proceeds of labour which are the total social product. Marx in his *Critique of the Gotha Programme* spells out that from these proceeds have to be deducted:

First, cover for replacement of the means of production used up.
Secondly, additional portion for expansion of production.
Thirdly, reserve or insurance funds to provide against misadventures, disturbances through natural events, etc.

These deductions from the 'undiminished proceeds of labour' are an economic necessity, and their magnitude is to be determined by available means and forces, and partly by calculation of probabilities, but they are in no way calculable by equity.

There remains the other part of the total product, destined to serve as means of consumption.

Before this is divided among the individuals, there have to be deducted from it:

First, the general costs of administration not belonging to production . . .
Secondly, that which is destined for the communal satisfaction of needs, such as schools, health services, etc. . . .
Thirdly, funds for those unable to work, etc. . . .

Within the cooperative society based on common ownership of the means of production, the producers do not exchange their products . . . Accordingly, the individual producer receives back from society – after the deductions have been made – exactly what he gives to it. What he has given to it is his individual amount of labour. For example the social working day consists of the sum of the individual labour hours; the individual labour-time of the individual producer is the part of the social labour-day contributed by him, his share in it. He receives a certificate from society that he has furnished such and such an amount of labour (after deducting his labour for the common fund), and with this certificate he draws from the social stock of means of consumption as much as the same amount of labour costs. The same amount of labour which he has given to society in one form, he receives back in another.

Calculating Labour Values

The certificates are not of course money except in one respect, that they serve as a unit of account. Like a railway ticket, they have no value after they have been used, except for accounting purposes. They would probably not even be transferable, since they would not circulate as a means of payment. Most important of all, they could not be accumulated like money as a store of value. They could not, in other words, create capital and become the basis for the inequalities of the capitalist system. This does not mean that there would be no investment. Certificates could be spent on buying tools and machines up to the limits of individual earnings and there would be deductions from credits for work done to provide for communal needs, both current and future.

This still does not tell us how compensation would be calculated for individual labour. No method is proposed for measuring and compensating social labour for social provision. How to replace individual choice in the market by a real development of democratic choice in social production and social provision is not spelled out by Marx or Engels. Their model of a socialist economy clearly requires social ownership of the means of production, social organization on a planned basis, a great extension of social provision *and* broad popular participation in the whole decision-making process at every level. But the connecting links in the model are not clear. We have individual labour times combined in cooperative production to form social labour, but the sum total of the value produced must inevitably be more than the sum of the individual parts. At the same time, we have to determine the value of the stored-up labour in the machinery and plant that goes into the value of the product. When we know this, then we know the basis for Marx's 'simple and intelligible' social relations of the individuals in production.

There is no doubt that with the aid of computers we could calculate what a modern economist in the Ricardian tradition – Piero Sraffa of Cambridge – has called 'dated labour' (i.e. labour time stored up in capital equipment as well as current labour time). Then we could build models in the econometric sense of shadow prices based on real costs of production. If these were openly and intelligibly published to reveal comparable estimates of value added, whatever the actual price in the market, most of the antagonistic conflicts could be removed.

Such conflicts certainly should be removed by the system of labour credits which Paul Cockshott and Allin Cottrell have proposed in their book *Towards a New Socialism*. This system takes into account the need to know at any time, no longer the market prices, but the up-to-date labour values of inputs, i.e. of direct labour, the labour that went into plant and machinery and raw materials, and the similar labour values of outputs of inter-mediate products. These two authors, respectively a computer specialist and an economist, demonstrate that with modern com-puters, teletext publication and continuous information from work-places of changes in labour values, it would be as easy to achieve this knowledge with a small delay as it is to achieve the instant information about money prices that is now available from stock markets, money markets and exchange markets (Cock-shott and Cottrell, 1993).

Their proposal assumes that the intention of establishing a socialist society along the lines suggested by Marx was only held back by the impossibility of calculating labour values except with a delay of several years. When actual attempts were made to introduce a measure of labour value added into wage determina-tion in countries attempting socialism, as in Yugoslavia, they came up against two kinds of objection. The first was that employers who introduced advanced machinery would be gaining an unfair profit, if workers agreed to accept only the average value added by labour when, as would probably be the case, the new machines required skilled machine-minding. Such a claim for skilled labour can be dealt with by allowing for a premium over simple labour. As regards the share of higher productivity from mechanization which should go, not to the worker involved, but to society as a whole, this will only seem to be just if two conditions are fulfilled: the calculation must be quite open and intelligible and the worker has a say in the way communal needs are met from the social fund. In Yugoslavia, workers felt that neither of these conditions was fulfilled. This does not invalidate Cockshott and Cottrell's argument, but it shows the problem of any incomes policy.

The second objection to the use of measures of labour value added in assessing compensation for work done is that fair remuneration should take into account the needs of different workers with different circumstances. Marx takes up both these points in his *Critique of the Gotha Programme*:

> One man is superior to another physically or mentally and so supplies more labour, in the same time, or can labour for a longer time ... Equal right is then an unequal right for unequal labour ... Further, one worker is married, another not; one has more children than another and so on and so forth. Thus with an equal output and hence an equal share in the social consumption fund, one will in fact receive more than another, one will be richer than another and so on. To avoid all these, rights instead of being equal would have to be unequal.

The Stages of Socialism and Communism

Hold on! some readers will cry. Does not Marx at this point stop and say, 'You are expecting the stage of communism to be reached before socialism has been built.' Did not Marx clearly indicate that there were two stages, that socialism would be followed by communism? The first stage would be distinguished by payment for work done, 'From each according to his ability; to each according to his work.' Only in the second stage would each receive 'according to his need'. In other words, generalized social provision would be appropriate to the stage of communism. One stage could be expected to lead into the other as free social provision steadily replaced money wages and money payments. The power and authority of government would be replaced by 'an association in which the free development of each is the condition for the free development of all'. 'The state would wither away' in Engels's famous phrase.

Suppose, however, that the power of the state had to be greatly expanded in order to build up the productive forces of a society in which workers undertook to build socialism from a low level of productive power; and suppose that exploitation, either open or behind the veil of money, had been almost inevitably involved in the accumulation of resources for developing such productivity, then the transition to open social provision and the actual withering away of the state might be long drawn out and extremely difficult. This was clear enough in the early 1980s, and indeed for many years before the whole Soviet model collapsed.

Marx had spoken of society carrying over into the building of socialism all sorts of hangovers of capitalism, even of other past social formations. In his *Critique of the Gotha Programme* he says:

> What we have to deal with here is a communist society, not as it has *developed* on its own foundations, but on the contrary, as it *emerges* from capitalist society: which is thus in every respect, economically, morally, and intellectually still stamped with the birthmarks of the old society from whose womb it emerges.

And he goes on to talk about the defects inevitable in the first phase of communist society, as it is when it has just emerged after prolonged birth pangs from capitalist society. But Marx is suggesting here a transitional stage of birth pangs even before we can talk of building socialism. It is not correct for the apologists of Soviet socialism to claim these extenuating circumstances. They should not yet be talking about socialism at all in Marx's sense. 'Between capitalist and communist society lies the period of the revolutionary transformation of the one into the other.' There corresponds to this also a political transition period in which the state can be 'nothing but the revolutionary dictatorship of the proletariat'. This concept was taken up by Lenin to justify what he had to do in 1917; but for apologists to do so seventy-five years later is to invoke what Marx would have called the power of ideology, in the sense of a false consciousness, to conceal from the people the reality of their condition. In the same way capitalism offers the ideology of the workers' freedom from either slavery or serfdom to conceal behind the veil of money the actuality of wage slavery.

None of this should be taken to suggest that the building of socialism, even from more advanced productive forces than existed in the Soviet Union, Eastern Europe or China, would be an easy task. There is a real problem, as yet unsolved, of discovering the model (or models) of a non-money economy which might replace commodity production for the market by conscious organization of production – not by the few but by the participation of the great majority of the people. Marx and Engels imagined a model of cooperative production units linked together by mutual exchange agreements. Since then the scale and complexity of production have enormously increased and the range of products we regard as essential has vastly proliferated. It might seem that such simple systems as Marx and Engels envisaged were now out of the question although Ernest Mandel in the late 1980s was still pressing the claims of a society of associated producers (Mandel, 1988).

We have two remedies: we could reduce the range of products without loss of satisfaction – as the Green movement recommends us to do – or we could use computers to present us with instant information about what is available and to help us to organize on a social basis the allocation of resources to meet our needs. Computers which as little as ten years ago were still mainly being used for planning by governments and giant companies have become the tool of nearly every man and every woman working in government and business or engaging in private correspondence. They could be transformed to become the instruments of popular decision-making and control. It is not at all necessary, and certainly not what Marx or Engels envisaged, that production should be concentrated in vast enterprises under socialism and subjected to centralized control with no room for small-scale private enterprise. It is significant that it should have been an economist, Allin

Cottrell, working with a computer specialist, Paul Cockshott, who have most daringly set out to rehabilitate Marx's socialism after the collapse of the Soviet attempt and that they should have drawn heavily on the democratic potential of the personal computer in so doing. We shall see in the next chapter how far these tools could have helped to solve the problems faced by the Soviet Union.

FURTHER READING

BARRATT BROWN, MICHAEL, *The Economics of Imperialism*, Penguin Books, 1974 (see Chap. 3)

BODINGTON, STEPHEN, *Computers and Socialism*, Spokesman, 1973

BOTTOMORE, T. B., and RUBEL, M. (eds.), *Marx: Selected Writings*, Penguin Books, 1961

COCKSHOTT, PAUL, and COTTRELL, ALLIN, *Towards a New Socialism*, Spokesman, 1993, Chap. 3

ENGELS, FRIEDRICH, *Socialism: Utopian and Scientific*, 1892 (first published in England 1907); Central Books, 1979

FREEDMAN, ROBERT (ed.), *Marx on Economics*, Penguin Books, 1962

MANDEL, ERNEST, 'The Myth of Market Socialism', *New Left Review*, No. 169, 1988

MARX, KARL, *A Critique of the Gotha Programme*, 1875; Lawrence & Wishart, 1938

NOVE, ALEC, *The Economics of Feasible Socialism*, Allen & Unwin, 1983

13 THE SOVIET MODEL

Economic models do not emerge from nowhere. They arise from the attempts of human beings to understand the world they find around them and thus to improve their control over it. The Soviet model can only be understood in relation to the whole stage of Russian history when the Bolsheviks seized power in 1917. We have already recognized that in Russia the level of productive forces, and the development of capitalism, were far below what Marx and Engels assumed would be necessary to provide the basis for building socialism. It was only fifty years since serfdom had been abolished in Russia; modern industry was only just being established and was mainly in the hands of foreign capitalists. Moreover, Russia's historical development had taken more the form of what Marx designated as Asiatic society than the feudalism of the rest of Europe. For this reason and because of the small working class and vast and backward peasantry Marx was not optimistic about the prospects of revolutionary change in Russia. Nevertheless he was sufficiently interested in some questions raised with him by Vera Zasulich, a Russian populist and revolutionary leader, to go to the lengths of learning Russian and studying its history. Vera Zasulich's questions concerned the possibility of the historic Russian village commune becoming the basis for a leap into socialism without an intervening stage of capitalist development. Teodor Shanin has published a collection of essays (*The Late Marx*, 1983) in which he discusses this whole question.

Although Russia did not share with other Asiatic societies a great irrigated river system like that of the Tigris and Euphrates, the Indus, the Ganges or the Yellow River, it did share with them an open frontier to nomadic Mongol invasions from the north and east. This encouraged the emergence of a powerful, centralized military authority at the frontier – in Moscow as at Persepolis, Delhi or Peking. The power of the Tsars, as of the Persian, Indian or Chinese emperors, was far greater than that of any European monarch. The nobles were much more the emperor's agents, without the local base of feudal barons. In place of a hierarchy of feudal services, taxes were collected by agents of the central state. Although from time to time the centre's power was challenged, invasion from the east soon led to its restoration under an Ivan the Terrible, a Peter the Great or (should we not add?) a Joseph Stalin.

The Bureaucratic Tradition in Russia

The result of such a history was that the Bolsheviks inherited not only a massive central bureaucracy, but a very limited tradition of local initiative compared with that which the knights and yeoman farmers gave to England. Even the merchants of the great market cities of Vilna, Minsk and Kiev or of the ports of St Petersburg, Riga or Odessa depended more on transit trade than local produce. The main initiative behind nineteenth-century Russian modernization came not from the merchants, nor from small-scale local craftsmen, but from the bureaucratic state itself calling upon foreign enterprise. Starting late and with a very limited industrial tradition, the model of a command economy was inevitably adopted as the only one on which to industrialize. This was likely to be a bad model on which to build a socialist society; and so indeed it proved. Even before Stalin, the Soviet economic model depended upon the most highly centralized planning system. Stalin himself was sufficiently sensitive about references to Russian centralism to stop a quotation from Marx's Preface to the *Introduction to the Critique of Political Economy*, cited in his *Dialectics of Materialism*, just before the sentence in which Marx refers to Asiatic society.

To compound the problem of a tradition of centralized bureaucracy there was the limitation of the small industrial base that had been established in Russia by 1914; and what there was had been much weakened by 1917. It was the aim of the Bolsheviks to build both an industrial and socialist society under the leadership of an extremely small working class in an overwhelmingly peasar.

country. The alliance of workers and peasants had only the most tenuous roots. The attempt to translate ideas of class struggle between owners and non-owners in industry to the countryside only alienated the peasantry. The overwhelming majority of these were working proprietors. Only a tiny number were big landlords and many of those families which owned no land had done so once and hoped to do so again. The party and the army became inevitably the substitute for a vanguard class in town and country, and resistance to civil war and invasion decimated the cadres of both party and army. For all these reasons centralization of power was the more certainly continued. It was still with them nearly seventy years later. (See Bahro, 1979, Chap. 3.)

It is not quite correct to speak of the continuity of a central bureaucratic tradition from Tsarist Russia into the Soviet Union. There were periods of Soviet history when a break was attempted. The first was in the very first two years after November 1917. This was a period during which, as a result of the absolute collapse of the Russian armies in battle with the Germans, the Bolsheviks had been able almost without a shot fired to occupy the power vacuum which that collapse had left. In this period soviets of workers and of soldiers and sailors were formed, repeating the experience of the 1905 Revolution, and began to build a new structure of political and economic decision-making throughout the towns and cities of Russia, but especially in Petrograd (the old St Petersburg, later renamed for a time Leningrad).

Invasion from outside in 1918, fomenting civil war, as so often before in Russian history, re-established the power of the centre. Apart from problems of local independence, outside the big cities the Bolsheviks were not always in a majority in the soviets. Lenin believed that central authority had to be restored. Old Bolsheviks like Alexandra Kollontai and others who were to form the briefly tolerated Workers' Opposition nevertheless protested. Although the invaders were defeated by 1920, soon nothing was left of soviets except the ideology – in the title of the new state and in the names of the various levels of representative assembly. The workers were in effect taken out of politics. 'You work well; we'll govern well,' as the Polish leader Gierek crudely put it fifty years later. The socialist innovation of a dual function, of a political *and* economic organ of government, was abandoned after 1919 – and not rediscovered except for brief but important periods in China and Cuba much later. Henceforth, economic organization was to be centralized in the hands of a central committee and its apparatchiks, in the now nationalized banks and industrial companies. These apparatchiks were often in fact the same bureaucrats who had occupied the government departments under the Tsars, as Lenin frequently complained.

The second break was not so much a break in the bureaucratic tradition as a relaxation of centralized authority. The years from 1918 to 1921 were described as a period of war communism marked by barter and requisition. The armed forces simply commandeered what was needed. The resources were found for resisting the allied invading armies and for re-establishing some of the railways and a very little of the basic industry that had been brought under state control. Re-establishing all that had existed before the destruction of seven years of war and developing new resources in industry and agriculture evidently demanded something other than military requisition. Many parts of Russia faced actual starvation and desperate measures were taken. Dictatorship of the proletariat had become dictatorship of the party. Lenin was only too well aware of the dangers of such elitism. Roy Medvedev has collected the evidence in his book *Leninism and Western Socialism*.

It was decided to free the market and encourage private enterprise in industry and agriculture. Basic industries including coal, electricity, iron and steel, transport – both rail and road – and foreign trade were retained in state hands but devolved to republics and local authorities. State plants also produced tractors for agriculture and managed their allocation. The rest was left to free enterprise. This was called the New Economy Policy (NEP) and there is no doubt that it produced results – some good, some bad. The good result was that by 1928 industrial output had been brought back to pre-war levels, and unrationed goods were returning to the shops again. The two bad results were, first, that agricultural recovery was extremely slow. The peasants were eating the extra food they produced and were not encouraged to market more since prices were kept down for the sake of industrial workers' needs and so as not to enrich further the rich peasants (kulaks). Secondly, and no less unfortunate, there was the emergence of a new capitalist class – the so-called 'NEP men' – whose obvious enrichment seriously undermined any socialist enthusiasm among the masses.

It was evident that an alternative model was needed that was not either the corporate wartime model or the old market model. Lenin (who died in 1924) and Bukharin believed that the growing superiority in productive efficiency of the state-owned enterprises and the increasing influence of the state's resources in providing tractors and farm machinery for agriculture would permit a steady subordination of the private (NEP) sector to the public sector in both industry and agriculture. But Lenin frankly saw the increased productivity of state enterprise emerging from the application of US technology. This even included welcoming not only American engineers to help in building electric power stations but also the ideas of F. W. Taylor ('Speedy' Taylor), the work-study founder from Bethlehem Steel Corporation, 'combining Soviet power and the Soviet organization of administration', said Lenin, 'with the up-to-date achievements of capitalism' (quoted in Braverman, 1974, p. 2). This marked a fatally narrow emphasis on the materialist base of productive power without the democratic consciousness to develop it to meet people's needs.

The Five-Year Plans

At first these matters were openly argued and discussed and, while the central planning bodies were encouraged to develop their overall direction of the economy, the policy towards the peasantry was marked by caution and pragmatism after the excesses of war communism. This mix of policies – the development of central planning and price control with small-scale free enterprise and peasant agriculture – was continued by Stalin for four years, but the open discussion was halted with the destruction of the Workers' Opposition and the banishment of Trotsky. In 1928 Stalin changed everything with his forced industrialization backed by compulsory collectivization and liquidation of the kulaks 'as a class'. It was a brutal measure and precursor of much more brutality to follow. But the process of changing age-old agricultural practices in order to raise productivity and of capturing the increase for accumulation has not anywhere been solved without violence. The enclosures of English common land, the clearances of the highlands of Scotland or of Kenya, the restriction of North American Indians or Southern Africans or Australian Aborigines to tribal 'reserves' all bear witness to this.

An industrial revolution presupposes an agricultural revolution. Not only do new industrial workers in the towns require to be fed from a surplus off the land, but where the population is overwhelmingly agricultural the surplus for investment for the future must come from the land. Preobrazhensky, a brilliant Bolshevik economist, whom Stalin murdered along with so many others, called this 'the iron heel of primitive accumulation' at the expense of the peasants.

It was nothing new, but the violence done to the Russian peasantry in the 1920s created a tradition of terror which lasted long after Stalin's death. Zhores Medvedev in his *History of Soviet Agriculture* has demonstrated how the seizure of food from the countryside during the famine of 1926 by agents of the state established a culture of violence which spread into every department of state and gave the secret police its special role in government (Medvedev, 1988). It was never possible, even after Stalin's death and Khrushchev's denunciation of the Stalin terror, for Soviet society and the Communist Party at its head to live down that terrible memory and start again – as Gorbachev was to discover.

With the wisdom of hindsight we can see that their view of the class struggle in the villages led Stalin, and Lenin too, to expect the poor and middle peasants to work for the Soviet state, when all they wanted was to own their own land. A slower and less brutal process of modernization of agriculture, through control of the commanding heights of industry and the development of state and cooperative enterprises in agriculture, such as Lenin and

Bukharin proposed, might well have worked far better in the long run. The disastrous effects of forced collectivization remained to plague Soviet economic development for fifty years in the flagging figures of agricultural output and the dependence on imported grain, where Russia was once, before 1917, a major grain exporter. In the short run, however, with Russian cities facing famine in 1926 and the first five-year plan only three years off its inception, it is possible to understand Stalin's impatience.

What then was the model of the Soviet economy as it was developed in the first two five-year plans running from 1928 to 1937? First of all, it was a model of command economy in which orders were transmitted from the top and the centre downwards and outwards to the localities and enterprises. The argument in the Soviet Union from 1925 to 1927 between what were called the 'geneticists' and the 'teleological' planners was won by the latter. In other words, those who wanted to follow objective tendencies of the market economy, and particularly of peasant attitudes as they evolved (genetically), and adapt them through financial controls were defeated by those who wished to set specific targets as the aims (teleologies) of industrial development to 'catch up' with the developed economies, and use physical controls in the process.

Central planning to replace the market, even with a private small-artisan sector, with private trading and a private sector in agriculture, implies four non-market relationships:

1. Coordination and articulation of enterprise plans in place of market anarchy or of bankers' financial management.
2. Social direction of priorities in place of the market indicators of prices and profits or of the giant companies' medium-term planning.
3. A long-term strategy to overcome the limitations of short-term profit calculations in planning investment.
4. Social motivation that replaces the motive of money-making.

We shall look at them each in turn to reveal the Soviet model.

The first of these elements is in part only a matter of adequate information and the calculation of coefficients of inputs and outputs by industry and enterprise, of imports and exports, of supply and money demand, and, therefore, of prices and wages, of jobs and available labour, of credit and activity. Without the aid of computers these equations involved large numbers of office workers collecting, organizing and calculating the data, but somehow it was done. Even with computers, mistakes are bound to be made in planning centrally the inputs and outputs of thousands of enterprises over the vast area of the Soviet Union. Coordination of enterprise plans, however, is even more a question of democracy, of an alternative to the information system of the market for discovering social needs as well as private wants.

There were three alternatives for the second element, the social direction of the economy. It could be highly centralized with output targets, material cost reductions, productivity increases, quality assortment, credit, employment ceilings, wage bills and allocation of materials all determined centrally for each enterprise; or these could be left to local decisions within a framework of *ad hoc* directives on interest rates, clearance of bottlenecks, stocking or destocking, labour utilization, etc.; the third alternative might be decentralization to enterprises to reach their own investment decisions within a much broader range of central policy decisions. In fact, within the first five-year plans no freedom was allowed for playing the market. Quantities and qualities of output were strictly fixed as the targets for every enterprise. Reforms in this area were not considered until the late 1950s in the Soviet Union.

In the meantime, the threat of Hitler's invasion had once more re-established war communism. Food was requisitioned. Factories were ordered to produce for the war effort to centrally determined standards and quantities. The German armies were held at Stalingrad in 1943 and then rolled back with terrible losses. Soviet industry, rebuilt behind the Urals, had produced the arms and the tanks to supply the soldiers. The first post-war five-year plans continued the command model in tackling the tasks of rebuilding a war-shattered economy. In this way they were remarkably successful. By 1950 the national product was 50 per cent above the level achieved in 1937; but, as priorities became less obvious and the range of peacetime needs proliferated, the simple central directives of a command economy became less and less appropriate.

The third aim of planning reasserted its importance. This, we said, was to replace the profit motive by a long-term strategy. The social direction of resources implies an aim beyond winning a great war or restoring the economy thereafter. Capitalist command economies could do that but no more. The aim of Stalin's five-year plans after 1928 had been to develop a base of heavy industry for the industrialization of the country. Investment was stepped up from 12 per cent of the national product in 1928 to 26 per cent in 1937. This was a remarkable achievement for a country with a national income per head only about a quarter of what it was in a country like Britain, since what was being set aside for tomorrow was what many would have wished to consume today. For, while communal consumption was increased between 1928 and 1937 (from 5 to 10 per cent of the national product), personal consumption did not increase at all and actually fell as a share of the national product, from 80 per cent to only just over 50 per cent. Some of the giant schemes can be criticized, particularly the canals and hydroelectric power plants for which Beria's concentration camps provided the labour. Although industrial output was trebled, output per worker was barely increased. But the industrial base was built. Far more of a problem was the failure to increase agricultural output, although here there was some increase in productivity as labour moved from agriculture into industry. (For these figures see my book *What Economics is About*, 1967, table p. 266.)

The aim of the strategy of Bulganin and then of Khrushchev after Stalin's death was, openly, to catch up with the capitalist West. But this involved increasing output per person in industry and increasing food production. Major improvements were made in both respects in the mid-1950s, first by decentralizing industrial decision-making to regions and enterprises and, secondly, by raising agricultural prices to increase the incentive for higher output. But the improvement was not maintained as new problems arose, once the basic needs of the population were met. Bulganin listed them in his reports to the Central Committee: above all, neglect of quality, production of unwanted goods, regional imbalances and concealment of stocks and reserves. It became evident that increasingly complex orders to enterprises about what to produce, how, when and with what resources, were being neglected by managers in favour of fulfilling whichever instruction carried most advantage for the enterprise. This was generally the achieving of the target of physical output. So, at whatever cost in quality, in hoarding of resources of labour and materials, in ignoring possibilities of expansion or of increased productivity, this at least was achieved – no less, but also no more, lest next year's target be set too high!

This is where the fourth aim of planning which we listed comes in – providing a social motivation that replaces the motive of money-making. What should this motivation be? The great patriotic war, national recovery, catching up with the West, improving quality and service – such motivations as they are listed here have descending orders of urgency and increasingly depend upon the sense of involvement of the workforce in the productive process and of all citizens in the decisions about what should be produced. So long as industrial investment is extensive – more plants, more workers – growth can follow from central commands, but when investment becomes intensive – more and better output from the same plant and from the same workers – then not only the planners but the workers and the management of plants must be motivated to make the increases in productivity and quality.

Two problems arise: the first concerns the motivation of the planners. Defence of the nation is more important than oral hygiene, and will attract the more ambitious and efficient bureaucrats. Brezhnev used to complain of the lack of toothbrushes. In the scale of national priorities they were bound to come low down. The second concerns the motivation of the workers, who must either believe in what they are doing, or be bribed – by moral or material incentives. Bribery may be by piece-work payment or by perks, plus upward mobility for a small elite. In either case, growing inequalities will arouse resentment among the majority left behind. Mistakes in planning will cause further alienation. For workers, and managers too, to believe in raising productivity

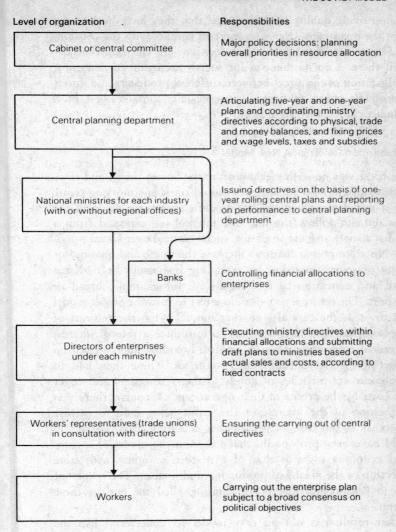

Level of organization	Responsibilities
Cabinet or central committee	Major policy decisions: planning overall priorities in resource allocation
Central planning department	Articulating five-year and one-year plans and coordinating ministry directives according to physical, trade and money balances, and fixing prices and wage levels, taxes and subsidies
National ministries for each industry (with or without regional offices)	Issuing directives on the basis of one-year rolling central plans and reporting on performance to central planning department
Banks	Controlling financial allocations to enterprises
Directors of enterprises under each ministry	Executing ministry directives within financial allocations and submitting draft plans to ministries based on actual sales and costs, according to fixed contracts
Workers' representatives (trade unions) in consultation with directors	Ensuring the carrying out of central directives
Workers	Carrying out the enterprise plan subject to a broad consensus on political objectives

Figure 10. Model of a command economy

and improving quality they must feel that they have both a real say in the investment decisions and real contact with the consumers. This will be difficult if major decisions are all made centrally and if there is no mechanism for social discussion to determine the allocation of resources between different producers and different products and to effect producer–consumer contact, to establish consumer choice. (See Figure 10.)

The Liberman Reforms: A New Model

Since there was no such mechanism in the Soviet Union and since the elite of party and bureaucracy would resist any move to create such a popular mechanism, the reforms that were made in the 1960s did not follow the line one might have expected from a socialist society striving to ensure social control over social provision. No attempt was made to increase the range and quantity or quality of social provision by extending free issues beyond free health and education to free supply of, for example, bread or transport. The reforms proposed in effect to turn the Soviet model back towards the capitalist market model. What the reforms of Professor Liberman intended was to introduce a rate of interest charged to enterprises, so as to control hoarding and to open up competition between supplying enterprises. These then had to make contracts for sales of goods to their customers and cover their costs by the profits of their operations. Of course, there was no question of the interest or the profit being paid to private owners as is the case in a capitalist economy. But the system would have been profoundly changed from the model of a command economy towards that of a market economy with state ownership of the means of production and finance. The revolts of 1968 in Poland and Czechoslovakia signalled the end of these reforms.

What resulted is not an easy model to understand like the market model or the command economy. The state through the Planning Department and the departments of industry at the centre still fixed prices and still controlled the banking system that made finance available and fixed tax rates for different industries.

It still, therefore, controlled the overall allocation of resources. Within this framework enterprises had a certain freedom to make their own bargains with their suppliers and with their customers. At first sight it may appear that this 'mixed economy' of plan and enterprise combines the needs of worker motivation and consumer preference. But it is a bad mix.

There are at least four reasons for this. First, the workers still do not know the value added by their labour. This was concealed behind money values which comprise a complex mix of production costs, taxes and subsidies. Workers might therefore well harbour doubts about increasing output without appropriate recompense. Secondly, the consumers still did not know what they might have had other than what appeared in the shops, how much disappeared under the counter for special customers and what services they might have had instead of goods. Thirdly, agriculture suffered from chronic under-investment, because, while state purchase prices were raised, the effect was to encourage not investment but retention of labour on the land. Many collective farms faced ruin when they had to buy the machinery from the tractor stations and essential fertilizers in the Khrushchev reforms of the late 1950s and 1960s. Agriculture had for far too long been financing industry's development and the arms build-up, and still lacked the incentive to innovate except on small private plots. The result was stagnating output. (See Roy Medvedev's biography, *Khrushchev*.) Fourthly, and most important, the whole system depended neither on a measure of real competition that forced enterprises to invest in new plant and new ideas or die – there was still a safety net for failing firms and a fixed framework of central resource allocation – nor on an openly argued, popularly understood and agreed social investment plan. It depended increasingly on enlarging the size of enterprises, as in the West, so that more decisions were taken inside the company. The average size of enterprises was actually larger in the East than in the West. Beyond the enterprise the system depended on a network of personal contacts and private agreements – what in Britain would be called the 'old-boy network'.

Before 1985, when Gorbachev came to power, the stories about what came to be published in the Soviet press showed that these formed but the tip of an iceberg. Glasgow University's *Soviet Studies* had provided a continuous flow of such stories from the Soviet Press. The reason for the corruption appeared to be the continuation of shortages. Where prices are fixed, rationing is by the queue or supply from under the counter; and apart from the injustice, this fails to encourage new and improved production. There is always a seller's market. In *The Revolution Betrayed*, Trotsky characterized the resulting situation very sharply:

> The basis of bureaucratic rule is the poverty of society in objects of consumption with the resulting struggle of each against all. When there are enough goods in the stores the purchasers can come whenever they want to. When there are little goods, the purchasers are compelled to stand in line. When the lines are very long, it is necessary to appoint a policeman to keep order. Such is the starting point of Soviet bureaucracy (Trotsky, 1930).

The result of such a system proved less disastrous for the Soviet Union when Trotsky was writing in the 1930s than it did thirty years later in the almost continuous relative technological decline from the heady days of the Sputnik in 1957 and the moon-shot a few years later. The Liberman reforms of the mid-1960s reduced the gap which opened up between the technology of the Soviet Union and the USA from fourteen years to four years; but after that the lag steadily widened again in computers, automated production, military armour and nuclear missiles. (See Amann *et al.*, 1981.)

Perestroika and *Glasnost* under Gorbachev

So far this chapter stands almost as it was written in 1983. The changes are mainly in the tense of the verbs. Practically no one in the West had then heard of Mikhail Gorbachev or knew the meaning of *glasnost* and *perestroika*. But there was an impending sense of collapse in the succession to Brezhnev of two dying men, prior to Gorbachev's election to the position of General Secretary of the Communist Party in 1985. It was becoming obvious to close observers that the arms race between the superpowers was becoming an intolerable burden which was weighing down the Soviet economy and that the people lacked the consumer goods that even a middle-income capitalist country could supply. Output of both agriculture and industry was growing in the early 1980s at half the rate of the 1970s, even according to official statistics, and there were reports of colossal waste of resources and rising discontent in the non-Russian-speaking republics.

The dissolution of the Soviet Union and Gorbachev's resignation as President at the end of 1991 drew a veil over the Gorbachev years. Yeltsin was left free to adopt a Western-style market economy as his model in Russia; and this further obscured the fact that Gorbachev had his own economic policy model. Gorbachev achieved fame outside the Soviet Union as an international statesman. It is recognized that he had a very clear understanding that an end to the arms race was a precondition for any Soviet economic policy, and history will remember him kindly for that. But the received opinion in the West is that he was a reluctant economic reformer and had to be replaced by someone more determined.

This may be a wilful misunderstanding arising from the fact that the Gorbachev model was certainly not the Western market model. It was therefore written off outside the country, but why did it fail inside? It is a matter of some importance, especially for socialists, to answer this question. It was not for want of advocacy or for intellectual support. The first half of Gorbachev's own book on *perestroika*, published in 1987, is devoted to reform and democratization of the economy; and it is presented in Gorbachev's own words as 'a carefully prepared programme, rather than a pompous declaration'. The details are spelt out at greater length in the work of his chief economic adviser, Abel Aganbegyan, significantly titled *The Challenge: The Economics of Perestroika* (1988).

That the economic programme was carefully prepared we learn from Aganbegyan. The group of men in their late fifties who came into power with Gorbachev had been students and youthful apparatchiks when Khrushchev was challenging the Stalin myth and introducing economic reforms. Khrushchev's replacement by

Brezhnev ended the reforms. As young men they saw the change as a disaster and separated out to build power bases in different parts of the Union to prepare for the day, probably twenty years on, when Brezhnev must be called to his fathers. In the meantime they met and planned for a restructuring – *perestroika*. At the centre of their plans was the absolute necessity for a new openness – *glasnost* – and for democratization of every part of the economy and of society at large. The people, working people, men and women, in towns and countryside, had to be given back the power that had been taken away from them for so long.

It sounded good, but what did it mean in fact? The whole command economy was to be dismantled and the task of the centre – the State Planning Committee and the ministries – reduced from detailed ordering and monitoring to a guiding role of establishing general allocations between sectors, balancing demand and supply and setting economic norms. This word 'norms', which is generally translated directly from the Russian as 'normatives', has no exact English economic equivalent, but corresponds more to the indicative planning by government of the operations of nationalized industries than to wartime regulation of industry.

Norms were to have the effect of laws applying to all, unlike the system of orders and contracts applying to specific enterprises. Within long-term norms of technological advance, increased labour productivity, minimum and maximum wage levels, investment policy, health and safety rules and social obligations, all enterprises were to be self-regulating. They had to find their own supplies, market their products, determine their prices (with the exception of certain basic products), allocate their wage funds and decide on investments as well as manage their day-to-day operations. Banks would allocate funds within overall Soviet and republic budgets. Increasingly, it was supposed that enterprises would be free to enter the world market and to keep a proportion of foreign earnings for investment.

The fundamental implication was that competition would be reintroduced and enterprises would have to be efficient to survive. Extensive growth – more plants and more resources – would have to be replaced by intensive growth – increased productivity.

Efficiency which had been so lacking in the past was to be, in Aganbegyan's words, the 'driving force of change', and that would inevitably mean the prospect of unemployment. Aganbegyan was opposed to the creation of unemployment as a deliberate act of policy and recommended that measures should be taken by state institutions at appropriate levels to organize the redeployment, either on training schemes or in new enterprises, of workers made redundant. The main source of improved efficiency, he believed, would come from the workforce, through better motivation and consultation about innovation, once full employment was guaranteed in general but not in existing jobs.

This model of economic organization is, of course, many miles from Marx's communist system of associated labour and the sharing out of labour credits, or of Cockshott and Cottrell's planning on the basis of computerized labour values. But Aganbegyan was able to show that in certain parts of the Soviet Union and in certain industries, notably the car industry, experiments along the lines that he was indicating had been made and had proved themselves successful. There was, moreover, in the writings and speeches of Gorbachev and of Aganbegyan a 'powerful ethical charge', as Teodor Shanin has described it, 'about justice, a better society, more humane human beings, concern for the truth' (Shanin, private communication, 1993). And this was not limited to rhetoric but informed all the restrictions on alcohol consumption and the deliberate switch of resources from military hardware to better food supplies, to health and education and other social provision.

What Went Wrong? Politics and Economics

So, what went wrong? Basically, the merging of models did not work. The political scene became polarized between what were called 'hardliners' who, in the main, wanted to hold on to the command economy and the so-called 'reformers' who believed in a total opening-up to market forces, with support from outside capital and advice from American academics. The coup against Gorbachev only deepened the division and Yeltsin's siege of the

Parliament two years later finally forced the middle-of-the-road followers of the Gorbachev model out of the picture. It appeared that all compromise between the old and the new had failed. Output of industry and agriculture fell, unemployment grew, living standards declined, there was less and not more in the shops for ordinary people – the freeing of prices released some supplies but at prices beyond their reach. The inflation rate soared and Yeltsin was forced to accept IMF loans and Western aid tied to free market conditions. The West became increasingly unpopular, but the divisions between marketeers and planners polarized still further and subtly changed their meaning.

Much worse was to follow as nearly all state-owned property was privatized, public services were starved and all state credits and subsidies went to launch the new private sector. But there was not a Russian bourgeoisie to take over the state property, including all manufacturing, commerce and distribution. It could not be sold at market prices, but was taken over by 'interested groups and individuals'. Sometimes this meant the management and workers; often it meant ministry officials, planners with nothing to plan; but also operators from the black market and the informal economy. The division between planners and reformers became increasingly a division between 'conservatives' and the mafia of the black market. The conservatives are not the old traditionalists, supporters of the Stalinist system, but new property-owners anxious to protect their gains from speculators and parasites 'eating their way through' the country's resources, as Kagarlitsky describes them (Kagarlitsky, 1994). Press reports speak of $20 billion every year being exported to Swiss banks and similar hideouts by 'legal means', but Kagarlitsky calls this the 'tip of the iceberg'. Since the conservatives, who need Yeltsin's presidential powers and control over the police and the army, have no entrepreneurial skills and the mafia use theirs for their own enrichment, the result is economic collapse.

Factories which were once producing goods at high levels of technology have been closing down. Locally produced industrial goods have disappeared from the shops. The public services of transport, heating, lighting and sewerage are collapsing. In the winter of 1993, there were outbreaks of diphtheria and even of cholera. Living standards have declined to the level of the 1950s, shortly after the war's end. The value of the rouble has sunk to practically nothing and the only currencies that can buy anything are dollars or deutschmarks. Moscow and St Petersburg begin to look like African capitals – Americans and Germans standing outside smart restaurants and hotels, while the markets are half empty and the streets are full of beggars, muggers and wideboys. It is a catastrophe on a colossal scale.

Revolution from Above

It is important to ask why the Gorbachev model did not work. Two main explanations are offered, each reinforcing the other. The first is that the Soviet bureaucracy resisted every change that would diminish their power; the second, that running down the military industrial complex and converting it to meeting civilian needs proved much more difficult than had been expected. The central bureaucracy had the support of the managers of most of industry. It became clear that it was much less risky for managers to go on contracting for orders from central government than to go out into the market and look for supplies and markets. To begin with, all high-tech supplies were in the hands of the military industrial complex. Industry had become so concentrated even outside the defence suppliers that there was often only one combine responsible for the total Soviet production. Sewing-machines were an example. Small firms could not even get started since they had no access to supplies, not even to spare parts for maintenance, except by bribery and corrupt practices.

At the same time, as Gorbachev was to concede, this was revolution from above, from the leaders of the Communist Party. Most factory workers and farmers were apathetic. They were not being involved in the changes and could only see the old apparatchiks benefiting from the loosening-up of controls. I worked for a time with Aganbegyan on the economic editing of the translation of his book, *The Challenge*, and I asked him where he saw the revolutionary forces coming from that would make the changes he envisaged. His answer was that change would come from the young and well-educated technical workers throughout industry and government. They were fed up with the old gang and ready for radical change. Why could they not make it, then? The answer must be that the young and well-educated workers either held on to their jobs with the factory managements or plumped wholeheartedly for the market. They had no organization except the Communist Party. Many were disillusioned with that and some regarded the Communist leaders as the enemy against which they were fighting. According to Simon Clarke, this was particularly true of the miners, who saw themselves as being engaged in a class war, albeit for their high differential wages (Clarke and Fairbrother, 1993).

None the less, the outlawing of the Communist Party was a fatal move for any chance of a revolution from above. As well as the time-servers, there were many thousands, if not millions, of honest members who were committed to radical reform; and without the party, Gorbachev lost his power base. He was not even an elected president. Yeltsin was – but of Russia. Therein lay the final explanation for Gorbachev's failure. He failed to hold together the old Soviet Union, even as a commonwealth of independent states. There was probably nothing that could be done by 1989 to maintain Russia's empire. That is how non-Russians and Russians alike perceived it. Lenin's principle of independence for all nations that wished it was never upheld, even by Lenin. Russian hegemony – in laws and language and ruling officials – had for seventy years been so overpowering that the harm could not be undone, short of a complete breakaway from the hegemonic state. For Russians the end of empire was the final blow, for which Gorbachev was given the blame and which Zhirinovsky could so easily recall in the ultra-nationalist appeal of his speeches.

This is the politics of *perestroika*, but was the economic model workable? Aganbegyan wrote of working collectives in enterprises responding to economic signals. Sometimes, he just said that enterprises will respond to such signals – that is, in place of the command economy, implying that the management would respond. But what kind of working collective did he have in mind? Workers' cooperatives have a lamentable record of failure, except in very small-scale enterprises. Yet productive efficiency, to generate and accumulate funds for new investment, was quite properly at the very heart of *perestroika*. Under capitalism, an individual owner strives for efficiency to ensure a return on his capital stake. Managers of joint stock companies are encouraged by the offer of bonuses for profitability and threatened with take-over in the event of a falling share price for their company on the stock market. The enterprise manager in a command economy had to carry out orders or find himself in Siberia. When this ceased, what incentive was being offered to the collective enterprise managers under the Aganbegyan scheme of self-management? This was certainly never made clear to the previous Soviet managers; most of them naturally voted to stay with the old system and when that was destroyed by privatization, to make their own way by purloining state resources or operating on the black market.

The economic signals which Gorbachev attempted to put in the place of total planning implied not only that the state fixed norms, but that movements of prices reflected supply and demand. Any diversion from market forces would require taxes and subsidies as sticks and carrots for management to respond to. But it was not established how the old structure of taxes and subsidies was to be changed and what part workers' representatives would have in such decision-making. In such a vacuum a dual economy, part market, part command, emerged. But it soon became obvious to all that the market could not be left unregulated, as sums of money began pouring out of the countries of the old Soviet Union into Swiss bank accounts wherever managers or ministry officials could get hold of saleable resources. Eastern Europe had more experience of market regulation, but it too had not been successful. We need to ask, why?

East European Models: Market Socialism?

The East European satellites had begun to declare their independence even before the Soviet Union broke up. At the end of 1989

Gorbachev had agreed to the withdrawal of all Soviet forces by 1991. In a largely peaceful revolution, except in Romania, elections were held throughout 1990 and new governments were formed, replacing over forty years of one-party Communist rule, and by the end of the year the unification of Germany took place.

All the East European countries had adopted, first, the centralized command model of the Soviet Union and later, after terrible upheavals in Poland and Hungary in 1956, some elements of the more decentralized Liberman model. None succeeded, even after the brief Prague Spring of 1968 and the Solidarity advances in Poland of 1980–81, in establishing political democratization that could have involved both workers and consumers in participation in the crucial decisions about resource allocation. Not that Solidarity's initial demands arose from a strongly felt lack of workers' participation. They arose directly from the failure of Premier Gierek's promise to 'rule well'. This had not been an empty boast; it had implied that Communist rule would guarantee full employment, rising living standards in terms of goods and social services, and all without price inflation or speed-up at the work-place. These were gains for workers that capitalist models had never guaranteed. The promise worked for a time and greatly impressed Western visitors; but, when the model failed in Poland in 1970 from falling productivity of old plants and again in 1980 from excessive investment and growing debts to the West for new plants purchased there, Polish workers turned to trade unionism to defend what they regarded as their social and economic rights. Only when their economic demands – more meat and a five-day week – were rejected, was the political issue raised of either socialist participation in planning production and distribution or a return to the market to allocate resources by the purse.

Some East European Communist rulers have done better in at least involving more party members in upward mobility and participation; some like Hungary had re-established the role of the market. (See MacDonald, 1983.) Hungary moved furthest back towards the market model, with small capitalist enterprise freed to employ labour in industry, agriculture and commerce. The advantage lay in the decentralization of decision-making, but the large enterprises were integrated into joint production with Soviet and Comecon enterprises; and there were many 'Buy Back' agreements with Western capitalist corporations. The world capitalist system was increasingly incorporating socialist as well as capitalist enterprise. The pressures of cost-saving and Marx's law of value operated on both. Enterprises could not survive in world competition under regimes of subsidy and state support. What Janos Kornai called 'soft budgeting' gave managers and their workers complete autonomy without responsibility since there was no real market competition. Political and economic criteria became quite hopelessly confused (Kornai, 1990).

It might seem that in Eastern Europe the Soviet model was increasingly converging towards the capitalist market model, with monopoly on an international scale. Giant enterprises in the East as in the West bargained with their national governments to protect and support their worldwide investment policies, and the limitations on each were the financial controls of their banking associates seeking to coordinate their individual initiatives. But this would be a false conclusion. The Soviet model was only a market model in that most goods were produced for sale and wages were paid for labour power. It was still primarily a command economy. There was no room for private enterprise in the Soviet economy.

The decentralization that emerged in Eastern Europe, and especially in Hungary, consisted of a kind of dual economy: a command economy and a tolerated private, grey or even black, economy of people seeking to escape from the ever-present tutelage, the very 'visible hand' of the bureaucracy. In industrial production managers sought to avoid the dangers of failing to fulfil the plan by hoarding labour and raw materials and eschewing the risks of innovation. In agriculture production on private plots was permitted, and even encouraged, so that there was food to buy in the markets. In these ways the alternatives of rationing by the purse or the queue for all but basic rations were avoided, but with goods under the counter and special shops for the privileged (Haraszti, 1977).

A perceptive Hungarian economist, Laszlo Andor, described the disintegration of Eastern Europe in the early 1990s in terms of 'an attempted leap from the utopia of advanced socialism to the utopia of the free market' (Andor, 1994). Economic realities destroyed both. Karl Kautsky, the Austrian Marxist writing with remarkable prescience in 1930 about the unavoidable disintegration of the Soviet Union, warned:

> If the Soviet state collapses, it will be the most urgent task of its successors to provide for the undisturbed continuity of production, the more so the more pitiable the economic conditions which they find. One can as little transform nationalized production into capitalist production at one blow without incurring danger, as vice versa. (Kautsky, 1930, quoted in Wollen, 1993)

This prediction was only too tragically realized in the Soviet Union, as we have seen; but in Eastern Europe, even before the Soviet collapse and the break-up of the economic links with Soviet industry through Comecon, there had been some experience of combining plan and market in what came to be called 'market socialism'. After the initial enthusiasm for the 'free' market and the gospel according to Von Hayek as preached by the IMF, the Eastern European elites – mostly ex-communists – rediscovered the role of the state. They had to; they had a triple crisis on their hands. The crisis in Eastern Europe consisted not only in the failure of the Soviet connection and the arbitrary, inefficient and corrupt rule of Communist governments. The Eastern European economies had for some time suffered also from two connected economic problems – the backwardness of their industrial plant and the result of trying to correct this by importing machinery from the West.

All the East European countries were heavily in debt as a result of borrowing from Western banks in the early 1980s. They had been caught, like other developing countries, by the scissors of falling prices of their raw-material exports and the rising prices of imported oil and machinery and rising rates of interest. The Soviet Union's terms of trade had not been affected in the same way because of the strength of Soviet oil exports, until oil prices fell; and foreign trade was a much smaller element in the Soviet economy than it was among East European countries. For them the drain of debt payments drew off a quarter to a third of their export earnings. Only Romania under Ceaucescu's regime carried out the IMF prescriptions to the letter by exporting everything the country produced to pay off the debt, leaving the population in a state of total destitution. In the USSR and Eastern European economies, according to UN statistics, even excluding Romania and Bulgaria, levels of productivity fell from about 80 per cent of those in West Germany in the 1950s to about 50 per cent in the 1980s. The proportion of fixed assets in industry which were under five years old declined from around 40 per cent to under 25 per cent between 1975 and 1988. In the Soviet Union the drop was from 45 per cent to 36 per cent.

The hope of the new post-Communist governments in the early 1990s was that foreign investment would come to the rescue of their ailing economies, and in the meantime the way could be cleared by state intervention in the market. The number of registrations of foreign investment grew very large, a cumulative 60,000 by the end of 1992 in the ex-Soviet Union and Eastern Europe as a whole. The actual capital invested was, however, still relatively small, some $14 billion, half of this in the former USSR. This figure spread over several years can be compared with total foreign direct investment flows from all countries in just one year, 1992, of $150 billion (figures from UNCTAD, 1993). Injections of capital were of no value if they were simply salted away in Swiss bank accounts. Foreign investors soon learnt that they had to be extremely selective, choosing to invest only in those resources which had worldwide potential and those regions where laws were enforced. A gap soon opened up between what came to be called the Latin Americanized countries – Slovenia, Poland, Croatia, the Czech republic and Hungary – where Western capital retained an interest, and the rest, which included Russia and most of the old Soviet Union, apart from the areas with rich mineral deposits.

Transformation Paths

Hugo Radice, the Leeds University economist who has been following the changes in Eastern Europe, has identified three possible transformation paths. None is yet to be found in its pure form, nor could they develop as such. All will have to adapt to the changing features and movements of global capitalism (Radice, 1993).

The first path is the neo-liberal path: opening up the whole economy to market forces, including currency convertibility, privatization of state industries and a generous welcome to foreign capital to work with local capital, facilitated rather than regulated by the state. This could hardly be called any kind of socialism, not even market socialism, and would probably require only a minimum welfare safety net, but strong curbs on the bandits' peculations and on the workers' rights.

The second path is the protectionist path, where a substantial state sector is retained for a considerable period into the future in close alliance with local capital. Foreign investment is limited, and selected local industries are protected by tariffs on imports and subsidies on exports until they can stand on their own in world markets. This again is hardly even market socialism but rather state-guided capitalism, such as has been working successfully in East Asia.

The third path can more truly be described as market socialism. Radice calls it the state-development path. A clear plan is mapped out for the future in which the state identifies and promotes sectoral objectives in production and trade which accord with the country's comparative advantages. The aim is a continuous upgrading of the level of technology. The choice of public or private, local or foreign capital is decided on pragmatic grounds. State expenditure on education, health and welfare is viewed as an input into dynamic expansion in the world market, not just a product of economic growth. There is little sign of such a path being followed in Eastern Europe, but it can be clearly seen in China.

We shall see how market socialism is working when we study the Chinese model, but we have warnings from Kornai in Hungary after 1968 (Kornai, 1990) and from the studies of Brus and Laski in Poland that market socialism requires a restructuring of economic institutions, in particular the devising of provisions to sustain the system with clear 'incentives' (for profit maximizing) and 'agencies' (for relating the state and the enterprises) (Brus and Laski, 1989). It requires even more all the state regulations and built-in controls that have been developed over the years in capitalist countries to prevent the worst abuses of the free market.

These several possible growth paths may be realistic scenarios, but they are very different from Marx's model of socialism. So were the command economies of the Soviet Union and the East European satellites. Writing in 1983, it was possible to foresee what was to come. This is how the original chapter on 'The Soviet Model' ended and I repeat my words verbatim:

> The links between lower-level and upper-level economic and political decisions have never been forged. Politico-economic organs have been aborted. Social provision has been checked. Workers' control has been lost in the bureaucracy of appointed managers and in the hierarchy of party and unions. The grass-roots initiatives of workers and citizens have been forgotten and only an explosion like that of Poland's Solidarity has revealed what has been seething below the surface – and what must break out once the state fails to deliver the promise upon which a political consensus has been built (MacDonald, 1983).
>
> These are harsh judgements, but the evidence is inescapable, in the growing dependence of the Soviet Union and of Eastern Europe on Western capital, technology and grain supplies, even more in the attempt to emulate capitalist production, 'catching up with the West', and not building a new society. It may be argued, as Nove (1983) argued, that there is no way of replacing the market except by the most arbitrary and inefficient central decisions over the allocation of several million products at any time. But the sheer number of permutations and combinations does not seem to be an adequate reason for not seeking an alternative to central commands if there were not advantages for the ruling elite in keeping things as they are. Here the major problem is that top priority tends always to be given to defence requirements, so that the military become the elite of elites.

We can now see that the prediction was correct. The arms race was fatal for the Soviet Union both by its call upon resources and by its perpetuation of a regime of violence. The model of a command economy is well suited to fighting a war, but the cold war between the USA and the USSR had to be fought not in the field but in the hearts and minds and bellies of the people. When it came to the crunch the Soviet Union, after only eighty years of industrialization, punctuated by two massive armed invasions, did not have the resources or the freedoms to compete with a United States that had been industrializing for 200 years and had never been ruled by terror and had never been invaded. The system of extensive development, moreover, failed to generate increased productivity or to conserve resources and protect the environment. The socialist attempt failed in the Soviet Union. We need to look at alternative attempts, and first of all at China.

FURTHER READING

AGANBEGYAN, ABEL, *The Challenge: The Economics of Perestroika*, Hutchinson, 1988

AMANN, R., *et al.*, *The Technological Level of Soviet Industry*, Yale University Press, 1977, 1981 rev.

ANDOR, LASZLO, 'Disintegration in Eastern Europe', in Carlos Berzosa (ed.), *La Economia Mundial en los 90*, Icaria, Barcelona, 1994

BAHRO, RUDOLF, *The Alternative in Eastern Europe*, New Left Books, 1979

BARRATT BROWN, MICHAEL, *What Economics is About*, Weidenfeld & Nicolson, 1970

BRAVERMAN, HARRY, *Monopoly Capital: The Degradation of Labour in the Twentieth Century*, Monthly Review Press, 1974

BRUS, W., and LASKI, K., *From Marx to Market: Socialism in Search of an Economic System*, Oxford, 1989

BUKHARIN, N. I., 'The Road to Socialism and the Worker Peasant Alliance' (1925), in R. B. Day (ed.), *N. I. Bukharin: Selected Writings*, Spokesman, 1982, pp. 209–94

CARR, E. H., *The Russian Revolution: From Lenin to Stalin*, Macmillan, 1979

CLARKE, SIMON, and FAIRBROTHER, PETER, 'The Workers' Movement in Russia', *Capital and Class*, No. 49, Spring 1993

COCKSHOTT, PAUL, and COTTRELL, ALLIN, *Towards a New Socialism*, Spokesman, 1993

DEUTSCHER, I., 'The Tragedy of the Polish Communist Party', in Martin Eve and Dave Musson (eds.), *The Socialist Register 1982*, Merlin Press, pp. 125–62

DOBB, M. H., *Socialist Planning: Some Problems*, Lawrence & Wishart, 1978

ELLMAN, M., *Socialist Planning*, Cambridge University Press, 1979

GORBACHEV, MIKHAIL, *Perestroika*, Collins, 1987

HARASZTI, MIKLOS, *A Worker in a Worker's State*, Penguin Books, 1977

KAGARLITSKY, BORIS, *Russia from Crisis to Catastrophe*, Labour Chronicle Russian Radio Show, 1994, available from Paul Cockshott, University of Strathclyde

KAUTSKY, KARL, *Bolshevism at a Deadlock*, 1930

KORNAI, J., *The Road to a Free Economy*, Norton, 1990

LEWIN, MOSHE, 'Society and the Stalin State', *Social History* (Hull), 1976

MACDONALD, OLIVER, 'The Polish Vortex: Solidarity and Socialism', *New Left Review*, No. 139, May–June 1983, pp. 5–48

MEDVEDEV, ROY, *Let History Judge*, Spokesman, 1976

MEDVEDEV, ROY, *Leninism and Western Socialism*, Verso, 1981

MEDVEDEV, ROY, *Khrushchev*, Blackwell, 1982

MEDVEDEV, ZHORES, *A History of Soviet Agriculture*, Macmillan, 1988

MOLYNEUX, MAXINE, 'Women in Socialist Societies', in Kate Young *et al.* (eds.), *Of Marriage and the Market: Women's Subordination in International Perspective*, Conference of Socialist Economists, 1981, pp. 167–202

NOVE, ALEC, *The Economics of Feasible Socialism*, Allen & Unwin, 1983

NUTI, D. M., 'The Contradictions of Socialist Economics: a Marxian Interpretation', in Ralph Miliband and John Saville (eds.), *The Socialist Register 1979*, Merlin Press, pp. 228–73

RADICE, HUGO, *Global Integration, National Disintegration?*, University of Leeds, School of Business and Economic Studies, 1993

SHANIN, TEODOR, *The Late Marx and the Russian Road*, Routledge, 1983

SIRIANNI, CARMEN, *Workers' Control and Socialist Democracy: The Soviet Experience*, Verso, 1982

TROTSKY, LEON, *The Revolution Betrayed*, 1930

UNCTAD, *World Investment Report*, United Nations, 1993

WITTFOGEL, K., *Oriental Despotism*, Yale University Press, 1957

WOLLEN, PETER, 'Our Post-Communism: The Legacy of Karl Kautsky', *New Left Review*, No. 202, November–December 1993

14 THE CHINESE MODEL

The origins of revolutionary societies are crucial to their specific development. We saw this in looking at the Soviet model that emerged from old Russia. The model that emerged from the Chinese Revolution was perhaps even more specifically Chinese. China was certainly one of the Asiatic societies as Marx defined them. The central authority of the emperor and his agents had been required both to manage the irrigation systems of the great rivers and the canals that connected them and to defend the Chinese people from nomadic invaders to the north. Many times in the more than two thousand years of Chinese history when central power was challenged by provincial war-lords, and the emperor's agents became local landowners, a new Mongol invasion from the north re-established this vast country's unity under centralized bureaucratic rule. In describing our own top civil servants as mandarins we recognize their Chinese prototypes. In China, the size of territory is smaller than in Russia but the number of people is even greater; the centralizing tendency was that much stronger.

China's National Liberation Struggle against Japan

In China, as in Russia also, the building of a socialist society was attempted upon a very small industrial base amidst a vast, largely illiterate and oppressed peasantry. In China as in Russia the first Communist revolutionaries nevertheless saw the tiny working class as the active force in making the revolution, accepted the party as its conscious vanguard and followed Lenin after 1917 and subsequently Stalin as leader. But one great difference separated the experience of the two countries. The victory of the Chinese Revolution followed only after eighteen years of national liberation struggle against the Japanese occupation and civil war. By contrast the Russian Revolution itself preceded three years of resistance and civil war, and many years of struggle with the kulaks.

What was most important for the Chinese Communists during their years of struggle was that a whole area of liberated territory in Yenan was maintained against the Japanese. In this territory it was possible for democratic political *and* economic forms of socialist life to be established although the territory was surrounded by an imperialist sea. Above all it was possible as the territory was expanded for peasants to be involved in struggle against the rich landlords and in developing new ways of cooperative farming. It was at this time, in the 1930s and 1940s, that the egalitarian practices were developed – of involving the leaders in manual work, of avoiding differences in rank and dress, of including women in the armed forces, of training an army that was not only drawn from the people but committed to the emancipation of the people. This revolution is faithfully described in William Hinton's book *Fanshen: A Documentary of Revolution in a Chinese Village*.

It is sometimes implied by writers on the Chinese model that the differences from the Soviet model arose because Mao chose to build socialism on a peasant and not an industrial proletarian base, that the Long March of the Red Army from Kiangsi in the south-east to Yenan in the north-west in 1934 was a deliberate abandonment of an industrial for an agricultural model. There is some truth in this, but Mao's Peasant and Workers' Army, organized in Hunan and established in Kiangsi in 1931, drew recruits not only from the peasants but from the miners of Hangyang and from intellectuals and workers among the insurrectionary troops of the Kuomintang (KMT).

Chiang Kai-shek, the KMT leader, had abandoned the original aims of Sun Yat-sen, the founder of the KMT and first President of China, and had turned on the communists in Shanghai in 1927. Instead of repelling the Japanese, he launched successive extermination campaigns against the communists; however, not only Sun Yat-sen's widow but the 'Young Marshal' Chang and other Chinese officers joined Mao. The crucial importance of Mao's 6,000-

mile Long March was that, though only 20,000 of the original 300,000 survived it, the Red Army had passed through provinces containing 200 million people, spreading militant propaganda, taxing the rich, reducing rents, expropriating the big landlords, and putting up the only resistance to the Japanese that was to be found throughout China. The anti-fascist struggle became also a class struggle, inevitably, because the big landlords and merchant capitalists trading with the West (compradors) were collaborators with the Japanese.

The model that emerged with the establishment in 1949 of the People's Republic of China was designed to carry the new-democratic class coalition that Mao had forged of peasants, workers, intellectuals, small capitalists and national capitalists (as opposed to the compradors) into the building of the socialist stage of the Chinese Revolution. It was designed to do what Lenin and Bukharin had believed could be done – to establish slowly but surely the dominance of the new islands of socialism in a mixed economy by strengthening the state industrial sector and the cooperative farms in agriculture. For some years the peasantry in southern China had still to settle accounts with their landlords and expropriate their property. For some years small business-men and traders were encouraged to develop their economic activities as in Lenin's New Economic Policy. But everyone soon knew that the struggle was launched in every aspect of Chinese life between the 'capitalist road' and the 'socialist road'.

The economic model in this mixed economy thus combined state enterprises in industry with a huge private industrial and agricultural sector of small owners. It functioned within a central planning authority that managed foreign trade, controlled all banking and finance, intervened in the regulation of wages and prices and directed accumulation mainly from agricultural produc-tion into new investment in basic heavy industry. The model worked: output increased in industry and agriculture; but it moved further and further towards the Soviet type of command economy, towards centralized decision-making and away from the decentral-ized political-economic organs which had grown up in the liber-ated areas. One must not exaggerate; some bureaucratization had already begun during the Yenan period. Moreover, one must recognize that the encouragement of a national bourgeoisie inevitably discouraged the political development of many industrial workers in the towns and cities, as with the NEP in the Soviet Union.

China's Break with the Soviet Model

Until Stalin's death in 1953, and for some years after that, Mao had presented himself publicly as Stalin's disciple. Khrushchev's denunciation of Mao in 1956 only confirmed Mao's apparent allegiance. Far from liberalizing, Mao strengthened the state's control. The role of the private sector was rapidly reduced from more than 50 per cent of industrial output in 1950 to less than 25 per cent in 1954 and almost nil in 1956. 'The people's democratic dictatorship became in essence', in Premier Liu Shao-chi's words, 'a form of dictatorship of the proletariat.' The central bureaucracy was strengthened along with the central power of the party. The cadres would act from now on as substitutes for the peasantry and the workers in making revolutionary change. Mao appeared to be siding with the apparatchiks with their close links to Moscow and belief in dependence on Soviet plant and technology for China's industrialization. Yet already in Mao's speeches in 1956, encouraging the blooming of the 'Hundred Flowers' and on 'The Ten Great Relationships', Mao was prefiguring a model for building socialism distinct from that of the Soviet Union. By 1958 he was promoting the 'Great Leap Forward', through small-scale industry, creative initiative at the grass roots and the establishment of communes in the countryside.

Because the 'Great Leap Forward' was absurdly over-ambitious and industrial output failed to grow much beyond the recovery levels of 1956, it has become accepted practice to laugh at Mao's 'backyard' iron and steel furnaces. Yet there can be no doubt that this experience, however limited, of industrial production actually *in* the countryside gave to the peasantry a confidence and understanding of the value of industrial development for them – in producing agricultural tools and equipment – that no similar development of industry in the towns and coastal areas could have equalled.

The break between China and the Soviet Union did not come finally until 1963 but it began with the appearance of two articles in April 1956 in the *People's Daily* on 'The Historical Experience of the Dictatorship of the Proletariat'. These warned clearly of the dangers of 'one-sidedly developing heavy industry without paying attention to the people's livelihood' – the mistake of 'some socialist countries', it said, which 'we have not committed'. The articles equally strongly warned against expropriating the factories' accumulation funds and taxing the peasants' surplus output without involving either workers or peasants in the decisions. (Quoted in Schram, 1974.) Between 1959 and 1962 Mao's speeches to the Chinese Communist Party and cadres increasingly involved open criticism of the 'Soviet revisionists' and determination to build a socialism distinct from that of the Soviet Union.

But Mao pulled back from the opening-up of free thought created by the 'Hundred Flowers' speech and thousands of intellectuals who had taken the opportunity to speak out were caught in the clamp-down that followed. It was almost as if the invitation had been a provocation. Over half a million men and women, mostly intellectuals, were declared to be 'rightists' and permanently silenced. It illustrates Mao's oscillation between positively imperial encouragement of the cult of personality, utopian expectations about what could be done in his own lifetime and a hard-headed understanding of the slow-moving doggedness of the Chinese peasantry.

Fortunately, the main emphasis of the alternative Chinese model on locating small-scale industry as well as agriculture in the countryside and on creative initiative at the grass roots was that it should develop popular power and combat bureaucracy at the centre. In his more cautious moments, Mao said that he was not worried if the building of socialism took a hundred years and not the fifteen years of which he had once spoken. If the process involved the full participation of the masses it would be done well. If not, it was worthless; and he still believed that 'light industry and agriculture can provide the greater and faster accumulation' in the end. The seeds of these thoughts are all to be found in his speech of April 1956 on 'The Ten Great Relationships'. It was a complete reversal of the Soviet model and not surprisingly implied Mao's challenge first to Liu Shao-chi and then to Lin Piao, who respectively represented the bureaucracy and the army and who, although chosen successors to Mao, stood for a return to the centralist, bureaucratic, party-dominated model that they had learnt from the Soviet Union.

The Cultural Revolution

In the decade between 1956 and 1966 it was, however, far from certain that Mao's thoughts would prevail or that Mao's own relationship to the bureaucracy and the army would leave much room for developing the power of the people. The Cultural Revolution, starting in 1966 and continuing for the whole of the next decade, was not as is generally supposed begun as Mao's reply to the bureaucrats. It is well understood that Mao supported the Red Guards, the young cultural revolutionaries, with Lin Piao's aid from 1968 to 1971; but he depended on the army to control the effects of his fomenting of endless struggle throughout the years of the Cultural Revolution. When Mao called on the youth of China to 'bombard the headquarters' and challenge the bureaucracy, he was seizing the initiative to put himself at the head of a movement that was already getting out of hand. The dissident leader Wei Jing-sheng has written to explain that it is wrong to refer to the Cultural Revolution

> as having started from the encouragement [from above] of Red Guards to rebel. I joined the Red Guards [he says of April 1966]. I know exactly why they rebelled – not because Mao encouraged them, but because they were indignant at seeing all the inequalities and irregularities in society and in school. That Mao later used them by giving them full support so as to achieve his personal aims is another story. (Quoted in Benton, 1980.)

What Mao, nevertheless, supported and encouraged was a movement which attempted, albeit in a Utopian fashion, to leap forward into a society where the divisions between mental and manual work, between town and countryside, between industry and agriculture, could be overcome and ended through class struggle and challenge to the bureaucratic elite. Thus, the bureaucrats and intellectuals were sent to labour in the countryside; peasants and workers were directed to universities; and, most significant of all, the communes were established and developed as economic and political organs combining both agricultural and industrial work. The word 'Utopian' is used, as Marx and Engels used it, to imply that such ideas did not yet have a real basis in advanced productive forces for their realization. The establishment of the communes was, none the less, a major achievement of the Cultural Revolution. It is clear that what developed in the countryside between 1966 and 1976 was a politico-economic model which enjoyed a certain immunity from the endless struggles at the centre. I can personally vouch for the statement in 1977 of a group of builders of the Red Canal, which now irrigates a large district in Shansi Province, that they had not taken any notice of changing instructions from Peking over the years.

The Communes

The nature of the Chinese commune has been widely misunderstood. It was not meant to imply some kind of communal living – though some kitchens were communal, the Chinese family remained the basic cell of Chinese society as much as ever, greatly to the regret of some Western feminists. The commune idea was not meant to imply that all communes had reached a stage where there was no private property and where the village teams and the brigades from several villages which formed one commune received goods and services *according to their needs* from the funds realized by the work of the whole commune. That would only have been true of the most advanced types of commune, which were often the least successful, having leapt precipitately without peasant consent from private to collective ownership. What follows describes how most communes looked in 1977.

The commune was first of all an organ of political government, a local authority for between 20,000 and 30,000 people. There were about 30,000 such communes in China, with responsibility for housing, education, health, local roads, water and drainage and many other environmental services. At the same time the commune was a self-governing collective, an economic organ responsible for the agricultural production of the villagers and for local industrial activities that did not, like major fertilizer plants, coal mines, sugar factories or refineries, come under the control of higher county, provincial or national authorities. In most communes the income might be earned by individuals or households but more generally by village teams which organized their own work and were paid according to a points system that related working capacity and work done.

This basic points system could be supplemented by production of handicrafts and of vegetables, chickens, etc. from small private plots, some of which produce could be sold in local markets. Village teams could also earn income by working on the 'mass line' on large-scale irrigation, road and rail schemes. In the more advanced communes not only household but team incomes were pooled in the brigade income. Out of household or production-team or brigade income the cost of purchases of seed and tools and the hire of equipment and other services like grain milling or fertilizer, bought from the commune, had to be paid for together with basic rations of grain, fats, sugar, cotton and fuel and house rent where villagers did not own their own houses. What income remained after such basic expenditures was available for some personal spending but mainly for social spending, and for accumulation for new investment by the commune. This was subject to a small land tax and to the requirement of sales of food to the state at fixed prices.

The investment decisions of the commune were accountable to popular control, which allowed for considerable variation in the services provided for health, education, housing and investment in agricultural or industrial development. The national prices set by the state for agricultural produce and for agricultural inputs – farm machinery, fertilizers, irrigation pumps, etc. – or in the service sector for books or medical equipment, determined the relative resources available for town and countryside. The aim was to provide an incentive for agricultural workers to raise the level of their productivity in order to increase the margin of profit in their activities from which extra social provision could be made. Private spending was discouraged. Egalitarianism was celebrated, especially in areas where the Cultural Revolution established its greatest influence. One of the essential strengths of the commune was that it promoted small-scale, light industry as well as agricultural production, so that villagers could see with their own eyes where at least some of the accumulation from their surplus production was going.

The Chinese communes thus provided a strongly decentralized model of political economy within a centralized command system of resource allocation by price-fixing and overall investment policy. The links in the model between decision-making at the commune level and those at county, province and national level were assured by the Chinese application of the principle of democratic centralism. There were no competing parties; all authorities at every level of government – in the countryside, towns and cities – were elected democratically from below, but subject to the regulation of the next higher authority. Indirect election of delegates from the lowest up to the highest level was the universal practice. The result was an extremely effective upwards and downwards line of communication of economic information and of political instruction, while it left the top with overall power.

The communes, however, as they developed posed a serious challenge to the party and state bureaucracy, and reasons would have been found by China's leaders for their dissolution, if they had been more successful in meeting China's urgent need for food for a rapidly rising population. As it was they could simply be branded as a failure since food production actually fell.

The weakness of the communes, which made them into what we called Utopian forms of organization, lay in the underdeveloped forces of production to support social provision of the kind we have described. In the countryside this showed itself in the communes in the proliferation of cadres – not only officials but health workers, teachers, creative workers – on an inadequate base of productive workers. It also implied slow growth in food production – too slow to meet the rapidly expanding population. This was for two reasons. First, egalitarianism meant that households and teams that were go-ahead or endowed with better land gained no advantage, as a result of the pooling of resources, and had no incentive to raise productivity. Secondly, Mao's embracing of the Dazhai model, when he called on all villages to learn from Dazhai Brigade in Xiyang county, not only elevated purely physical effort above skill, but encouraged the development of the poorest areas and not the richer lands. Khrushchev in the Soviet Union had also believed in extending agriculture by opening up virgin land in Siberia rather than intensifying production on the best lands. In both cases the results were disastrous.

The weaknesses in industry that resulted from the Cultural Revolution were even more serious. 'Better a socialist train than one that runs on time' sounds an attractive slogan where time does not matter much and improved efficiency is not crucial for economic development. So does the 'iron rice bowl' with its guarantee of jobs for life for regular workers in state enterprises, but it did little or nothing to encourage innovation or to raise productivity. The replacement of both management and trade unions by revolutionary committees brought forward new cadres and challenged bureaucracy, but the general disparagement of experts and of efficiency was counter-productive. Industrial output and foreign trade stagnated, although large construction projects of railways, shelter belts, canals and irrigation works continued. Fear of enemy attacks led Mao to establish industries, especially for arms production, in the interior of the country and far from the centres of population and communications. They became costly white elephants.

The Chinese came to refer to the years of the Cultural Revolution as 'ten wasted years', but this seems to those who visited China in those years like Professor Joan Robinson of Cambridge to be far too strong a reaction, and to neglect important advances in small-scale and intermediate technology at commune level that retained some humanity in the productive process and served to increase production even if productivity failed to rise. It also underestimates the importance of the Cultural Revolution criticism of an elite of full-time workers who were trade-union or political leaders with salaries and privileges far beyond those of the mass of unorganized part-time workers in industry and commerce.

The disparagement and even persecution of experts was, however, particularly serious in science and technology. Here the criticism of elitism had some justification but, when places in universities and technical colleges were filled with workers and peasants who had little or no prior education, this meant that they were able to benefit little from the courses, and advanced studies almost disappeared. At the same time, sending the professors with the bureaucrats to do manual work in the villages was a good corrective of their mandarin attitudes (the mandarins of old China wore their fingernails long to show that they did no manual work); but as a permanent measure it was wasteful of their knowledge and stifled all dissenting criticism.

The best result of the Cultural Revolution was probably that tens of thousands of current students were dispersed all over the countryside either with the Red Guards or at their summons. In this way they learnt not only to do manual work but to know something of China outside the big cities. It is they without doubt who created a tradition of protest from the Cultural Revolution that was irreversible. Their return either into intellectual work or often into factory work, so as to find employment, at least of some sort, in the cities, provided a whole movement of Chinese dissidents that was to become something approaching a real opposition. At least, Mao and the Gang of Four did not kill off most of their opponents as Stalin did. For, the new leaders of China after Mao grouped around Premier Deng Xiao-ping were survivors from the more bureaucratic Communist leadership of the 1950s.

China after Mao

The situation in China described so far is how it appeared to a visitor from outside ten years ago. What happened after Mao's death and the overthrow of the 'Gang of Four' is now clear. During his last years Mao declined into a state of senility and

China was governed by the group that came to be called the 'Gang of Four'. This included Mao's wife, Chiang Ching, who acted in every way like a traditional Chinese empress. These four were uncompromising supporters of the view of the need for continuing class struggle in the Cultural Revolution; all opponents and critics were labelled class enemies and many were imprisoned and executed. The Gang's extreme democratic and egalitarian rhetoric did not prevent them from behaving personally in the most authoritarian and elitist manner. The result was a rising tide of criticism and contempt of authority, in which both the good and bad in the Cultural Revolution were equally rejected. Corruption became widespread. Officials fudged the statistics but output began to fall and food shortages appeared in many places.

After Mao's death criticism of this period consisted, first, of a simple attack on the persons – the Gang of Four; and this was in time extended, secondly, to a critique of the theory of continuing class struggle, especially in the Resolution of the Central Committee of the Communist Party of China of 27 June 1981. This left Mao's reputation intact as a 'great Marxist and great proletarian revolutionary' whose contribution 'far outweighed his mistakes'. Su Shaozhi, who was formerly the director of the highest Chinese party school, the Institute of Marxism-Leninism and Mao Zedong Thought in Beijing, has summed up the man:

> I think that Mao Zedong, in the end, could not free himself from peasant influence, and that he had always inwardly cherished the idea of conquering and ruling the country. With the prestige of the party, and of Mao Zedong personally, rising to unprecedented heights, and everyone heartily singing 'East is Red', he did not feel that the 'great saviour' was an unproletarian idea ... He began to think and act more and more like an absolute monarch. Mao Zedong had a description of himself: 'I am a man who defies laws human and divine.' He ignored the party and the state institutions and made all decisions by himself (Su Shaozhi, 1993, p. 55).

Mao's own personal self-aggrandisement only partially explains how Mao's new road to socialism failed to produce the economic development the country needed. Four answers can be given: the first must be the worship of the strong state ('big state; small society') and the elevation of state ownership as the highest form. Combined with the monopoly of power in the hands of a small group at the centre, this encouraged the resort to violence and the subordination of local initiatives to central dictation. The struggles that Mao encouraged, to be waged by country against town, by manual against non-manual, by poor peasantry against rich, by people against bureaucrats, the socialists against the capitalist roaders, descended at the end of the Cultural Revolution into senseless faction fighting, denunciations, imprisonment and even liquidation of opponents as in the Soviet Union.

The second cause of failure arose from the fact that the growth of population moved ahead of the growth of food production, allowing no margin for disasters. Mao's hope of establishing a slow rate of agricultural development proved unrealistic. Moral incentives to increase production through the sharing of income by teams (households) and brigades (villages) in the communes proved inadequate. The return to more individual material incentives was a natural development, although this was never openly argued in any forum of discussion but was imposed from above by bureaucratic edict.

The third cause of the Chinese model's failure was the breakdown in fraternal relations with the Soviet Union and the conviction among China's leaders that Soviet 'social imperialism' would lead to aggression across China's borders and require a huge diversion of resources into armaments and defence, including underground bunkers for all town populations. This analysis was again never openly argued, and the need to modernize was often expressed in terms of China's weakness in face of potential attack. The fourth problem was that the process of industrialization and urbanization, partly because it was widespread and not narrowly concentrated, led to a gross loss of an estimated 30 per cent of agricultural land. Even after allowing for the opening up of new (often poorer) land the net loss could be over 15 per cent. With less land to work on, machines must replace human beings to maintain and increase agricultural output.

The growth of the population – by 75 per cent in thirty-three years – meant not only more mouths to feed but a vast underemployed population as the children grew to adulthood. Small rural towns and low-technology industry were supposed to provide the solution, but some bigger cities with concentrations of skills and high technology were required for the modernization of industry, science, agriculture and defence that the Chinese embarked upon. As the cities grew, only a firm ban on travel could prevent the irruption of shanty towns like those in India and Latin America. The problem was described most vividly by Dr Richard Kirkby of the Architectural Association, who spent four years in China studying urbanization problems. He called it the problem of finding 300 million new jobs.

Already in the 1980s it did appear that the model of the economy we have been looking at had changed in certain important respects, while remaining quite unchanged in other ways. What was unchanged was the centralized control above all, in society over information and discussion, and in the economy over prices, credit and investment, not only for industry but also for agriculture, transport and services like health and education. Also unchanged at first was the restriction on renting land, hiring labour, speculation and private lending of money at interest. The Chinese economy became increasingly a market economy, but there was no 'Big Bang' as in Eastern Europe.

Vella Pillay, an economic adviser to the Bank of China over many years, has distinguished (in a personal communication) several stages in the reform of the original Maoist model. The first stage paved the way for what was to follow. From the state plan making use of the market economy at the beginning, by the end the market economy was making use of state planning. In the first stage, the following changes took place:

1. In industry, agriculture, education and health services, respect everywhere for the expert was restored and with it the emphasis on efficiency and skill rather than mass mobilization of sheer labour power.

2. Material incentives increasingly replaced moral incentives and social goals. This took place both in the spread of piece-work in industry and of differential income paid for household-team and brigade work in agriculture.

3. Basic units of production in industry and agriculture were granted much more freedom to buy and sell in the market within overall credit and investment policies operated by the state banks, and subject to central price-fixing which applied to basic materials, rationed goods and agricultural deliveries to the state. This was called the 'dual track' price system.

4. The central government deliberately granted aid to selected counties and enterprises which could be seen to be growth points for applying advanced technology in industry and agriculture. Such agricultural growth centres were near to major urban areas wherever local conditions were suitable, so that their needs were met.

5. Private ownership of the land was reaffirmed at each level – team, brigade and commune – and the communes were being deprived of their political administrative function so that they became what were called 'agro-industrial commercial companies', making family contracts with the peasants. The communes had powers of coordinating and stimulating economic activity and cooperation; but this had to depend on voluntary participation and not on administrative command. Even though the commune might have state funds for investment as a lever of control, the main levers were the market and the system of state prices.

6. Special enterprise zones were established to promote exports and to attract foreign investment. In time as many as fourteen coastal cities had been opened up for such foreign trade and investment. The state monopoly of foreign trade was ended.

The whole concept, then, of the politico-economic organ was modified, not only for the commune but also for the town or city district. Agriculture and industrial enterprise were separated from local popular control – agriculture returned more and more to private or cooperative ownership, industry to the state subject to trade-union and market influences. Behind this, Mao's insistence throughout the Cultural Revolution on the need for the continuation of class struggle was abandoned.

The opening up of the economy to market forces increasingly involved not only private ownership of the land but private ownership of capital. For a time in the mid 1980s it was still unclear whether different forms of ownership – private, cooperative, or state – would be combined in what was a predominantly socialist economy. In the event, the capitalist elements came to dominate. Critics of the whole reform process, like William Hinton (Hinton, 1991), believe that this was the intention of Deng Xiaoping and his associates all along. The received authority of Marx was preserved for the development of productive forces as a 'first stage of socialism'. The official argument of the Chinese leaders was that they were 'feeling out the stepping-stones in order to cross the river'. Socialism was still the goal, but the key question concerns democracy, what the students in Tiananmen Square called the 'Fifth Modernization' after Deng's 'Four Modernizations' – of industry, agriculture, technology and defence. Should it be 'after' or should it be 'before'?

Politics or Economics in Command?

The reform movement in Communist China, as in the Soviet Union and Eastern Europe, combined demands for both political and economic reform. Many of the reformers rejected the monopoly of power at the centre in the hands of the party, both in the state administration and in economic organization. As Mao had once said, 'Industry, agriculture, commerce, academy and military; east, west, south, north and central, all is under the leading role of the party.' Reform implied opening up the party's monopoly to political pluralism and freeing the economy from state controls for market forces to work. But the emphasis placed either on the political or the economic reforms varied, and equally the decision whether they should be attempted at the same time or with one preceding the other. Gorbachev chose political reform first and Eastern Europe followed suit. While Mao had always spoken of putting 'politics in command', the Chinese reformers who followed him chose to start with economic reforms.

The advisers from the industrialized countries have always recommended a combination of political and economic reform for developing countries, and this has been the advice of the international financial institutions – the IMF and the World Bank – in the structural adjustment programmes that they made a condition for financial aid, particularly in Africa. After the massacre in Tiananmen Square in 1989, the demand for political reform became a major issue between the United States and Chinese governments. But capitalist and socialist views of democracy are somewhat different. Capitalist democracy implies diffused political power for the people but narrowly limited economic power. Socialist democracy would have to imply both economic and political power for the people, as Chen Erjin and the Chinese Democracy Movement insisted (Chen Erjin, 1984). When the main agencies in the economy are under social ownership, the separation of powers between party and state must, they believe, be observed.

Where economic and political reforms have been attempted together within a capitalist framework, the results have disappointed the architects of reform. In most of Africa, the actual situation is that economic reforms of centralized state power have failed, but there has been success in political reform, in part – ironically – as a result of the economic failure. In Russia and Eastern Europe, there have been radical political changes but economic reform has progressed haltingly. There were none of the institutions and commercial agencies in place to make a market economy work. By contrast, in China a market economy has been established stage by stage as the agencies and institutions were established, but under an unreformed party and a continuing authoritarian state administration.

There were Chinese dissidents like Wei Jingsheng who put political reform before all else. But most of the political reformers like Su Shaozhi, whose student followers died in Tiananmen Square, wished to see political and economic reform running together – 'a real market economy and democratic political pluralism' (Su Shaozhi, 1993, p. 55). They were looking to reproduce in China, in place of authoritarian commands, the 'checks and balances of economic liberalism' which existed in capitalist economies, and without which they feared that the market would become anarchic. The fear was justified by the inflation and disruption that followed the exaggerated pace of economic reform attempted by Hu Yaobang and Zhao Ziyang which led to the explosion in 1989. After that experience, Deng Xiao-ping combined extreme political conservatism with a period of economic retrenchment and reassessment. Controls were reintroduced to curb inflationary price increases and speculative investment activities. In Vella Pillay's analysis, which we noted earlier, this comprised a distinct stage lasting from 1988 to 1992. It was followed by stimulative monetary and investment policies and radical movement towards a market economy, with a further stage envisaged in which banking and finance would be increasingly liberated from state control.

This sequence appears to be similar to that of the East Asian model which we studied in Chapter 7, where we saw that a free market economy was established by strong authoritarian governments. We had then to note that the market economy was not introduced overnight, by simply dissolving state ownership and controls. The authority of the state was required in order to maintain order and repress revolt in a situation of unaccustomed competitive struggle and increasing unemployment and inequality. That is the rationale for an authoritarian state, in the view of some China-watchers like William Overholt (Overholt, 1993), although he recognizes the egalitarian instincts, for all their authoritarianism, in the leaders of the South Korean and Taiwanese economic miracle. But state power was not only required for policing; its economic role was crucial. What Overholt fails to appreciate sufficiently is the extent of economic control that was exercised by the East Asian governments prior to the opening up of their economies to the world market. The same failure is typical of IMF and World Bank advice to African and East European governments, which has driven them out into world competition before their economies were able to withstand its pressures. The Chinese have not made this mistake.

A question mark remains over the assumption made among those who expect economic reform to lead on to political reform, that market competition will create the conditions for political pluralism. It is true that, as South Korea and Taiwan have prospered economically, their centralized authoritarian regimes have been relaxed and democratic practices have been introduced. Hong Kong, as a British colony until 1997, must be regarded as a special case, but Singapore is more a benevolent dictatorship than a democracy and Malaysian and Indonesian dictatorships are not so benevolent. Growing inequalities inside society and between regions are typical of market economies and do not lend themselves readily to the relaxation of authority.

China is, moreover, so very much bigger than any of these newly-industrializing countries. Rising living standards have developed very unevenly in China, the coastal provinces moving ahead at twice the pace of those inland (with the exception of Xinjiang, the land of the Uygurs). This is not to say that there is therefore a danger of China breaking up, as the Soviet Union and Yugoslavia did, in the face of growing inequalities. The Han people make up 94 per cent of China's population. However, as a result of the distribution of benefits from the economic reforms, there is a vast contrast in lifestyles between the new rich in China, often the sons of the old party leaders, and the mass of the people. Those who have suffered most are those in the more backward rural areas, who have been forced by the privatization of the communal farms either to labour for a wage or to leave the land and seek work in the towns.

For critics of the reforms, like William Hinton, the privatization of landholding takes China right back to the days of landlord rent, bound feet and superstitious beliefs. But these critics were also convinced that it simply would not work – after the initial release from the straitjacket of a bureaucratic power structure and the initial wave of money-making with anything that could be sold off privately from the accumulated resources of the communes. Hinton records that he wept when he flew over central China in 1983 and saw all the old ribbon strips of private landholdings re-established. Such fragmentation, he believed, could never produce a decent living for the peasants.

In the event, food production increased and ten years later the strips had been joined up again – only in part, as Hinton would have wished, in collective farming. Many smaller landholders had become labourers for the larger owners, or had emigrated to the cities in search of work. The emigration has been described as one of the largest migrations in history – out of the countryside and into the cities. There is no doubt that there was much overpopulation and underemployment in the countryside, but the two phenomena have simply been transferred to the urban areas, where food is short, jobs are scarce and crime is rising. In Chinese government thought, what was the solution to this growing problem? Agricultural reform based on cooperative management evidently could not succeed without much wider economic measures (Bowles, 1994).

Chinese Market Socialism

The Central Committee of the Chinese Communist Party, meeting on 14 November 1993, was moved to declare:

> The socialist market economic structure is linked with the basic system of socialism . . . this structure aims at enabling the market to play the fundamental role in resource allocations under macro-economic control by the state. To turn this goal into reality, it is necessary to uphold the principle of taking the publicly-owned sector as the mainstay . . .

The Central Committee's decisions on this occasion refer further to

> the need to transform management mechanisms of state-owned enter-prises, and to establish a modern enterprise system which meets the requirements of the market economy and in which the property rights and the rights and responsibilities of enterprises are clearly defined, *government administration and enterprise management are separated* [emphasis added – MBB] and scientific management is established.

Vella Pillay, reviewing these decisions from the standpoint of an official of the Bank of China, asks whether what is said to be 'necessary' can in fact be assured, i.e. whether the state-owned sector has the means to provide the 'mainstay' when resource allocation is left to the market, and government administration and enterprise management are truly separated (Pillay, 1994).

There is no doubt that the failure to separate political and economic criteria in enterprise management, and the practice of state subsidies, soft loans and tax relief for state enterprises, led to grotesque inefficiencies and squandering of assets in China, as in Eastern Europe. Exposing enterprises to market competition for capital and for other resources could provide a necessary discipline, but what then would be the criteria for macro-economic control by the state? Under a capitalist system, the stock market combines the threat of bankruptcy or take-over to supply the necessary discipline. But these constraints on decision-makers fail to take account of negative externalities, such as pollution, advertising of noxious products, etc., or of uneven development in growing income inequalities and in the monopolistic positions of increasingly concentrated capital in giant companies.

It was undoubtedly the fear of such untoward developments in a capitalist market economy that led the Chinese Communist Party to seek to retain macro-economic control. None the less, by 1994 China was moving towards a fully-fledged capital market and private banking system with openings for foreign capital. A Foreign Exchange Market was being established; foreign banks were already operating in China on behalf of foreign companies. On the Shanghai Stock Exchange in 1994, foreign-owned shares were still distinguished as 'B' shares from Chinese-owned 'A' shares, but the distinction was to be ended. Even more remarkable, the issuing of shares in former state properties, not only to Chinese residents but also to foreigners, was under consideration. What would then be left of socialism in the market? What direct power would the government have over the economy when, as was proposed, the Central Bank was to be made 'independent under leadership of the State Council'? How was this different from any capitalist economy with a government employing the indirect measures at its disposal to influence the decisions of capital-owners, national and foreign, within the overall pressures of the going rate of profit?

European experience would suggest that a strong regulatory force at the centre is required, both to prevent growing inequalities between regions and the development of a whole range of negative externalities, once the protective powers of the nation state are challenged by the capital movements of transnational corporations. Resistance to the strengthening of federal powers in the European Union, as exhibited by governments like that of Mr Major in Britain, must be expected to collapse in the face of the realities of the balance of power worldwide between giant companies and governments. The population and land area of China are nearly three times those of the European Union. The need to establish strong central control over the economy is that much greater, and more possible to achieve. The Japanese model could be replicated in other East Asian countries by similar close cooperation between government ministries and the major groupings of big local capital accumulation under Japanese tutelage. That option is not available to China, if only because neither Chinese sentiment towards Japan nor the interests of non-Japanese foreign capital in China would permit it.

The implication of this discussion is that in China a much stronger and more extensive state direction of the economy is needed than the Japanese combination of cooperation and competition in order to prevent inequalities and negative externalities emerging. The Chinese leadership appears to place much faith in the strengthening of the role of the Central Bank; and Vella Pillay has elaborated a proposal for state-owned main investment banks to act as the chief monitoring agency over associated groups of enterprises in each industry. Already in China by 1994, associations of enterprises with input-output linkages had been created along the lines of the Japanese and South Korean conglomerates. Pillay's argument is that the Central Bank could prevent overheating by maintaining a balance between supply and demand, as the Central Committee decisions of November 1994 required. But the main investment banks would be needed to achieve the absolutely essential prerequisite of development, as he describes it: 'efficiency in production (rising productivity of capital, labour and other factors of production) ... leading to higher levels of capital accumulation and employment growth, through a finance-driven approach based on main bank monitoring and supervision supported by competitive product markets' (Pillay, 1994).

Pillay's belief is that this system of control by the main state-owned banks, pursuing the 'broad economic strategies of the state', would provide a 'rational mechanism whereby the social surplus' could be 'devoted to planned improvements in the level of social consumption and of investment in the infrastructure and the expansion of productive capacity ... in conditions which bring about a more egalitarian distribution of income'. There is no doubt that bankers in China as elsewhere could develop the skills to monitor and supervise the efficient use of capital and even of labour, but the efficient use of other resources, especially of fuel and energy, and the avoidance of negative externalities in environmental damage require other kinds of controls and controllers. Nor does Pillay give any evidence for his belief that such a regime of what we may call 'bankers' socialism' would do anything to prevent the emergence and perpetuation of inequalities.

Efficiency versus Equality

We are back to the old problem in China since the revolution – that investment in the most productive persons and regions ensures efficiency and faster growth, but at the expense of equality. Some other instrument of social cohesion and income redistribution will be needed beyond the fiat of bankers, if the conditions for a more egalitarian distribution of income are to be established. And this cannot just be a matter of catching up after the event, as with the fiscal policies of most capitalist governments. If Pillay's main investment banks are to be the agent of government overall strategic policy, they will have to operate not only financial criteria but also non-financial criteria – for the development of backward regions, for energy conservation and environmental protection, and for export promotion. The use of subsidies and unsecured credit may well need to be controlled and limited in duration, but the abandonment of all such support for weak sectors of the economy can only spell growing inequalities and frustration, leading as in Africa to outbreaks of violence and civil war.

It has to be recognized, however, that Mao's dream of an egalitarian way of economic development from an agrarian to an industrial society was quite simply utopian, a romantic failure. The necessary growth in productivity had to come from those men and women and from those regions most capable of achieving it. Middle-ranking peasants who had gained full rights to their land from the old landlords knew how to increase output with the aid of water control and new tools and equipment. They did not see why they should share the increase with the landless and the less efficient farmers. Those in the towns and cities who had some expertise in the professions and in commerce and industry did not accept that much of their time should be spent on manual labour and under the direction of those much less capable. No industrial revolution has ever been carried through without some element of force and some encouragement of unequal rewards for unequal contributions. China is no different.

No one will doubt the immensity of the task that Mao attempted and the magnitude of his achievement in uniting the Chinese people against the Japanese invasion and in liberating them from an oppressive feudal society, so that they could begin to build anew. Like all previous emperors of a new dynasty, his greatest claim to fame must be that he brought the great rivers of China once more under control. The mass line may have seemed to those who toiled on it little different from the slavery of old, but it is the basis of all the current increases in food production. Failure to maintain China's irrigation system in the mad chase to make money would soon lead to disaster. China cannot, today, any more than earlier in its history, survive without a strong central power, to control the rivers and hold the several regions together.

It is no more than a Marxist would expect if we find in China that the new society could not be built without enormously increased productive forces and without all the hangovers from an old society to hold it back. There is a special need in relation to China to understand the nature of the inheritance of the Asiatic mode of production and its distinguishing characteristics, which China's great historian, Wu Dakun, has emphasized differentiate it from the European or Japanese feudalism out of which capitalism emerged (Wu Dakun, 1983). The overriding problem for the

Chinese people today remains the absolute necessity, while developing new forces of production, to bring the requisite central power under democratic control. That was never achieved, or even attempted, throughout Chinese history, but it is a condition of Chinese progress today.

FURTHER READING

AZIZ, S., *Rural Development: Learning from China*, Macmillan, 1978

BENTON, GREGOR, 'China's Oppositions', *New Left Review*, No. 122, July–August 1980, pp. 59–78

BOWLES, PAUL and XIAO-YUAN, DONG, 'Current Success and Future Challenges in China's Economic Reforms', *New Left Review*, No. 208, November–December 1994, pp. 49–77

CHEN ERJIN, *China: Crossroads Socialism. An Unofficial Manifesto for Proletarian Democracy*, Verso, 1984

ELVIN, MARK, *The Pattern of the Chinese Past*, Stanford University Press, 1973

FALCONER, ALAN, *New China – Friend or Foe*, Naldrett Press, 1950 (Books That Matter)

HALLIDAY, FRED, 'Marxist Analysis and Post-revolutionary China', *New Left Review*, No. 100, November 1976/January 1977, pp. 165–92

HINTON, WILLIAM, *Fanshen: A Documentary of Revolution in a Chinese Village*, Monthly Review Press, 1967

HINTON, WILLIAM, *The Privatisation of China: The Great Reversal*, Earthscan, 1991

JUNG CHANG, *Wild Swans: Three Daughters of China*, Flamingo, HarperCollins, 1993

LEW, R., 'Maoism and the Chinese Revolution', in Ralph Miliband and John Saville (eds.), *The Socialist Register 1975*, Merlin Press, pp. 115–59

LING, DING, *The Sun Shines over the Sanggan River* (trans. Gladys Yang), Foreign Languages Press (Peking), 1954

LOCKETT, M., 'Managing China's Industry', *China Now*, May–June 1980, pp. 18–20

OVERHOLT, WILLIAM H., *China, the Next Economic Super Power*, Weidenfeld, 1993

PILLAY, VELLA, 'China's Banking and Financial Reforms' (mimeograph), March 1994, personal communication

PILLAY, VELLA, 'A Banking and Finance-driven Approach to the Application of "Market Socialism" in China' (mimeograph), Conference of Socialist Economists, July 1994

ROBINSON, JOAN, *The Cultural Revolution in China*, Penguin Books, 1969

ROBINSON, JOAN, *et al.*, 'Mao and the Cultural Revolution', *China Now*, July 1981

SCHRAM, S. (ed.), *Mao Tse-tung Unrehearsed*, Penguin Books, 1974

SELDON, MARK, *People's Republic of China*, Monthly Review Press, 1979

SU SHAOZHI, *Marxism and Reform in China*, Spokesman, 1993, p. 55

VAN GINNEKE, W., 'Employment and Labour Income Trends in China (1978–86)', in Van Ginneke (ed.), *Trends in Employment and Labour Incomes: Case Studies on Developing Countries*, ILO, 1988

WHEELWRIGHT, E. L., and MACFARLANE, B., *The Chinese Road to Socialism*, Monthly Review Press, 1971

WU DAKUN, 'The Asiatic Mode of Production in History as Viewed by Political Economy in its Broad Sense', in Su Shaozhi *et al.*, *Marxism in China*, Spokesman, 1983

15 THE YUGOSLAV MODEL

One of the important differences between the background to the Russian and Chinese Revolutions, we said earlier, was the fact that a national liberation struggle *preceded* the Chinese Revolution. A great liberated agricultural area in Yenan in north-west China was established for many years in which experiments in building a new society could be made before the revolutionaries faced all the problems of the cities and their links with the capitalist west. The Bolsheviks in Russia, by contrast, had to struggle against invading armies *after* the Revolution; and this struggle did not involve a class struggle in the countryside as it did in China. The Yugoslav experience in the Second World War was nearer to that of the Chinese than of the Russians. The Yugoslav partisans freed themselves from the German armies of invasion in the Second World War in a way that cannot be said quite of Russia after the First World War or of other Eastern European countries after the Second World War. In doing so the Yugoslav partisans were involved in a class struggle in the towns and countryside similar to that of the Chinese communists; but – and it is an important but – the liberated areas held by the partisans were never held by them for long enough for the growth of democratic practices to become firmly based inside them.

There is no doubt that local resistance movements in all parts of Yugoslavia involved major struggles with collaborating industrialists, landowners, Chetniks and others, so that a revolutionary base for a new society began to emerge. That such a base was never firmly established was the result, first, of the need of the partisans to build a hierarchical army to fight the Germans and, later, of the eclipse of the 'terenci', those who belonged to the people and knew the terrain, as soon as the Germans withdrew permanently from an area and the army moved in. Yet, when the German armies were finally evicted from Yugoslavia, a socialist state *was* established and capitalists as well as collaborators had their property taken from them.

Yugoslavia's revolutionary experience thus lies somewhere between the Soviet and Chinese. On the one hand, the partisans fought their own war of liberation; on the other hand, they never had the chance to build their own model of a new society in liberated territory. Despite this, not only dissidents on the democratic socialist wing of the Chinese Communist Party but also more centrally placed Chinese intellectuals began in the 1960s to look to Yugoslavia as a model for social transformation in a backward economy. What both parties had in common was the experience of breaking with the Soviet party, the Yugoslavs in 1948, the Chinese after 1963. Both had thereafter to find a new model of the economy that would continue to develop the class struggle in the villages, raise agricultural output and consolidate workers' power in industry and agriculture. This last was the most difficult without allowing workers in the technologically advanced sectors or on richer lands to improve their position at the expense of those with less advanced capabilities and in more backward areas.

The Yugoslav partisans' great achievement was not just that they crippled large numbers of German, Italian and Bulgarian divisions and assorted local collaborating forces, but that in doing so they succeeded in uniting the several different peoples of which Yugoslavia was composed. All the six main nationalities are Slavs, but they have had different histories and inherited three different religions — Catholicism, Orthodox Christianity and Islam. In addition to the six nationalities, there are sizeable numbers of Hungarians in the Voyvodina and of Albanians in Kosovo. Uniting all these peoples was the more remarkable because the Germans, like the previous occupying armies of Hungarians, Turks and Austrians, had exploited their differences in order to divide and conquer; and the German occupation had begun with the most horrendous massacre of Serbs, Jews and gypsies by the Croat quisling regime which the Germans had established in Bosnia. At least 200,000 died in the extermination camps and the number may have been nearer a million.

Socialist Self-Management

The Yugoslavs began their recovery after liberation in 1944–5 by introducing a command economy, with a five-year plan following in 1947 on the Soviet model. Land was redistributed and collectivization begun, while industrial and commercial enterprises were given precise output targets prescribing down to the last pin and nail what was to be produced. One-year rolling plans provided some flexibility but the targets were set by the central planning authorities, and the provinces and localities were expected to conform. The break in 1949 was complete not only with the Soviet Union but with central planning and collectivization. A major attack was launched by the Yugoslav party on what they called statism, i.e. the use of state authority to issue commands, and on the bureaucracy that went with it. Decentralization became the watchword. In late 1949 workers' councils began to be established with great enthusiasm in industry throughout Yugoslavia. The law on the management of state economic enterprises followed in 1950 and was soon extended to non-economic activities like hospitals, government offices, etc., and incorporated in a new constitutional law in January 1953. By this law social ownership of the means of production, together with self-management by producers in the economy and self-government by the working people in the communes, municipalities and districts, were all established as 'corner-stones of the socio-political order of the country'. Local authorities at various levels increasingly became what we have called political and economic organs.

It is important to try to understand what this law actually meant for the workers involved. Not only in industrial and commercial enterprises but in every other government and service activity workers in groups both large and small were given a budget to spend in the way they thought best, albeit within a rigid framework of controls, which all related to their integration with other workers in other enterprises or departments. The continuing restriction of these central controls led to the demand from enterprises and local authorities that they be lifted. The main change demanded was that the distinction between wages and profits should be eliminated and that a common income of the enterprise, to be shared by agreement between all the workers, should take its place.

Such decentralization was established by the late 1950s and meant a great reduction in the intervention of state bodies in the distribution of incomes both inside and between enterprises. The allocation of enterprise income for investment remained firmly within the control of the federal parliament and, in effect, of the central planners. Moreover, taxes for social and public services at local and provincial levels remained firmly fixed. Workers began to demand greater freedom, complaining that what they were left to allocate from the value they added at work, after all the fixed deductions, was almost worthless – a basic wage, a small bonus and a share in the social welfare fund, altogether much less than half the enterprise's net profit before paying wages. From that personal income, moreover, they still had to pay out almost a half in federal taxes, social insurance and contribution to house-building funds. (See Barratt Brown, 1970, tables pp. 274 and 276.)

Once more we are face to face with a model that is Utopian in its expectations at a low level of productive capacity and consumption possibilities. Workers are simply not prepared to increase their productivity when they *know* that deductions from the value they added by their work would include (even as Marx said they should) provision for: (a) public services such as science, health, education, etc.; (b) reserve funds for financing sales, especially exports, and for new investment in the enterprise; (c) central (federal) funds for accelerating the development of underdeveloped regions and republics; (d) general public needs of the local community in which the enterprise operated; and (e) collective social consumption of housing, etc., in addition to private consumption of goods and services.

Nevertheless, the model had the advantage we have already seen to be so important of combining political, administrative and economic organization at a decentralized level. Enterprises in Yugoslavia in the 1960s were owned and managed by local authorities at different levels: province, county, district or town. Managerial appointments were made jointly by the local authority and the elected enterprise management committee, with the latter having a veto. The requirements of federal and local government were established by law within an overall national plan of redistribution between rich and poor regions. The essence of the model, then, was that enterprises and other units of organization of 'associated labour', as the Yugoslavs called it, were united through their agreed joint plans.

To quote the standard statement of Premier Edward Kardelj on the system of socialist self-management in Yugoslavia (see Boskovitch, 1980):

> The Plan must provide the right and possibility for a worker in the basic organizations of associated labour to have a continual insight into the results of the pooling of his [sic] labour and resources into the jointly earned income, i.e. into the management of income at all levels of associated labour and within the overall process of social reproduction; and to have control and the right of decision-making on how this income is used, while being at the same time responsible for the economic results of this management, and for the material effect of this management on his personal remuneration.

This is a long way from the command economy or even the mix of command and market economy of the Soviet Union. It was a model that had some similarity with the commune model in China; but in place of the centralized planning either of China or of the Soviet Union, the Yugoslav model implied a plan that did not direct but merely coordinated the initiatives of self-managed enterprises within national laws that required deductions to be made for social provision and investment. The essential elements in the model described in the quotation from Kardelj were, first, the possibility for 'a worker . . . to have a continual insight into the results of . . . his labour' and, second, the need for planning to go upwards and downwards with the basic organization of associated labour as the focal point.

On the first element, my own studies of enterprises in Yugoslavia during a visit in 1959 convinced me that the majority of workers certainly had an insight into the results of their labour. The problem was that this knowledge led those whose work had a high market valuation to question whether they wanted so much of the value to be transferred to support less productive enterprises and regions. The argument was developed in the first two issues of *New Left Review* (January–March 1960). The coordination of plans was the result not so much of compacts between enterprises as of agreements between the enterprise owners. These were the districts, counties and national authorities, ownership being distributed according to the importance of the enterprise. These responsibilities were all changed in 1963 when socialist self-management was made, in the Yugoslav leaders' phrase, the 'dominant production relation'.

Self-Managed Enterprises in a Market Economy

The argument of the Kardelj article from which we quoted earlier was that prior to 1963 the ownership of enterprises by state authorities at different levels, and the narrow range of real decision-making power open to workers in commercial and industrial enterprises and government offices alike, constantly reinforced the authority of the state and the bureaucracy. The new constitution of 1963 and the economic reforms of 1965 were designed to guarantee self-management in production and in public services as an 'inalienable right' of the Yugoslav working people. Ownership of economic enterprises was transferred to the workers themselves. Similar autonomy was granted to educational, health and other social institutions. The power of central planning bodies was delegated to parliamentary commissions or to state banks and other public financial institutions acting within the law of the land and the working of the market. Only foreign affairs and national defence, foreign-exchange control and the reallocation of resources between the several republics of the Yugoslav federation were retained at the centre.

What was rather more remarkable, the Yugoslav economy was opened to the world economy, in effect the capitalist world system, through the adjustment of Yugoslav prices to world prices and the opening of investment opportunities to foreign capitalist companies within strict limitations of control over ownership. This implies a reason beyond the protection of self-management in the reforms of 1965. The reason was in fact not far to find; it lay in the collapse of an alternative non-aligned, Third World trading bloc for the Yugoslav economy to relate to. In the early 1960s mutual trade agreements had been reached between Yugoslavia, India, Brazil, Indonesia, Algeria, Ghana, Cuba and Egypt to enable all these countries to establish a major element of independence from either the Soviet bloc or the European Economic Community Common Market.

In 1962 such a third force seemed a real enough possibility for it to form part of the policy prescription I proposed for a Labour government which might be elected in 1964 (see Barratt Brown, 1963). The failure of that government when elected to join in a Third World trading bloc must be regarded as at least part explanation for the subsequent rapid collapse of the bloc. The fact is that within a few years Nehru had gone, and Goulart, Sukarno, Ben Bella, Kassim and Nkrumah had all been overthrown with help from the CIA. Only Castro and Nasser remained to support Tito, and Nasser was soon to go. Evidently, with hindsight we can see that my prescription failed (see my analysis in the Preface to the second edition of After Imperialism, 1970). What happened to the Yugoslav economy was disastrous (witness, for example, the impact on plants that had been established for converting timber to rayon for a far larger market than the fifteen million Yugoslavs).

There were two alternatives for the Yugoslav economy: to return to Comecon, the trade organization of the Eastern European bloc, or to reach some accommodation with the Common Market. The first was unthinkable after the experience of 1946–8; the second was entertained. But the price was high: opening the Yugoslav economy to world prices and to world capital, and in particular to Western European capital. Foreign markets were soon established for Yugoslav agricultural produce: wine, hops, timber, canned fruit. Subcontracts were obtained for Yugoslav manufacture of components, especially of motor-car components for Fiat. Agreements were made with Hilton and other American and European hotel companies to establish joint ventures to cater for the rapidly growing tourist trade. The principle of social ownership was assured as to 51 per cent of the capital, the principle of self-management was retained for every enterprise within the limits of the views held by the foreign owners of the 49 per cent. Enterprises and cooperatives that enjoyed high productivity in industry or agriculture flourished and their workers' incomes grew. The gap between these and the small suppliers' and small peasants' incomes grew even faster.

It became a common sight in the richer provinces to see a Mercedes outside the houses of cooperative workers producing wine or hops for export or of workers in electrical and mechanical factories, while down the road there were still houses with mud floors and tin roofs. Getting a job in the first rather than in the second sector became a matter increasingly of bribery or family and ethnic 'protection'. Workers in the more advanced concerns had a 'clear insight into the results of their work'. Perhaps the others had too; for tens of thousands of them left for Western Europe as migrant workers. There is no incentive for a workers' collective to share their income with extra labour. Competition in the market became once more the allocator of resources. Only the League of Communists and the Chambers of Commerce and the banks and large trading concerns provided respectively the ideological and the technological coordination for reconciling the plans of the autonomous self-managing enterprises. What had begun as a model that gave full freedom for associated self-managing enterprises to plan together through compacts and agreements became step by step a market model with competing self-managed companies operating subject to the control of a party apparatus.

The Struggle for a Socialist System

The adoption of major amendments to the Yugoslav constitution in 1971 and the promulgation of a new constitution in 1974 inaugurated a third phase in the development of the Yugoslav model. On the one hand, it gave to the economic enterprises and other 'organizations of associated labour' in industry, commerce, finance, health, education, government offices, etc., even more freedom to manage their own affairs, including decisions on investment, subject only to payment of tax, and within the frame-work of a competitive market – the marketing having an international as well as a purely national extension. On the other hand, a massive ideological struggle was embarked upon to encourage workers to criticize not only centralism (statism) and bureaucracy but also all forms of corruption and self-seeking. That this last might often mean simply dissidence from the party line has to be recognized. It is only too easy to understand that ideological struggle is often the attempt to impose a false consciousness, in Yugoslavia as in China or the Soviet Union, where the reality of continuing power at the centre is concealed behind the rhetoric of democratic fervour and the veil of money in the market.

The most important proposal for change in the Yugoslav model after 1971 arose from the influence of Ota Sik who fled from Prague to Belgrade when the Prague Spring ended in 1968. Ota Sik had been vice-chairman of the Economic Council in the Czecho-slovak government prior to the Russian invasion. The Yugoslavs learnt from Sik the idea of introducing into their pricing and wage policies a system of rewards that took into account not only current hours of labour but also the past labour incorporated in the machinery and plant the worker was working with. Great inequalities had been emerging, as we noted, between workers' wages in industrial and agricultural production employing advanced technology and in those with backward technology. Marx had written about 'socially necessary labour time' as that which was needed to produce goods with average current levels of technology.

We saw earlier that a Cambridge economist in 1960, Piero Sraffa, following some of Ricardo's as well as Marx's ideas of machinery as 'stored-up labour', had developed the concept of 'dated labour'. This was materialized in the various stages of the development and production of productive machinery and in its utilization in the labour process. Sik built on this concept a computerized model of dated-labour inputs from which he deduced a set of 'shadow prices' for output from different industries at different levels of technological development. This enabled the Yugoslav planning departments to supply the political leaders –

the League of Communists – with ammunition for them to criticize the workers in enterprises having the most advanced plant if they used the resulting high levels of productivity to claim much higher wages for work hours of no greater length or intensity than that performed by workers in less advanced plants. Workers could in a real sense then know what the value added by their work amounted to. It was much less easy to apply this to agriculture; and in industry they did not like what they knew.

To a considerable extent the Yugoslav League of Communists had always acted behind the scenes rather than openly, at least at local level, in providing both ideological cover and actual organizational coordination for economic activities in both industry and agriculture. The League henceforth became a more open advocate of the proposition that for the same 'socially acknowledged work' – i.e. socially necessary labour time – which was how it was described at the 1971 congress of self-managers of Yugoslavia, 'approximately the same living standards should be secured for the workers'. At the same time, trade unions were increasingly expected to help 'coordinate the different interests which come to the surface in the sharing of income and personal remuneration'. The basis of this sharing was now said to be the 'pooled production potential in the form of living and *past* labour' (my emphasis – M.B.B) and 'their part in the joint financial risk'.

This recognition of the contribution of past labour to socially necessary labour time, as well as of a risk-taking element, was designed to persuade members of those enterprises with more advanced technology, higher incomes and greater security to contribute more to the financing of collective needs and to the development of other enterprises with less advanced technology and greater risks, especially in the poorer regions. This is an incomes policy that has proved unacceptable in a capitalist economy. It is only the 'clear insight', as Premier Kardelj called it, of workers into the value of the work they do at different levels of technology that makes it remotely possible to advocate it in a socialist economy. Even there, Kardelj admitted that workers could not be expected to agree to invest funds in new technology which made them redundant unless they received some compensation in financial reward or redeployment. How this worked in practice can best be studied in Milojka Drulovitch's book *Self-Management on Trial*, not ignoring the implications of its title.

After reading Kardelj's statements, doubts linger about an ideology that perhaps spreads a false consciousness around the real calculations of past and present labour in the distribution of incomes. It would be hard to imagine an economy as backward as that of Yugoslavia in the 1950s progressing within thirty years to a point where workers would voluntarily give up nearly a half of the value they add by their work to providing for social needs and investment in future development in the poorer regions. So much was clear enough in the early 1980s, but the subsequent disintegration of Yugoslavia was not, I think, foreseen by anyone. Explanations range from the appeal to historic ethnic conflict which the 1945 federal constitution could not contain, via denouncement of unassuaged Great Serb nationalism to wholesale dismissal of the viability of all communist political and economic regimes in Eastern Europe.

The Disintegration of Yugoslavia

The most widely accepted explanation for the tragic events in the early 1990s in what had been Yugoslavia is that ethnic tensions which had a long history in the region became uncontrollable once the repressive authority of communist rule had been broken. This is the view presented by the journalist Misha Glenny in his widely influential book, *The Fall of Yugoslavia* (Glenny, 1993). He characterizes the war in Bosnia-Herzegovina in 1992–4 as 'a continuation of the struggle between 1941 and 1945 . . . a revival of unresolved conflicts, prejudices and vendettas on a local level'. The impact of the Second World War on Yugoslavia Glenny describes as 'a genocidal struggle between Serbs and Croats . . . felt most keenly in Bosnia . . . a nationalist religious war, whose violence surpassed that of all other wartime conflicts in the region'. Glenny insists that 'Bosnia has always survived by dint of a protective shield provided either by a Yugoslav state or the

Austrian or Ottoman empires.' By a 'Yugoslav state', he explains that he means 'the inter-war royal dictatorship' and what he calls 'Titoism'. When these broke down, he says, in 1941–5 and after 1990, the results were inevitably horrifying.

This explanation must be faulted on two counts. First, the so-called 'mediating powers' providing the 'protective shield' in fact, with the exception of Tito, sedulously practised the arts of divide and conquer – the Turks encouraging conversion to Islam and enrolling local leaders as *capetans*; the Hungarians moving Serbian soldiers up to the military frontier in the north of Bosnia, the *krajina*, in territory that was part of historic Croatia. The result was to create the divisions that could be exploited by the German occupation in 1941–4 and that became acute again in 1990. Secondly, it is now fashionable among right-wing historians to decry the national liberation war of Tito's partisans, which succeeded, as Glenny admits, in bringing the Yugoslav peoples together for the next fifty years. But to describe it as a 'nationalist religious war', a 'genocidal struggle between Serbs and Croats', as Glenny does, is to run counter to all the evidence. The question, in any case, remains as to how the Titoist 'protective shield' was broken.

Noel Malcolm in his *Bosnia: A Short History* (Malcolm, 1994) offers some rather dubious evidence for the diminution of the claims for Tito's partisans in resisting the Axis occupation. At the same time, he builds up the strength of Mihailovic's Chetniks to the extent of dating their first collaboration with the Germans as late as September 1943 – that is, after the Italian surrender, which delivered huge quantities of arms into partisan hands. This enables Malcolm to claim that the struggle was chiefly among Serbs themselves – between partisans and Chetniks – Tito's main aim being to establish Communist rule over Yugoslavia, at whatever cost in lives and property, so that the Titoist shield was never a strong one. Malcolm shows no sign of having read the official record on the British decision to switch support from Mihailovic to Tito, which predates Chetnik collaboration to long before 1943 (Auty and Clogg, 1975). He further denies that Tito's forces ever 'pinned down' any large number of German divisions, asserting that at the beginning of 1943 there were only four German divisions, of low calibre, in the whole of Yugoslavia. (In August of that year they were joined by two reserve divisions of trainee recruits, and one burnt-out division from Stalingrad; and a few more were brought in towards the end of the year after the surrender of Italian forces in September.)

How many was 'a few more'? The crucial issue relates to the period just before the Allied landings in France in June 1944, and Prime Minister Churchill informed the House of Commons on 24 February 1944 that the partisans' 'guerilla army of over a quarter of a million men . . . is holding in check fourteen out of the twenty German divisions in the Balkan Peninsula, in addition to six Bulgarian divisions and other satellite forces'. The point that has to be noted is that this army was not what Glenny always calls an army of 'Serb dominated partisans' but drew support from all the Yugoslav peoples. Tito was himself a Croat and, while the largest element in the high command was Serbian and Montenegrin, there were powerful leaders from Croatia, Slovenia and Macedonia, and a most distinguished Jew. Bosnian Moslems were less well represented, but among the political commissars there were many sons of rich Moslem merchants and landowners who had studied in Paris or Vienna.

No one is going to deny that appalling crimes were committed by the Croat fascist Ustashe at Kozara and Jasenovac in 1942, with German connivance, resulting in the murder of at least 200,000 Serbs, Jews and gypsies. Nor can one deny the partisans' murder of several tens of thousands of Yugoslav prisoners of war discovered with captured German divisions and handed over by the Allies at the end of the war. It still cannot be claimed that the partisans' war was anything less than what they called it, a 'war of national liberation from the Axis occupation', involving in that struggle all nationalities and all parts of the country. What Tito created was a Yugoslavia in which people could live together in relative ease and freedom. Given that, why then did it all disintegrate after fifty years?

Economic Collapse

The view of Croat nationalists about the cause of Yugoslav disintegration, which has become widely accepted not only in Germany but in the wider compass of the media, is that it was the result of the unbounded and unassuaged ambitions of Great Serb nationalism, embodied in the persons of Slobodan Milosevic and Radovan Karadjic. But the fact is that no attack was mounted by Milosevic against Croatia until after Croatia and Slovenia had declared their decision to secede from Yugoslavia. The Yugoslav army, effectively under Milosevic's command, moved in to retain the two republics. Both escaped by means of German recognition. The recognition of Slovenia came first and was widely supported in Europe, because Slovenia was not only the richest Yugoslav republic with the closest physical and historic links with Austria, but also had a largely homogeneous population. The Yugoslav army withdrew.

Recognition of Croatia was another matter. There were similar links with the West as in the case of Slovenia, but Croatia contained large Serb minorities and there were many groups of Croats spread throughout Bosnia. The Yugoslav army attacked in Dubrovnik and in Slavonia, where there was a considerable Serbian minority. Fighting ended with the recognition of Croatian independence by Germany, followed reluctantly by the rest of the European Union, and without guarantees for the Serb minority or for Bosnia's integrity.

The result was inevitable: that the nationalist leaders of Serbia and Croatia should seek to divide up Bosnia between them, and at the expense of the Bosnian Moslems. The war which followed worked upon all the national and religious differences engendered by Bosnia's long history of foreign occupation. But the reason why the federal constitutional arrangements broke down is still unexplained. The resurgence of Great Serb nationalism, which had been successfully contained for fifty years, must have had some occasion. Malcolm recognizes that the occasion was related to the collapse of the Yugoslav economy, something that Glenny never mentions. He rightly sees the falling standard of living in the 1980s and the particular fall in the relative position of Bosnia and of other less developed regions as a cause of rising frustration and tension, which Milosevic could turn to his own advantage by playing on the supposed unjust treatment of the Serbian peoples under the Tito constitution. It is interesting to note how those who criticize the Serbian 'Chetniks' today are the same as those who have been trying to rehabilitate Mihailovic's wartime Chetniks who had the very same Great Serb ambitions.

While Malcolm recognizes Yugoslavia's economic weakness in the 1980s, he asserts that a 'weak and malfunctioning economy' was 'guaranteed under the Yugoslav communist system'. This really won't do, because for thirty years, after the most destructive war, economic growth *per capita* had averaged 5 per cent a year. This was equal to that in other East European countries and well above that in the capitalist economies, both developed and developing. In the 1980s the whole progress of economic development in Yugoslavia stalled and standards of living actually fell, with the worst falls taking place in the poorest regions, including Bosnia. Nor can the same reasoning, based on the failure of communism, be applied to the Yugoslav collapse as to the concurrent collapse in the rest of Eastern Europe. The economic models, as we have seen, were entirely different. If we are to learn anything from distinguishing these models, we need to discover either a common cause or separate causes.

A common cause might appear to be the existence of one-party rule. This undoubtedly made it difficult, if not impossible, for problems to be discussed and alternative solutions formulated when the crisis came. But there were wide limits in the Yugoslavia of the 1980s for free discussion and the publication of alternative views, even while the monopoly of political action was retained by the Communist League. Some views were suppressed, including the publication in 1983 by Izetbegovic, the man who was to be Bosnia's president, of an *Islamic Declaration*. The authors were briefly jailed, although they pleaded that they had no intention or desire to create an Islamic state in Bosnia. Similar action was taken against Croat and Serbian nationalists, with the clearly stated aim of defending the federal constitution.

The original federal constitution introduced by Tito at the end of the war had guaranteed all the six Slav peoples of Yugoslavia a large degree of self-government in their own republics, with a measure of autonomy given to the Hungarians and Albanians in the Vojvodina and Kosovo respectively. After 1974 the constitution was considerably modified to allow for decentralization of almost all decision-making to the republics, including the autonomous regions of Vojvodina and Kosovo. Control of the army and foreign policy and of some basic prices remained with the federal authorities, in whose leading ranks Serbs were greatly over-represented in relation to their population. It can indeed be argued that this decentralization was an important cause of Yugoslavia's disintegration, but what was done in 1974 cannot have been the immediate cause of what happened in 1990.

The other problem that Yugoslavia shared with East European countries and with many developing countries in the 1980s was the overwhelming weight of military expenditure against the threat of cold war becoming hot war, and associated with that the growing burden of foreign debt. Although Yugoslavia was not a member either of NATO or of the Warsaw Pact, the country lay historically along the fault line between East and West. Arms expenditure in the 1970s was taking a quarter of Yugoslav national income, at the expense of the country's development, although Bosnia benefited from the siting of arms factories in this republic, which is the furthest of all from external borders.

Yugoslavia's debts to foreign banks and international institutions were incurred, not only to pay for arms, but also for industrialization. The problems of repayment arose first in the mid-1970s for oil-importing countries like Yugoslavia with the rise in oil prices, and then for raw-material exporters with the fall in commodity prices during the 1980s. All the time the prices of manufactured goods imported from the industrialized countries were rising, and interest rates rose to high levels and stayed there. The price-scissors cut into the country's foreign balance. Agreements to reschedule debts simply increased the size of the original borrowings and of the annual servicing payments required. Yugoslavia's debt of $6 billion in 1975 rose to $20 billion in the 1980s, demanding a rising figure of annual payments, which by 1989 reached 30 per cent of all the country's export earnings.

The results of the rising debt were inevitable. As goods were increasingly produced for export, and wages were paid without corresponding goods in the shops, inflation rose from an annual rate of 15 per cent in the 1970s to 40 per cent in 1981–3, thence to an average 200 per cent in 1985–8 and finally to 1,300 per cent in 1989. Such a rise of 100 per cent a month made the Yugoslav currency worthless. As usual, those with lower incomes fared worst, but in Yugoslavia, as in some other indebted countries, there was a particular discriminating cause. Some people had foreign currency – in Yugoslavia's case, Deutschmarks, earned individually by working in Germany (there were a million such migrant workers in the 1980s) or by their company's earnings from joint ventures and from the tourist trade. These people, who lived mainly in the north – in Slovenia and Croatia – were largely immune from inflationary pressures. As so often in the Third World, those who suffered most from the country's debts were driven into crime and violence and in the end into civil war.

This differentiation between the republics was exacerbated in Yugoslavia by uneven regional development, manufacturing concentrated in the north, raw-material production continuing in the south. A central element in the federal constitution had been the required redistribution of income from the rich north to the poor south. During the 1980s the Fund for the Development of the Less Developed Republics was reduced to 2 per cent of the social product of the more developed republics; and the central budget for the support of social services throughout the country to 1 per cent of national income. (In the UK it is nearer 30 per cent.) And this was at a time of falling incomes and rising unemployment, mainly in the less developed regions (Hashi, 1992).

By 1989, the average income in the richest republic, Slovenia, had risen to more than double the Yugoslav average, while that of Kosovo, the poorest, fell to one quarter of the average. That is a 7:1 difference; in the 1950s the gap had been only half as wide. Unemployment rose in Yugoslavia to 17 per cent of the labour force in 1989, but the rate in Kosovo rose to over 50 per cent; in

Bosnia, Macedonia and Montenegro the rate was between 20 per cent and 30 per cent, having quadrupled since the 1960s, while the rate in Slovenia had doubled to a mere 3.5 per cent. The perception of the citizens in the rich and poor republics was, however, that each was suffering at the expense of the other. The rich saw their manufactures being exported to pay the debt while the poor were contributing nothing. The poor saw their raw materials being sold at lower and lower world prices for export and for processing in the industries of the north.

The Serbs, who live in the middle both geographically and economically, saw themselves running the country but getting no benefit from their efforts. Yet the centre was blamed for mismanagement, since it was responsible for issuing the currency, managing the debt and fixing basic prices. The fact was that the centre had little or no power over the separate republics' imports and export earnings and capital movements. Each republic had developed its own industries, each insisting on having its own steel industry, oil refineries, sugar factories, etc. Only one-third of national output and a fifth of capital movements had by the late 1980s come to circulate between the republics; the rest moved inside each republic or, in the case of the northern republics, mainly with the outside world. Yugoslavia had ceased to be a national market and could no longer be managed from the centre (United Nations Economic Commission for Europe, 1990).

In these circumstances the break-up of the federation was inevitable. Only the party and the army were left to hold the country together; and when the separate republics' Communist Parties fell apart, that left only the army, which was predominantly officered by Serbs. To strengthen the political centre meant strengthening Serbia. As a strong man appeared in Serbia, the army backed him, at first quite genuinely, to save the federation. If the strong man had great Serb ambitions, that was inevitable in the circumstances. Neither he, nor the original federal constitution, nor Great Serb nationalism, can be blamed for the disintegration of Yugoslavia. The blame must lie with the debt, the price-scissors and the demands of the Western bankers for their pound of flesh.

Still less can it be said that the Yugoslav model of political economy had failed, at least in the form it had taken before it was distorted by separatist ambitions in the north when the debt payments began to bite. It is often said, for example by Martin Woollacott in *Bloody Bosnia* (Scott and Jones, 1993), that the West betrayed the Yugoslavs – for not arming the Bosnian Moslems or for not intervening against the Serbs. It is doubtful whether either action would have helped the people of Bosnia, but what is certain is that there would have been no bloodshed if the West had forgiven the Yugoslav debt in 1990. The last Yugoslav prime minister did in that year bring the rate of inflation under control and took steps to revive the economy, but he received no support from the West. He was forced to give way to the men of arms. It was the same in Nicaragua, Peru, Bolivia, Somalia, Rwanda and Algeria at different dates. National models of political economy have to survive in an extremely hostile world.

FURTHER READING

AUTY, PHYLLIS, and CLOGG, R. (eds.), *British Wartime Policy towards Resistance in Yugoslavia and Greece*, Macmillan, 1975

BARRATT BROWN, MICHAEL, 'Workers' Control in a Planned Economy', *New Left Review*, No. 1/2, January–March 1960, pp. 28–31

BARRATT BROWN, MICHAEL, *What Economics is About*, Weidenfeld & Nicolson, 1970

BARRATT BROWN, MICHAEL, *After Imperialism*, 1963, 2nd edn, Merlin Press, 1970

BARRATT BROWN, MICHAEL, 'The War in Yugoslavia and the Debt Burden', *Capital and Class*, No. 50, Summer 1993

BOSCOVITCH, B. (ed.), *Socialist Self-Management in Yugoslavia*, Belgrade, 1980

DAVIDSON, BASIL, *Special Operations Europe*, Gollancz, 1980

DRULOVITCH, M., *Self-Management on Trial*, Spokesman, 1978 (see esp. the Afterword)

GLENNY, MISHA, *The Fall of Yugoslavia*, Penguin, 1993, p. 140

HASHI, IRAJ, 'The Disintegration of Yugoslavia', *Capital and Class*, No. 48, Autumn 1992

LOCKETT, M., 'China and Yugoslavia', *China Now*, No. 98, September–October 1981

MALCOLM, NOEL, *Bosnia: A Short History*, Macmillan, 1994, pp. 181–4

SCOTT, NOLL, and JONES, DEREK (eds.), *Bloody Bosnia: A European Tragedy, The Guardian* and Channel 4 TV, 1993

SIK, OTA, 'Socialist Market Relations and Planning', in C. Feinstein (ed.), *Socialism, Capitalism and Economic Growth*, Cambridge University Press, 1967

UNITED NATIONS ECONOMIC COMMISSION FOR EUROPE, *Economic Survey of Europe in 1989–90*, United Nations, 1990

VANEK, JAROSLAV (ed.), *Self-Management*, Penguin Books, 1975 (see esp. the chapters by B. Horvat, 'An Institutional Model of a Self-managed Socialist Economy', pp. 127–44; Jaroslav Vanek, 'Decentralization under Workers' Management: a Theoretical Appraisal', pp. 352–68; and D. D. Milenkovitch, 'The worker-managed enterprise', pp. 423–9)

16 THE AFRICAN MODEL

The models of capitalist economies that we looked at in the first part of this book were primarily theoretical models – different ways of looking at the same economy, although they led to different ways of managing it. The economic models we have looked at in this part have been primarily empirical models – different ways of managing different economies, in attempting to build socialism. Although these did involve theoretical differences, they arose chiefly from the specific historical, political and economic structures of the different societies in which the attempt was being made. To talk about an 'African model' is to depart from such specificity. First, a model that is distinctly African remains a hope, in some places an expectation, but hardly anywhere realized. Secondly, the historical inheritance – political and economic – of African societies varies widely – so widely that one ought, perhaps, not to talk about *one* African model. Nevertheless, African societies, in some of which attempts were made to carry through a socialist transformation, do all have certain common characteristics that permit us to group them together.

The Common Heritage of the African Peoples

The first characteristic that is shared by the whole of Africa is that all its peoples had developed social formations, in many cases to a high Iron Age level, prior to invasion by Europeans who then sought to eliminate all evidence of a pre-colonial history. The second characteristic is a common experience of European colonial rule and behind that of the slave trade, with its depopulation of West and Central Africa. Even Ethiopia, which was an empire itself, was for a brief period under Italian rule. South Africa provides a special case (one shared by Algeria, Kenya and Rhodesia) of European settler rule.

The third characteristic is almost equally widely shared: the overwhelming proportion of the African population, apart from the white settlers and plantation workers, are peasants. That is, they not only have some claim to the land they work on, but they live and work together, in households, mainly to feed and clothe and house themselves and, only secondarily, to produce cash crops for the market. The predominantly agrarian nature of African society remains the norm today. There have for long been great cities in Egypt and in the Mediterranean states, and to these have been added burgeoning capital cities in most of the African states, whose exponential growth can be expected to result by 2015 in half the population of the continent living in urban areas.

The fourth common characteristic follows from the first two. African peasant societies are extremely poor, many of them still working the land with the simplest tools, 'slashing and burning' the forests to make soil for crops, following herds of sheep and cattle over poor grazing land. Despite the glories of ancient African civilization in Egypt and Sudan, Uganda, Zimbabwe and Mali and on the Mediterranean and the east and west coasts, little was left after European slavery and looting but fairly primitive, albeit skilful, forms of peasant agriculture.

The fifth common characteristic is that what development had taken place in Africa was of products for export to Europe: tropical food products like cocoa, coffee and tea, palm oil, groundnuts and bananas, textile fibres like cotton and sisal, and minerals – copper, gold, bauxite and most recently oil. This development was often at the expense of the local population – the best land used for export crops, the men driven into the mines.

The sixth characteristic is that the frontiers had been drawn quite artificially by the European powers, cutting across language and ethnic divisions. Ports and railways were built with one aim, to facilitate the export of what was often in each colony just one crop or mineral for the benefit of the colonial power. Such dependent development had created a quite artificial world division of labour which provided cheap raw material imports for European industry and a captive market for European manufacturers.

The last common characteristic followed from this dependent trade relationship. Above the peasantry there had emerged a *petit bourgeois* class of state officials and traders committed to the export–import business with the European power and designated as the heirs to the colonial rulers when they withdrew or were expelled.

National Liberation Struggle and Socialist Aims

The different nature of the process of decolonization provides the main variant in the recent experience of African societies. Algeria, Kenya, Zimbabwe and the Portuguese colonies had to fight for their freedom over many years of national liberation struggle. The peoples of South Africa, Angola and Namibia and of the Ethiopian empire were still fighting in the 1980s. The others were granted their freedom more or less peacefully. The result in most of these latter cases was what the colonial powers hoped for: the replacement of the colonial administration by a local elite that would carry on the same dependent trade relations. Many of the elites had been educated in Europe – at Eton and Oxford or Sandhurst or their equivalents in France, Belgium and Portugal. There has in most African states been a succession of elites – the first elite of national liberation leaders was within a few years usurped by a colonially trained military and these were followed by what Basil Davidson calls 'pirates' (Davidson, 1992), like Mobutu of Zaïre, with their personal clienteles; and finally a [World Bank–IMF] 'adjustment elite has emerged: a class of speculators and wheelers and dealers in currencies, cars and drugs who have been elevated to the status of pillars of society, symbolizing, as they do, the "freeest" of market forces' (Adedeji, 1993, p. 216).

Where freedom had involved a national liberation struggle, the result was in most cases different. In Algeria and in Kenya a social revolution was aborted by the colonial powers. In the former Portuguese colonies, in Zimbabwe and in the territories occupied by Ethiopia the attempt was made to carry through a social revolution after liberation. Socialist aims were attempted for much longer in Tanzania and in Ghana; and in Ethiopia and certain states which had been French colonies – Benin, Burkina Faso, Congo, Madagascar, Mali – so-called 'Marxist' regimes were established with a degree of Soviet protection, although their currencies remained linked to the French franc.

It is not at all inevitable that a movement of national liberation should set itself socialist aims. Indeed, although the founders of Africa's national liberation movements were mainly committed socialists, the aims of the struggle for liberation had to be broad enough to draw upon the widest possible support. This had to include both *petit bourgeois* groups, whose commitment to socialism was limited, and a peasantry which had little or no understanding of the meaning of the commitment. A national struggle in Africa had to reckon with the intervention of South Africa in the front-line states, which prolonged the fighting long after the Portuguese had withdrawn. From the beginning, it had to involve not only struggle against the local trading class that was acting as agents of the colonial power but also struggle against the many divisions of the nation (within the artificial frontiers drawn by the European powers) not only of class but of tribal, religious and language groups. Historically some of these had dominated others; some had been richer than others; some had been more closely associated with the colonial power. There was no other way of fighting than by democratic mass participation. Amilcar Cabral (1969) in describing most clearly the social structure of Guinea-Bissau revealed the basis for united struggle against the Portuguese.

The advantage possessed by those movements which had been engaged in the armed struggle was that over long periods of time large areas of the country had been liberated. Inside these liberated areas experiments in democratic social transformation were initiated, as they had been much earlier in China's Yenan province. Also as in China, what emerged were organs of political and economic power, taking not only administrative but economic decisions. Under the most arduous and dangerous conditions men and women had to find ways of working and fighting together so that mutual trust was perfect and the common aim of victory unsullied. Nothing less than equality and the full sharing of the heaviest tasks by all would ensure survival. The outstanding example is the Eritrean People's Liberation Front (see Firebrace and Holland, 1984), but much the same could be said of the armies of liberation in the Portuguese colonies (Davidson, 1981). Those who were most backward – the peoples of the forests, the women, the nomadic groups, the forced labour in mines and on plantations – were taught to read and write and encouraged to form their own associations to contribute to the common effort. The strength of the women's organizations is most particularly marked in the Eritrean People's Liberation Front.

Wartime Aims and Peacetime Practice

When victory is achieved and the colonial powers evicted and the guerrillas come down from the mountains and forests into the towns, then comes the moment of truth. Only too easily can the leaders of the armed struggle slip into the administrative posts evacuated by the departed colonial administrators and their local agents. Where there had been no armed struggle this is just what did happen; and even in Tanzania where the aim was to build a socialist society the actual commitment of the more educated classes to socialism was minimal. Indeed, the very concept of socialism built upon means of production which were often hardly advanced beyond the Iron Age must seem absurdly Utopian, especially to a Marxist. The programmes of the liberation movements in Guinea-Bissau or Eritrea, for example, did not speak of building socialism but only of destroying colonial and feudal exploitation, ending corruption and class divisions and establishing a national and democratic structure.

When the inevitable counter-attack came from South Africa, and from the transnational companies, to turn back the successful revolutionary actions against the colonial powers, the problem of revolutionary leadership became acute. This arose for Tanzanians in 1971 in relation to their response to Idi Amin's coup in Uganda; but the same problem arose in all the former Portuguese colonies facing South African military invasion. The role of an organized and structured political party had to be established – to guarantee the unfolding of the programme of advance against exploitation to 'raise the cultural, social and economic life of the masses', as Davidson phrases it (1980, p. 56; and more fully described by him in *Southern Africa: The New Politics of Revolution*, p. 70). That Angola and also Mozambique survived the South African attacks in 1976 was largely thanks to the Cuban intervention, but South African support for counter-revolutionary groups continued for many years, distorting and often destroying all attempts at reconstruction.

That the fruits of liberation struggles were so generally disappointing cannot be entirely blamed upon outside intervention. The political and economic model adopted in Africa did not differ greatly from state to state, whatever the apparent ideological commitment of the leaders. It was not a model which was at all suited for building upon African democratic traditions or for transforming societies distorted by colonial rule.

The Centralized State

It was the aim of all African liberation struggles to remove white men from the seats of colonial power, and the aim of the nationalist leaders to occupy those seats. This had been the ultimate goal of which, through all those years of humiliation under colonial rule, they had dreamed. 'Seek ye first the political kingdom!' had been the advice of Kwame Nkrumah, first President of Ghana, to his fellow nationalists in the 1950s, 'and the rest will be added unto you.' The kingdom might be small, one of over fifty ex-European colonies each averaging a few million people, but it would be yours, the resources, the state revenues and above all a share in the profits of mines and marketing boards. The colonial state which these nationalist leaders inherited had been highly centralized, bureaucratic and designed for one purpose only – the extraction of raw materials and of profit from their export.

It so happened that the command structure of the centralized state had been recommended to Africa's nationalist leaders also by the example of the Soviet Union. It was not Soviet Marxism that attracted them so much as Soviet success in industrializing a

Third World country, epitomized in the 1960s by the launch of the first sputnik. The power of the central authority in African states was strengthened even beyond what it had been under colonial rule. Whatever remained of pre-colonial traditional organs of local cooperation was degraded or destroyed. All power was concentrated in the hands of a Party and ultimately in a single leader and his clientele. The result was unmitigated failure. Such centralization led in the end to disaster in the Soviet Union, but in that vast country for a time a highly educated and experienced bureaucracy deploying vast resources maintained an impressive rate of economic growth. No African state had anything approaching either the cadres or the resources on the same scale.

The failure of the centralized state in Africa was made very much worse by the collapse in world prices of Africa's export products. As each of the African colonies had been designed by their European colonial rulers to deliver two or three products as raw materials for European industry, the value of these raw materials for export made up a large proportion of the income of most of the post-colonial states. While prices remained buoyant in the 1950s and 1960s, *per capita* incomes grew and the revenues from the mines and marketing boards supplied finance for increased expenditure on education and health, and on improved infrastructure, as well as lining the pockets of the elite. Little was done to diversify from this concentration on primary production for export; the African elites were tied in to this trade as merchants and farmers or as government officials on marketing boards. The result of falling prices from the middle of the 1970s to the early 1990s was to reduce the average *per capita* income of African states by about 1 per cent a year to little more than three-quarters of what it had been, low as that was.

Debt and Structural Adjustment

The falling prices of Africa's products during the 1980s was compounded by the foreign debt which African states had contracted in the 1970s to pay for imported machinery for industrialization, and in the case of the non-oil-producing countries for the higher cost of oil imports. Africa was caught in a price-scissors of falling prices of its commodity exports at a time when manufactured goods' prices and interest rates on borrowed money were rising. Servicing the debt came to take up an ever increasing part of export earnings and inflows of investment and aid came to be overtaken by outflows of debt service payments for many of Africa's poorest countries. The tragedy was that most of the industrial development projects supplied, financed and staffed by the industrialized countries were quite inappropriate in scale and design for African needs, and became costly and under-utilized white elephants, while nothing was done to make small-scale advances in the technology of the great mass of the African peasantry.

The weakness of African economies was still further impaired by the policies of structural adjustment which were imposed upon those African states which sought assistance from the international financial institutions – the World Bank and the IMF. In the belief that the cause of Africa's problems lay entirely with the centralized state structures of economic management, these institutions made their aid and rescheduling of debt conditional upon governments agreeing to privatize state agencies, reduce state subsidies and open up their economies to the world market. At the same time, they were encouraged to expand their commodity exports to repay their debts. The result could have been predicted. Since all producers were encouraged to expand commodity exports simultaneously, stocks built up and prices fell even more sharply, with catastrophic effects on producers' incomes and on government revenues. (The evidence is compiled in Barratt Brown and Tiffen, 1992.)

Privatization and reduced state spending in their turn created economic chaos and first halted and then reversed the advances in health and education that had been achieved. The offer to sell state agencies to private investors failed to attract foreign interest because of the loss of state protection and the public subsidies which had underpinned African economies. All the independent studies by United Nations agencies and academic researchers alike indicate that, far from easing the debt, these measures aggravated the burden (UN Economic Commission for Africa, 1989, and Mosley *et al.*, 1991). Increased exports left fewer goods available to meet demand, inflation grew and the local currency collapsed. As we saw happening in Yugoslavia, those who had access to foreign currency, often by illegal activities, survived. The rest were driven increasingly into the grey and black economies and into other forms of crime, and ultimately into inter-tribal fighting. It was not by chance that massacres followed in the Sudan, Somalia and Rwanda, countries which had the highest ratio of debt to national income in Africa. By 1994 Algeria's debts exceeded these, with debt service payments due amounting to the whole of a year's export earnings. Algerians receiving remittances from families in France could survive, the rest taking to the streets and killing, in protests led by Islamic fundamentalists.

The African People: the Forgotten Alternative

It is widely supposed that civil war in Africa is only a continuation of age-old ethnic conflicts. To suppose this is, as Basil Davidson insists, to ignore all Africa's pre-colonial history. Before the fearful irruption of the Atlantic slave trade into the African continent, the many peoples of Africa had found ways and means of living together in peace and productive activity. It was the European powers who exploited ethnic differences to divide and conquer, even to the point of inventing tribes, as Professor Terry Ranger has pointed out (Ranger, 1983). Far from being unskilled in meaningful and effective participation in political affairs, as Europeans came to suppose, Africans had developed their own parliaments and systems of accountability. Davidson quotes in one place the Asante Parliament and judicial system and in another an outline of the governance of the *Asiwaju* (traditional prime minister) of Ijebu, in what is now modern Nigeria:

> a society where the monarch reigned rather than ruled, where there was decentralization of power, public accountability, and economic and political empowerment . . . democracy which involved the participation of the people prevailed . . . and government rested on consent and consensus (Davidson in Adedeji, 1993, p. 25).

Extremes of climate make Africa a hard continent, which has encouraged the instinct of cooperation rather than competition to ensure human survival and development. Claude Ake, one of Africa's most distinguished political economists, has emphasized the 'profoundly participative character of African culture'. 'Africans', he writes, 'do not generally think of themselves as self-regarding atomized beings in essentially competitive and potentially conflicting interaction with other such atomized beings. Rather their consciousness runs in the direction of belonging to an organic social whole.' He points to the way Africans regard participation as being themselves 'an organic part of the process of making decisions and of shaping policies and events ... not just exercising the right of assenting or dissenting from outputs or options that are already predetermined by processes over which one has no control whatsoever'. This notion, he believes, 'is most conducive to sustainable development'. 'In the African view, participation is a matter of sharing tangible things, namely the rewards and sacrifices of community membership.' (Ake, 1990, p. 14.)

Claude Ake claims that there is 'no lack of popular participation in development projects and, even more generally, in economy and polity in contemporary Africa', but it is not to be found in the official programmes either of governments or of aid agencies. It is what he calls 'the forgotten alternative', based upon the culture, value and interests of the African people themselves, which have for so long been overlaid and disregarded. I have tried in another place to collect together examples of such alternative activity as he claims still survives (Barratt Brown, forthcoming) and the evidence is overwhelming. It is to be found at the grass-roots of all societies – in peasant associations, in women's self-help groups, in savings clubs, in African non-governmental organizations (NGOs), and throughout the informal economy in the cities and urban areas, which accounts for incomes amounting in many countries to more than the official national income.

Africa's tragedy is that for many years after independence was achieved, the traditional associations of the people and existing cooperatives were neglected and even proscribed in favour of centrally organized agencies of the ruling party. In pursuit of European models of modernization – whether from the West or from the East – organizational forms with which they felt no identification but only alienation were imposed upon the people. The household farm, the women's work groups and marketing networks were all broken up either for waged work or for wider collectivities that had no meaning for the people. The most tragic example was the establishment of *ujamaa* villages in Tanzania, which were seen by President Nyerere as the answer to elitism, but became a model of centralized bureaucracy.

Ujamaa Villages and Poder Popular

There was an obvious attraction for African socialists in the Chinese experience of building socialism on a peasant base, since an even higher proportion than in China of the population of African societies (85 to 90 per cent) were peasants at the moment of liberation. How far Julius Nyerere of Tanzania consciously adopted Chinese experience is unclear. Chinese engineers and workers were invited in to build a new railway line from the centre to the coast. The concept of socialist villages or socialism in villages (*ujamaa vijijini*) could equally well have had more than a little in it of a glance back to Vera Zasulich, or Robert Owen, whose writings Nyerere read as a student in Edinburgh. It certainly was intended to suggest that socialism could be built on the basis of the cooperative working and living of the traditional peasant household. All the programmes of the national liberation movements had peasant cooperatives included in their aims as the basis for 'agricultural development and for the production of those consumer goods which peasant crafts could encompass. All insisted that the cooperatives must be formed on the basis of free consent.

Ujamaa villages were established often by force rather than by consent and with little or no respect for the democratic rights of the peasants to decide what they would do with their land and where and how they should settle. The whole sad story is admirably documented by Andrew Coulson (1979). In the one-time

Portuguese colonies the influence upon liberation leaders came from Cuba rather than from China; and the Cubans did much to defend the new regimes from attack by South African forces and South African armed guerrillas. The parties which had led the liberation struggles, PAIGC in Guinea-Bissau, Frelimo in Mozambique, MPLA in Angola and later ZANU in Zimbabwe, were all inspired by the Cuban revolution and committed to the concept of *poder popular*, 'people's power'.

Poder popular meant development through mass participation in government, agriculture, industry, commerce, culture, education and health. *Poder popular* in Portuguese is the same as the Spanish *poder popular* which the Cuban Revolution has made its own. Cuba's population was predominantly peasant, like most African societies, with one large capital city in which capitalist development was concentrated. It was Cuban revolutionary policy to develop the countryside at the expense of Havana. *Poder popular* was first tried out in 1974 in Matanzas province, next door to Havana, not the poorest but not the richest of the thirteen provinces outside the capital. Its success in that province led to its wide adoption. It has to be added that subsequently its effectiveness was limited by a great extension of the central planning system. The similarity of name does not imply that the African societies in the liberated Portuguese colonies borrowed the concept from Cuba. But certainly their belief in it was reinforced by Cuban military support and more than that by the democratic style and manner of the hundreds of Cuban doctors, health workers and technicians working in Angola.

In African societies after liberation, as Basil Davidson described it (1980, p. 57), the concept of people's power had three elements to it: (a) the extension of the powers of local government – village, district and town assemblies with their own executives and with more and more responsibilities allocated to them, both political and economic; (b) the promotion of trade-union structures, not only protecting workers and their families but organizing better systems of production and exchange; (c) the encouragement of other forms of mass participation and particularly of the women in their own organizations at the grass roots.

It is not pretended by Davidson, nor by anybody else, that this process of 'self-liberation' is automatic or guaranteed. There were mass organizations, including trade unions and women's organizations, in Cuba as well as in Africa which appeared to friendly critics to be lacking in real grass-roots activity (see O'Sullivan, 1982). Getting the goods produced, increasing agricultural productivity, investing in new plant, defending the country against invasion – whether in Africa or in Cuba – began to impose their own priorities and organizational structures. We have seen it in China and we saw it in the Soviet Union. In Africa, at much lower levels of productive capacity and with fewer cultural and educational resources, self-liberation was that much more difficult. To take emergency measures, as in China or Tanzania, by sending the officials out into the villages and enforcing village organizations through the supply or withdrawal of essential supplies, may work for a time. It does not ensure long-term development, let alone generating political consciousness with which socialism can be built.

Africa's Own Model

In 1987 a group of African scholars from many disciplines met together in Kericho, Kenya, under the auspices of the Nairobi-based African Academy of Sciences and the Dakar-based Council for the Development of Economic and Social Research in Africa (CODESRIA), to discuss a number of papers prepared previously by several participants on their vision of Africa in 2057, a century after Sudan and Ghana achieved independence from colonial rule. They established the Beyond Hunger Project as a counter to what they called the 'self-fulfilling' prophecies of an Africa in permanent crisis. They challenged all the conventional wisdom on Africa – of state-centred, directive, donor-fed, capital-intensive projects – and proclaimed a vision of grass-roots oriented, supportive, locally initiated, people-intensive programmes. They saw no future in the projection of current perspectives, but saw levers for change in the delinkage of African economies from primary production for export, in South Africa's democratization, in more pluralist political associations and in the liberation of women, intellectuals and ethnic minorities from neglect and oppression, in new adaptations of technological innovation to African conditions and, finally, in broader regional associations and new forms of pan-African unity.

It was an inspiring vision, but it did not remain a dream. Within two years, the UN Economic Commission for Africa (UNECA) had responded to a self-satisfied World Bank report on *Africa's Adjustment and Growth in the 1980s* with its own *African Alternative to Structural Adjustment Programmes: A Framework for Transformation and Recovery*. This emphasized that human beings and not institutions or markets must be the 'fulcrum for development', which must involve 'the extended family for the cooperative spirit of self-help development and traditional sanctions on leadership'. The programme has been criticized for its lack of practicality and its continued reliance on government intervention in place of the market (Pickett and Singer, 1990). Such criticism simply ignores the thirty-one practical measures proposed in the Alternative Programme and the important role assigned for the market and for private enterprise within a framework of public regulation.

Nor was the UNECA Alternative Programme a single shot across the bows of the international institutions. It had been preceded by a whole series of all-African declarations by the Organization of African Unity (OAU) and Action Programmes prepared with UNECA officials, and was followed by still more declarations, programmes and charters. The OAU was founded in 1963 in response to Nkrumah's call for 'Africa to Unite, or Perish'. At its silver jubilee twenty-five years later, its historian, Kwesi Krafona, concluded that there was 'nothing to celebrate but misery to harvest'. Yet in the next six years, between 1988 and 1994, much was accomplished in the development of regional organizations and continent-wide policies.

In 1980, the Lagos Plan of Action for Africa's development towards economic unification by the year 2000 had been prepared for the OAU. It was a response to the failure of African governments to obtain protection against the declining world prices of their exports through help from a Common Fund for Commodities, which was to have been established by the UN Conference on Trade and Development (UNCTAD). The Lagos Plan was a major step towards common action by African governments. It was countered immediately by a World Bank report proposing to supply funds to individual governments which adopted structural adjustment programmes. The African initiative was stalled, but was renewed at conferences in Abuja between 1985 and 1987 to discuss a common African position on external debt. These produced Africa's Priority Programme for Economic Recovery (APPER), adopted by the UN General Assembly, against the single dissenting vote of the United States, as the UN Programme of Action (UN-PAAERD). The Abuja conferences were followed by the Khartoum Conference in 1988 on the 'Human Dimension of Africa's Economic Recovery and Accelerated Development' and finally in 1989 by the UNECA Alternative Programme.

The response of the World Bank was once again immediate and dismissive. A vast new report with several appendices was issued as a *Long-term Perspective Study of Sub-Saharan Africa*, which borrowed much of the language of the UNECA programme, but proposed the continuation of structural adjustment programmes country by country, under the Bank's surveillance, which were said to be working successfully. It was greeted with outrage by African governments, although most of them had apparently entered willingly into such programmes in order to obtain rescheduling of their debts. An expert group was called upon by the UN Secretary-General to consider Africa's commodity problems and propose a solution. This reported once again in favour of a world-market, export-led strategy for Africa's products, despite falling world prices. The World Bank's reports on *Adjustment in Africa* became more self-critical, but held to their presumption that recovery must come through individual private enterprise in the national and world markets and through the reduction of state involvement in the economy, although in South-East Asia the Bank's experts were conceding that such involvement was the foundation of the 'Asian economic miracle'.

In the meantime, conferences were being held by the OAU throughout Africa on how Africans envisaged their own way forward: implementing the UN Charter on Women's Rights and establishing the importance of the role of women in development; proposing an Agenda for Action on the Environment; drawing up a Plan of Action on Population Control; and, most significantly, preparing an African Charter on Popular Participation. These declarations and charters were in part at least in reaction to a continent-wide explosion of demands for democratic reforms in African governance. Single-party governments with leaders of such long standing and eminence as Nyerere in Tanzania and Kaunda in Zambia were forced to hold elections, in which opposition parties gained power. Even tyrants like Mobutu of Zaïre were put under pressure to give way to demands for change.

The crucial question emerged: could all the conferences and the opening-up of government to opposition groups taking place at the top of African societies be linked to the grass-roots organizations in the villages and the informal economy in the urban areas? The view of the World Bank had always been that this could only be accomplished by Africa's private entrepreneurs in commerce and industry. It was the firm conviction of the Bank's experts (Marsden, 1992) that, with state controls removed, these burgeoning African capitalists had begun successfully to fill that 'gap in the middle' of African society which has been so widely noted. They expected them largely to displace both dwindling peasant associations and a declining informal economy. The prevailing view of Africa's own experts is that the gap is being filled by plundering privateers and that the cooperative principle must establish itself in both rural and urban economies, not necessarily as an alternative to the private entrepreneur, but as the leading force in the empowerment of the producers upon which Africa's development depends (Adedeji, 1993, pp. 215ff.). This will mean at local level the strengthening of African NGOs to hold together smaller associations on a democratic basis, sometimes working in partnership with foreign NGOs, and at a regional level the breaking-down of barriers between nation states and the reuniting of ethnic and language groups in market networks that are large enough to be viable.

The choice or degree of combination of these different views will depend upon the varying resources and development of the separate African countries. The problem for all will remain the same as that which we found in looking at China's modernization. In order to establish a process of rapid growth in agriculture and industry, peasant cooperatives and capitalist private entrepreneurs operating in competitive national and international markets must depend at first upon powerful supporting structures of the state, and of a state large enough alone or in combination with others to take the strain. State intervention will then be needed to redistribute wealth from the rich to the poor, since economic growth widens the gap between rich and poor and between developed and backward regions, thereby narrowing the market in the long term. It tends also to be ecologically unsound in the short-term abuse of the environment, unless regulatory measures of conservation are enforced. For development to be sustainable, as the African people have learnt over centuries of experience, it has to be pursued through institutions of cooperation and popular participation. No development of any sort, however, will take place today without the cancellation of the foreign debt. Only then will a new model for Africa be able to include the means to ensure survival in a world economy in which immensely powerful forces are at work.

FURTHER READING

ACHEBE, CHINUA (ed.), *Beyond Hunger in Africa: Africa 2057 – An African Vision*, James Currey, 1990

ADEDEJI, ADEBAYO (ed.), *Africa within the World: Beyond Dispossession and Dependence*, Zed Books, 1993

AKE, CLAUDE, 'Sustaining Development on the Indigenous', in World Bank, *The Long-Term Perspective Study of Sub-Saharan Africa*, Background Papers, Vol. 3, Washington, 1990

BARRATT BROWN, MICHAEL, *Africa's Choices: After 30 Years of the World Bank*, forthcoming

BARRATT BROWN, MICHAEL, and TIFFEN, PAULINE, *Short Changed: Africa and World Trade*, Pluto Press, 1992

CABRAL, AMILCAR, *Revolution in Guinea*, Stage I, 1969

CABRAL, AMILCAR, *Unity and Struggle*, Heinemann, 1980

COULSON, ANDREW (ed.), *African Socialism in Practice*, Spokesman, 1979

DAVIDSON, BASIL, *Cross Roads in Africa*, Spokesman, 1980

DAVIDSON, BASIL, *The People's Cause: A History of Guerillas in Africa*, Longman, 1981

DAVIDSON, BASIL, *The Black Man's Burden: Africa and the Curse of the Nation State*, James Currey, 1992

FIREBRACE, JAMES, and HOLLAND, STUART, *Never Kneel Down: Drought, Development and Liberation in Eritrea*, Spokesman, 1984

KRAFONA, KWESI (ed.), *Organization of African Unity, 25 Years On*, Afroworld, 1988

MARSDEN, KEITH, 'African Entrepreneurs – Pioneers of Development', in *Small Enterprise Development*, Vol. 3, No. 2, ITD Publications, June 1992

MOSLEY, PAUL, *et al.*, *Aid and Power: The World Bank Policy Based Lending*, Routledge, 1991

MUNSLOW, BARRY, *Africa: Problems in the Transition to Socialism*, Zed Books, 1986

ONIMODE, BADE, *A Future for Africa: Beyond the Politics of Adjustment*, Earthscan, 1992

O'SULLIVAN, SUE, 'Women in Cuba', *Spare Rib*, 20 August 1982

PICKETT, JAMES, and SINGER, HANS (eds.), *Towards Economic Recovery in Sub-Saharan Africa*, Routledge, 1990

RANGER, TERENCE, 'The Invention of Tradition in Colonial Africa', in Eric Hobsbawm and Terence Ranger, *The Invention of Tradition*, Cambridge, 1983

UN ECONOMIC COMMISSION FOR AFRICA, *African Alternative to Structural Adjustment Programmes: A Framework for Transformation and Recovery*, Addis Ababa, April 1989

WORLD BANK, *Sub-Saharan Africa: From Crisis to Sustainable Growth, a Long-Term Perspective Study*, Washington, November 1989

WORLD BANK, *Adjustment in Africa: Reforms, Results, and the Road Ahead*, Oxford, 1994

3 WHAT MODELS DO WE NEED NOW?

17 MODELS FOR UNDERSTANDING TRANSNATIONAL CAPITALISM:
(1) WHAT COMES AFTER THE NATION STATE?

The development of capitalism into a worldwide economic system took place side by side with the consolidation of the power of the nation state. In reality, most states are not single-nation states, but, like the United Kingdom, made up of several nations. State formation under a central government, the unification of the market within a certain territory, with a common currency and taxes, weights and measures, and laws governing the ownership and protection of property, was a necessary condition for capitalist progress. Yet once their power was established, owners of capital did not want the state to interfere in their business. So there was invented the story of the United Kingdom as a kind of 'nightwatchman' state with governments pursuing policies of *laisser-faire*. It was a myth.

The nation state, even such a one as the United Kingdom in the nineteenth century, provided for a central bank, roads, railways, postal service, land enclosure, company laws, regulation of trade unions, health and sanitation services, and a system of schools and law and order, with prisons, a police force, an army and a navy that patrolled the seven seas to protect overseas investments and, finally, the government of a network of colonies round the world which came to incorporate a quarter of the earth's land surface. Some nightwatchman! But there was much more to come, as the state was used to protect industries with tariffs, nationalize industrial undertakings, provide a comprehensive health and education service, housing, pensions and social security – all the provisions of what we now call the 'welfare state'.

Each nation state prided itself on its sovereignty, that is, its freedom to make its own laws, issue its own money, raise its own taxes, protect its own land and people, defend its own frontiers. Being a colony or other form of dependency meant being unable to do these things and having them done for you by an outside power over which you had no control. Some states started large and contained many nations comprising hundreds of millions of people. Some were small and might contain only one nation and comprise no more than a few hundred thousand people. What they all have in common is their sovereignty, whether they have a sovereign king or queen or state president.

Some states emerged with a single unitary system of government under which all power was held at the centre, even though some might be delegated to lower bodies, as in the UK. Some of the larger states were created with a federal system of government under a constitution by which power was divided between the centre and the regions or localities, as in the USA. In some federal states, each of the regional bodies, which had powers granted by the constitution, represented a single nationality, as in the republics of the Soviet Union and in part in what was Yugoslavia. Some nations, like the Kurds, have no state. Some states' frontiers cross the boundaries of nations, as is often the case in Africa, where on gaining independence states were based on colonial frontiers which had ignored ethnic groupings.

Sovereignty at Bay

Large or small, unitary or federal, every state has the same responsibility for its economy and is separately represented in international institutions. The Charter of the United Nations begins with a flourish: 'We the people . . .', but ends with establishing an organization of states without any *direct* representation of peoples. The first principle of the United Nations Organization clearly established the 'sovereign equality of all . . . members' and spelt this out by insisting that 'nothing in the Charter is to authorize the United Nations to intervene in matters which are essentially within the domestic jurisdiction of any *state*' (emphasis added). Thus the World Bank and the International Monetary Fund, for example, treat separately with each individual member state.

None the less, the sovereignty of nation states has been under challenge from several directions – sideways from transnational companies, from above by the new super states like the European Union, and from below by rising national consciousness in many multinational states like the Soviet Union. As early as 1971 Raymond Vernon, a Harvard Professor of Economics, had written a book entitled *Sovereignty at Bay*, which contrasted the growing size and power of the transnational companies with the limited grasp of the nation state. At the same time, the nation states of Western Europe were engaged in forming a European Community and economic union to respond to this growing power of the transnationals. Such a union detracted from the sovereignty of its members in many different respects, to such an extent that in some states, and particularly in the UK, the concept of 'subsidiarity' was invented to protect the powers of the nation state against usurpation from above. An even more powerful challenge was coming from below – from the separate nations within each state. This led to the actual disintegration of the Soviet Union, Yugoslavia, Czechoslovakia and Ethiopia, and to secessionary movements in the UK, Spain, Sri Lanka, Nigeria and other African states.

It appears on the surface of these developments that a contradiction was growing between the capitalist market, which was becoming ever more a global market, not only for goods, but for capital and labour, and the governments, which were regulating the market, but which remained national, even narrowly national. The old models of nation-state management, whether by nightwatchmen, Keynesian or monetarist governments, appeared to be losing their meaning as more and more economic decisions are made by large companies operating transnationally. But beneath the surface the change is not so great as it appeared. Capital has always been international, the law of value tending to equalize profits worldwide. While land and labour and certain goods were always relatively immobile, capital could move across borders. Indeed, it was an essential element in the working of the capitalist system, that capital could move anywhere at any time.

National and International Money

The way in which capitalism developed, based upon separate nation states each with its own money, gave a misleading impression. It appeared that each state should, and could, manage its own money and with it stake out its own economic development. All the separate states' currencies were, however, linked in a hierarchical order to the other currencies through exchange rates and were in effect only subdivisions of the dominant currency. Thus it was the chief role of the pound sterling and then of the US dollar to create the necessary conditions for the mobility of capital. The fact that these national currencies were in the last resort convertible into gold gave them additional security, but gold could not in itself be a world currency. World trade needed a strong world money in constant circulation.

This is the one nugget of truth in the arguments of the monetarists and of those who have emphasized the commercial element in British imperialism (Barratt Brown, 1994). The power of money had to be preserved for the system to survive and there had to be one form of money that was secure. The fallacy in the arguments lies in the belief that any national currency performing the role of a world money could be sustained and made secure only by monetary measures. We saw earlier, in Chapter 6, that the power of money in capitalism comes from real things – the capacity of money to set labour to work with machinery to produce profit, its truly productive capacity, and not any speculative or trading profit that emerges solely from the sphere of circulation. Thus when the British economy ceased to produce a surplus, except from investment and trading in the productive activity of other, rival economies, the pound sterling could no longer command respect. The US dollar faces the same humiliation today, and, unless the US economy can re-establish a surplus with the rest of the world, a new world currency will have to be found to guarantee the effective working of the system.

Within the separate nation states, governments used their power to issue and manage money, to tax and to spend, as instruments for the general strengthening of their economies. It appeared that they really could do this; but there were limits, of varying degrees for different states. That there is a hierarchy of national currencies becomes obvious if one looks at the different rates of interest which you have to pay to borrow the money of different nation states. The range of rates for six-month borrowing on 24 February 1994 was: Japanese yen, 2.25 per cent; US dollar, 3.8 per cent; Swiss franc, 4.0 per cent; Canadian dollar, 4.1 per cent; German Deutschmark, 5.2 per cent; pound sterling, 5.3 per cent; Dutch guilder, 5.5 per cent; French franc, 6.1 per cent; Danish krone, 6.2 per cent; Italian lira, 7.7 per cent; Spanish peseta, 8.2 per cent; Portuguese escudo, 10 per cent.

There are no prizes for guessing which are the stronger currencies, reflecting the stronger economies at that moment. The currencies that can be borrowed at lower rates are those which can be expected not to depreciate during the period they are held, because the economy behind them is believed to be capable of sustaining them. The weaker economies are not trusted so that those with funds to invest have to be bribed with higher rates to hold the money of these economies.

This has a major significance for national sovereignty in money matters, as we saw in Chapter 6. There are many who believe that the sovereign power of a British government to manage the country's economy depends on control over the currency, and that cannot be abandoned. It has been said, not entirely in jest, that British sovereignty lasts for a few hours only, after the German Bundesbank changes the interest rate that it will pay on Deutschmark borrowings. The British government and the Bank of England have time to discuss whether they should follow suit at once or somewhat later with a corresponding change in the British rate. And both largely depend on the US rate and the US rate on the Japanese rate. The importance of this limitation is that management of interest rates was always in the past an important tool in any government's locker for speeding up or slowing down private investment and economic activity in the national economy. UK governments can now no longer afford to reduce interest rates to encourage economic recovery, if the result is that money-holders will simply stop holding British currency. If enough do that, the value of the currency goes down and that creates further problems for the government from a rise in the price of imports.

Those who argue in favour of defending even the vestiges of national sovereignty over money often complain that the alternative is to place the nation totally under the sovereignty of another state. Keynes's alternative was a group of faceless bankers who, he hoped, would come to 'take a world objective outlook'. Such illusions have been destroyed by the actual experience of the World Bank, although in Keynes's defence one has to say that the Bank was a United States creation from the start and not at all what Keynes had envisaged. The alternative of joint action among sovereign states to take the necessary steps to manage the world's money has been tried at regular meetings of the ministers of finance of the major powers and at similar meetings in the European Community. It seems clear that these have been wholly ineffectual either in maintaining economic growth or in keeping down interest rates.

Joint Action or Common Action

The explanation is that joint action is not the same as common action. Joint action is applied as the government of each state sees fit and generally in such a way as to extract some national advantage. This was unsatisfactory in the 1930s, when it led to just the beggar-my-neighbour policies which Keynes's international banking proposals were designed to prevent. Joint action in money matters is even less likely to be effective today because of the speed at which changes take place. All holders of capital, whether governments, private individuals or large corporations, are having to face a radical acceleration in the mobility of capital, not only across national boundaries but across types of assets. This is not entirely, or even mainly, the result of speculative activity, which has certainly increased much faster than the growth in productive activity; it is because of the enormous range of alternative temporary resting-places for profits before they are converted into long-term productive assets. Money flashes round the world at electronic speed, faster than the speed of sound. For the financial managers of the large companies that generate profits worldwide, there is at every single moment a question about where to put their company's money.

When at the end of February 1994 there was heavy selling of European government bonds, especially of UK government gilts, because it was believed that US interest rates might be raised, one leading dealer commented: 'This sell-off is completely unwarranted on fundamental grounds [i.e. any problems in the European economies themselves]. What we're dealing with has very little to do with economic fundamentals – it's about the preservation of capital' (*Financial Times*, 25 February 1994). The fact that he was quite wrong is irrelevant – it had very much to do with the fundamentals of the Japanese economy – but what mattered was that the dealers believed that it was all part of a game in the Casino of world money markets.

For governments to catch money on the wing for short-term or long-term stay is an anxious and frustrating activity in which only the major players can participate. It is not only, however, that most governments have lost the power to control the movements of money, there is now not even one government that has that power. The days of a world currency that is also a national currency are numbered. If the capitalist world is not to descend into chaos, a new world money will be needed that is no one country's national currency. Keynes knew this fifty years ago, but the United States dollar was then still preferred to Keynes's 'Bancor' as a common currency. We shall return to the question of the world's money in the next chapter. There is a halfway house for the European states that has now to be examined, and that is the prospect of a common European currency.

The European Community moved steadily throughout the 1980s towards a single market for goods and services, with common accepted standards for production and for labour, and with the final aim of an Economic and Monetary Union. It was hoped that the twelve member economies would converge by the end of the century to a point where they could have just one currency, the ecu, in place of twelve (if other states were added by then, they would add their strength to the ecu). It was clear that the management of the currency would have to be a common task and not a joint task. A European Central Bank would have to be authorized by all the members to act on their behalf in the fast-moving monetary world. But this was a prospect to terrify all the nationalists other than the Germans, since all – including the Germans – assumed that the Bank's president would be a German.

The problem of controlling a Central Bank is a real one, even where there is only one money that is not an individual nation's money but is one that is accepted by all members. The advantage of having one nation's money as a common currency was always said to be its management by a powerful government and the accountability of that government to democratic control. Keynes's international bankers running the world's money were not acceptable to the United States Senate, but there were doubts about them also in the minds of every good democrat. In 1944 the United States took on the job of world money management, but by the 1980s the dollar, even a Euro-dollar, was no longer regarded as totally acceptable outside the USA. There is nothing democratic about the situation that followed. It was then the finance directors of the giant transnational companies who took over control of the world's money, although not in any collective or coordinated manner.

Ken Coates, the Euro-MP, has summed up the contradictory imperatives which face any democrat:

> One: national independence and autonomy must be upheld as still the most basic area of democratic advance;
> Two: the growth of transnational economic power, and the weight of accompanying crisis, demand measures of international coordination which can best be undertaken within a democratic framework. (Coates, 1988)

Democratic Frameworks for Social Cohesion

The question is: what democratic framework? Coates, in the article from which the quotation is taken, was arguing for a directly elected assembly of the people within the United Nations Organization to bring real people's power to bear upon the haggling of the representatives of states worldwide. But, as a Member of the European Parliament, he has argued elsewhere for the democratic framework of the European Union to be strengthened. Just as the smaller individual nations have looked for greater independence within their multi-nation states, so they have at the same time recognized the importance of economic coordination at a higher level. Thus the Scots in the UK and the Catalans in Spain are fervent advocates both of a greater measure of national self-government and also of stronger powers for the European Parliament and Commission.

The need for measures of international economic coordination is twofold. The first need is to counteract the power of the transnational companies to divide and conquer, state by state, and to accumulate capital in a limited number of regions, marginalizing the rest, which turns out to be the majority. The second need is to correct uneven development and growing inequality both between states and inside states. Whether we take a Marxian, Keynesian or Myrdal-type model, all show that capitalism tends to polarize wealth and poverty. One of the main tasks of the nation state as it has developed over the years has been to maintain social cohesion. This it has done in part by celebrating a national interest through a common flag, national anthem and historic anniversaries. But for this to be more than ideology, it has had to effect some redistribution of wealth and income – from the rich to the poor. This has not been from altruistic or humanitarian motives among the rich, but rather from fear of social breakdown and of failing purchasing power.

Where such systems of redistribution built into political constitutions break down, as they did in Yugoslavia, not only the economy but the whole social order collapses. Inequality between states can equally lead to breakdown. The increasing amounts of foreign debt to be paid to developed countries from the export earnings of the developing countries have already led to economic collapse and military rule in many Latin American and African countries, of which Algeria is the latest and most tragic example. Algeria and Yugoslavia illustrate the way external inequities aggravate internal inequalities. In both countries those who had access to foreign currency – Deutschmarks or francs – from tourism and migrant labour could manage to live. The rest, holding a local money that was increasingly worthless, could only survive by slaving, prostitution, stealing or in the last resort killing.

The redistribution of income from rich to poor, to create a more balanced economy and to sustain purchasing power, proved to be impractical in Yugoslavia and has broken down over the debt settlements of the developed and developing countries. It has been argued that this is because the gap between the incomes of rich and poor was too wide in these cases – 1 to 7 between the poorest and richest states in Yugoslavia, 1 to 60 between the average low-income economy and average high-income economy in the world as a whole. Within the UK, the gap in income per head is only 1 to 2 between Northern Ireland and Greater London, and inside Europe only 1 to 3 between Greece and Germany. Levelling-up in Europe is regarded as an attainable goal. This is what is being attempted between East and West Germany, albeit attended by many problems.

A Single Currency as the Unifying Force

The German example showed that adopting a single currency was a quick if drastic way of achieving the desired result of unification. With only one money, and no possibility for economic activities in East Germany to be protected, most East German firms were uncompetitive with those in West Germany and collapsed. Financial transfers from the West were at once required – in the short term, to pay unemployment benefit, in the long term to invest in new plant and equipment. It has placed a heavy tax burden on the West German people and kept their interest rates high because of the need for borrowed money. Similar action to support the poorer European states – Greece, Portugal, Ireland and Spain – would not be easy, but those who favour such a policy can point to strong arguments.

The strongest argument in favour of a single European currency is, no doubt, the power that it could wield in the world monetary arena, to face up to the dollar and the yen, not just for competitive advantage, but in order to win support for a new world money. Such a new world order is the subject of the next chapter. Inside Europe, the great advantage that is proposed is the possibility of embarking upon a common programme of economic development, to reduce unemployment and increase welfare, without each separate state holding back in case it found itself alone out in front with higher taxes and interest rates and unable to compete with the others. This is always the danger of 'joint action'. It happened when the French socialist government on acceding to power in 1984 proposed to carry out the essential stages of a programme drawn up by an all-European socialist group and entitled *Out of Crisis: a Programme for European Recovery*. Goods flooded into France from the other European countries and capital flooded out, until the French government called a halt and proceeded to put the machine into reverse, adopting thereafter the most restrictive fiscal and deflationary monetary measures.

A particular advantage of common action with a single currency is that all Europeans can make immediate comparison between the social and welfare provisions which are available in each state. At present these are concealed behind the different currency labels and the difficulty of knowing whether to translate these according to current exchange rates or purchasing power parities (i.e. what a household can actually buy with its money in different countries). While governments may attempt to level such social costs downwards in order to steal a march on others by making their national costs more competitive, as the British government attempted to do in opting out of the 'Social Chapter' of the Maastricht Treaty, European working men and women will seek to level *upwards* to the best standards available anywhere in Europe.

If it is then argued that such levelling upwards will make the whole of Europe uncompetitive with the rest of the world, and particularly with the USA and Japan, there are two answers generally offered from the other side. The first is that there is no evidence that countries with high levels of taxation and welfare expenditure have fallen behind the others in production and exports. On the contrary, they have been in the lead. This is not

surprising since higher labour costs will have encouraged investment in new plant and machinery, while availability of cheap
labour holds back such investment.

The second answer that is given to those who would cut
European social costs to compete with non-European suppliers is
that European support, especially from the trade unions, will need
to be given to overseas suppliers to enable them to raise their
standards. The alternative is that beggar-my-neighbour policies by
governments are reproduced in cut-price labour competition by
producers. There is always a danger that a united Europe, of the
North and the West, could become a fortress Europe. Already
largely self-sufficient (only 7 per cent of the needs of the European
Union are met from outside), such a wealthy community could
seek to cut itself off from the rest of the world. This is hardly
likely with so many European companies operating worldwide.
Nor would it make sense in terms of the subsequently reduced
purchasing power in those non-European markets, upon which
European manufacturers have always relied. But that is the subject
of the next chapter.

The Role of Bankers and Economic Policy-Making

There is no doubt that bankers have a bad image. They borrow at
one rate and lend at another and make a profit in the process.
They take their cut from all the profits of productive industry
without contributing anything to production. They appear to
regard small businesses as not viable unless they have saleable
assets, and have decided that some small countries are what they
now term 'non-bankable'. They sought and obtained tax concessions from the state for defaulting borrowers, including many
from the developing countries, but did not write off these countries' debts in their own books. In Britain, though not in Germany
or some other countries in Europe, they take a short-term view of
the return on capital, which precludes the kind of long-term
investment that Japanese industry can rely upon.

Central bankers are seen as older and more conservative even
than other bankers and to be counted on to put the reduction of

the rate of inflation before any consideration of reducing the rate of unemployment. In the UK there is a particular problem, that the City of London, which is the heart of the banking world, is widely perceived – and not only on the left – as having for long had far too much power at the centre, at the expense of British industrialists, who have mainly worked and lived in the English provinces, in Scotland and Wales. This is a half-truth, like the story of the nightwatchman state. The bankers in Britain originated from industry and shipping and, while they did not put up risk money for industry, they provided overdrafts and credits, and financed overseas mining and railways investment.

The links between banking and industry in Britain were always much closer than is suggested by historians who have sought to revise the traditional Whig and Marxist interpretations. But, as the City showed in its antagonism to Chamberlain's call for tariff reform and imperial preference at the end of the nineteenth century, it had a much wider view of the system of world capitalism than one limited to trade and investment in the British Empire. It was only when British economic power was waning after the 1930s that the narrower range of empire trade and a sterling area became important City concerns. The outflow of investment capital from Britain since 1979 is a function not of the City's predilection for overseas investment, but of the opportunistically international interests of modern transnational companies. Whether they are registered in the UK or elsewhere, they will invest without consideration of their national origins.

What then is proposed to make the bankers accountable to a wider interest than that of the major money-holders? This question has become one of the first importance in relation to the development of the European Community towards an Economic Union. Euro-sceptics in the UK have resisted every step that took Europe nearer to federalism, but the federalists have not always been as open as they should have been in revealing the federalist implications of their proposals.

The arguments around the creation of a central banking system for Europe are a case in point. The chief aim of a central bank, as it is of its chief money-holders, is price stability, that is to say in European Union terms, maintaining the strength of the ecu. This was accepted in the European Commission's Basic Document on Economic and Monetary Union for the operation of the European System of Central Banks (ESCB), but the terms of reference for the ESCB state:

> without prejudice to the objective of price stability, the ESCB shall support the general economic policies in the Community with a view to contributing to the objectives of the Community as laid down in article 2 [of the Maastricht Treaty].

Article 2 in effect therefore provides the bankers with their guidelines. This article specifies that

> The Community shall have as its task, by establishing a common market and an economic and monetary union ... to promote throughout the Community, a harmonious and balanced development of economic activities, sustainable and non-inflationary growth respecting the environment, a high degree of convergence of economic performance, a high level of employment and of social protection, the raising of the standard of living and the quality of life, and economic and social cohesion and solidarity among Member States.

Article 2 refers also to implementing under article 3

> the adoption of an economic policy which is based on close coordination of Member States' economic policies, of the internal market and on the definition of common objectives.

Stuart Holland, in drawing attention to the careful drafting of these articles, has sought to answer those Euro-sceptics who complain that member states are being asked to give up their own power to manage their economies without any institution at European level taking over the responsibility. It is obvious that a bank – the one new European institution that is being proposed – cannot make economic policies; it can only be required to abide by them. Stuart Holland, in pressing the case for a European Recovery Programme, therefore proposes that the Economic Policy Committee of the Council of Ministers (i.e. of the separate national governments) should be formalized as a 'Standing Committee for Cohesion' (Holland, 1993).

The fact is that bankers are only to be feared as makers of economic policy if there is no clear line of economic policy being pursued by government. If European governments are to combine their economic policy-making, then the logic of this is that they will need to create institutional forms for such common action. For these to have the necessary legitimacy, they need to be democratically accountable. That means the acceptance of the federal principle and the strengthening of the European Parliament as both the forum for discussion of economic policy and the instrument for ensuring that the bankers stay within their guidelines. A constitution is no better than the commitment of its constituents to it, but without a federal constitution it is meaningless to pretend that there can be any advance from ineffectual promises of joint action to effective planning of common action in Europe's economic development.

FURTHER READING

BARRATT BROWN, MICHAEL, 'Away with all the Great Arches: Anderson's History of British Capitalism', *New Left Review*, No. 167, January–February 1988

BARRATT BROWN, MICHAEL, *European Union: Fortress or Democracy?*, Spokesman, 1991

BARRATT BROWN, MICHAEL, 'Commerce as Imperialism', in *End Papers*, Spokesman, 1994

COATES, KEN, *Think Globally, Act Locally: The United Nations and the Peace Movements*, Spokesman, 1988, p. 148

COATES, KEN, and BARRATT BROWN, MICHAEL (eds.), *A European Recovery Programme*, Spokesman, 1993

GRANT, WYN, *The Politics of Economic Policy*, Harvester Wheatsheaf, 1993

HALL, PETER, *The Political Power of Economic Ideas*, Princeton, 1989

HOLLAND, STUART (ed.), *Out of Crisis: A Project for European Recovery*, Spokesman, 1983

HOLLAND, STUART, *The European Imperative: Economic and Social Cohesion in the 1990s*, Spokesman, 1993

VERNON, RAYMOND, *Sovereignty at Bay*, Macmillan, 1971

18 MODELS FOR UNDERSTANDING TRANSNATIONAL CAPITALISM
(2) OLD SPHERES OF INFLUENCE OR A NEW ORDER?

It has been the great advantage of capital, compared with any other form of property, that it can move freely across the whole world, wherever the highest yield may be gained. Capital never before moved so fast and so far and in such large amounts as today. Nor was it ever so free of state controls. This was the message of the last chapter. Capital still has to be incorporated, at least for a time, in machinery and land and materials and labour, to yield a profit that is not just a sharing-out of someone else's profit. Control over capital – for investment in plant, for loans to buy materials, for credit to finance operations – is what gives power. The question that has to be answered is why capital flows just where it does and nowhere else.

Most of the world's capital is held by a small number of very large transnational companies. That we know from Chapter 3. It is the ability of these companies to move their capital around and not just the companies' size and the size of their undertakings that is the foundation of their power. The working model of capital is dynamic; it cannot be static. Capital that is not earning profit every minute of the day, every day of the week, every week of the year is in effect making a loss. It is no longer ownership of the means of production that now gives most profit, but control over markets, not just in distribution but in the whole chain of commercialization that realizes the value added by labour.

It was David Ricardo's insight into the nature of capital when it was *fixed* in machinery that showed that capital cannot then be 'switched', and cannot therefore be said to *justify* a certain rate of profit. The value of capital is determined by the rate of profit and not vice versa. But Ricardo also saw that the amount of capital fixed in machinery can be reduced for a given output and is being continually what Marx called 'cheapened'. Then, the rate of profit can be increased. The key to capitalist success is the economy of time. Capital must yield its return in the shortest possible time, in order to be 'recycled' for further accumulation and investment. Where the capital flows will depend on the value added by labour in the time available. The argument between those who hold to different models of the flow of capital is about different forces of attraction.

Models of Development, Dependency and Underdevelopment

(1) The Leninist Model

In Chapter 8 we noted how Lenin, writing on the eve of the Russian Revolution, summed up what he saw as the Marxist model of imperialism in the era that succeeded the 1870s as follows: concentration of production in monopolies, the merging of banking and industrial capital, the export of capital rather than goods, the sharing out of the whole world between the great monopolies, the territorial division of the world among the capitalist powers, in which the state was increasingly integrated with the barons of finance capital. Thus capitalist super-profits from the colonies were said by Lenin to support not only the capitalists, but also a labour aristocracy in the decaying imperial powers, at the expense of the impoverishment and oppression of more than half the world's population. This was a model of the nation-state imperialism of the great powers, which ruled the world in the first half of the twentieth century.

What we have to consider now is the continuing effect of such economic imperialism on the development of the world economy. When Lenin after the Russian Revolution offered to a wider audience his essay on *Imperialism, the Highest Stage of Capitalism*, written originally in 1916, he especially emphasized in the Introduction to the French and German editions of 1920 the connection between decay at the imperial centres and exploitation of the overseas colonies. In so doing he was deliberately placing the Soviet Union at the head of the underdeveloped countries of the world and appealing for support for the young republic. His earlier hopes of revolutions in Western Europe, supporting the Soviet Union, had been abandoned.

In following the Marxist model of the capitalist world economy in Chapter 8, we recognized the economic pressures behind the spread of capitalism from Europe outwards throughout the nineteenth century. We saw the unequal development of different centres of capital accumulation, first in Europe then in the USA and Japan. Lenin's model of imperialism predicted only too accurately the outbreak of further wars between the colonial powers and much less accurately their decline and decay. Such expectations were widely accepted, however, especially in the underdeveloped countries, and they gave hope and faith to generations of revolutionaries in the colonial and ex-colonial lands, as Lenin intended that they should. Once the parasitic and moribund imperialist powers were thrown out, then the way would be open, so it seemed, for true economic development.

The Leninist model has, however, to be criticized, both on empirical grounds (it doesn't fit the facts) and on theoretical grounds (the model wouldn't work). The empirical objections are of three kinds. I argued these at length in my *Economics of Imperialism* (Chap. 8). First, the colonial empires were built during the most dynamic periods of capitalist economies: the British empire in the 1850s and 1860s, German and French colonization in the 1880s, the US expansion at the turn of the century. Secondly, there is no evidence that monopoly positions in Germany or the USA led to capitalist decay, in the sense of technological decline. Rather the opposite. Thirdly, the greater part of the export of European capital was not a real outflow from a dying market but reinvestment of a part of the earnings from earlier overseas investments; and this capital investment was not mainly in the colonies but in the independent countries – first the USA, then Canada, Australia and New Zealand, South Africa and Argentina as they developed their economies with European capital.

The theoretical objection to the Leninist model only confirms this factual judgement. Why, it must be asked, should capital which could not find investment opportunities because of the declining market at home, find openings in the still more impoverished colonies? A small part of the investment was of course in the exploitation of cheap labour in mining and plantations in Africa and South-East Asia and the Caribbean. By far the greater part was in fact in industrial development in North America, Australasia and Europe itself. Without this real development European capitalism would have indeed ground to a halt in the nineteenth century. Similarly, without the flow of gold from the USA after the Second World War and the loans to developing countries, there would have been no post-war boom. In Greek mythology Midas died from starvation after surrounding himself with great piles of gold that he could not eat and in the end could not climb over. This was the theme of an earlier book of mine, *After Imperialism* (1963), in which I suggested that a new international framework of trade and aid was equally in the interests of the working people of developed and of underdeveloped countries.

(2) The Core-Periphery Model

Some who held on to the Lenin model extended it to argue the very opposite thesis: that the capitalist system had always pumped wealth from the peripheral countries to the core of advanced countries and continues to do so today. If there were a few semi-peripheral countries in which some development was taking place, this was wholly dependent upon the core countries' capital and technology. It was, therefore, impossible for such development to get beyond the creation of a limited elite market for the core countries' industrial products, while leaving the rest of this semi-periphery, like the periphery itself, as impoverished suppliers of primary products. The major argument of this school of thought, in the writings of A. G. Frank, Samir Amin and Immanuel Wallerstein, is that exchange is unequal between the core countries' industrial products and the periphery's food and raw materials. More labour is obtained for less. This may be true of direct labour, but a Marxist has to ask about socially necessary labour, that is, labour applied to the average technical means of production; and the fact is that relative wages do not appear to be lower than relative levels of productivity comparing developed and underdeveloped countries. (See my *Economics of Imperialism*, pp. 232–3.)

The Frank–Amin–Wallerstein argument would not necessarily be refuted by this fact. Their contention is that whatever improvements are made in productivity, as for example in modern factories in poor countries, wages will be held down there by the workers' weak bargaining position. The raising of oil prices and higher wages in OPEC countries have then to be regarded as exceptional. So has the wider impact of 'Fordism'. This means the simultaneous reduction of costs through higher productivity, e.g. in motor-car manufacture, and the improvement of wages, e.g. of workers in the motor-car industry and associated industries, so that both production and consumption of key durable consumer goods like motor cars can be expanded in Third World countries, if only among a quite limited proportion of the population. Despite this limitation the extension of numbers of consumers is evidently not unimportant to the giant companies.

Yet Wallerstein in an early essay (in Amin *et al.*, 1982) writes that, while 'in an expanding world system there is always some room at the top (or in the middle) . . . viewed globally, the "more at the top" is far smaller than the "more at the bottom" and the gap has grown steadily greater across the centuries'. This could be interpreted in several ways: (a) for every x number of people made better off, $x + 1$ were no better off; or (b) $x + 1$ were actually worse off; or (c) $x + 1$ were better off but not so much better off so that the gap widened. Wallerstein goes on to say, however: 'It is undoubtedly the case that few 16th century rural producers worked as hard or as long for so little as do rural producers in today's Third World.' We are still not given any evidence of something that we could measure. That the gap has been growing between the standard of living of most people in developed countries and most people in the underdeveloped can be shown to be true by looking at averages in both cases. But both the average and the median (i.e. allowing for specially advantaged groups pulling up the average) in both developed and underdeveloped countries, even excluding those attempting to build socialism, can be shown to have been rising.

What is the importance of this playing with numbers? The answer is that Wallerstein is arguing that capitalism can no longer meet the needs of an increasingly large proportion of the world's peoples and is therefore in global crisis. As the total world population increases, this statement could be true, i.e. that capitalism cannot meet the needs of increasing numbers of people. But his argument is that for every extra mouth to feed better, capitalism needs more than two hands to exploit worse. Wallerstein fails to suggest a proof for such a model and I cannot think of any facts that could be advanced to support it. All the statistics show increases in living standards for both developed *and* underdeveloped countries, at least throughout the 1960s and 1970s, and there was even some sign of a narrowing of the gap between them in the 1970s. The gap widened again in the 1980s, with the developing countries as a whole barely increasing their income per head and those in Africa, Latin America and West Asia actually falling back. Much of the fall was due to falling oil prices after the oil price hike of the 1970s and to the general continuing fall in primary product prices. By the end of the 1980s and in the early 1990s, the recession had spread to the developed countries, partly, at least, just because of the declining purchasing power of many developing countries.

The rich countries were suffering and not gaining from the impoverishment of the poor. At the same time, we also had to notice that China and most of South and East Asia were leaping ahead. There is no evidence that increased exploitation in the South was enriching the North. Rather the contrary. Lenin's model of worsening exploitation of the Third World is no more defensible than Marx's model of 'increasing immiseration', though Marx was generally careful to suggest that the polarization of wealth and poverty was subject to many counteracting forces.

The implications of this critique of the Lenin model and core-periphery model are important for the possibility of building unity between the working people of developed industrial countries and the peasantry of the underdeveloped lands. If it were the case that the rich countries were rich because the poor were poor, then the interests of the peoples of each would be in conflict. Such a model of exploitation by rich countries and peoples of poor countries and peoples, however, completely misses the class differences inside each. There are probably far greater differences of income, wealth and power between the classes in underdeveloped countries even than there are inside the developed. What is true is that workers in the underdeveloped countries are paid far less for the same hours of work than are those in the developed countries. Both are exploited by the giant transnational companies, which divide and conquer, picking up cheap labour where they can. But their policies are based on a synergy, as they call it, developing raw materials and production in one place, drawing on skilled labour and technical expertise in another, using cheap labour for a part of the productive process in a third, marketing the product in a fourth.

A New World Division of Labour

There is no doubt that the historic division of labour between countries producing manufactured goods and those producing food and raw materials was wholly artificial. Europe and North America simply got in first. In terms of resources of coal and iron and land for cotton-growing as well as in the supply of skilled weavers India should have been the seat of the first industrial revolution. But Indian armies had been defeated in 1757 by British armies and Indian merchants bought off by British traders. The textile industry of India, which had supplied all Europe with cotton goods up to the end of the eighteenth century, was destroyed by machine-made textiles, and as a British governor reported the result, 'the plains of Bengal were bleached white with the bones of the weavers'. One after another – from the towns and villages of Yorkshire to the towns of Latin America, China and Japan – the craftsmen's products were replaced by manufactures. England, Europe and later North America became the centres of industry; the rest of the world was reduced to becoming an agricultural field. Only the independent countries which had been settled by Europeans and then, much later, Japan, East Asia and Russia with central planning succeeded in wrenching themselves free from this artificial world division of labour. Marx had supposed, not only in the case of India but much more generally, that capitalism would none the less succeed in effecting the spread of industrialization. Even Lenin speaks in his *Imperialism* essay of 'the export of capital . . . expanding and deepening the further development of capitalism throughout the world'.

Marx had always assumed that the backward echelons would follow the forward contingents. 'The country that is more developed shows to the less developed, the image of its own future.' So Marx wrote in the Preface to Volume I of *Capital*. In 1853 he had written about the East India Company that England was fulfilling 'a double mission in India: one destructive, the other rejuvenating . . . The means of irrigation and internal communication . . . the immediate and current wants of railway locomotion' could be 'the forerunners of modern industry'. This quotation has been seized upon by those who have wanted to encourage the belief that imperialism was a progressive force in worldwide economic development, although Marx himself cautiously added: 'The Indians will not reap the fruits of the new elements of society scattered among them by the British bourgeoisie, until in Great Britain itself the now ruling class shall have been supplanted by the industrial proletariat or till the Hindus themselves shall have grown strong enough to throw off the English yoke altogether.' (Quoted from Marx's letters on India in the New York *Daily Tribune*, July 1853.)

Until the emergence of the East Asian 'dragons', it did not seem that, after Japan, capitalism would give birth to any new centres of capital accumulation. The centrally planned economies of the Soviet Union and China were establishing the new models of industrialization. However, one writer in the Marxist tradition, Bill Warren, proclaimed his belief in the 1970s in the universality of capitalist development. In a controversially entitled book, *Imperialism: Pioneer of Capitalism*, Warren argued that economic development was not only a fact in the underdeveloped capitalist countries but a theoretically inevitable fact of capitalism (Warren,

1980). He claimed to show that capitalist development was occurring in Brazil, Iran, Mexico, Malaysia and Singapore, Korea, Peru, Taiwan and Zambia, as well as in Israel, Japan and Spain, just as it had done much earlier in the USA, Canada, Australia, New Zealand and South Africa. Warren was followed by others, who were quite explicitly critical of Marxist models. Peter L. Berger celebrated the victory of what he called, in a book so entitled, *The Capitalist Revolution* (Berger, 1987).

For Marxists, this was not a new argument. The Communist International (the Comintern) in 1928 concluded that imperialism was a retarding force both of industrialization and capitalist development of the productive forces in the colonies. In doing this they rejected both Marx's views and the advice of the Indian and British delegates. The result was not only to establish Soviet leadership of the anti-imperialist forces in the East but to encourage belief in the strength of a nationalist struggle in the colonies against the imperial powers and their local agents, such as would embrace all classes and not only the workers and peasants. Bill Warren's thesis was that this adoption of Lenin's model blinded Marxists to the actual facts of economic development in the ex-colonial territories after the Second World War. Underdevelopment, he said, was a fiction and the evils of dependent development a myth propagated by nationalist intellectuals who failed to see the really pioneering role of capitalist industry and agriculture in the Third World. Warren used the concept of a Third World to distinguish very precisely the developed capitalist world model, the Soviet-type model and his own model of capitalism pioneering economic development.

What actually happened in the 1980s after Warren had died was that, while in East Asia capitalist industrialization firmly established itself, the growing points of development in southern and western Asia, in Latin America and in Africa shrivelled. In Chapter 7, we found special reasons for the success of industrialization in East Asia. Development elsewhere was held back by the artificial division of labour between primary producers and manufacturers. Most developing countries were primary producers, caught in the price-scissors of the 1980s – falling primary-product prices and rising prices of manufactured goods; and this was exacerbated by the growing burden of debt, incurred to finance industrial development when primary-product prices were high and having to be repaid when these prices had collapsed. Only the East Asian countries had succeeded in escaping from the artificial world division of labour and establishing themselves as producers and exporters of manufactured goods.

Even in East Asia, a distinction must be drawn between the several developments taking place: on the one hand, in South Korea and Taiwan, and to a lesser extent in Malaysia and Indonesia, where self-generated capitalist accumulation was taking place, and, on the other, in the free-trade zones like Colombo and Manila, and even in the more prosperous territories of Hong Kong and Singapore, which were no more than enclaves of wider hinterlands. These zones were being used by the big transnational companies for their cheap labour, like the *maquiladoras* in Mexico. Within duty-free zones huge concessions were offered to the giant transnational companies: tax concessions and tax holidays, cheap labour, but an educated labour force, no unions, free movement of goods and capital, structural support for new company investment. Each of the new zones was offering its own package of attractions for the giant transnational companies. By the end of the 1980s something like one-seventh of all manufacturing output in the world was taking place in such developing countries. Before the collapse of the Soviet and East European economies in 1989, they together with China were producing twice that much; and the pace of China's industrialization was by 1994 rapidly making up for the lost output in the ex-Soviet Union and Eastern Europe.

There is much anxiety in Europe and North America at the threat to Northern industries from imports of goods manufactured with cheap labour in the South. In certain sectors – clothing, shoes and electronic assembly – the special capacity of well-educated young women in East Asia to perform highly complex tasks for very low rates of pay has set a pace which Northern workers cannot compete with. But the penetration of Northern markets by Southern manufactures is still well below 10 per cent of overall consumption. Far more serious for Northern manufacturing companies is the development, which we noted in Chapter 7, of advanced, capital-intensive industrial undertakings in South Korea and Taiwan, generating their own capital accumulation from their own profits.

Capitalist Convergence

The difference between this development and what has been happening in the free-trade zones and in Africa and Latin America consists in the different application of the profits. In South Korea and Taiwan, and increasingly in Malaysia and Indonesia, the profits have been ploughed back into local investment. In the case of other developing countries, the profits have flowed out, well beyond the rate of incoming investment. Capital accumulation was taking place elsewhere. We begin to understand the meaning of this condition in Britain today now that it is mainly *outside* Britain that the giant companies which were originally based here are investing their capital today. Unemployment rises and imports of goods replace home products. Growth is limited to a few products – North Sea oil and gas in Britain's case – and even low wages are not enough to attract capital back because skills are low and the market is poor. Capital may still be attracted to pick up privatized parts of nationalized industries at bargain prices.

There is a question whether an improvement in the terms of trade and an increase in the export earnings of primary-producing countries would lead to a resumption of the industrialization process which collapsed in the 1980s. There appears to be a major obstacle: too many of the ruling elites in Latin America, Africa and South Asia are tied in to the trade in primary products, whether as landowners, traders or beneficiaries of the system of marketing boards. If there were enough of them so that their purchasing power increased to the point where it became an attractive market for the transnational companies, even attracting companies to invest in local manufacturing, then some development would follow.

For industrialization to take off as a cumulative process,

however, local industrial enterprise would be required and this appears to be beyond the capability of local elites outside East Asia. We can test this by employing the model which Hamsa Alavi (1982) proposed in his analysis of the colonial mode of production or what he calls the peripheral capitalist mode. He contrasted it with the feudal mode (and we might add the Asiatic mode), the remnants of which survive in many underdeveloped countries. In doing this he provided a chart (see Figure 11), which I have somewhat modified to take in elements from the text of his analysis. The chart suggests a model of relationships in each of these modes, assuming that we are taking from Marx his model of social formations, which we looked at in Chapter 1. But we need to add a further dimension which Alavi's analysis omits. There should be a last line that indicates the role of ideology. What the transnational company transmits is not the military power and religious authority of feudal or Asiatic society, nor simply the racial claims of colonial regimes, but the growth path of capitalist technology, the hard sell of the transnational company's economic and cultural hegemony.

From this table it can be seen that the peripheral capitalist mode is shown in crucial respects as moving towards the capitalist mode. How far this actually goes will depend on the particular conditions in particular countries and the interest of the transnational companies in maintaining their hold on particular countries for their capital accumulation. In the crucial question of extracting a surplus the peripheral mode is shown to be moving towards the capitalist mode, but accumulation for reproduction remains specific to the peripheral mode. The reproduction takes place elsewhere and the superstructure remains to keep it that way, with overwhelming ideological support. Only the countries building socialism with command economies and Japan's East Asian associates succeeded in retaining the greater part of the capital accumulation *inside* their economies. The scale of capital ownership and control necessary for operating in world markets today implies that nothing less than giant transnational companies or very large-scale state enterprises can survive. This is the central weakness of the World Bank's model of small-scale private industrial entrepreneurs

	FEUDAL MODE OR ASIATIC MODE	CAPITALIST MODE (CMP)	COLONIAL MODE OR PERIPHERAL CAPITALIST MODE
LABOUR	Unfree: serf or peon, tied to land, share-cropping Or: peasant proprietor or village commune (Asiatic)	Free of feudal control but with no means of production. Proletariat	Mixed: serf/peasant/proletariat Moving to CMP but NB landless members in the countryside
SURPLUS EXTRACTION	By extra economic force: tribute or tax (Asiatic) or interest (moneylender)	Wage labour Economic coercion	Mixed: non-economic and economic force Moving to CMP but NB plantations
NATURAL ECONOMY OR COMMODITY PRODUCTION	Limited market but mainly self-sufficient natural economy	Total market with generalized commodity production	Specific to mode: export-market cash crops destroying local self-sufficient economy
ACCUMULATION FOR REPRODUCTION	Surplus wholly consumed	Surplus partly invested in extended reproduction	Specific to mode: outflow of profit leading to reproduction elsewhere but some surplus consumed and invested locally
SUPERSTRUCTURE	Fusion of economic and political power at all levels necessary for coercion by non-economic means	Separation of economic (class) power and political state power; bourgeois state, bourgeois law, etc.	Specific to mode: fusion of merchant and landed economic and political power in state and army

Figure 11. Labour, surplus, commodity production and superstructure in four modes of production (after Alavi in Alavi and Shanin, 1982, pp. 178–9)

from developing countries competing in world markets without some state support. The fact is that they can't.

Uneven Development

The model of the new world division of labour seems then to be one in which capital moves inside a few hundred giant transnational corporations. If a government can offer tax concessions, free-trade zones or high rates of interest, it may attract the investment of these corporations. Wherever enough capital sticks, the market will grow and a cumulative process of growth can take place. Wealth attracts and poverty repels. In many underdeveloped countries there is in effect a dual economy: first, a small rich elite involved in the trading of imported finished manufactures for exported primary commodities and, secondly, a mass of peasantry with enclaves of mines, plantations or cheap labour for manufacturing processes. For long this was the condition of Japan and Italy. Indeed, Italy still has a rich industrial north and an impoverished rural south. The UK has its Celtic fringe. Only the wealth of Britain and the most severe measures of protection in the command economies of fascist Italy and Japan and of the countries attempting to build socialism succeeded in breaking through the freeze of such a dual economy. Japan's Asian associates followed suit.

Why should other countries not do the same today? Bill Warren said they could and did. 'Fordism' describes, as we saw, a process by which an elite in Third World countries can afford to buy the products of the subsidiaries of giant transnational companies in these countries, where costs have been reduced by a combination of automation and cheap labour. Spain was the first example, but many South American countries have followed after. The difficulties, however, become increasingly overwhelming as time goes on. First, the scale of capital required for investment in new technology is much greater. We have seen that the plant and equipment at the command of a Japanese worker in the 1980s was estimated to be four or five times that available even to a British worker. Secondly, the concentration of capital in the hands of a few giant companies means that they have been able to demand high rates of interest for loans to governments. The Mexican and Polish governments in their bid to break out of their dual economy borrowed funds at rates which were for a time absorbing all of their export earnings. Thirdly, the long post-war boom based on US spending came to an end. Industrial development in a period of stagnant markets is a desperately competitive business.

It was being suggested in the early 1990s that the flexible automation of 'post-Fordism' could overcome the problems of mastering the technology and achieving the necessary scale of funds facing newcomers to industrialization. Plant could be smaller and cheaper and its operation could draw upon innovatory designs through networks of information technology. This is what we saw to be providing the foundation for the industrial advance of countries in East Asia, associated with Japanese economic development. If these advances are not occurring in other regions, it is because they are being held back by their inability to enter world markets controlled by the giant transnationals and sometimes by deliberate protection of the industries of the existing industrialized countries. We have also had occasion to notice the continuing involvement of the ruling elites in many developing countries with primary production and small-scale trading and as prices of primary products have been falling, the subsequent perpetuation of a vicious circle of declining incomes and failing investment.

Anxiety about the failure of the underdeveloped countries to develop has spread from concerned economists, humanitarians and socialists to the political establishments of the capitalist world. The widening gap between rich and poor not only between countries but inside many underdeveloped countries has aroused the alarm of many political leaders whose faith in the free market is less than perfect. When we looked at the monetarist model we saw that this was fundamentally a revival of the free-market model which in effect left the giant companies free to exercise their money power without government controls. The politicians who have been most concerned about the deep divide between the rich and poor countries, the North and South as they see it, have mainly been Keynesians. The authors of the report entitled *North–South: A Programme for Survival* (1980) included Willy Brandt,

319

Edward Heath, Olaf Palme and Pierre Mendès-France, all ex-prime ministers, as well as ministers and bank governors of thirteen other countries – all men of a distinctly Keynesian mould. They followed this in 1983 with *Common Crisis*, a further appeal for North–South cooperation for world recovery. Finally, a team led by Willy Brandt, working under the auspices of the Socialist International, published *Global Challenge: From Crisis to Co-operation. Ending the North–South Stalemate* (Brandt *et al.*, 1985). In this the Brandt team emphasized more strongly even than before the absolute necessity of income redistribution from rich to poor and the replacement of 'beggar-my-neighbour' policies with a commitment to 'better my neighbour'.

These political leaders saw the Keynesian model as having broken down because of the failure to manage the international economy. They looked to new institutions and new measures to replace the dollar as a world currency. They pleaded for new and increased aid from the rich countries to the poor to revive the failing purchasing power of those who had suffered worst from rising oil prices and falling prices of other commodities, and for coordinated action to start the process of recovery. The fact that these same politicians did not take these actions when they had power before the monetarists took over detracts from the effectiveness of their appeal but not necessarily from its logic.

For the dangers are certainly greater in the 1990s than they were in 1978 when the *North–South* report was prepared. It is not for nothing that they called the report 'a programme for survival'. They truly feared a revolutionary explosion in the poor countries if all hope of an improvement in their condition disappeared; and they linked this with fears of the massive build-up of armaments that both take resources away from meeting urgent needs and set the stage for nuclear holocaust. The years after the report was written saw the outbreak of wars between the Soviet Union and Afghanistan, between China and Vietnam, between Iraq and Iran, between Ethiopia, Eritrea and Somalia, between South Africa and Angola, between Britain and Argentina, between Israel and Syria. It is a frightening record of accelerating violence, reproduced in the 1990s with even greater violence in civil wars in the former Soviet

Union, in Yugoslavia, in Somalia, the Sudan, Angola, Mozambique, Rwanda and Algeria, and in Nicaragua, Peru and Colombia.

It cannot be by chance, as we have noted earlier, that all these countries, where law and order descended into violence and civil war, had foreign debts that were nearly equal to their annual national income and were taking up to half their export earnings in servicing payments. And this burden of debt was, in nearly all cases, undoubtedly the cause and not the result of the outbreak of violence. It was not hard to understand. The debt and the attempt to repay it led to rising inflation, the local currency rendered worthless and the economy collapsed. Those who had access to hard currency – Deutschmarks or dollars or French francs – could survive. The rest, we saw, were driven to extremities.

What the authors of *North–South* recommended was unfortunately as inadequate as Bill Warren's prescriptions – and for the same reason, because they both assumed that, without doubt, capitalism can everywhere generate economic development. Both were working with an economic model in which capital investment spreads to fill any and all gaps in the world economy. The rising mountain of Third World debt was recognized by the Brandt Commission as the major challenge to such assumptions. The Frank–Amin–Wallerstein model we looked at earlier in this chapter assumed that capital investment will mainly avoid poor countries and only the few rich will benefit.

The model we seem to be moving towards in our thinking in this chapter comes down half-way between each of these extreme models. Capitalism tends to uneven development. Capital *can* be attracted and held in less developed countries in one of two alternative situations: (a) that governments are established which are determined to provide a strong supportive framework for local and foreign capital in the country which protects infant industries and subsidizes their first entry into world markets without encountering protectionist resistance from already industrialized countries; (b) that governments – and this really means radical, even revolutionary socialist governments – can reach agreement among themselves to create an alternative framework of planned trade exchanges outside the ambit of the giant companies;

this implies, as we have learnt from the Soviet experiences, that there can be what Steve Bodington (1982) described as an accumulation of political consciousness that parallels Preobrazhensky's iron heel of primitive accumulation of economic resources. Neither of these situations is likely to obtain so long as the world economy is suffering a major recession, with no international attempt being made to advance a programme of economic recovery.

The weakness of the economic model of the new economic order as exemplified in the Brandt Commission is that it depends on two quite different assumptions: on a sort of voluntary tax by the governments of the rich countries to help the poor (out of fear for their own skins) and on the belief that the governments of the poor countries would be capable of carrying through an economic development programme. Both assumptions are open to question. Even if some governments of rich countries were prepared to increase their aid to the poor, this would be severely limited by their expectation that others would not. Yet without any form of international authority the basis of an international Keynesian policy is missing. This is that the rich will agree to a smaller share of a larger cake because that way their slice will not be reduced. It is a more serious problem that the so-called neo-colonial regimes in most underdeveloped countries are far too deeply tied into current trade relations with the developed countries to challenge the existing world structure of economic relations and to change the paths of economic development which these relations have established.

One further limitation has to be taken into account in reviving Keynesian international policies. This is that economic growth can no longer be pursued without consideration for the ecological constraints upon the continuation of current growth paths. Since these are the only paths that the system of private capital accumulation has shown itself able so far to follow, the question is raised whether a new route can be opened up without first destroying the system. Regulation of private capital by nation states has in the past protected communities from the worst effects of unqualified profit-making. In the last chapter, however, we saw reason to doubt the capacity of the nation state today to bring the system under control. At the same time, states in which the economy was organized on the basis of state accumulation in the attempt to build socialism rather than on that of private accumulation were found to be destroying their natural environment with even fewer restraints.

Self-reliance or Mutual Reliance

What would a model of sustainable world development look like? There are two candidates for consideration. One we looked at briefly in the chapter on the Green model. This is that development, as we understand it, should in effect be abandoned as a dead-end. Each group of peoples, nations or other formations should be encouraged to follow a policy of self-reliance, largely cutting themselves off from others, and certainly from others at any distance or at different levels of economic development. Trade should be reduced to an absolute minimum, and the complexities of modern technology dispensed with. This is called 'the New Protectionism' by its advocates. It finds favour with those who have become wholly disillusioned with life in modern industrial societies. But the rejection of all exchanges throws out the baby with the bathwater, the benefits with the disadvantages, and some of the supposed disadvantages do not survive close scrutiny.

It is said, for example by the SAFE Alliance, that moving goods across the oceans of the world is extremely wasteful of energy (Raven, 1994). But, in the very paper that argues against the lengthening of 'food miles', it is shown that UK imports of food from Europe have increased at the expense of imports from Australia, New Zealand and South America; a table is reproduced showing that it requires less and not more energy to carry a tonne across the Atlantic or the Pacific or Indian Oceans, in a giant modern container ship, ore carrier or tanker, than it does to carry a tonne across the British mainland. It is argued, moreover, that long-distance trade encourages agricultural specialization in the developing countries, especially the growing of cash crops by agri-businesses with heavy investment in chemical fertilizer. In fact, I have shown elsewhere that in Africa there has been no increase in the proportion of land devoted to cash crops, and most Third World agricultural production comes from small-scale farmers who intercrop their cash crops with their staple subsistence food. Ironically it is the farms nearest to the European and North American consumers which are now agri-businesses, dependent on petroleum products for tractors, fertilizers, pesticides and herbicides. (Barratt Brown and Tiffen, 1992.)

There is still a case to be made for increasing trade between developing countries, but the argument in favour of autarky comes mainly from the well-to-do in the industrialized lands, and the main objections to such proposals come from those who have not yet seen many of the benefits of modern technology, which it is proposed to abandon. The obvious benefits include the reduction in burdensome heavy-labouring tasks of carrying water, collecting firewood, digging coal, hoeing and harvesting by hand, carrying produce to market. The no less considerable benefits of travel and communication of ideas should not be overlooked. One of the main causes of bargaining weakness among primary producers is their ignorance of conditions beyond their horizons, of world prices and market requirements. It can be of no benefit to millions of craftsmen and farmers to keep them ignorant in the name of self-reliance, let alone in honour of some romantic glorification of the simple life.

The alternative both to autarky and to the present forms of unequal exchange lies in the establishment of common policies and actions between producers in different countries of the same commodities, so that the bargaining position of the small farmer and craft worker, and equally of waged workers in mines and factories and on plantations, is raised to a level commensurate with that of the owners of land and capital, whether private or state. With such collective bargaining strength, it would be possible as well as necessary for trade exchanges to be subject to some international planning, both to ensure fair exchanges and to protect the environment. It is widely argued by governments of industrialized countries in the General Agreement on Tariffs and Trade (GATT) and other international forums that only free trade ensures a result that is to the advantage of all. But we have seen that free trade does not benefit all equally and we know that it does nothing to protect the environment. Planned trade exchanges are nothing new, nor a peculiarity of command economies.

Governments that do not appear to be planning their trade exchanges in any positive way are generally doing so negatively, by the imposition of tariffs and non-tariff barriers against outside producers and by subsidies and grants in aid of their own producers. Through GATT most of the world's nation states have agreed to negotiate down the barriers to trade, but they still seek to retain those forms of protection that they regard as most important for their own economies. Common markets and regional trade agreements are in effect forms of planned trade, sometimes, as with the European Union's Common Agricultural Policy, of the most complex and restrictive kind.

The present situation is that the giant companies plan their own transnational exchanges, but governments act unilaterally, if at all. Each government acts on its own to reduce its country's imports either directly by import controls or indirectly by general deflation of the purchasing power of the country. This simply means that other governments follow suit and the whole level of world trade is set far below what it could be. To expand such trade exchanges would require that governments should agree on a planned growth of mutual trade. The more governments involved the better. It was an important factor in the successful economic growth of West Germany, Austria and Finland that each had an important proportion of its foreign trade guaranteed by long-term planning with the Soviet Union and Eastern Europe. If this principle had been widely generalized beyond Eastern Europe the whole level of economic activity could have been expanded.

When we looked at the model of a unified European economy in the last chapter, we saw the advantages that were claimed for a single market, in which goods and services moved freely. But we concluded that the free market's tendency to uneven development had to be regulated by active measures to redistribute income from the economically more advanced to the more backward areas. On a world scale the disparities are still wider and the need to support trade with aid still greater. One of the particular strengths of a unified Europe would be the external power that such a community of nations could bring to bear in advancing common policies in negotiation with the other world powers – the USA, Japan and China.

A New Bretton Woods

It was the European allies who pressed most strongly towards the end of the Second World War for international institutions and policies which would support nation-state commitments to full employment of people and resources. In Chapter 5 we saw how Keynes's proposals for a World Bank and Monetary Fund and a world money were associated with an International Trade Organization (ITO) to expand world trade and support economic recovery. After the Bretton Woods meetings, in subsequent agreements among the Allies, ITO became no more than a General Agreement on Tariffs and Trade (GATT), with the limited aim of promoting free trade, the Bank and Fund became agencies of US policies and the US dollar became the world's money. None of this should have caused surprise, since the United States emerged from the Second World War with almost all the world's gold, most of the world's manufacturing industry and much of the surplus grain. Today, the hegemony of the United States is under challenge – from Japan, from Germany and even from China. The necessity and the possibility exists for building new international institutions fifty years on from the Bretton Woods agreements, although the special circumstances of the world war alliance, and at the same time the threat to the capitalist order from the Soviet Union, are quite absent today.

'Fifty years is enough' was the slogan of a worldwide campaign in 1994 to express the conviction of non-governmental organizations that the development policies pursued by the IMF and the World Bank have been inimical both to the interests of the poor and to the natural environments of the Third World and Eastern Europe (*Bankcheck*, June 1944). The single-minded pursuit of debt collection throughout the 1980s had, they argued, left the world's poor poorer and the natural resources of the world devastated. This was not only because the international financial institutions had required from debtors an export-led strategy to service their debts, but because they had insisted on cutting back public spending on health, education and food subsidies. The consequent collapse of the entire economic and political structure in many countries led to the withdrawal of foreign investment and the marginalization of whole regions, including most of sub-Saharan Africa.

The sad fact is that the Bretton Woods institutions have come to be seen by most Third World people as an alien force – 'just another clan', as a Somali leader described the UN force in his country. From the very start, the combination of a US citizen as President of the Bank and Managing Director of the IMF, US Congress nominees on the Executive Boards, a voting majority of the G7 on the Council and the Bank's dependence on the US capital market for its funds has retained the institutions as agents of United States foreign policy.

If Third World confidence is to be re-established in these institutions and indeed in the United Nations, a new Bretton Woods will have to go beyond the promises of their managers, welcome as they are, that there will be more openness and more concern for the condition of the people and the conservation of the environment in their policies. Proposals have come from Greenpeace and other NGOs for making the institutions subject to public monitoring of their impact, not only on economic growth and financial stability, as now, but on movements in the human development index, in natural-resource accounts, in employment and income distribution, in measures of fair trade and citizen participation, and promotion of women's access to resources (NGO Working Group on the World Bank, 1994). That none of these indicators would show a positive response after many decades of activity reveals the width of the gap between the original declared aims of the Bretton Woods agreements and their realization in practice.

These proposals could be reinforced by requiring the institutions to adhere to two of the original Articles of Agreement respecting Independent Advisory Bodies. These were to include:

– an Advisory Council – selected by the Board of Governors to include representatives of banking, commerce, industrial, labour and agricultural interests . . . with *as wide a national representation as possible* (emphasis added);

– Committees for each loan – to include an expert selected by the Governor *representing the member in whose territory the project is located* (emphasis added).

Neither of these has ever been operated. This led one senior IMF consultant from Trinidad to resign in 1989, after making proposals for a major reduction in Bank and IMF staffs and in their exorbitant salaries, and to use the funds released to finance new watchdog bodies. His proposals included:

– an Advisory and Review Commission to receive and adjudicate complaints; Regional Coordinating Committees to coordinate individual country programmes in the same region; a Programme Watch Committee composed of representatives from interested bodies in the loan-receiving country to monitor programmes; and Environmental Impact Committees from nationals in each region to study the ecological effects of IMF/Bank programmes in their region (Budhoo, 1990).

Most developing countries would settle for a great reduction in IMF/Bank interference and for the separation of the International Development Association (IDA), the Bank's soft-loan facility, and the Global Environment Facility (GEF) from the Bank's control and their establishment under more accountable UN procedures.

A new model Bretton Woods would have to involve the writing-off of Third World debt, at least that of the least developed countries, not just its rescheduling, which leaves the debt bigger with the unpaid interest added to the principal. It would also require that international aid should be stepped up to the UN recommended level of 0.7 per cent of the rich countries' incomes. It was running throughout the 1980s at less than half that level and was frequently tied quite improperly to financing the donor countries' exports. One proposal for a new Bretton Woods involves a new approach to aid. Instead of financing individual projects for individual countries – often prestige projects benefiting only the contractors from the industrialized countries – international aid should be directed to strengthening the bargaining position of primary producers in world markets.

This could be achieved in two ways. First, the Common Fund for Commodities could be revived. This was established by UNCTAD in the early 1980s to help finance stocks of commodities when supply exceeded demand. The scheme failed because stocks grew beyond the funds that the rich consuming countries were prepared to make available for financing them, *and* the stocks were in the hands of companies in the consuming countries. In fact these companies had no real interest in a scheme designed to keep up the prices of the raw materials they purchased on the world market and, according to one insider, Suzette Macaedo, had done all they could to sabotage the Common Fund. At the same time, the producing countries had no funds to operate their own stockholding, although coffee-growers had begun to operate a coffee retention scheme, until the frosts in Brazil suddenly sent the world price shooting up again after its long fall.

It was being argued in the middle of 1994, when coffee prices doubled, that the coffee-growers' problems were at an end and other commodity prices would recover as the world recession ended. But there have been short-run blips in the chart of coffee prices before – in 1975–6 and 1984–5; the trend of prices has been consistently downwards. The free-market model of the commodity markets guarantees this downward trend because of the weaker bargaining position of the producers and, just because the violent ups and downs in the market give the speculators their opportunity, such free markets encourage overproduction. If adequate stocks had been held by the producers in the 1980s, this would have checked the fall in prices which was so disastrous for the growers, and the stocks could have been used to fill the gap caused by bad harvests from frosts or drought. But no single group of producers has had the funds to carry large stocks and they have been unable to agree together in face of the divisive actions of the transnational buying companies and the international financial institutions.

The second benefit to be derived from the holding of stocks of commodities by primary-producing countries is that these could then be reckoned, like gold or hard currency, as an asset against which developing countries could borrow funds for their development. The marginalization of primary-producing countries as 'unbankable' could be ended. Such a scheme was proposed by three distinguished economists, Professors Hart, Kaldor and Tinbergen, at the first meeting of UNCTAD, as a Keynesian response to the weakening purchasing power of the developing countries in the 1970s. But such thinking was not in line with the aims and operations of the giant transnational companies or of the monetarist policies of the governments of the industrialized countries. I have described this argument at length in my book on *Fair Trade* (Barratt Brown, 1993).

New Forms of Trade Exchange

An essential element of the world order emerging from a new Bretton Woods would be an international trade organization. This would not simply monitor trade flows and identify obstacles, as is proposed for the GATT World Trade Organization; it would positively support new trade initiatives. These would be particularly valuable if they could develop trade beyond the current concentration inside the spheres of influence of the three centres of economic power and encourage linkages in a triangle of exchanges between the industrialized countries, the ex-members of the Soviet bloc and China and other semi-developed countries, and the great mass of developing countries. This would require, first, that the new international financial institutions would be prepared to deal with groups of developing countries wishing to work together and not just with individual nation states, and, second, that they would help to finance agreed trade exchanges and not simply rely on exposing each individual country to the vagaries of the world market.

For any such international trade model to be introduced, it would be necessary for some new extra-market pressures to be brought into action. Two potential forces for change could be mobilized for a positive movement in the development of trade exchanges, both of which have taken up defensive postures in the past. These are the organized industrial workers in the industrialized lands and farmers' organizations in developing countries. In the industrialized countries the trade unions in each country press for tariffs and import controls against goods coming from every other country and especially from those where wages are low. The transnational companies stand back, happy to divide and conquer. Free trade is the answer proposed by the most technically advanced producers and accepted for services as well as goods, agriculture as well as industry, in the latest round of GATT negotiations. But this only drives down labour costs everywhere and forces the least advanced producers out of the market without providing alternative jobs. What is needed is an element of international planning along the lines suggested above. At the same time, the basic rules of the ILO have to be enforced. These are not about defending any particular wage levels but about protection against forced labour, child labour and denial of the right to organize.

Most people in the developing countries are farmers. A few farm on a large scale and have been able to protect themselves, with the help of their governments, against the subsidized production and export of agricultural products from other countries – mainly the developed countries. The overwhelming majority of Third World farmers, who are smallholders and tenants – subsistence farmers with a small cash crop to sell – have had no protection against dumped grain from the developed countries or against falling world prices for their cash crops. You might think that the people of the developed countries benefited from getting their coffee and tea, rubber and cotton more cheaply; but it does not seem that reductions in world commodity prices are reflected in the shops. Consumers have begun to ask who gets what in the prices of the goods they buy and to discover how little the growers get in the make-up of the price of goods that come from poor countries.

A new agency of change has begun to emerge in the consumers' movements in the rich industrialized lands. After the spread of a 'green' movement for ecologically acceptable products, there followed the 'fair trade' movement. This movement of consumers is still not united with organizations of industrial workers, but the logic is there for this to happen. Falling purchasing power in the developing countries means declining demand for goods produced in the industrialized countries. Both small farmers in developing countries and industrialized workers in the developed would benefit from agreement on expanded trade exchanges. These possibilities will be the subject of the next two chapters.

FURTHER READING

ALAVI, HAMSA, 'The Structures of Peripheral Capitalism', in H. Alavi and T. Shanin (eds.), *Introduction to the Sociology of Developing Societies*, Macmillan, 1982, pp. 172–94

AMIN, S., *et al.*, *Dynamics of the Global Crisis*, Macmillan, 1982

BARRATT BROWN, MICHAEL, *After Imperialism*, Heinemann, 1963; Merlin Press, 1970

BARRATT BROWN, MICHAEL, *The Economics of Imperialism*, Penguin Books, 1974

BARRATT BROWN, MICHAEL, 'The New Industrial Division of Labour', in H. Alavi and T. Shanin (eds.), *Introduction to the Sociology of Developing Societies*, Macmillan, 1982

BARRATT BROWN, MICHAEL, *Fair Trade: Reform and Realities in the International Trading System*, Zed Press, 1993, pp. 143 ff.

BARRATT BROWN, MICHAEL, *Africa's Choices: After 30 Years of the World Bank*, Penguin, 1995

BARRATT BROWN, MICHAEL, and TIFFEN, PAULINE, *Short Changed: Africa and World Trade*, Pluto Press, 1992, pp. 32–3

BERGER, PETER L., *The Capitalist Revolution*, Wildwood House, 1987

BODINGTON, STEPHEN, *The Cutting Edge of Socialism*, Spokesman, 1982

BRANDT, WILLY, *et al.*, *North–South: A Programme for Survival*, Penguin Books, 1980

BRANDT, WILLY, *et al.*, *Common Crisis: North–South Cooperation for World Recovery*, Pan Books, 1983

BRANDT, WILLY, *et al.*, *Global Challenge: From Crisis to Cooperation. Ending the North–South Stalemate*, Socialist International, Pan Books, 1985

BUDHOO, DAVIDSON L., *Dear Mr Camdessus – Enough is Enough*, New Horizon Press, 1990

FRANK, ANDRÉ GUNDER, *Crisis in the World Economy*, Macmillan, 1980

HOLLAND, STUART (ed.), *Out of Crisis: A Project for European Recovery*, Spokesman, 1983

HOLLAND, STUART, *Towards a New Bretton Woods: Alternatives for the Global Economy*, Spokesman, 1994

INTERNATIONAL RIVERS NETWORK, *Bankcheck*, No. 8, June 1994

LENIN, V. I., *Imperialism, the Highest Stage of Capitalism*, 1916; Central Books, 1978

MADDEN, PETER, and MADELEY, JOHN, *Winners and Losers: The Impact of the GATT Uruguay Round on Developing Countries*, Christian Aid, 1993

MARX, KARL, *On Colonialism* (articles in the New York *Daily Tribune*, 1853), Lawrence & Wishart, 1960

MURRAY, ROBIN, 'Underdevelopment, International Firms and the International Division of Labour', in Jan Tinbergen (introd.), *Towards a New World Economy: Papers and Proceedings of the Fifth European Conference of the Society for International Development, The Hague, October 1971*, Rotterdam University Press, 1972, pp. 159–248

NGO WORKING GROUP ON THE WORLD BANK, 'Draft Letter to M. Camdessus at the IMF', *Information Packet* No. 44, IC, 1994

RAVEN, HUGH, *Food Miles*, Safe Alliance, 1994

THOMPSON, E. P., *et al.*, *Exterminism and Cold War*, Verso, 1982 (see esp. N. Chomsky, 'Strategic Arms, the Cold War and the Third World')

WARBURTON, DAVID, *Economic Détente*, General and Municipal Workers' Union, 1979

WARREN, BILL, *Imperialism: Pioneer of Capitalism*, Verso, 1980

19 MODELS OF SOCIAL TRANSITION

The model of the world capitalist economy which we have attempted to outline is a model of uneven development – uneven between more-developed and less-developed areas and uneven between the several more-developed centres themselves and equally uneven *inside* the developed areas, and *inside* the less-developed areas. The worldwide slump of the 1980s consequently has affected these different areas unequally; it has nevertheless to be seen as a major crisis in the system with unemployment, slump and preparation for war more threatening than at any time since the 1930s. In Marx's model such crises would be expected to spell the end of the capitalist system and its replacement by a social formation capable of developing all the productive capacities of modern technology for the benefit of ordinary people and not for mutual destruction. The crisis of the 1930s, however, ended in fascism and war. It was not inevitable that the working class in Britain or elsewhere would take the opportunity of such a crisis to overturn the system. Lenin described the great capitalist powers as 'moribund' in 1916 and Trotsky continued to write fatalistically of 'the epoch of decaying capitalism' in 1936, expecting a second world war to help the revolution, if revolution did not first prevent a war (see *The Revolution Betrayed*, 1972 edn, p. 231). But capitalism did not die, and appeared triumphant after the collapse of the Soviet Union.

If crises did not create the occasion for the transition to socialism, an alternative view emerged in the 1970s that perhaps capitalist development and full employment might generate the organization and confidence of workers to step up their demands beyond what the capitalists could concede, and that this then would lead to a growing challenge to the system. No such event was realized, and renewed slump evidently weakened working-class organization and confidence, particularly in one of the weaker capitalist states like Britain. There were no inevitable roads to socialism; and socialists began to give thought in estimating the possibility of social change in any country to the two elements of agency and space – agents of change and room in which to manoeuvre. Agency is seen in terms of classes; space in relation to the respective power of the state and of transnational capital.

The main theme of Part One of this book was that economic power – in a capitalist society the power of the owners and controllers of capital – has become concentrated in the hands of a smaller and smaller number of larger and larger companies. We explored their power on a world scale in the last two chapters. At the same time, we saw that the political power of the nation state, although it was exercised in much wider range and greater depth than ever, was inadequate except in the case of the super-states – of the USA and perhaps of Japan – to stand up to the economic power of the transnational companies. In Western Europe the Common Market, or European Community and European Union, as it was successively known, had come into existence to remedy that weakness. At the same time, the giant companies had become increasingly opportunistic in their relations with the nation states, even with the super-states. The old ties of the state with finance and industrial capital, of which Lenin had written in *Imperialism*, had been largely broken.

The exceptions to this challenge to nation-state power were found in Japan and the East Asian states, where a form of state capitalism emerged. This is not to say that inside the European Union the old nation-state capitals, especially in Britain, did not attempt to resist the growing power of the wider union. This divide between nation-state political power, however, and corporate economic power rendered inoperative the models both of the neoclassical market and of Keynesian demand management on a national scale in the developed equally with the developing economies. Nothing less than a global framework of political power could contain the giant transnational companies.

In the second part of this book we considered the case of those states where political power had been seized from the capitalists.

The main theme was the weakness of a Marxist analysis of the possibilities of real social change developing from a previous capitalist formation in underdeveloped countries at levels of living and political consciousness far below what Marx assumed to be necessary for building socialism. Again and again we saw that, where the productive capability in societies attempting to build socialism was inadequate for developing socialist relations of production, what resulted from revolution was a command economy with larger or smaller elements of the market model retained in it. Where the process of industrialization could not be carried through in part by the capital investment of giant companies with state support, it could be done wholly by state investment. In every case the process of accumulation for economic growth meant inevitably that some degree of economic or political force had to be used to extract for growth tomorrow what working people on the land or in industry, and especially on the land where most of them lived, would gladly have consumed today. In either case, the power of the world capitalist market in defining the technology, dictating the products and centralizing the capital became impossible to resist.

In an increasingly polarized world, socialists have asked what chances there are of breaking out of the system of uneven development; and what advantages there would be for workers or peasants in so doing. In the last chapter, we saw reasons why peoples of the Third World had been led to doubt the benefits of a policy of extreme self-reliance. But this is not to say that increased bargaining power for disadvantaged groups should not be the aim of all movements for social change. For such groups every opening, however small, in the structure of power has to be taken advantage of.

A diagrammatic model (see Figure 12) can be used to show some of the variables that create space for change. According to the strengths of interest of the transnational companies and the relative level of industrialization of the country, we can suggest four extremes (shown in the boxes) and indicate what might happen in less extreme cases. In the middle ground the unity of different class groups in struggling for change and for independ-

MODELS OF SOCIAL TRANSITION

ence will be crucial. At the extremes the unity and aspirations of the predominant class will be crucial.

The most interesting revelation of this model is the possibility (bottom right-hand box) that might seem to arise for social change and independence in an industrial nation in which transnational companies were losing their interest. Britain in the 1980s might have been an obvious example, if we could disregard the

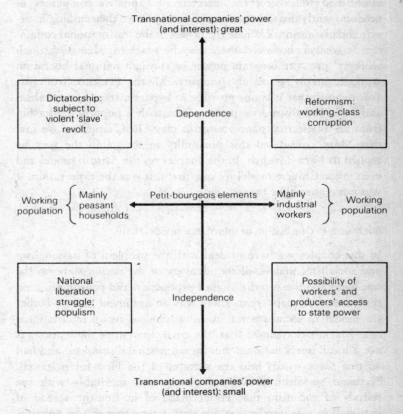

Figure 12. Models of space for fundamental social change in nations, according to transnational-company power and interest and level of industrialization of the working population

wealth of North Sea oil. The question of the agency of change has then to be looked at. Where nation states are pursuing development dependent on investment by transnational companies, space will be limited and agency will be crucial. The unity of industrial workers, with the support of intellectuals and some elements of local capitalists, might make some possible challenge to the power of the transnational companies and of the world market. Space for social change will be more limited where dictatorships are established to protect the interests of capitalist companies in predominantly peasant countries (i.e. to protect their mining interests and plantations). Where the power of the transnational companies is weaker, however, there may be space for change through workers' pressure on state power or through national liberation struggle, involving mainly peasants. All the evidence from the 1980s shows that it is not possible to bypass a stage of capitalism and build socialism on a peasant base with a populist leadership from an intellectual *petit bourgeois* class. In Chapter 12 we saw that Marx considered this possibility in Russia in the way he replied to Vera Zasulich. In the chapter on the African model and even in the Chinese model we saw that this was the expectation. It was not realized in either.

Socialism in One Nation or International Socialism

In this chapter we have to deal with the problem of nationalism and socialism, that is, of the ideology of the nation state on the one hand and the socialization of production and consumption on the other. For many years there was an argument as to whether the model of socialism was to be a national or an international one. Marx had assumed that 'the emancipation of the workers is not a local, nor a national, but an international problem' and had written these words into the statutes of the First International. National socialism came to be associated inevitably with the parody of socialism that Hitler made of it. But the spread of nationalism was unrelenting. Up until a time that can be precisely dated as 10 June 1943, the world socialist movement – at least as seen by communists – was an international movement.

The First International collapsed with the defeat of the Commune and the Franco-Prussian War in 1870, and with Marx and Bakunin locked in argument over the claims of anarchism. The Second International, led by the German Social Democrats, disappeared in August 1914 under a tide of wartime nationalism. Lenin's Third International, the Comintern which Stalin ended in 1943, was established from the start as an organization which 'subordinated the interests of the movement in each country to the common interest of the international revolution'. The executive committee of the Comintern became the general staff of the Communist movement designed to ensure the worldwide advance of communism at the expense of any national presumptions. This created a problem for the Comintern from the start and allowed it to become by the late 1920s in Stalin's hands an instrument of Soviet state policy. On the pretext of defending the central bastion of socialism (supposedly the USSR) any deviation was treated with summary execution.

Why then was it that *after* the Red Army's defeat of the German forces at Stalingrad, *after* the Allied Armies' victory in North Africa in 1943, and with every prospect of the defeat of fascism, in which the possibility opened up of turning anti-fascist war into a socialist revolution, as Lenin and Rosa Luxemburg had always predicted, why was it then of all moments that Stalin dissolved the Comintern? The way the Comintern behaved had always been an affront to national consciousness, and Stalin had used it to murder rivals; but to reject any international organization was surely going too far. The Trotskyists responded by establishing the Fourth International to continue the struggle for international socialism through an increasing proliferation of breakaway groups.

Stalin's reasons were reasons of state. He saw the state as a nation state, engaged in fighting what he dubbed 'a great patriotic war', not a socialist crusade. Fernando Claudín, the Spanish Communist leader, argued in his study of the Communist movement (Claudín, 1975), that the immediate aim of the dissolution was simply to facilitate negotiations between Stalin, Churchill and Roosevelt over the division of the world into 'spheres of influence'.

All the evidence suggests that Stalin was just as fearful of revolution in Europe as were the leaders of the Western Allies. The actual carve-up took place at the meeting in Yalta of the Big Three in 1945. It has been bitterly criticized equally from the Right and the Left for freezing a division of the world that suited only the political interests of the two super-states. But the dissolution of the Comintern leaves behind it a still unanswered question about socialism and nationalism.

The question of socialist internationalism is too easily and too often reduced to the question of the possibility of 'socialism in one country' and what is said – quite wrongly – to have been the basic disagreement between Stalin and Trotsky. Both had, in fact, for long assumed with Lenin – and following Marx – that a Russian socialist revolution could only occur in the wake of and as an integral part of socialist revolutions throughout Western Europe. All three later realized that the Russian Revolution could, at least by 1920, be defended without supporting revolutions elsewhere. The change in view was not just a reflection of the fact of the Soviet's survival when German and Hungarian and other revolutionary movements collapsed; but arose from a difference in the meaning assigned to the word 'revolution' – a difference which has remained to confuse us to this day.

It is essential to remember that Marx and Engels and the Russian Bolsheviks were thinking before 1917 of a social revolution – an entire epoch in which socialism would be built, destroying as it advanced the whole power of capitalism as a world system. The Russian Revolution was in effect a political revolution, in which the previous ruling class was replaced, but socialism was not yet built. It was, however, in Lenin's interest, and still more in Stalin's interest, to confuse the two meanings of revolution and appeal both to workers in the West and to the oppressed peoples of Asia to support the new Soviet state as a bastion of socialism. Lenin had always seen Russia as a link between proletarian-led revolutions in Western Europe and capitalist (bourgeois democratic) revolutions in Asia. The first had not yet been realized but the second might still be mobilized if only an international party as instrument for advance in Europe and Asia could be fashioned. The Comintern was to be just that. If the Bolshevik model had worked, then others could follow their example.

Lenin assumed that the only reason why what he believed to be a 'dying capitalism' still retained workers' support was the corruption of a reformist labour aristocracy, bribed by colonial tribute. Once this was removed, the workers of the old colonial powers would revolt – as long as selected and trusted leaders like the Bolsheviks in Russia were trained to carry through Comintern policy. What Lenin forgot or never understood was the commitment of Western European workers to the national democratic institutions that were not just a part of the ideology of capitalist rule but also represented actual gains won by working-class struggle. He forgot especially the role of the trade unions in Western Europe as the army of that struggle and not just as instruments of incorporation in capitalist political economy. Reformism was not a mere function of colonial tribute but a deep-rooted national phenomenon in Western Europe. If a social revolution was to be made, then, in Western Europe, it would have to be in a form that took account of and built upon that national reformist tradition, just as revolution in Asia (or Africa or South America) would have to have at its centre a broadly peasant-based national liberation struggle.

While the Comintern failed to take account of such national differences, socialists in each of the nation states failed at the same time to see the importance of international organization to challenge a world capitalist system. The Soviet Union was not itself able to offer an alternative world system but only an Eastern bloc and a military defence system. Stalin's attempt to replace the Comintern with the Cominform in 1947 broke up after his death in 1953 and in the defection of Yugoslavia, in the criticisms of the Italian party and the purges of Communist leaders in Czechoslovakia, Hungary and Bulgaria, and finally in the revolts in 1956 in Hungary and Poland and the beginning of China's break with the Soviet Union in the same year. Soviet political leadership was rejected and only imposed in Eastern Europe by Russian tanks.

Nothing, however, replaced the Cominform except Comecon –

a purely economic organization for mutual cooperation in foreign trade between the Soviet Union and the Eastern European countries. Of course, there are the trade-union internationals. These maintain rather tenuous links between national industrial unions. There have been *ad hoc* international associations: against nuclear weapons, against environmental pollution, against the worst acts of US imperialism in Vietnam, in Angola or in Nicaragua. There is no longer, however, in the minds of socialists any model of an international movement.

What does exist is a plethora of voluntary associations with international links, NGOs concerned about the environment, about world poverty, famine, fair trade, the debt burden – both campaigning bodies and aid agencies. They are loosely linked by various networks and through the International Council for Voluntary Associations (ICVA) and its offshoot, the NGO Working Group on the World Bank, but they are not linked to the trade-union internationals. This means that effectively there is no international challenge to the power of the giant international accumulations of capital, but only scores of very divided, separate challenges. More than anything else, it is an international working people's association that would have to be rebuilt, if this power is to be challenged. Those who share a common enemy have to find forms of effective collaboration.

A Monolithic Party or Political Pluralism

If there is no model of one international socialist movement, still less is there any single clear model of the agency – a political party at national level, adequate to carry through a major social change. In almost every nation state the model is now different. Under the influence of the Comintern and later of the Cominform it was holy writ that the model of the Russian Bolshevik Party, which emerged out of conditions of illegality, repression and exile in a backward country with a vast peasantry, a strong intelligentsia and minute industrial working class, must be the model for all to follow. In this model, power descended from the centre and the so-called principle of 'democratic centralism' allowed only for discussion of the proper application of 'the line' at lower levels. Such a model was hopelessly inappropriate to the pluralist democratic tradition of the developed capitalist nation states, even where the industrial workers were in the overwhelming majority. It was still less appropriate in the underdeveloped nation states where, even on Leninist principles, the next stage of political development was bourgeois (capitalist) democracy. It had little or no meaning at all where a political revolution had been achieved, as in China, and a social revolution required a major change in consciousness on the part of vast masses of small farmers.

Once more we have to distinguish between political and social revolution. Political revolution in the Soviet Union and China, in Yugoslavia and most African states has been overturned and one-party rule displaced. There was in all of these countries more than one class to be represented. They were all in fact characterized by large peasant populations, a very small industrial working class and a quite large *petite bourgeoisie*, including intellectuals. It will not be denied that the unity and discipline of a monolithic party was a necessary condition for leading a national liberation struggle. What was always in question was whether such a party could build socialism.

In the early years of the Soviet Union we saw that a Workers' Opposition existed; and elsewhere, in revolutionary periods, associations of peasants, of women and of intellectuals have been encouraged to take their own initiatives along with the trade unions, but later, when power was established by revolutionary parties, have been expected to act mainly as agents of the centrally determined single-party line. By contrast in most developed and developing capitalist societies there has generally been a plurality of parties dedicated not only to reformist or revolutionary aims but to conservative and reactionary aims and representing between them a whole range of interests: working-class, peasant, *petit bourgeois*, intellectual, industrial capitalist, landowning, etc. Action for social change will require class alliances of the Left.

It is clear that there will be no single model of agency for social change in developed countries. It will have to represent not only local and national traditions but a wide range of interests of those who feel some commitment to changing the capitalist social order. It is worth noting the capacity of the leaders of successful liberation struggles in economically backward countries to analyse the class structures of their societies. We can say this equally of Lenin, Mao, Tito, Ho Chi Minh, Castro, Cabral, Neto. If they did not succeed in establishing a permanent revolution, they created the conditions for social change.

In the more developed countries there is a class structure which gives a common understanding of waged employment to the greater part of the population. Equally important is the plurality of interests in the population, since this consists not of a homogeneous mass, but of employees of the private and public sectors, of production, commercial and service industries and so on. In most developed countries the employing class and self-employed make up a small proportion of the total. Even in countries with a large remaining peasantry like France and Italy the proportion is now less than one-tenth. Within even the major nine-tenths, however, the plurality of interest has to be recognized and any movements for social change built upon it. The variation of interest may be due to nationality, location, occupation, ethnic origin, gender, education, culture, etc. Despite all the studies of the sociologists, it is surprising how rarely these variations have been analysed in terms of their predisposition to social change.

One of the major weaknesses in the monolithic, single-party model of social change is that its language and expression tends to be masculine and male-centred. In some cases this is the work of the translator rather than of the German or Russian original. From Marx's 'Man himself is the basis of all his material production' to his 'for socialist man the whole of what is called world history is nothing but the creation of man', there is, as in all nineteenth-century political writing, only one human gender. It is no different in Lenin, writing at the end of *What is to be Done* that it is when 'Russian social democracy will emerge from the crisis in the full strength of manhood, that a "new guard" will arise'. The programme of the Communist International ended with a single-gender appeal, 'working men of all countries, unite!' The Soviet Union's propaganda spoke of creating 'the new man'.

For Frantz Fanon, the African revolutionary, 'Decolonization is the inevitable creation of new men.'

It is not only that half the world is missing from the language of these appeals, at least in their English translation; more than this, the concepts of new guards and vanguards, of 'man's' struggle for survival, of workers' militancy, of cadres and echelons and party discipline – all draw upon predominantly male experience of armies and wars, of domination and violence. I am certainly not arguing that a gentler, more pacific, let alone passive view of the world is either necessarily feminine or necessarily more suited to movements for social change. I am saying that male language and expression tends to exclude and to alienate women and not to draw upon the contribution which women have to make. The women's movement in the last decades has shown to all socialists that it can build forms of non-sectarian, collaborative and comradely organization and action, which the rest of us neglect at our peril. The women's protest has become widespread – in Britain in the camps against Cruise missiles on Greenham Common, in Chile in the demonstrations against the Pinochet dictatorship, in India in the Chipka movement, hugging trees against deforestation, in grass-roots movements throughout Africa (Sachs, 1992).

Centralized and Decentralized Models of Social Change

We have seen enough of command economies in the hands both of capitalist and post-capitalist regimes to know that they offer a most uncertain if not absolutely nugatory road to social change. Decentralization combined with abrogation of all central direction to market forces we found equally inadequate as a response either to the giant transnational company or to the failures of excessive centralization of the economies that followed after political revolution. Yet the outstanding characteristic both of developed and developing economies is the enormous range of local economic activity that takes place outside the market. In developing economies this mainly has always consisted of the subsistence economy, peasant households' production for their own needs that have not yet been wholly subordinated to the demands of cash crops.

Added to this, there has been the more recent growth of the 'informal economy' in the towns, which we have found in developing countries and especially in Africa. In developed economies the non-market activity ranges from vegetable allotments and gardening through every kind of 'do it yourself' activity to a huge area of sports and recreational clubs. More than this, the satisfaction of work for most people in such societies comes far more from the comradeship and sense of solidarity of the work-place than from any pleasure derived from the work tasks themselves. Though a few jobs retain the old rewards of skill and craftsmanship and personal initiative, and there are new and exciting jobs in computer design, these are today in the minority.

Above all, the greatest satisfaction in many people's lives comes not from work at all, or even from the nuclear family and private recreational activity. It comes from some form of voluntary public service. We have already noted the growth in the activity of northern NGOs in the international arena. Statistical evidence is sparse in this area, but it does seem that something like two-thirds of the adult population, in Britain at least, is involved in some kind of voluntary social activity, not simply as passive members or spectators but actively taking some social responsibility and initiative. The evidence is to be found in the section on 'Participation' in the annual issues of *Social Trends*. In the early 1980s, we could still write of these activities in an optimistic way as a voluntary complement to shorter hours of employment. Ten years later, a decade of high unemployment combined with longer hours at work for those employed have made such activities into an involuntary alternative to work.

What all this was beginning to mean was that in the developed capitalist countries a standard of living had been reached for most people at which, as Marx expected, men and women could begin to see beyond the immediate needs of survival to preparing for a richer future and combining in a day's work both mental and manual activities. By contrast it has been the whole experience of capitalism, especially since the 1880s, that the division of labour in industry has separated out the mental work into the offices and the manual work into the workshops. That this has been a quite deliberate process of 'divide and conquer' initiated by capitalists is completely documented in Braverman (1974). That those who lost their skills at work sought for alternative activities in the trade-union movement and outside the work-place is less well documented. But Eric Batstone was able to show in the 1970s how the demands for worker control and participation were sought for as compensation for the de-skilling of labour (Batstone, 1977).

Marx and Engels declared in the *Communist Manifesto* that capitalism produces its own grave-diggers in the revolutionary proletariat. Later, in a famous passage towards the end of the first volume of *Capital* (end of Chapter 32) Marx wrote:

> Hand in hand with this centralization, or this expropriation of many capitalists by few, develop, on an ever extending scale, the cooperative form of the labour-process, the conscious technical application of science, the methodical cultivation of the soil, the transformation of the instruments of labour into instruments of labour only usable in common, the economizing of all means of production by their use as the means of production of combined, socialized labour, the entanglement of all peoples in the net of the world-market, and with this, the international character of the capitalistic regime. Along with the constantly diminishing number of the magnates of capital, who usurp and monopolize all advantages of this process of transformation, grows the mass of misery, oppression, slavery, degradation, exploitation; but with this too grows the revolt of the working-class, a class always increasing in numbers, and disciplined, united, organized by the very mechanism of the process of capitalist production itself. The monopoly of capital becomes a fetter upon the mode of production, which has sprung up and flourished along with, and under it. Centralization of the means of production and socialization of labour at last reach a point where they become incompatible with their capitalist integument. The integument is burst asunder. The knell of capitalist private property sounds. The expropriators are expropriated.

The concentration of production, the increasing size of plants, the growth of a collective proletariat, the organization of trade unions in large plants, the socialization of labour, as Marx termed it, proceeded apace in every industrialized country right up to the 1960s. But all the evidence of the 1970s showed that, while the scale of capital and the share of total industrial output of large companies has continued to grow, the number of workers in each plant has been sharply reduced. The process accelerated during the recession of the 1980s. The revolution in information technology has made possible the coordination and control of large numbers of smaller groups of workers in more capital-intensive plants scattered around the countryside in the industrialized countries and spread across the world in newly industrialized enclaves like Singapore or Hong Kong. In this way the giant company has broken up the concentration of collectively organized labour and taken advantage of reserves of labour where both the tradition and the capacity for organization were weaker. The evidence was presented in the 1970s for the Italian economy in an article by Fergus Murray (1983) and for the UK by Tony Lane (1982). That the trend towards decentralization in the 1980s need not necessarily weaken all forms of workers' organization was shown by Mike Best in his study of 'The New Competition', which we shall review in the next chapter (Best, 1990).

There was always a weakness in Marx's argument that the collective proletariat would necessarily develop a revolutionary class consciousness and form a revolutionary party. The connections between groups of workers and class consciousness and class parties do not have the inevitability that followers of Marx have often ascribed to them. This weakness was fully explored by Göran Therborn in an essay on problems of class analysis (1983). But Therborn underestimated the effectiveness, at least in Britain and Germany, of the multiplant combine committees which developed a considerable capacity to hold together, in one organization, workers in a wide range of separate plants and unions. The connections between such committees and effective political action are much more tenuous.

In Britain there is only one party which has sought to represent both the range of social activists we have just described and the trade-union movement. This is the Labour Party; but its whole history is ambivalent on the issue of whether it is concerned with change to improve the place of workers inside the capitalist system or with the overthrow of the system itself. Violent overthrow has for long been excluded; forms of peaceful but radical social change have nevertheless been propagated inside the Labour Party by socialists from Sidney Webb to Tony Benn.

The failure of the Labour Party as a party of social change was more than ever evident after three successive victories by the Conservatives in British general elections. This failure cannot be simply categorized in terms of reformist leaders corrupted by colonial tribute – still less now than in Lenin's time. The failure stems largely from the weakness both of parliamentary democrats and of trade unionists to think through, create and propagate a model of political economy which would link government and parliamentary activity at the central planning level with the real interests and expectations of people on the ground – in the demands of trades councils, of special interest groups, tenants' associations, sports clubs, etc. – working independently or in relation to organs of local government.

The argument between those who work inside the Labour Party and those who reject such accommodation is generally conducted in terms of parliamentary versus extra-parliamentary activity. That this is a fatal dichotomy can be shown in the British case from every single successful action by working people to resist capitalist attack: from the People's Charter, the Ten Hour Acts and Reform Acts and social-security legislation to the struggle over appeasement of Hitler, over the National Health Service, over Tory Industrial Relations Acts or abortion-law reform and free access to family planning. The weakness of extra-parliamentary struggles on their own is that they are negative, like trade-union activity mainly defensive. In the minds of workers engaged in such struggle there is no positive model of social change, nothing of what the Italian communist, Antonio Gramsci, called 'hegemonic consciousness'. By this he meant the belief among working people in their capacity to become the new ruling class, challenging both capitalist ideology and capitalist economic power, which jointly provide its current hegemony.

If working people in a developed industrial economy like Britain's have failed to develop this consciousness, despite the overwhelming size of the working class, its long history of struggle and the single centre of the trade-union and labour movement, this can be attributed in part to the model of reformism that offered an advance for an aristocracy of labour, in part to the nationalist consciousness of an ex-imperial nation, in part to the real advances that workers have won. It has to be added at the end of this chapter, however, that the main causes of this failure must be, first, the narrow space left by a successful capitalist class powerfully linked to the state in which a movement for social change could manoeuvre; secondly, the failure of working-class leadership to develop a model of an alternative social formation to capitalism that would inspire working men and women to work together for its realization. Marx largely left the vision of a new society that would follow after capitalism for his successors to depict, when they approached the moment of change. His indications of its central features were sparse. Those who hope to find the will to work together for a radical social change will need a clearer vision of an alternative model to any we have seen so far in the market or command economies of our time – one that offers a central framework for decentralized action.

Recovering from the 1980s Depression

For a time in the 1970s it seemed that the trade-union shop stewards' struggles in Britain over productivity bargaining might lead to the firm establishment of more positive actions through workers' cooperatives and factory combine committee plans, such as the Lucas Aerospace alternative production plan. Trade unions were linking up with community development programmes under local authority initiatives encouraged by the Greater London Council and other metropolitan regional authorities. The thrust of these actions had four main elements: the extension of trade-union bargaining beyond wages and conditions to challenge managerial prerogatives on manning, hiring, firing and investment decisions; the claim that production should be to meet social need and not merely market demand; the forging of links with trade-union organizations in other countries in Europe, mainly inside transnational companies; there were even the beginnings of horizontal linkages with socialist authorities in other countries – the GLC with Paris, West Midlands with Milan, Sheffield with Harare in Zimbabwe. All this was ruthlessly destroyed by the Thatcher government, but something of the intention remained.

A crucial element in the strength of these movements was the development of the nationalist orientation – in Scotland and Wales, in the Basque country, in Catalunia and Galicia in Spain, in Emilio Romagna in Italy. Such nationalism has been a very effective stimulus to local workers' cooperatives, pre-eminently in the case of Mondragon in the Basque country and of Benetton in Northern Italy. Local and regional movements have been supported by the feminists and equally by the Greens. They have come together on ecological campaigns for conserving the environment, combined with advocacy of small-scale technology and slower rates of economic growth – less for the rich, but more for the poor.

In the 1980s the Labour Party withdrew from some of these commitments in the interest of winning middle-of-the-road votes, but the Social Democratic parties in the European Parliament have been proposing programmes which would tackle rising unemployment and at the same time repair and improve the damaged social infrastructure that has been left behind after a decade of underspending in the name of monetarism. Public support for such programmes can, however, be judged by the very mixed performance of Social Democratic parties in the European parliamentary elections in June 1994. The monetarist policies of governments in the 1980s can bear much of the blame for the collapse of the advances made by trade unions and local community organizations in the 1970s. High rates of unemployment undermined the very foundations of trade-union strength, cuts in government spending reduced the resources available to local authorities, and in Britain a seemingly vindictive attack was launched upon trade-union privileges and local government powers. But a large part of the public voted for such monetarist policies; and this has to be explained.

Looking back to the years of near full employment from 1945 to 1975, it is hard not to feel a sense of nostalgia for a lost era of peace and contentment, when Britain was regarded as a very pleasant land to live in. The living conditions of the overwhelming mass of the people, not only in Britain and Europe generally but in North America and throughout the world, improved steadily year by year and hope of continued improvement into the future was widespread. With ups and downs, world production and world trade expanded and the inequalities between regions and inside each region seemed to be slowly reducing. What went wrong?

No one now doubts that the capitalist world in the 1970s entered a downswing in the long economic cycles, which were first described by Kondratieff. As rates of profit fell, those with capital sought to strengthen the power of money, to cut labour costs, reduce taxes and public expenditure and privatize state assets. Competition was rife, mergers and take-overs proliferated, those who could not protect themselves found the price of their labour or of their produce falling. The gap between rich and poor opened up again – in each country and worldwide. In the richer, industrialized countries, a much larger proportion of the population benefited than had done so in previous depressions. It is true that unemployment rose to over 10 per cent of the UK workforce, as three million full-time jobs were lost and a million and a half part-time jobs gained. But the average earnings of those in the UK who stayed in employment rose fourfold between 1976 and 1991, while retail prices rose only threefold. The top 40 per cent of households increased their share of post-tax income from 60 per cent to 66 per cent, and the top 40 per cent of owners their share of marketable wealth from 80 per cent to 90 per cent. It was only necessary for this top 40 per cent to vote for the Conservative Party to win for it a majority in the House of Commons (see *Social Trends*, annually).

If the Conservative government of Mr Major had reached the nadir of its fortunes by mid-1994, with only 20 per cent of the vote in the opinion polls, it is because many of the 40 per cent had begun to suffer. They had borrowed beyond their means and especially in taking out mortgages on houses whose value, having trebled on average between 1980 and 1989, began to fall thereafter.

And on top of this they were beginning to feel the loss of public services, particularly the impoverishment of the National Health Service, and to fear the rising levels of theft and criminal violence in the city centres spreading outwards into the towns and villages. Even if economic recovery continued for some years after the low point of 1992–3, it was not expected that employment would really increase, however much the official figures of the unemployed were reduced. The reason for this prediction was the labour-saving implications of all new investment in industry and commerce. When demand expands, most of the extra output can be obtained without increased labour. This is becoming true even in the service sector. Nothing less than a wholly new attitude to working hours and to work-sharing would serve to reduce unemployment. Despite an official 40-hour week, the actual average number of hours worked by employed men in the UK in 1989 was 44; in the rest of the European Union the figure was only 40. In the UK, 40 per cent of men regularly worked over 40 hours, and among the self-employed 40 per cent worked over 50 hours (*Social Trends*, annually).

The call today from government and employers is everywhere for labour flexibility, which generally means longer and more inconvenient hours for the workers. Competitive pressure has driven employed against unemployed, part-time against full-time, women against men, Third World wages against those in the First World. No individual nation can stand out against the rest. So all must suffer and all the work that desperately needs to be done to conserve energy and improve the environment is not done, while millions of men and women are paid to do nothing. Governments vie with each other to reduce taxes, which would have served to employ men and women on useful work at a decent wage. Yet work at social security levels of pay is unacceptable, since this would drive all wages down. It is a seemingly insoluble problem, until those who are better-off and employed agree to share their wages and their jobs with those who are worse-off and unemployed. Is there the faintest chance that this could come to pass?

It is undoubtedly true that in a system which runs on the rate of return on capital, the owners of the capital will see to it that all costs are cut to maintain the going rate of profit worldwide. Those whose enterprise fails to deliver that rate will go out of business, but the going rate may be high or low. What keeps it up is the combination of labour-saving machinery and reserves of cheap labour. The social change that would end the division of labour has always been seen by socialists as one that would end private ownership of capital. The Soviet Union has shown us that public ownership of capital can be at least as exploitative of labour and of the environment as private capital. In the upswing of the long trade cycle it might be possible for a cumulative expansion of incomes and jobs to take place and for inequalities to be reduced. But it is not necessary that that should happen. How can the socialists' aim of greater equality be assured? What would make both the 'haves' and the 'have-nots' work together to share more equally the jobs and incomes that are available? To make it more realistic, our model at the beginning of this chapter (Figure 12) needs the addition of a third dimension which would register the level of full employment, without which no social change appears to be possible.

We attempt some answers to that question in the last chapter, but it needs to be emphasized here that anything that helps the recovery of employment and the reduction of inequalities must create the conditions for social change. The opposite – rising unemployment and growing inequalities – will not lead to the breakdown of the system in the way that Marx envisaged. The result of such a conjuncture will be once again, as in the 1930s, the rise of fascism and preparation for war, which could in the present state of world armament turn out to be terminal for the human race. It should be enough to recall the absolutely clear correlation between the impoverishment and inequality caused by the rising burden of debt in Third World countries and the outbreak of violence and civil war. Violence spreads from the poor to the rich and no one is safe from acts of terrorism. Peace is indivisible and so is prosperity.

It may still be questioned whether such thoughts are enough to encourage the acceptance of social change among men and women whose instinct is to look cautiously at all proposed changes. There were special circumstances at the end of the Second World War to urge upon the Allies the necessity for making a major commitment not only to preserving peace in the future but to establishing social justice. A ferocious war had been fought and cruel dictators overthrown. In the process promises of a better future had been made to the men and women called upon to risk their lives and their possessions; and alliances had been made by the capitalist powers with their one-time socialist enemies. At the same time, the chief of these, the Soviet Union, had emerged as a great power with strong supporters in all the capitalist countries and in their colonies. It was an absolute imperative for the survival of the capitalist system that the needs and expectations of those who had seen little or no benefit from the old system should be in some way satisfied.

The circumstances fifty years later are very different. There has been no disruptive war and no serious threat of major wars, the threat from a socialist rival has been dismissed and the majority of the people of the more advanced capitalist countries have for many years enjoyed an undreamt-of measure of prosperity. If more than half the world's people have barely benefited, there may be some feelings of regret and some stirrings of conscience among the lucky ones. But it is very much to be doubted whether that is enough to generate a general willingness among the 'haves' to embark upon changes for the benefit of the 'have-nots'. And yet there are many who feel that the task should be attempted, if only there were some clear alternative model to replace both the tragic regress of the only forms of the socialist ideal that were on offer and the apparently self-destructive progress of capitalist reality.

FURTHER READING

BARRATT BROWN, MICHAEL, *European Union: Fortress or Democracy?*, Spokesman, 1991

BATSTONE, ERIC V., *Shop Stewards in Action*, Blackwell, 1977

BEST, MIKE, *The New Competition*, Polity Press, 1990

BRAVERMAN, HARRY, *Monopoly Capital: The Degradation of Labour in the Twentieth Century*, Monthly Review Press, 1974

CENTRAL STATISTICAL OFFICE, *Social Trends*, HMSO, annually

CLAUDÍN, F., *The Communist Movement: From Comintern to Cominform*, Penguin Books, 1975 (see esp. Chaps. 1–3)

COATES, DAVID, *Labour in Power? A Study of the Labour Government, 1974–1979*, Longman, 1980

COATES, DAVID, 'On Labourism and the Transition to Socialism', *New Left Review*, No. 129, September–October 1981, pp. 3–22

COATES, DAVID, 'Space and Agency in the Transition to Socialism', *New Left Review*, No. 135, September–October 1982, pp. 49–63

COATES, KEN (ed.), *How to Win*, Spokesman, 1981

COATES, KEN, and TOPHAM, A. J., *The New Unionism*, Penguin Books, 1974

COATES, KEN, *et al.*, *Planning the Planners*, Spokesman, 1983

COOTE, ANNA, and CAMPBELL, BEA, *Sweet Freedom*, Picador, 1972

HODGSON, GEOFF, 'On the Political Economy of Socialist Transformation', *New Left Review*, No. 133, May–June 1982, pp. 52–66

LANE, TONY, 'The Unions Caught on the Ebb Tide', *Marxism Today*, September 1982

LENIN, V. I., *Imperialism, the Highest Stage of Capitalism*, 1916; Central Books, 1978 (see esp. the Introduction to the French edition, 1920)

MURRAY, FERGUS, 'The Decentralization of Production – the Decline of the Mass-collective Worker', *Capital and Class*, No. 19, Spring 1983

SACHS, WOLFGANG (ed.), *The Development Dictionary*, Zed Press, 1992

THERBORN, GÖRAN, 'Problems of Class Analysis', in Betty Matthews (ed.), *Marxism: A Hundred Years On*, Lawrence & Wishart, 1983

TROTSKY, LEON, *The Revolution Betrayed*, 1936, 5th edn; Pathfinder, 1972

WAINWRIGHT, HILARY, *et al.*, *State Intervention in Industry*, Coventry Trades Council, 1980

MODELS FOR BUILDING
A NEW SOCIAL ORDER

In a highly provocative pamphlet entitled *Advanced Capitalism and Backward Socialism*, two socialists, Bill Warren and Mike Prior, in 1975 emphasized the absolute necessity for socialists in their manifestos to be able 'to gather all aspects of human life together in one knot' because this was how capitalism succeeded in presenting itself today and why it was so successful. It was not, they said, enough for the Left to 'parcel out the various issues – that for middle class intellectuals, that for women and students, that for the working class and so on . . .' An integrated strategy was required. The failure to provide this from the Left must account for the continued survival of capitalism and for the continued strength and influence of the Right, most recently manifested in the support for Conservative governments in Britain despite at least three million unemployed, a crumbling industrial base and the destruction of the Welfare State as we have known it. What Mrs Thatcher offered was a totality of political and economic aims which appeared to have a central coherence, at least for the 80 per cent of workers who were still employed, for those who dreamt of winning the pools and buying a corner shop, for all house-owners and for those households on pension which had private superannuation schemes to support them. The core of this 'knot' was a private income, private health insurance, private education, personal initiative, personal responsibility, personal choice of goods and services, and a private morality.

Utopian socialists were criticized by Marx and Engels a century ago for believing that the mere idea of a society in which freedom and equality and fraternity were realized would be enough to attract men and women to change the social order. Capitalism should have, in fact, reached a stage where it had created resources adequate to support a new and just order but had shown itself no longer to have the capacity to develop further resources to meet the just needs of men and women. Nevertheless, Marx and Engels shared the optimism of their nineteenth-century contemporaries, and their faith in human reason and natural goodness. Thus, men and women only needed, first, the clear evidence of exploitation, injustice, waste and mutual destructiveness, and, second, the confidence of class struggle, to liberate themselves from the fetters of an outmoded society.

This must all seem very distant from the scenario today, but even in the 1970s such optimism was outdated. The psychologists had been recalling for us a sense that human beings all shared in the original sins of unreason, aggression, acquisitiveness and cruelty, a sense which belonged to an earlier Christian and pre-Christian tradition. It was already fundamental to the beliefs of the Green movement that our personal greed must be kept in check if we were to survive. Love of our fellows, belief in equality, for women and men, the desire for freedom, may after all not be strong enough to overcome the sins of greed and selfishness for those who can safely benefit from 'sinful' behaviour. Mrs Thatcher gave her imprimatur to this impoverishment of the human spirit when she proclaimed: 'There is no such thing as society: only men and women and families.' Self-advancement was to be the rule, with no concessions to Adam Smith's 'moral sentiment'. Television provided the one link which she wanted between Her Mistress's Voice and the family round the box; no subversive meetings and demonstrations.

Given that the 'knot' of capitalist forms and ideology – with no little help from the media – continues to hold the majority of the population in its grip and may not so easily be untied, what would be the nature of an alternative 'knot'? We may distinguish three main elements: cooperative production in place of exploitation, social provision to replace reliance on the market for private goods, opportunity for all-round human activity instead of the narrow divisions of labour into town and country, men's and women's, mental and manual, skilled and unskilled occupations, supervisors and supervised, with all the specialisms that go with these divisions. In such a commonwealth all that Marx meant by alienation would then be replaced by fulfilment – the alienation of the work-place, the alienation of the market, the alienation of a divided society. But we need now to look at working models for such a fulfilling commonwealth.

Cooperative Production and New Technology

The first and most obvious source of dissatisfaction with the capitalist 'knot' lies in the exploitation of the work-place. Again and again, men and women have turned to cooperative production in order to escape from that exploitation, but only to find that they had not escaped from the grip of the capitalist market. To survive in competition with others they have exploited themselves. Marx and Engels criticized the Utopian socialists for supposing that such cooperatives could be established, first, without the development of sufficient productive capacity; only then would it be possible to have expanded production that did not depend on exploitation; and, second, without the ending of private capitalist ownership of the land and all the means of production.

Given these two conditions, Marx and Engels envisaged a cooperative commonwealth based upon contracts of mutual exchange drawn up between independent, self-governing factories and cooperative farms and shops. Goods and services would be exchanged according to the labour time incorporated in them. Each member of society would receive, wrote Marx, 'paper checks, by means of which they withdraw from the social supply of means of consumption a share corresponding to their labour time. These checks are not money. They do not circulate.' The 'veil of money' that conceals the real social relations of exploitation in production is drawn aside and at the later, communist, stage of society the social supply, while it will still be measured by labour time for planning and accounting purposes, will provide for consumption according to men's and women's needs and not according to their work. (See *Capital*, Vol. II, Chap. 18.) Is this still a feasible proposition?

In the hundred years since Marx and Engels wrote, the whole scale of production has enormously increased, the influence over all economic activity of the world market has been greatly strengthened and the complexity of the network of trade exchanges with all their ramifications thereby intensified. As a result of these developments it has seemed that there could be no alternative model in a world dominated by giant transnational companies except the model of a command economy with similar enormous enterprises, such as we saw operating in the Soviet Union and in the corporate bureaucracies of capitalist states. In both, there is the same highly centralized, hierarchical and authoritarian model of economic management. What is more, the giant capitalist company and the large Soviet enterprise equally managed their widespread and various activities and locations in much the same manner, although in the one the profit flowed to the private capitalist and in the other to the state. At the very start of this book we posed the question whether such an apparent substitution of one authority for another could be expected to attract men and women in capitalist countries to seek to build a new society. It is clear now that it did not. We have confirmation enough of the privileges and perquisites available to the top officials of the Soviet state, and of the absolute absence of any widespread diffusion of decision-making power in the Soviet Union, and in the other centrally planned economies, that would have encouraged broad participation. Whole societies simply collapsed from lack of motivation to make them work.

To many the dream of creating a society based on decentralized decision-making seemed to have become totally unrealizable. The best that could be done, it seemed, was to change the leaders and bureaucrats at the top and concentrate on trying to make them somewhat more accountable and more conscious of the waste, inefficiency and destructiveness of an economy not genuinely subject to popular control through re-establishing the role of the market. Democracy, so it was argued, required a market economy to make it work but this was no guarantee of economic democracy.

It is a fortunate fact that the development of computers and especially of the microchip has changed everything. It has generated an information revolution which provides us with the capacity to receive, analyse and comprehend vast masses of information at any moment from all over the world. It provides also the possibility for any individuals or groups not only to have access to such information but to have the power to feed in their own choices and responses to the decision-making process. It is no longer necessary that electronic communication should be the one-way process that haunted Winston Smith in Orwell's vision of 1984.

Technology is, however, not neutral. Under the laws of motion of capitalism technology has always been applied both to cheapen costs and to preserve the power of capital. Thus the application of machinery to productive processes during and since the industrial revolution has always involved a division of labour which separated manual and mental work, detail work and decision-making, men's and women's work, employment and unemployment. It did not have to be that way, that women were herded together in great numbers on the floors of vast mills and factories as machine-minders, with men doing the more skilled work and the design and planning taken upstairs into offices.

At first it seemed that the invention of the computer further increased the scale of operations and degraded the skills and decision-making capacity of the operatives. But there are compensations. It seems certain that some operations can now be almost wholly automated, so that machine-minding is eliminated. This is the case with most refining processes and with milling, grinding, polishing, welding, printing, paint-spraying, etc. It is devoutly to be desired that automation may soon replace the exhausting and debilitating women's work of etching the circuitry on the micro-chips and assembling them on their platforms. The Green movement, we saw, rejected such devout hopes and it does appear that computers have tended to replace skilled rather than unskilled labour.

Political and Economic Democracy

The cheapening and micro-scaling of the computer have meant, at the same time, the opening up of new possibilities for decentralized, small-scale production of a whole range of less standardized processes and less standardized goods, such as instruments, china, decorations, shoes, personal belongings of all sorts. Ten years ago it had already been realized that the micro-computer could become an invaluable tool not only for communications, but for aiding the learning process in schools and colleges and for aiding diagnosis in medicine. Above all it was correct to see that it could aid the decision-making of small groups. Where the robot replaces the human agent, of course, jobs have been lost, but where the micro-computer supports the human agent jobs are gained.

It has already happened that there is no further building of larger and larger plants with fewer and fewer workers and a highly centralized and authoritarian planning system as the norm of computerized industry. This does not mean that capital is not still being centralized and workers laid off, but the scale of production is being reduced and actual operations decentralized. Small was not only seen to be beautiful – by Schumacher in 1973 – but in the 1980s found also to be feasible. Mike Cooley, as one of the authors of the Lucas Aerospace Combine Shop Stewards Corporate Plan, had already in the 1980s written in his book *Architect or Bee?* of the alternatives in the social organization of microtechnology as well as of the alternatives in socially responsible systems and socially useful products that were being rendered possible.

The fundamental question for socialists to ask is, 'What difference does the introduction of the new technology make to the exploitation of workers in employment?' Quite contrary to Marx's expectation that the increasing size of a dispossessed proletariat and its organization in larger and larger units would give workers the power to challenge the capitalist system, some modern socialists have proposed that this power will come from the possibilities opening up as a result of computerized and decentralized systems of production. Productive processes, it is argued, no longer require great concentrations of capital. Anyone can own the means of production. The case for such new thinking has been made most effectively by Geoff Hodgson (Hodgson, 1984).

The centralization of capital nevertheless continues apace worldwide and the market power of the largest transnational companies grows relentlessly. This is not, as we saw earlier, because they control the productive processes, but because they control the commercialization of production, through which labour is exploited. Small-scale producers may be proliferating everywhere, not only as always in agriculture, but throughout mining, industry and transport. But unless they can by some means combine together, they have little or no bargaining power against the finance houses and the giant traders in the commodity markets and the supermarkets. It was one thing for a small number of oil-producing countries to form OPEC and jack up the oil price. It is quite another for millions of coffee farmers to agree on a retention scheme, although this has been happening. Mostly they are held within the commercial grip of state marketing boards or giant trading companies.

We have to imagine a model which would hold together a large number of small cooperative units but was not the centralized, hierarchical model of either a department of state or a giant trading company. The sheer difficulty of imagining such a model is reduced by the information that the computer can make available at great speed and in an easily understood analytical form. The coordination of any large number of small enterprises still requires, first, some system of mutual exchange and, second, some calculation of relative values of products and services. Neither of these is impossible to obtain so long as information is available on the total mix of products and services (or rather several total mixes of products and services) available from the productive resources of a country, taking into account its imports and exports, and on the dated-labour time involved in their production.

A distinction has here to be drawn clearly between current-labour time added and the stored-up labour time incorporated in plant and machinery that both enter into the value of a product. When we looked at the Yugoslav model we saw the possibility of introducing this labour–time calculation for a just distribution of income; and the unfortunate effect of this information *not* being publicly available, so that enterprises with more capital equipment (stored-up labour) could earn very much higher incomes than those with less, and not be challenged. Great differences of income, therefore, emerged in the same way as in the capitalist system between those companies with monopolistic positions and advanced technology and those in the less advanced, more competitive sector. To correct such inequalities requires not only coordination and income adjustment between enterprises but publicly debated decisions about the allocation of resources between different sectors and geographical areas and different demands for public and private consumption, in effect what we called in the last chapter a horizontal integration to balance vertical hierarchies.

Experiments in Popular Planning

It is not enough for socialists to argue that there should be in a socialist society a greater proportion of national resources devoted to social provision than obtains under a capitalist system. It is necessary to propose means by which the whole population can be involved in decisions on this proportion and on its application. The argument in favour of the usual capitalist-economy mix of state taxation for social provision and of wage bargaining for personal consumption is that at least, in that way, the worker/consumer has some influence on the allocation of resources. The danger that is widely recognized in any society that moves towards a larger proportion of people's income going to state spending on social provision is that the decision on the allocation of resources will be made by bureaucrats and planners who are not in any way accountable to the people.

Social provision, to take a familiar example, cannot be a matter of a Health Service supplied from on high by consultants and managers or of educational and social services unilaterally supplied by headmasters and local-government officers, or even by councillors. Without forging links between the suppliers and users, between the caring services and the community, it will not be possible to determine what are the social needs of the people and therefore to meet them adequately. It is the remoteness and bureaucratic organization of the public services that makes so many people feel alienated from them today and attempt if they can to make private arrangements rather than seek social provision.

How then can the felt needs of men and women as both producers and consumers be identified and brought together if not by the market or by central authority? The difficulties may seem overwhelming but some experience already exists in the 1980s, when drawing up popular plans for social needs became central to thinking in the labour movement in Britain. A group of trades councils and trade-union combine committees in the 1970s explored the implications of such popular planning and some of this experience was applied by the Industry and Employment Department of the Greater London Council in the 1980s. These explorations emerged from a process of debate and discussion and joint activity developed over many years, in conferences and publications organized by the Institute for Workers' Control and the Conference of Socialist Economists. In such forums shop-stewards' combine committees, community groups and socialist academics could come together to share experiences. They all emphasized the grass-roots-upwards direction in economic organization.

The fact that a few of the grass-roots organizations supported by the GLC held widely unacceptable ideas gave the whole experiment a stigma, applied by the press as the 'loony Left', and gave Mrs Thatcher's government the excuse for closing down what was a standing challenge to her belief in the exclusive capacity of private enterprise to supply all the goods and services which a family could need. Similar experiments were closed down by the withdrawal of funds from local enterprise plans: to provide socially useful employment launched by local councils in the West Midlands, Sheffield, Cleveland, etc.; and to support other local community initiatives to identify and define the social needs of their communities, taken by women's groups, tenants' associations, community associations, ethnic-minority groups, youth clubs, sports clubs and the whole range of voluntary societies for supporting those in special need – the old, the very young, the disabled and handicapped.

The defeat of the first experiments in popular planning suggests two lines for democratic development: first, giving new power to local government, not only returning the powers that in Britain Mrs Thatcher took away, but adding more; and, second, changing the whole nature of parliamentary government to incorporate some real democracy. The fact is that, while we have seen a decline in the membership of political parties, there has been a great increase in support for voluntary bodies, both those participating in association with government and those demonstrating their protest against government – tenants' and residents' associations, women's refuges, Age Concern, CARE, Shelter, Child Poverty Action, Christian Aid, to mention but a few.

Any discussion of local services inevitably raises in people's minds their own picture of the existing structure of local government. Often this is not only highly bureaucratic and authoritarian, even sometimes corrupt, but almost always it appears somewhat remote. The lowest tier of local government in Britain with any real powers is the district council. Parish councils have more power than they generally exercise but they depend entirely on higher authorities for their funds. The average population of a district or borough or county council is somewhat under half a million. There are in Britain roughly one hundred of these in ten regions. Districts may vary in population size from 40,000, in which councils enjoy limited powers within the framework of counties, to 250,000 in the larger, metropolitan districts.

The powers of the counties in Britain have been downgraded in the general Conservative attack upon local government and arrogation of power to the centre. Some structure of regional authorities, corresponding to the Euro-constituencies, has been proposed as the alternative to such measures of centralization (Martin, 1991). Equally important for making good the democratic deficit is the case for empowering a lower tier of government (see Barratt Brown, 1976). This lower tier would correspond to the ward or parish with a population of around 2,000 people, say 500 or 600 households, in a village or on an urban housing estate. For these to be effective some spending power would need to be delegated to them by statute, subject only to inspection. There was an important precedent for this in Britain. Certain universities and voluntary organizations like the Workers' Educational Association, residential colleges and women's institutes were deemed by the Department of Education and Science, as it then was, to be 'responsible bodies', to which government funds were allocated subject to budgeting limits and inspection.

Ironically, while these bodies have been brought under more centralized control by recent Conservative governments, the governors of schools that have 'opted out' as Grant Maintained Schools (GMS) have obtained just that responsibility. Unfortunately, while some of the governors of GMS schools are elected by parents, the founding governors were not elected by anyone but 'emerged' out of the local power structure. Local elections to such bodies and to the even less accountable Hospital Trusts, Development Corporations, Training and Enterprise Councils (TECs) or Housing Corporations could convert a quite arbitrary system into an extension of local community democracy. It would not be difficult to extend the democratic principle more widely in place of the proliferation of QUANGOs which have been the Conservative Party's substitute for elected government.

The case for central power to redistribute income is unanswerable on economic and moral grounds, if it is to be from the rich beneficiaries of a market system to the poor. But the spending of this income cannot be determined centrally if it is to meet real needs. In Britain, local government is shackled by laws about what is *ultra vires* (beyond their powers). Democracy requires that such shackles be removed. Whatever complaints there may be about the inadequacy and even the corruptibility of local councillors, they are more easily made accountable for their actions and will know, as central government cannot, what are the local priorities – housing in some places, jobs and training in others, economic opportunities combined with reduction of violence and crime in still others. Local needs, resources and traditions are everywhere different, even in areas of deprivation and special needs, as David Donnison has amply demonstrated (Donnison, 1994).

The problem of criteria for resource allocation between central government and such bodies and local authorities remains. The great advantages of locally provided services are that they are plainly visible and they can be made accountable to the expression of popular local needs and opinions. The present disadvantages are that local authorities have no horizontal links and have limited resources of their own and are subject to central controls which tend to make the local state a mere step in the hierarchy of the central state. While Conservative governments have decentralized industry by selling off the profitable parts of the public corporations, they centralized the social services by setting stricter limits to the spending and taxing powers of local authorities which already depended heavily on central government for their funds. A step towards a new order would be to move in exactly the opposite direction, by permitting local authorities to raise more income themselves and by extending their municipal trading powers.

New Forms of Democracy

The fatal weakness of such local economic-political organs as we studied them earlier was just this, their lack of resources – both economic and inspirational – to stand up on their own to the pressures either of the world market (in Yugoslavia and China) or of the central state (in the Soviet Union and Cuba). We suggested then, and it has been a thread running right through this book, that we do not have a model that links workers' self-management and popular power in determining social needs with the coordinating function of central planning. Socialists tend to fall back on a mixture of market model and command model. This is a really disastrous mixture, as we saw, because, while commodity exchange in the market means that the veil of money wages and money prices conceals from the worker the real value added by his or her labour, at the same time the central commands conceal from the people in general the basis for the allocation of resources between different needs and areas of provision. New forms of democracy are needed if large numbers of people, and not just a small elite, are to take part in decision-making on major policy issues.

It is the involvement of workers' control and people's power in both central and local decisions about resource allocation that is then the crucial problem for socialism. To say that we are democratic socialists and want democratic decision-making is only to say that we want to apply workers' and people's power where it matters. It is usual to propose several ways of doing this at the centre. First, it is evident that electing a Parliament which chooses a prime minister who chooses a government does *not* ensure popular control, but only prime ministerial control. Electing a Parliament which chooses a government with *control over the prime minister* might improve the situation, but the powers of patronage might still be such as to negate Parliament's powers. Secondly, then, giving to Parliament powers to establish committees which would have planning responsibilities in different areas and sectors would certainly increase popular power. Thirdly, a second chamber which, instead of being composed of a hereditary aristocracy and geriatric parliamentarians, industrialists and trade-union leaders, consisted of work-place representatives on a regional basis, has something to commend it if it were associated with a general strengthening of the powers of the first chamber in relation to ministerial power.

Parliament, as the word implies, is only a talking-shop. It is better than dictatorship, but it is not democracy in its original sense of 'rule by the people'. As individuals, we only vote for a new Parliament once every four years or so, and we can only influence MPs' voting behaviour and government ministers' policy decisions through collective action outside Parliament – lobbying, demonstrations and campaigns on particular issues. For these reasons a number of political economists have returned to the concepts of Athenian democracy. For example, Paul Cockshott and Allin Cottrell in their latest book, *Towards a New Socialism*, quote the work of the historian Moses Finley and of political scientists John Burchin and David Held (Cockshott and Cottrell, 1993, p. 191).

Aristotle, the Greek philosopher of the fourth century B.C., drew a clear distinction between the choice of governors by lot as the democratic way and choice by election as the oligarchic way. In an election, he argued, the rich and members of the political elite will always be chosen; but the majority of the people, the underclass of poor farmers and craftsmen, will only win sovereign control of government if *any* citizen can be chosen to govern, and the term of office is short; and that can only be ensured by drawing lots. The only example of this practice in Britain is jury service, which only falls on a voter once in a lifetime, but may fall on anyone (subject to vetos which counsels for the prosecution or defence may insist on, to rule out any possibility of prejudice). Professional advice and technical knowledge can be put at the disposal of any assembly of governors or court of justice, but decisions should be made by ordinary citizens.

In Athens the citizenry did not include the slaves, but it included the overwhelming majority of the population – the small farmers, traders and craftsmen, the minority being the slaves and rich slave-owners. Marx and Engels spoke of raising the proletariat to the position of the ruling class in order to win the battle of democracy, and they meant by 'dictatorship of the proletariat' a mass democracy unconstrained by property ownership. Lenin expected every cook to be able to govern in a workers' state, but failed to see that representatives of the people in elected so-called 'soviets' were not the same as direct involvement of the people in the original soviets of workers and soldiers.

If doubts remain about the prospect of government by the ignorant and inexpert, these may be assuaged by David Donnison's paraphrase of Aristotle, 'The poor majority know most and are most expert about poverty' (Donnison, 1994). Choice of rulers by lot offers an excellent guarantee of true and direct democracy, but it is criticized because it is said that it could only be applied in a small city state like Athens, where everyone knew everyone and the boundaries were no wider than one could see from a high building. Much larger societies making up nation states require, it is said, the formation of parties representative of different interests and coalitions of interest groups to form governments. Organized groups of workers form one such interest; organized consumers another.

Trade Unions as Agencies of Social Change

Organized workers have some real power in the work-place, but, outside, the power which workers can deploy is largely negative – to stop things happening, not to make them happen; and for this reason they have formed socialist parties to champion their interests. In most nation states there is some link between socialist parties and trade unions. The tendency during the years of monetarist counter-revolution against trade-union power has been for social democratic parties to distance themselves increasingly from their original base among organized workers and to make their appeal to voters as individuals. This so-called 'modernization' process was completed in Britain in 1994 by the election of Mr Blair to the leadership of the Labour Party and by his immediate statement on election that the unions, whose members had been involved in voting for the leader for the first time on an individual basis and not collectively, would have no 'special or privileged access' to a future Labour government but 'would have the same access as the other side of industry. In other words,' he added, 'they will be listened to.' The link between the unions and the Labour Party has been a particularly strong one in Britain ever since the party was founded as the Labour Representation Committee of the Trades Union Congress. So, this statement marked the end of an era. There was never any doubt about the privileged access to the Conservative Party of the 'other side'; but that is part of what Mr Blair was saying. His appeal was henceforth to the whole nation.

The 'whole nation' is, however, held in a structure of property ownership that is grotesquely unequal and generates similarly unequal incomes. The official figure is that 25 per cent of the people in the UK own 80 per cent of the marketable wealth (excluding dwellings) and receive 60 per cent of the national income. Parties were originally based on economic class – owners and managers, self-employed and workers – because these divisions represented the major differences of interest. In the Marxian socialist model, the capitalist state was controlled by the capitalist class in the interests of the owners of property, through various forms of persuasion, including violence and corruption. In a socialist society the distinction between owners and owned would disappear, the state would wither away, its allocative and coordinating functions being controlled by the people through an assembly of representatives of associated producers elected from their work-places to decide major allocations of national resources between sectors and uses, present and future. We have seen that none of the societies which attempted to build socialism by ending private ownership of capital were able to put an end to state power; rather the reverse.

The model of a workers' state appears to have failed, not only for economic reasons arising from the problems of replacing the market with other forms of resource allocation, but for political reasons, which Aristotle would have understood very well. Representation of interests through elections does not give power to the people. This is not only because of the method of election in choosing governors but because the class division of interests between owners and workers is not the only division about which people feel strongly; there are divisions of gender, race, religion, nationality, age, occupation and many special interests as well as class divisions. We have seen these at work in many of the models in this book. At the same time, the stubborn fact remains of human exploitation resulting from the extremely weak bargaining position in the market of the great majority of the people even in the richer industrialized lands of the world.

Socialists have always seen the collective power of organized workers as both a defence of the individual worker's bargaining position and a lever for altering the whole balance of power. Those who see an advance towards a more equal and more democratic society coming through the action of organized workers at the places where they work have to recognize that even at the work-place the power of workers is narrow, and limited to the special interests of a particular group. Workers can refuse to work on particular jobs and they can go on extended strike against management decisions or in support of pay claims. The existence in any enterprise of a union structure of shop stewards and committees provides important protection for individual workers against intolerable exploitation, but it has not proved to be an effective base for an overall challenge to the power of capital.

For a time in the 1970s, unions in Britain pushed out to establish workers' control over a wide range of management prerogatives. It was part of the Thatcherite revolution to roll this back. Despite the legal limitations that have been placed on its employment in the UK and in many other countries, the strike remains a powerful weapon, of which anyone who wished to go by train in Britain or fly to the Mediterranean was well aware in the summer of 1994. But it is a weapon that can only be employed where the workers have won the public's sympathy – something not so easy to win against a determined government, an orchestrated media barrage and massive police deployment, as the British miners discovered in 1984–5. Many trade unions, in particular those in Germany, have decided that there is more advantage to be gained from involvement in the structure of management to improve a company's performance than from industrial action to wrest a larger share of the earnings. Such incorporation within the capitalist system is regarded by some socialists as a betrayal rather than an advance, but the subsequent strength of trade-union organization combined with the threat of strike action as a weapon of last resort has given German workers, as well as German employers, undoubted power in the world market.

Workers' power at the point of production is under challenge not only from owners and managers; it is being reduced everywhere by the steady diminution of the productive labour force through the introduction of automated machinery; and it is far from being treasured by those who have no such market power but are consumers of the products of what appear to be highly privileged workers. It was once an argument of better-paid workers that they helped to raise the wages of the others; the 'others' did not always see it like that. Today, when an increasingly large part of the workforce is reduced to part-time work or occasional employment or unemployment, the benefits of the fully employed are not perceived as being fairly shared. That most workers in full employment work several hours a week of overtime is not well regarded by those who have no work.

It is not only the unemployed and part-time workers in industrial countries and peasants in developing countries who regard the interests of organized workers as largely if not wholly selfish. This is increasingly the view of the consumers in industrial countries. The higher wages of factory workers appear to push up prices in the shops and social service officials appear to care more for their rates of pay than for their clients. It is a constant complaint, even of experts in the field, like David Donnison, who are not at all disposed to diminish the important role of trade unions in protecting individual workers, that the public sector unions are part of the problem of unequal power in our society, not an answer to it. He believes that 'social services (created by labour leaders and often controlled by trade unions) have become powerful monopolies and landlords', part of what he terms the 'imperialism of the public sector' that has replaced the capitalist enterprise as 'monopolies which impinge most directly upon people's lives' (Donnison, 1991, p. 75).

Consumer Power and Networking

The challenge to the power of producers coming from consumers is, however, aimed mainly at the big companies' profits rather than at their workers' wages. Consumers have found recently that they have an extremely powerful weapon in their hands if they choose to use it – the boycott or refusal to buy certain goods. Cases where the boycott has been most effective include products from South Africa under apartheid and babies' milk powder pressed upon mothers in Third World countries where clean water is not available. Saying 'No!' to unfair or unclean trade has now been reinforced by saying 'Yes!' to the 'fair trade mark' and to 'green label' goods. The market for fair-traded and organic produce has moved out from the Oxfam and Traidcraft shops and the health-food stores and into the mainstream supermarkets. This is the direct result of the spread of 'ethical consumer' magazines and of advertising campaigns alerting the public to the possibility of getting an excellent product *and* giving a better deal to the workers and peasant producers, while saving the rain forests, not growing coca, etc.

Market enthusiasts have always argued that the great advantage of a market is that consumers can choose goods that they think are worth the money and reject those they believe are not; and, as a result, producers of what is wanted survive and the rest who fail go to the wall. The weakness in the argument lay for many consumers in their lack of money and for all consumers in the difficulty of knowing what was in the product and what alternatives might have been on offer, but were not. The Trade Descriptions Act and all the consumer magazines have increased the knowledge available and the Green and Fair Trade movements have added the possibility of buying an alternative that may be a bit more expensive but is fair and/or green. One of the great advantages of this 'alternative trading' is that it is based on a system of networking which brings the actual producers and consumers into more direct contact than is usual in the market. The producers of coffees for *café direct*, for example, have been shown how to get their green beans direct to the processors in Europe, so that the profits of the local middleman and giant traders are cut out. Many more products, and especially those that can claim to be organic, are likely to come onto the market in this way.

The big transnational companies have been using a system of networking for many years, but always as a conduit of profit to the centre. The system can be used for other purposes. The basic principles involved are that linkages are horizontal and freely entered into; contracts are long-term and allow for independent development of products or services, within agreed specifications. Examples are St Michael's products made to order for Marks & Spencer, and Original Equipment Manufacture (OEM) orders for Japanese firms. The networking system thus differs both from the vertical linkages of a combine with its subsidiaries and from arm's-length trading through the market on a short-term order basis. The big company at the centre maintains its control in the network by requiring exclusivity. To win anything near to equal exchange for small contractors, the requirement of exclusivity has to be broken. Non-exclusive trading is a key element in the international Alternative Trade movement. The essence of this network is that bids and offers are made openly but establish long-term partnerships.

Such networking relationships could easily be created in any locality where the residents, for example of a block of flats or a housing estate, wished to act collectively in arranging for maintenance services, installing heat-conservation measures, ordering fuel and other supplies used in common, caring for parks and gardens, managing recreational facilities, or providing crèches and home helps. At present, these matters are all attended to either by a local government authority or independently by individual households. Much local government provision has been rejected because it was bureaucratic and inflexible; individual household arrangements allow for freedom of choice and flexibility, but may be both expensive and wasteful. The community-run collective alternative such as the LETS system is becoming increasingly popular, especially as cuts are made in local government provision. The networks require a networker or group of networkers to make linkages, explore alternatives, tie up loose ends, collect monies and make payments – acting on behalf of the whole community and within the community's agreed terms of reference. To expand, they will need a framework of local government or other state support.

Diane Elson has proposed a system of consumer networks in the form of one or more national consumer unions, each having its own network of suppliers. These unions would act not only as information centres, like the Consumers' Association which produces the *WHICH?* publications, but as actual initiators of production. Her proposal came as a direct riposte to Ernest Mandel's Marxian view of resource allocation by representatives of groups of associated workers. Elson argued that, by drawing upon consumer interest, the varied needs and preferences of men and women in different regions could be represented and a strong element of mutual trust could be engendered to bind together the producers and consumers. At the same time, Diane Elson is so concerned at the dangers of excessive decentralization that she proposes the establishment at the centre not only of an Economic Planning Office, but of a Regulator of Public Enterprise and a Prices and Wages Commission (Elson, 1988). Unfortunately, it is not made clear on what criteria these bodies would make their decisions. Under predominantly capitalist ownership, the criteria would be bound to be determined by profitability. Under social ownership, which Elson is assuming, new social criteria would be needed.

Communities and Communes

Community is a much misused word; it is used now for any group which is treated as such rather than as individuals or families – thus community work, community care, community councils (in Scotland), or, for example, the Asian community. When Mrs Thatcher decreed that 'there is no such thing as society, only families and individuals', she was reflecting the fact that community has lost its sense of living and working together. This has been destroyed in most industrialized lands by the universality of market relations, except where we could still speak in some places of the mining community. What is proposed here is to revive the community as a real expression of shared cooperative activity. The proposal was for a ward or parish of about 2,500 people – up to 1,000 households. Some have argued that this is too large for any real community sense to exist.

Cockshott and Cottrell recommend the formation of communes of up to a hundred people. They have in mind the deliberate replacement of the family, not only for housing, cooking, child-minding, care of the elderly and recreation, but as an economic unit. Communards would be allocated labour tickets for hours of work performed in the commune and would contribute their earnings from work outside. Cockshott and Cottrell are assuming that payment for work in a socialist society is made according to the hours of work put in, with different labour values according to skill needed and machine time. In the commune, therefore, the external labour credits and internal work units would be aggregated and deductions made for taxes, collective purchases, maintenance costs and a reserve fund, leaving (hopefully) a surplus for individual or collective spending (Cockshott and Cottrell, 1993, pp. 165ff.).

Cockshott and Cottrell are following Marx's model which we looked at in Chapter 8, but they have added to it the notion of a computerized and continuously updated calculation for every product or service of the amount of socially necessary labour time required both directly and indirectly for their production. All goods and services would carry a bar code plus both their calculated labour value and the current price in labour units which retailers are actually charging in response to movements of supply and demand. Buyers and sellers would find labour values perfectly simple and intelligible because they would know just what everything is worth by the number of hours or parts of an hour it takes them to earn the equivalent. Cockshott and Cottrell have taken into account not only labour skills and dated labour but also environmental and natural resource considerations, as well as discounting for time by incorporating the average growth rate in labour productivity as the discount rate. But they rely on popular discussion and collective decision-making to determine how much to allow for differential skills, for rates of resource depletion and for expenditure on conservation.

One of the advantages of Cockshott and Cottrell's concept of labour values being calculated for all products and services is that this could be done now, short of any change in social formations. Some of the information needed will be regarded as a commercial secret and it would not today be possible to make it a legal requirement on companies to divulge such information and regularly to update it. None the less, much information could be made available about inputs of dated labour from input–output tables, as well as of current labour payments, in order to begin to calculate both the socially necessary labour values of a worker's time and of the goods and services produced.

It will be much more difficult to construct the institutional forms for cooperative work and cooperative living. It is an unfortunate but undeniable fact that most workers' cooperatives and most communes have ended in unmitigated failure. Cockshott and Cottrell suggest that the main reason for this has been inadequate and inaccurate calculations of the participants' true labour contributions from work inside and outside. I doubt it. My own personal view is supported by careful studies of worker cooperatives, which show that they work only when those who came together to form them were already friends or relatives and they wanted something to do together (Harper, 1992). Larger communities where people do not do everything together but share certain common services and activities have a much better record of survival. Examples are farmers' organizations of cooperative buying and selling and machine-sharing, and tenants' associations having common maintenance, laundering, child care and recreational provision. David Donnison believes that a housing cooperative works best serving 200 to 300 households, an urban secondary school needs a catchment area of at least 50,000 people and a modern health centre three times that number.

It has to be borne in mind in this connection that many communities throughout the world, and even in parts of Britain, have become what David Donnison has called 'multiple disadvantaged' – concentrations of poverty in what are in effect exclusion zones, composed of people driven there for many reasons: recent immigrants, single pensioners, older workers, young people who have never had a proper job, lone parents and people with disabilities of various kinds. They are not communities, but aggregations of people who have no shared interests, who move in and out of one or other such area and are not part of anything that could once have been called the *working* class. They typify, in Donnison's view, the great divide in modern society between those on the one hand who have jobs, join unions and other organizations, who can exercise rights, be patients of fund-holding GPs and have their children educated at opted-out schools, and on the other hand the marginalized and excluded remainder which accounts for a larger and larger proportion of the population – perhaps a fifth to a quarter in the UK, perhaps three-quarters worldwide. In some mining areas in Britain, the condition of the people is no better than it was in the worst years of the 1930s. They need special help, which can only come from national, federal or international measures of redistribution (Donnison, 1994).

Beyond the community level as we have envisaged it, there is a district level of some 50,000 souls – a small town or large village. At this level there will be many common services that are now either provided by local government, and increasingly in Britain by central government, or privately for those who can afford it. A few local shops, public houses and restaurants will have survived the encroaching spread of the multiple stores and tied houses. There may be some alternatives – branches of aid agencies like Oxfam and Traidcraft and cooperatives supplying wholefood and specialist goods. Ironically, the Conservative government in Britain, in its anxiety to destroy local government and establish its own placemen (*sic*) in QUANGOs, has opened up the possibility for the emergence of real local community power – in the management of schools, hospitals, health centres and clinics, libraries, galleries and theatres. But to occupy this space, popular organizations would need their own funding under constitutional arrangements and the power to retain the surplus on rents from housing and other services. Otherwise they would be totally subject, as today, to central government control of funding and decision on allocations.

Subsidiarity and Money Power

Beyond the bounds of a district of some 50,000 population it is not realistic to talk about a community. Yet the principle of decentralization, what is now called 'subsidiarity', still applies: nothing should be done at a higher level if it can be perfectly well accomplished at a lower level. This principle has only been applied by nation-state governments – particularly the British – to the withholding of powers from a federal European authority. Nation states are in a strong position to do this because they have the power to raise taxes and to borrow money with state backing. In states with a federal constitution, such powers are available to a limited extent to the separate authorities within the federation. In a unitary state like the UK, all local authority finance is subject to central government control, even the raising of funds from the rates for their own expenditure, as UK local government bodies have discovered under a regime of rate-capping by Conservative governments. The chief complaint of the Scottish people against the government in London, and the reason for their enthusiastic support for a European federation, is that they elect a crushing majority of anti-government MPs, but have no power to manage their own money in Scotland. Although the notes have the names of Scottish banks printed on them, London decides how many should be printed.

The importance for any elected authority to be able to raise taxes is that parties to the election can seek votes on a programme of local expenditure. For many years, until prevented by a Conservative government, South Yorkshire local authorities sought votes and won overwhelming support for a wide range of local services, including a subsidized public transport service. Even without rate-capping, there are limits for any local government's funding of expenditure from taxes and borrowing, so long as it has no control over the issuing of money and money movements outside the area of its authority. It is the loss of these powers that the British Conservative government is most fiercely resisting in its opposition to European Monetary Union.

Of the three main uses for money – as unit of account, means of payment and store of value – it is the last which causes the problem. This is because money can be accumulated as capital in a few hands and is also transferable at some rate of exchange from one area or one country to another. This problem could be avoided by any authority which obtained the support of its electors for issuing non-transferable vouchers which, like railway tickets, lost their value as soon as they were used. Such vouchers could be issued in payment for services provided to the authority, for example for local employment schemes, and could be spent at any store that wished to participate. The authority would have to agree to redeem the expended vouchers from the stores at a rate in national currency that it had announced in advance. A rate which gave a small premium to the purchaser and a corresponding discount to the store might still be acceptable to many stores because of the expansion of their sales. A socialist authority might experiment in calculating the socially necessary labour value of the goods and services as earlier defined and could set the rate accordingly.

It may seem to be a rather unfortunate recommendation for such a scheme that something similar already exists in the British prison service. Work vouchers are issued to prisoners for work performed, in this case at lower rather than higher levels of socially necessary labour values, because prisoners' living costs are subsidized. The vouchers represent hours of work spent in producing goods in prison workshops, gardens, farms, etc. These goods are then mainly marketed throughout British prisons at values related to prison wages plus cost of machine time, raw materials, energy used and other inputs. Some of the goods are sold outside and used to buy in necessary inputs. The vouchers have no value outside the service, but are used by prisoners to buy cigarettes and other goods from the prison stores. It is not inconceivable that prisoners' living costs might no longer need to be subsidized if enough hours could be devoted to productive activity; and it may well be that this little-known development in the prison service is the main reason for the interest shown by private companies in taking over the management of privatized prisons. It is not at all the case that China is the only country where prison labour is keeping down the price of goods put on the world market. So there are evidently some problems in applying the prison model to the world outside, but the idea as a basis for employing the unemployed on useful work has already attracted the attention of Labour Party politicians.

The LETS system has shown that the introduction of local currencies into a national money economy can easily be imagined on the scale of a city or a prison population, but beyond that the challenge to the nation state's powers and to private capital accumulation would become unacceptable. Preventing local monies from becoming part of the national currency is not so easy, since surpluses of local money obtained by individuals or firms will inevitably come to be exchanged at some rate for the national currency. John Roemer, in his proposals for establishing a form of market socialism, has suggested that commodity money (used in exchange) and stock money (capitalized for transfer) should be separated by law. He is not entirely convincing in his belief that a black market could be avoided (Roemer, 1994). National or federal currency-issuing authorities are likely to clamp down at once on any such subversion of their power to control the money supply.

Municipal enterprise offers an alternative way of giving independence to local authorities, if they are not to be permitted to issue their own currencies. There is a long history in Britain of municipal socialism, where cities like Birmingham, counties like South Yorkshire and regions like Strathclyde have owned or controlled their own productive enterprises. Most of these have not survived the onslaught of the Thatcher years on all public enterprise and the obsession with economies of scale in labour saving at whatever cost in externalities. There are great advantages, however, to be gained from decentralization in energy saving and environmental protection, as can be seen in the case of local heat and power units when these are compared with giant power stations releasing their heat into the atmosphere. There is the further advantage of exercising democratic control to relate investment decisions to local needs.

We have to be warned from the experience of Yugoslavia that decentralization can be taken too far. The transfer of ownership and control of enterprises from local counties and regions to the workers themselves, combined with reduction of the power at the centre to coordinate resource allocation and to redistribute income from rich to poor regions, started the break-up of the national market and then of the federal state itself, which was to have such terrible consequences. What we are looking for is a model which would reconcile popular control and local initiative with overall coordination and the correction of unequal development. Central to such a model would be an information system which recorded and published computerized calculations of current and dated labour time to establish socially necessary labour values for goods and services produced throughout the country. The advantages of producers working with better land, better locations, more advanced machinery, etc., would at once be clear to everyone. This was recommended in the first edition of this book as a set of shadow prices against which to judge actual market prices. Since then, Cockshott and Cottrell have carried the argument further in their proposals for a planned economy based upon labour-time accounting, with a central marketing authority to reconcile labour values and market clearing prices (Cockshott and Cottrell, 1993, pp. 121ff.).

A Democratic Model for Resource Allocation

Such information about socially necessary labour time made open and widely available would ensure a firm basis for challenging profiteers and identifying the underpaid; but the allocation of resources between one use and another would still need to be made at different levels by democratic decision, if both commands and market allocations are ruled out as inadequate means for doing this. Allocations between different services – education, health, environment, roads, housing and amenities – should be made at district and regional level, if local opinion is to be fully engaged. Already in the Highland Region of Scotland district plans for development in the economy, housing, mains services, community needs and the environment are drawn up only after meetings in every town and village at which local residents are invited to give their votes for or against particular possible developments by placing markers on a large-scale map of the area. The resources which the Region is able to deploy from local rates and central government grants are quite small. If cities, counties and regions were to publicize their plans with a system for voting for or against proposed developments, much of the criticism of the arbitrariness and bureaucracy of local government, such as has permitted central governments to arrogate more and more power to the centre, would disappear.

The key requirement in a decentralized economy is that at each of the levels of government, as they are shown in Figure 13, there are adequate funds at the disposal of the authorities, both from the sales of their own enterprises and from grants from higher authorities and from the centre, for them to have some real independence of action. Each layer of authority should have

LEVELS AND AVERAGE POPULATION	RESPONSIBILITIES	RESOURCES
Wards/ parishes 2,500	Small workshops. Land and housing. Gardens and small parks. Recreational facilities. Home helps, nurses and crèches.	Own produce and rents *plus* grants from districts
Districts 50,000	Shops, hotels, restaurants. Smaller factories and offices. Streets, sewers, parks. Libraries, galleries, theatres, radio. Education to fifteen and adult. Clinics and doctors. Local employment centres.	Own income from production *plus* grants from centre
Counties 1,000,000	Larger factories and farms. Planning, roads (except trunk). Hospitals, fire service. Universities, polytechnics, technical colleges. Local courts and police.	Own income from production and services *plus* grants from centre
Regions 6,000,000	Major factories (high technology). Regional banks. Institutes of science, medicine, culture, TV. Power supplies, ports, rivers, water, forests.	Own income from production, subject to national taxation
Nation 10 to 30,000,000	National enterprises (in steel, heavy engineering and chemicals). Parliament and committees. National planning. Posts and telephones. Railways and trunk roads. National courts. National institutes.	Own income from production and taxation, from which grants payable to lower levels
Federation 400,000,000	Federal enterprises (air, sea, energy). Parliament and committees. Federal planning. Currency and banking. Defence and foreign policy. International transport. Federal courts.	Income from own enterprises, taxation and borrowing.

International links: On the basis, not of international planning, but of international agreements, supervised by United Nations agencies for planned exchanges.

Figure 13. Model of a decentralized economy with social ownership and democratic control of executive responsibilities

responsibility for those matters most effectively dealt with at that level. Figure 13 gives a rough indication of how these might be divided up. However much responsibility is devolved, there is an absolute requirement at national or federal level for democratic control over those major allocations which we have found in all the models we have examined to pose the greatest problems – between poor regions and rich regions which have greater growth potential, between consumption today and investment for tomorrow, between old labour-intensive and new capital-intensive production, between private goods and public services, between development and conservation.

With all this in mind, we should now be in a position to begin to summarize the central principles of a democratic model of political economy.

We can say with certainty that the first prerequisite is that possibilities should exist for a wide variety of size and type of ownership of the means of production and distribution – from large-scale, state-owned enterprises in, for example, steel, coal, railways, oil and heavy chemicals, through municipal enterprise for local services and medium-sized cooperatives for mass consumer goods, right down to small-scale individual and family concerns for specialized goods and services with freedom to employ up to a dozen or so workers. Competition should be allowed for, subject to strict limits on advertising expenditure. The second is maximum divulging of information with alternative mixes of possible resource allocations fully calculated and simply presented for discussion and debate. The third requirement must certainly be involvement of the widest possible range of people – individuals and groups – in the decision-making process, to which the executives must be made responsible. There still remains the problem of working out and agreeing upon the criteria for making choices. It is these which the managers of command economies and of transnational companies keep most closely secret. At first sight it appears difficult to determine such criteria from the point of view of public benefit, once the demands of state power or of company profit are removed, and without either the market to determine prices or bureaucratic decisions taken from on high.

The simplicity of the model lies in the principle of mutual exchange within a framework of agreed minimum social standards and resource limits. Mutual exchange is established by horizontal contracts agreed between producing units and consumer groups at different levels. Many of these would be on a local level – producing units in a town or district producing goods or services for groups in the same area – and could, as we suggested earlier, be on the basis of free supply.

A further problem remains of criteria for balancing immediate satisfactions, on the one hand, and conservation of resources and protection of the environment, on the other. The answer given by one political economist who gave the question the most profound study over a lifetime of practical experience in Germany, India and the USA is that we need a framework of objective minimum standards. With the help of scientists, engineers and statisticians these could be determined by popular agreement. Here is what this political economist had to say about minimum standards (Kapp, 1978, pp. 294-5):

> Maximum permissible limits of concentration of pollutants in the air and water, rates of utilization short of the point of irreversible exhaustion of fuel resources, minimum standards of sanitation, education and medical care, standards of land utilization which incorporate our technical knowledge concerning the proper use of land which maintains soil fertility without setting the stage for erosion, waterlogging salinization and a higher incidence of malaria . . . the location and size of large multipurpose projects . . . guided by availability of raw materials, nearness to markets, access to transport facilities and the presence of energy resources. The principle of social economy demands, moreover, that investment be made in such a fashion as to overcome the cumulative tendencies towards inequality and regional backwardness.

In some cases, there would be no argument about minimum standards. We do not need to have competition in the supply of water, because the standard is obvious – clarity without taste. In other cases this last 'principle of social economy', as Kapp calls it, would need to be met by discussion and agreement at national or federal level about the limits of resources available to any region or area or sector.

To illustrate the working of such a model we might take the example of energy provision. Electricity generation is at present no more than 30 per cent efficient. Half the energy goes into the cooling towers as steam and the rest goes up the chimney to pollute the surrounding land and air. To reach even this efficiency, power stations have to be gigantic and near to rivers to draw upon adequate supplies of water. This is said to produce the lowest cost in market terms. A combined heat-and-power unit like the Chelsea Power Station, the steam from which provided central heating to nearby flats and houses, wasted only 30 per cent and not 70 per cent of the energy. The initial cost is greater in laying down the pipes for central heating. The return on capital invested takes longer to obtain (as it does with hydroelectric power because of the great cost of dam-building) but the long-term costs are less. The Kapp model would be based on a minimal requirement of conversion efficiency being set for all power stations. To calculate such resource limits, measurement could be made both in labour time and in use of physical resources: energy consumed, minerals and other raw materials used up, etc.

Employing Computerized Models

The main problem in replacing market decisions will be to find democratically controllable mechanisms for connecting the expression of social needs as well as private wants with the allocation of overall (national or regional) resources. All the horizontal mutual-exchange contracts would have to be registered in an electronic memory bank with necessary details recorded, so that all economic activity could be monitored, and totals calculated. Mismatches and gaps could be publicly considered and agreement reached on how to rectify them.

We have already seen that it has been argued by economists that there are far too many items of goods and services in daily use to allow for any such process of calculation and correction. And we have been reassured by Cockshott and Cottrell that the numbers were quite manageable. In any case, it would not be necessary for *all* such details to be published. Only the totals of labour and materials used up in each region and district would have to be made public, and the possible breakdown between different needs, between current and future use, imports and exports, etc.

That this is not an idle dream can be discovered by reading Stafford Beer's book *Designing Freedom* (1974). Beer set up a computerized model of the Chilean economy for the Allende government in 1973. Information was fed into the model from movements of economic activity: production and employment data, imports and exports, wages and prices, public and private consumption, etc. From this data a simplified, continuously up-dated visual display was presented of the state of the economy. This was made widely available not only to central- and local-government offices and trade unions and other popular organizations but also to factory, farm and office workers through TV links, where they existed. The effects of alternative policies could be simulated and decisions taken about resource use and priorities on the basis of up-to-date and comprehensive information made widely available. The system is described by Dave Elliott and Tony Emerson in their essays in Barratt Brown *et al.* (1976).

Similar principles could be applied to develop a model for international trade exchanges. Indeed, they were proposed many years ago by a Nobel Prize winner in economics who was awarded that now dubious honour long before Professor Friedman. In 1948 Professor Ragnar Frisch of Oslo described a multilateral trade clearing agency, for which he provided in 1967 a computerized model. Each country would draw up lists of imports and exports and the growth of volume in each over a period of years that it would like to see. These would be computed and published. Corrections would be made by agreement to achieve mutual consistency. Overall volume growth could be assured, because no country would need to cut back its imports when its exports were failing. Governments would have to guarantee plan fulfilment or pay compensation and, given the current world-market price structure, prices would need to be renegotiated each year. (See Frisch, 1967.)

At this same time, in the 1960s, a Hungarian economist, Dr Andreas Goseco, a staff member of the UN Food and Agriculture Organization (FAO), put forward a proposal for a supplementary payments mechanism of multilateral bartering, to make up for the developing countries' lack of hard currency. I have described Dr Goseco's parallel trading system elsewhere (Barratt Brown, 1993, pp. 146ff.) and noted that in this system the bids and offers of goods and services submitted to a central clearing agency, for which credit notes would be issued, could be made much more effective by use of 'E' Mail bulletin boards. A system of trade centres having the same aim was launched under UNCTAD auspices in 1993 to bring together at one place in each region all the necessary services to assist small businesses to engage directly in international trade. Interconnection was established between the centres by 'E' Mail, so that they offered a base from which to pioneer alternative trade exchanges distinct from the operations of the transnational companies. All these experiments have foundered on the rock-like opposition of the big trading and financial companies, who can see their monopoly positions being challenged. Alternative trade is none the less steadily spreading and an International Federation for Alternative Trade (IFAT) comprising alternative trade organizations from both the industrialized and developing countries has been in existence for some years to coordinate its members' activities. 'E' Mail information on prices and markets is already becoming widely available to peasant and artisan associations in all the continents.

In time it should be possible in the international economy as well as in national economies to replace the prices of the capitalist world market by values based upon dated-labour inputs. Today these prices fluctuate with speculation but move according to, first, the pressures of supply and demand and, second, the bargaining strengths of the parties, which themselves follow from relative positions of competition and monopoly in the market. In the last analysis the law of value ensures that rates of profit are equalized, cheap labour compensating for low levels of productivity. As a result a peasant producing groundnuts in Africa with no stored-up labour in the form of plant and machinery will be exchanging, when he buys a bicycle, many hours of current-labour time for a few minutes of current-labour time of an industrial worker in Britain, who has many hours of stored-up labour to work with. As mechanization permeates throughout agriculture and as industrialization spreads, and the mutual advantage of expanded trade exchanges at fairer prices becomes more widely understood, the unequal price system of the capitalist world market can be expected to wither away. This is the only long-term answer to the questions we raised in Chapter 18 about unequal exchange.

Work and Leisure for Men and Women

We have been looking at a new social order in terms of the goods and services we might enjoy, but this is itself to accept the money values of the market and to omit from our thinking the real meaning of work and leisure.

The model that most men and some women have in their minds of their working lives in an industrial society is that they should have a job for eight hours a day, at least on five weekdays, in order to make money to spend on essentials for their families and on their leisure-time occupations. These last may range from drinking and betting to gardening and sports via running a car, watching telly and playing cassettes and videos, to holidays in Spain. All involve money, and most involve some private possessions, leisure goods, a car, a garden, etc. The social provision and the social costs we have been considering are conspicuous by their absence. Public parks and swimming baths, council housing, recreation grounds and public transport, libraries and education centres might certainly be of interest to some. Pollution of land and air and water, traffic snarl-ups and congested roads and sordid housing might concern rather more. Their hope would be to earn more money to move to a better part of town or into the country. But only the very, very rich can buy clean air, pure rivers, uncongested roads, parks and gardens. Nothing less than a stately home can offer all this. It is perhaps not surprising that the minister who made the greatest cuts in public spending in Britain – ironically entitled Secretary of State for the *Environment* – lived in one such stately mansion.

It needs to be emphasized that the model of privately possessed leisure facilities paid for by money from work is seen rather differently through the eyes of women. Full-time paid work is not the all-important element in the lives of most women, but it could be with more flexible hours. Two thirds of all women between sixteen and sixty may have a job – and in Britain without employment rights – but for most this is a part-time job. The full-time job for nearly all women is still in the home and the hours of leisure are very few. The conclusion that women might reach about money to buy a private environment for living and leisure could well be the same as the man's – it will be even more important for them – but the possibility of finding social provision to ease the manifold tasks of housekeeping and child-rearing is likely to appear much more attractive.

It is well to start this section with the contrasting views of men and women in their approach to work and leisure, because what we have to say is that the working man's view has suddenly ceased to be typical. To start with, in Britain there are two million unemployed men and perhaps another million older men and youngsters who would register for jobs if they thought there were any. Three million is one-fifth of the men between the ages of sixteen and sixty-five. To go on with, the possibility that all men between sixteen and sixty-five will have full-time jobs for forty hours a week in the future can safely be regarded as nil. In 1994, however, there were over half a million women officially registered as unemployed, and thereafter at least as many others who would take work if they could find it. It is not, however, only that unemployment rates are unlikely, short of a major social change in economic organization, to be reduced. More than this, a technologically advanced society based on socialist principles would itself simply not need such long hours of work – either in each week or in each lifetime – even after major social changes have been effected. A new social order would imply a new model of work and leisure and a new distribution of each between men and women.

If such a new order were to be envisaged, there would be the most urgent need to prepare popular consciousness for accepting

shorter working time. Ken Coates, MEP, following up a suggestion of Frank Cousins (one-time leader of the Transport and
General Workers' Union), has proposed a target of 1,000 hours a
year. The present average in the UK is nearly double that and in
Japan hours are longer still. It would be impossible to introduce
such a measure on a national basis. International agreement
would be needed. Modern automated methods of production,
finance and distribution make such a reduction both possible and
necessary. But a massive promotional programme would be required and a great expansion of educational opportunity to fill the
spare hours, if it were to be realizable. At the same time, there
would need to be international agreements on minimum earnings
and equally effective controls through taxation of maximum earnings, as has been proposed by Professor Peter Townsend
(Townsend, 1994) and others.

The dictates of capitalist accumulation demand continuous
labour-saving investment to increase productivity and maintain
profits in a competitive market. The tendency is at all times, but
especially in a slump, to shed labour. Because of the overhead
costs – of National Insurance, superannuation, redundancy and
training funds and other employers' costs – workers are dismissed
instead of having their hours reduced. Overtime is always more
profitable than short-time working. Similar tendencies operate
even where the motive of private profit no longer exists, in
enterprises that have still to compete for markets and show a
return on their capital funds. Legislation against redundancies and
state-backed full-employment policies may nevertheless lead to
overmanning and failure to reduce hours of labour. The only
corrective for this can be the most open publication of the
proportions of current-labour time and past-labour time, in any
enterprise, in the dated-labour calculations upon which the valua-
tions of exchanges of goods and services are based. Informed
choices can then be made between those goods and services for
which maximum automation seems desirable and those for which
the care and creativity of human labour are desired; and rewards
can be made according to work done rather than technical
productivity.

There has been a continuing argument among socialists about whether work should be seen as a burden or a boon. Not all work can be pleasant and satisfying all the time. Revising these chapters, preparing the index and making the original notes was often boring, frustrating, time-consuming, hard grind, but infinitely preferable to most factory jobs. The creativity of work, whether it is in designing or producing goods and services that meet real human needs, caring for health, education and welfare of people, evoking and stimulating new responses to the human condition through the arts and crafts, or taking part in the whole decision-making process of a truly democratic society – all this is the first need of every man and woman. But narrowing of the work ethic to the mainly manual skills of male wage labour was a product of capitalism that has nothing to do with the joys and satisfactions of a new social order. We do not then need to look for an alternative to the threat of starvation that will keep people at work.

Labour can become a pleasure but, more than that, the rich variety of activity of men and women in a society where machines have taken over the most burdensome toil can provide total human fulfilment. I can only end this book by asserting that what I am already able to enjoy can with the full use of our technological capacities be enjoyed by all. Today I have been writing in the morning, gardening in the afternoon, reading the newspapers and sitting in committee in the evening. One hundred and thirty years ago in *The German Ideology* Marx already imagined how it would be, drawing, rather amusingly, on the model of a country gentleman:

> In communist society, where nobody has one exclusive sphere of activity but each can become accomplished in any branch (s)he wishes, society regulates the general production and thus makes it possible for me to do one thing today and another tomorrow, to hunt in the morning, fish in the afternoon, rear cattle in the evening, criticize after dinner, just as I have a mind, without ever becoming hunter, fisherman, shepherd, or critic.

To these I must personally add that I will need in future to help prepare the meals and look after the (grand-)children, so that the model of a new social order is truly one for women as well as for men.

What I, however, can appreciate as a privilege and a special chance must always be clouded and flawed by the thought of those who do not have that privilege and did not enjoy those chances. Only by sharing it does any pleasure retain its taste and the more who share, the richer the taste. Lest there be some misunderstanding here, I am not saying in any patronizing way that others should learn to appreciate all those pleasures that must seem now to be the preserve of the middle classes. Fred Hirsch (1977) has reminded us that we cannot all have a house with a view and may not all wish to listen to Beethoven sonatas and read poetry. If these things are what people want, as I do, they must not be denied them, but they need not and could not all be supplied through individual access to private goods and services.

Socialism is ultimately about the quality of life and not the quantity of goods. Those who wish to feel their way towards the sight, the taste and the smell of a new social order, and at the same time face up to the desperate struggles that lie between where we are now and where we could be then, will do better to stop reading political economy and studying economic models and turn to the great socialist poets and creative writers.

For the English, and perhaps for all English-speaking peoples, William Morris should be their guide and *News From Nowhere* their inspiration. No book which ends with a section on work and leisure would be complete without a few lines from Morris's Utopia:

The speaker is living in London a hundred years hence and answers a question from Morris about the pleasurableness of work:

> All work is now pleasurable; either because of the hope of gain in honour and wealth with which the work is done, which causes pleasurable excitement, even when the actual work is not pleasant; or else because it has grown into a pleasurable habit, as in the case with what you may call mechanical work; and lastly (and most of our work is of this kind) because there is conscious sensuous pleasure in the work itself; it is done, that is, by artists.

Morris is amazed and asks how this happy condition could have come about. The answer comes by way of criticism of our present system, which the speaker ironically calls 'civilization'. The speaker has this to say of 'the last age of civilization':

> They had reached a wonderful facility of production, and in order to make the most of that facility they had gradually created (or allowed to grow, rather) a most elaborate system of buying and selling, which has been called the World-Market; and that World-Market, once set a-going, forced them to go on making more and more of these wares, whether they needed them or not. So that while (of course) they could not free themselves from the toil of making real necessaries, they created in a never-ending series of sham or artificial necessaries, which became, under the iron rule of the aforesaid World-Market, of equal importance to them with the real necessaries which supported life. By all this they burdened themselves with a prodigious mass of work merely for the sake of keeping their wretched system going.

Lest it may seem from these quotations that Morris should be claimed only as the precursor of the Green movement, some words of warning have to be added in conclusion. Morris is deliberately vague about the details of how the houses and ovens were heated, how enough food and clothing and good housing and transport for all was produced. In what must seem a highly elitist manner the population of London seems to have shrunk; there is room for all to enjoy peace and quiet and a walk out of their homes into the countryside. Morris had no intention of overlooking the problem; he knew that his Utopia was the end result of long and bitter struggle to change the course of technology. It was the quality of life that he wished to transmit to his readers – the sense and feel of a society that was using its technology instead of being used by it.

In the end the models that each of us works out for the society of our dreams will probably be highly eclectic, drawing from many that we have studied in this book. There will probably be some residual but declining use of money in the market, some central planning of horizontal exchanges subject to popular controls, including international agreements on trade exchanges, space everywhere for self-management of groups at work and for choice in social provision, independence and equality for women and men in the home and at work, small-scale crafts, workshops and garden produce where appropriate, as well as large, automated, computer-controlled technology for basic materials and energy supplies and for transport and communication services. The mistake of nearly all model-makers in the past has been to suppose that there was one single cause of all our troubles and therefore one solution for them, instead of a plurality of causes and of ways of prospering.

It was the rich diversity of cultures that we emphasized in studying the models of socialism as they were attempted in Russia, China, Yugoslavia and Africa. The models of any new society will only emerge from the actual life and work of men and women living in the old and willing a change for the better. In the meantime it is important not to despair. To quote William Morris again: 'Ill would change be at whiles, were it not for the change beyond the change.' There is much that can be done now, to experiment with the new information technology, to build prototypes of new forms of social organization, to discuss these problems with our fellow workers and neighbours. In doing so, we will do well to remember the words of a Nigerian scholar, writing about renewal in Africa: 'Make it democratic and let it be small!' (Ake, 1990).

FURTHER READING

AKE, CLAUDE, 'Sustaining Development on the Indigenous', *Long-Term Perspective Study of Sub-Saharan Africa: Background Papers*, Vol. 3, World Bank, 1990, p. 19

BARRATT BROWN, MICHAEL, *From Labourism to Socialism*, Spokesman, 1972

BARRATT BROWN, MICHAEL (ed.), *Resources and the Environment*, Spokesman, 1976

BARRATT BROWN, MICHAEL, *Fair Trade: Reform and Reality in the International Trading System*, Zed Books, 1993

BEER, STAFFORD, *Designing Freedom*, Wiley, 1974

BENN, TONY, *Arguments for Socialism*, Cape, 1979

BODINGTON, STEPHEN, *Computers and Socialism*, Spokesman, 1973

BODINGTON, STEPHEN, *The Cutting Edge of Socialism*, Spokesman, 1982

COATES, KEN, *Heresies*, Spokesman, 1982

COATES, KEN, *Think Globally: Act Locally*, Spokesman, 1989

COATES, KEN, and BARRATT BROWN, MICHAEL, *A European Recovery Programme*, Spokesman, 1992

COCKSHOTT, PAUL, and COTTRELL, ALLIN, *Towards a New Socialism*, Spokesman, 1993

COOLEY, MIKE, *Architect or Bee?*, Hand and Brain, 1980

DONNISON, DAVID, *A Radical Agenda*, Rivers Oram Press, 1991

DONNISON, DAVID, *Act Local*, Commission on Social Justice, 1994

EATON, JOHN, *The New Society: Planning and Workers' Control*, Institute for Workers' Control, 1972

ELSON, DIANE, 'Market Socialism or Socialisation of the Market', *New Left Review*, No. 172, 1988

ENGELS, FRIEDRICH, *Socialism: Utopian and Scientific*, 1882; Central Books, 1979

FREEDMAN, ROBERT (ed.), *Marx on Economics*, Penguin Books, 1962 (see Part III, 'The Nature of a Communist Society')

FRISCH, RAGNAR, 'A Multilateral Trade Clearing Agency', *Economics of Planning (Oslo)*, Vol. 7, No. 2, 1967

HARPER, MALCOLM, *Their Own Idea*, Intermediate Technology Publications, 1992, p. 143

HIRSCH, FRED, *The Social Limits to Growth*, Routledge, 1977

HODGSON, GEOFF, *The Democratic Economy*, Penguin Books, 1984

KAPP, K. W., *The Social Costs of Business Enterprise*, Spokesman, 1978

LETS *Systems Guide*, 23 New Mount Street, Manchester M4 4DE

MARTIN, DAVID, *Europe: An Ever Closer Union*, Spokesman, 1991

MARX, KARL, *German Ideology*, International Publishers, New York, 1947

MORRIS, WILLIAM, *News from Nowhere*, 1890; Thomas Nelson, 1941

NOVE, ALEC, *The Economics of Feasible Socialism*, Allen & Unwin, 1983

ORWELL, GEORGE, *Nineteen Eighty-Four*, Penguin Books, 1954

PARTY OF EUROPEAN SOCIALISTS, *A Socialist Manifesto*, European Labour Forum, Spokesman, 1994

ROEMER, JOHN, *A Future for Socialism*, Verso, 1994

SCHUMACHER, E. F., *Small is Beautiful*, Blond & Briggs, 1973

TOWNSEND, PETER, 'Social Policy Objectives', *European Labour Forum*, No. 13, 1994

TRADES UNION CONGRESS and the LABOUR PARTY, *Economic Planning and Industrial Democracy*, 1982

WARREN, BILL, and PRIOR, MIKE, *Advanced Capitalism and Backward Socialism*, Spokesman, 1975

SUBJECT INDEX

Africa
   continent, xiv, xxiii, 3, 269, 270,
      275–6, 278, 397
   culture, 278, 397
   declining income, 297, 310
   independence, 271–2, 341, 397
   informal economy, 346
   marginalized, 40, 88, 93, 137, 275,
      291, 297
   model, xxii, 281ff., 285, 313, 338
   Organization of African Unity, 282–
      3
   South Africa, 111, 269, 272, 307, 313,
      374
   superpower clients, 137
   United Nations Economic Commis-
      sion, 282–3
accumulation, *see* capital
agriculture
   African, 270
   agribusiness, 171, 324
   British, 19–20
   Chinese, xvii, 227, 232, 241, 246
   European, 23, 215
   mechanization, 391
   Russian collectivization, 199, 205, 241
   Southern, 170, 325
Albania, 250, 264
Algeria, 277, 297, 320
alienation, 106–7, 358–9
alternatives, *see* economic alternative
   strategy; trade
America
   Latin, 40, 65, 93, 111, 297, 307, 310,
     311, 313, 318, 341
   North, *see* Canada; United States
Antarctica, 128, 161
Arabs, 170
arms
   economy, xxiii, 48, 59, 115, 123ff.,
     128
   exports, 132

   nuclear, 136, 160, 206
   race, xvii, 137, 206, 219, 320
   spending, 130, 232, 275
artificial fibres, 172–3
artisans, 172–3
Asia
   East, xxiii, 39–40, 88, 90ff., 166, 240,
     283, 310, 316, 318–19
   'Dragons', 88, 90ff., 316–17
   revolution expected, 341
Asiatic mode of production, 192ff., 223,
     246–7, 316–17
Australia, 111, 166, 307, 313, 323
Austria–Hungary, 250, 262
automation
   flexible, 99–100, 361
   and growth, 168–9
   revolt, 100–101, 373
   and socialism, 362–3, 393
   and trade cycle, 117

bankers, 126–7, 300–304
   international, 296
banks in China, 236, 242–3, 244–5
   of England, 43
   German Central, 52, 301–2
   Japanese, 102
   merchant, 43–4
   role in Soviet planning, 202–3, 208
   and state, 111–12, 289, 385
   West–East, 216
'Bennery', 45, 349
Bolsheviks, 193ff.
booms, *see* trade cycle
Bosnia, xx, 136, 250, 260, 266, 267
   Izetbegovic, Alija, 263
   Karadjic, Radovan, 262
bourgeoisie, *see* capitalist
Brandt report, 299, 319–22
Brazil, 40, 160, 313
   Amazon, 159
Bretton Woods, 68–9, 70

AUTHOR INDEX

Achebe, Chinua, 3
Adedeji, Adebayo, 271, 277, 285
Aganbegyan, Abel, 207ff., 211, 220
Ake, Claude, 278, 285, 397
Alavi, Hamsa, 316–18, 336
Althusser, Louis, 118
Amann, R., 212, 220
Amin, Samir, 308–9, 332
Amsden, Alice, 155
Andor, Laszlo, 215–16, 220
Aristotle, 170, 369–70, 372
Auty, Phyllis, 260, 267
Aziz, S., 247

Bacon, Francis, 170
Bahro, Rudolf, 158–9, 163–4, 165–6, 167, 176, 195, 220
Bankcheck, 326, 332
Barbier, Edward, 175, 177
Barnett, Anthony, 124
Barratt Brown, Michael, xx, xxv, 26, 29, 41, 89, 121, 126, 138, 177, 201, 220, 252, 254, 255, 276, 278, 285, 292, 303, 307, 308, 309, 324, 330, 332, 355, 366, 389, 397
Barrett, Michele, 152, 155
Batstone, Eric, 347, 355
Beddoe, Robin, 77, 89
Beechey, Veronica, 155
Beer, Stanford, 389
Benn, Tony, xi, 9, 45, 349, 397
Benton, Gregor, 228, 247
Berger, Peter L., 39, 42, 104, 121, 313, 332
Best, Mike, 42, 97, 102, 348
Beveridge, William, 78, 115
Blackaby, Frank, 131, 138
Bodington, Steve, xi, 10, 160, 177, 322, 398
Boskovitch, B., 253, 267
Bottomore, Tom, 192
Bowles, Paul, 242, 247
Bradby, Barbara, 150

Brady, Robert A., 53
Brandt, Willy, 299, 319–21, 322, 332
Braverman, Harry, 197, 220, 355
Brundtland, Gro Harlem, 177
Brus, W., 218–19, 220
Buarque, Christovam, 160
Budhoo, Davidson, 328, 332
Bukharin, N.I., 197, 220

Cabral, Amilcar, 272, 285
Campbell, Bea, 356
Carr, E.H., 220
Carson, Rachel, 158
de Castro, Josué, 158
Catephores, George, 105, 121
Cavanagh, John, 42
Central Statistical Office (*Social Trends*), 346, 355
Chamberlain, Joseph, 35
Chen Erjin, 239
Clairmonte, Frederick, 42
Clarke, Simon, 212, 220
Claudín, Fernando, 339, 355
Coates, David, 356
Coates, Ken, xi, 37, 44, 53, 54, 89, 296, 303, 356, 398
Cockshott, Paul, xxv, xxvi, 110, 121, 154, 155, 188–9, 192, 221, 369, 377–8, 384, 388, 398
CODESRIA, 280
Cohen, G.A., 10
Cooley, Mike, xi, 362, 398
Coote, Anna, 356
Cottrell, Allin, xxv, xxvi, 110, 121, 154, 155, 188–9, 191–2, 221, 369, 377–8, 384, 388, 398
Coulson, Andrew, 279, 286
Cousins, Frank, 393
Crouch, Colin, xxi, xxvi

Darwin, Charles, 118
Davidson, Basil, 125, 271, 274, 277, 280–81, 286, 287

415

READ MORE IN PENGUIN

In every corner of the world, on every subject under the sun, Penguin represents quality and variety – the very best in publishing today.

For complete information about books available from Penguin – including Puffins, Penguin Classics and Arkana – and how to order them, write to us at the appropriate address below. Please note that for copyright reasons the selection of books varies from country to country.

In the United Kingdom: Please write to *Dept. JC, Penguin Books Ltd, FREEPOST, West Drayton, Middlesex UB7 0BR*.

If you have any difficulty in obtaining a title, please send your order with the correct money, plus ten per cent for postage and packaging, to *PO Box No. 11, West Drayton, Middlesex UB7 0BR*

In the United States: Please write to *Consumer Sales, Penguin USA, P.O. Box 999, Dept. 17109, Bergenfield, New Jersey 07621-0120*. VISA and MasterCard holders call 1-800-253-6476 to order all Penguin titles

In Canada: Please write to *Penguin Books Canada Ltd, 10 Alcorn Avenue, Suite 300, Toronto, Ontario M4V 3B2*

In Australia: Please write to *Penguin Books Australia Ltd, P.O. Box 257, Ringwood, Victoria 3134*

In New Zealand: Please write to *Penguin Books (NZ) Ltd, Private Bag 102902, North Shore Mail Centre, Auckland 10*

In India: Please write to *Penguin Books India Pvt Ltd, 706 Eros Apartments, 56 Nehru Place, New Delhi 110 019*

In the Netherlands: Please write to *Penguin Books Netherlands bv, Postbus 3507, NL-1001 AH Amsterdam*

In Germany: Please write to *Penguin Books Deutschland GmbH, Metzlerstrasse 26, 60594 Frankfurt am Main*

In Spain: Please write to *Penguin Books S. A., Bravo Murillo 19, 1° B, 28015 Madrid*

In Italy: Please write to *Penguin Italia s.r.l., Via Felice Casati 20, I–20124 Milano*

In France: Please write to *Penguin France S. A., 17 rue Lejeune, F–31000 Toulouse*

In Japan: Please write to *Penguin Books Japan, Ishikiribashi Building, 2–5–4, Suido, Bunkyo-ku, Tokyo 112*

In Greece: Please write to *Penguin Hellas Ltd, Dimocritou 3, GR–106 71 Athens*

In South Africa: Please write to *Longman Penguin Southern Africa (Pty) Ltd, Private Bag X08, Bertsham 2013*

READ MORE IN PENGUIN

BUSINESS AND ECONOMICS

North and South David Smith

'This authoritative study ... gives a very effective account of the incredible centralization of decision-making in London, not just in government and administration, but in the press, communications and the management of every major company' – *New Statesman & Society*

I am Right – You are Wrong Edward de Bono

Edward de Bono expects his ideas to outrage conventional thinkers, yet time has been on his side, and the ideas that he first put forward twenty years ago are now accepted mainstream thinking. Here, in this brilliantly argued assault on outmoded thought patterns, he calls for nothing less than a New Renaissance.

Lloyds Bank Small Business Guide Sara Williams

This long-running guide to making a success of your small business deals with real issues in a practical way. 'As comprehensive an introduction to setting up a business as anyone could need' – *Daily Telegraph*

The *Economist* Economics Rupert Pennant-Rea and Clive Crook

Based on a series of 'briefs' published in the *Economist*, this is a clear and accessible guide to the key issues of today's economics for the general reader.

The Rise and Fall of Monetarism David Smith

Now that even Conservatives have consigned monetarism to the scrap heap of history, David Smith draws out the unhappy lessons of a fundamentally flawed economic experiment, driven by a doctrine that for years had been regarded as outmoded and irrelevant.

Understanding Organizations Charles B. Handy

Of practical as well as theoretical interest, this book shows how general concepts can help solve specific organizational problems.